Dimensions of Literacy

A Conceptual Base for Teaching Reading
and Writing in School Settings

Dimensions of Literacy

A Conceptual Base for Teaching Reading and Writing in School Settings

Second Edition

Stephen B. Kucer

Fordham University—Lincoln Center

Routledge
Taylor & Francis Group
New York   London

Senior Acquisitions Editor: Naomi Silverman
Assistant Editor: Erica Kica
Cover Design: Kathryn Houghtaling Lacey
Textbook Production Manager: Paul Smolenski
Full-Service Compositor: TechBooks
Text and Cover Printer: Sheridan Books, Inc.

This book was typeset in 10/12 pt. Times, Italic, Bold, Bold Italic. The heads were typeset in Zapf Humanist, Zapf Humanist Bold, and Zapf Humanist Bold Italic.

First Published by
Lawrence Erlbaum Associates, Inc., Publishers
10 Industrial Avenue
Mahwah, New Jersey 07430
www.erlbaum.com

Reprinted 2008 by Routledge

Routledge   Routledge
Taylor & Francis Group   Taylor & Francis Group
270 Madison Avenue   2 Park Square
New York, NY 10016   Milton Park, Abingdon
                                   Oxon OX14 4RN

Library of Congress Cataloging-in-Publication Data

Kucer, Stephen B., (date)
    Dimensions of literacy : a conceptual base for teaching reading and writing in school settings / Stephen B. Kucer.—2nd ed.
        p.   cm.
    Includes bibliographical references and index.
    ISBN 0-8058-4940-8 (case : alk. paper)—ISBN 0-8058-4941-6 (pbk. : alk. paper)
    1. Language arts.   2. Reading.   3. English language—Composition and exercises—Study and teaching.   4. Literacy—Social aspects.   5. Sociolinguistics.   I. Title.
    LB1576.K83 2005
    428.6—dc22

                                                                      2004016811

Printed in the United States of America
10   9   8   7   6   5   4   3

Contents

III: The Cognitive Dimension of Literacy

Preface

Since my days as a doctoral student, the field of literacy and literacy education has expanded significantly. In fact, until recently, referring to literacy as a field or a discipline was not commonplace. Today, however, literacy studies—under a variety of names—can be found at most major universities across the United States. Accompanying this ongoing expansion of the domain of literacy—as well as promoting it—has been an evolution of our understanding of literacy itself. I entered graduate school when cognition was all the rage, having recently supplanted or at least overshadowed the linguistic revolution for those of us with an interest in text processing. Since leaving graduate school as a student and returning as a faculty member, literacy has continued to evolve from a language process to an act of cognition, and currently, to a sociocultural expression. What has been lacking in this evolutionary process, however, is a synthesis of what we know—or at least what we think we know—literacy to be. Too often, each new view of literacy has replaced rather than extended and reformulated prior views. Conceptualizing literacy in a more harmonic and holistic manner, therefore, is the primary goal of this book.

Paradoxically, although this book highlights theory and research more than practice, teachers and teacher educators are its primary audience. Never in my lifetime have educational institutions, and teachers in particular, come under such scrutiny by the public. In many respects the standards movement, high-stakes testing, and leaving no children behind are holding classrooms hostage, determining what is taught, when it is taught, and how it is taught. If teachers of literacy are to have a voice in these policies, it is critical that they have an understanding of what literacy entails. Although politicians may understand literacy in reduced ways, teachers have an intuitive sense of the complexities of the literacy processes because they work with students who are reading and writing on a daily basis. This book attempts to make this teacher knowledge explicit and to more fully develop it.

The book is organized around four interrelated themes: linguistic, cognitive, sociocultural, and developmental. Each theme represents an aspect or dimension of literacy that is utilized as readers and writers construct meaning through written language. These dimensions of literacy, however, operate in a transactive and symbiotic manner—each impacts and is impacted by all the others. The challenge in writing this book, therefore, has been to fully explain each dimension in a comprehensible manner, yet also to demonstrate the interrelations among them. I have tried to meet this challenge by progressively drawing on information discussed in previous dimensions as later dimensions are introduced and addressed. Concluding the book is a discussion about what all of this theory and research means for the classroom, for the teacher, and most of all, for the students.

THE SECOND EDITION

In writing the second edition, I have tried to be cognizant of the needs of the reader as well as where the field of literacy is taking us. To these ends, the second edition:

- addresses the nature of language and oral–written language relationships in two chapters rather than in one;
- similarly separates the discussion of the reading process and reading comprehension into two distinct although interrelated chapters;
- adds recent theory and research on technology and literacy throughout the relevant chapters;
- expands the discussion of the "reading wars" and the points of contention among the participants;
- more fully addresses instructional issues and implications throughout the book rather than primarily in the final chapter; and
- updates the references throughout the entire book.

ACKNOWLEDGMENTS

In true sociocultural fashion, many individuals and institutions have contributed to the writing of this book. First, I acknowledge the early contributions of my Indiana University graduate school mentors, Jerry Harste and Carolyn Burke, who expanded my view of literacy beyond simple letter, sound, and word recognition. My colleagues in the Graduate School of Education at Fordham University–Lincoln Center have been immensely supportive and encouraging. Angela Carrasquillo first urged me to submit for review the chapters I had drafted rather than wait until I had written the entire book. Rita Brause's continued faith in my ideas for the book gave me the confidence necessary to keep writing when I hit that wall known as writer's block. I would be remiss if I failed to highlight the friendship of faculty members Eric Chen and Fran Blumberg. They not only provided me with intellectual liveliness, but more important, they provided camaraderie and good times.

I am also indebted to the diligent work and support of graduate student assistants in the Division of Curriculum and Teaching. Tim Gerken, in particular, tirelessly searched for bibliographic information, contacted authors and publishers, and created—and recreated!—many of the figures found throughout this book. In a more general sense, I thank the students—undergraduate and graduate—whom I have taught. Over the years I have used with my classes many of the ideas, activities, and tables and figures found throughout the book. The opportunity to "field test" my thinking before sharing it with a wider audience helped immeasurably. Additionally, student feedback on the first edition provided me with valuable information for revisions in the second edition.

The initial reviewers for the first edition of the book—Mary Heller, Kansas State University, and Sally Oran, Northern Arizona University—as well as the reviewers for the second edition—Sara Ann (Sally) Beach, University of Oklahoma, and Choon Kim, St. Cloud State University—contributed significant insights and suggestions for revision. I am grateful for their time and efforts. Finally, I thank my editor, Naomi Silverman. Naomi's respect for the concept of text ownership and her collaborative stance continually amazed me. It was also largely due to her prodding that a second edition was undertaken. She truly is a demonstration that some of "the Sixties people" have made it into the new millennium largely intact.

Dimensions of Literacy

A Conceptual Base for Teaching Reading
and Writing in School Settings

I
Introduction

1

A Multidimensional View of Reading and Writing

The interest in the nature and consequences of literacy and its instruction has exploded during the last several decades. This explosion goes far beyond the perennial educational concerns about why Johnny (and Susie) can't (or won't) read. Disciplines as diverse as linguistics, cultural studies, and psychology have all come to view an understanding of the processes of reading and writing as critical to their fields. Not surprisingly, there has been a tendency for each discipline to create literacy in its own image. Linguists emphasize the language or textual dimensions of reading and writing. Cognitive psychologists explore the mental processes that are used to generate meaning through and from print. Socioculturalists view acts of literacy as expressions of group identity that signal power relationships. Developmentalists focus on the strategies employed and the patterns displayed in the learning of reading and writing.

Historically, these various disciplines have had a significant impact on how educators both define and teach literacy in classroom settings. This has been particularly true for those teachers working in elementary schools. During the 1960s, due largely to the seminal work of Noam Chomsky (1957), the field of linguistics rose to prominence. The discipline explicitly rejected the long-standing behavioristic paradigm for understanding the nature of language and documented the rule-governed and transformational nature of oral language production. Educationally, the rise of linguistics in the academic community resulted in the development and use of so-called linguistic and dialect readers that emphasized the teaching and learning of letter–sound patterns, morphological features, and the syntactic relations represented in the language. Similarly, instructional strategies such as sentence combining were touted as avenues through which to improve student writing.

Following and building on the ground broken by the linguists was the ascendancy of cognitive psychologists, who began to document how readers and writers construct meaning through written language. Emerging from this research was a

3

fuller understanding of the active role of the individual in meaning making and of the critical differences in the strategies employed by proficient and less proficient readers and writers. Strategy instruction that helped students access and use appropriate background knowledge and to self-monitor their unfolding worlds of meaning as they interacted with print soon found its way into the curriculum. Reader response groups and process writing conferences also became commonplace in many classrooms.

Most recently, with the increasing acknowledgment of the linguistic and cultural diversity within the United States, various researchers have begun to examine the sociocultural dimension of literacy. The ways in which literacy is defined and used as a social practice by various communities (e.g., cultural, occupational, gender) are being documented. The nature of knowledge, its production, and its use as linked to literacy, ideology, and power are being uncovered. The educational impact of these explorations has been an increased sensitivity to the range of socially based experiences and meanings that students bring to the classroom. Additionally, educators have worked to ensure a more diverse representation of knowledges in the curriculum and more equitable access to these knowledges. Culturally responsive instruction and critical literacy are two routes through which this new sensitivity to diversity has been explored.

Accompanying and paralleling these trends were developmentalists' explorations of how young children construct the linguistic, cognitive, and sociocultural dimensions of written language. This examination has helped educators understand and appreciate the active, hypothesis-generating, testing, and modifying behaviors of the learners they teach. As a result of these new understandings, developmentally appropriate curricula and instructional mediation through scaffolding have come to be seen as critical components in the teaching of literacy.

Of course, these historical trends are not as linear as they may appear—nor are they isolated by discipline. Obviously, various fields have investigated literacy at the same time. Also, each discipline has drawn from other disciplines when necessary. For example, cognitive psychologists utilized linguistic analyses of texts as they attempted to understand readers' interactions with various types of written language. Similarly, socioculturalists have drawn on text processing research as they have explored how various cultural groups define and use literacy to mediate their interactions with the world. Consequently, we have psycholinguists, developmental linguists, social psychologists, and the like. Even so, if one looks at the trends in literacy instruction during the last several decades, it is fairly easy to discern which discipline was dominant at any particular point in time.

If literacy education is to be effective, it is important that literacy be conceived as dynamic and multidimensional in nature. Becoming or being literate means learning to effectively, efficiently, and simultaneously control the linguistic, cognitive, sociocultural, and developmental dimensions of written language in a transactive fashion. In a very real sense, every act of real-world use of literacy—that is, literacy events—involves these four dimensions (Kucer, 1991, 1994; Kucer, Silva, &

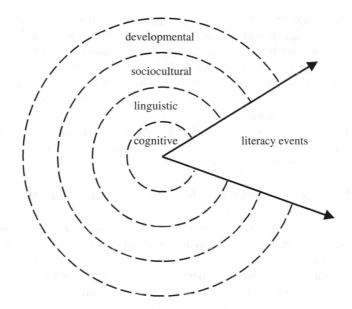

FIG. 1.1. Dimensions of literacy. From Kucer, S. B., Silva, C., & Delgado-Larocco, E. (1995). *Curricular conversations: Themes in multilingual and monolingual classrooms* (p. 59). York, ME: Stenhouse.

Delgado-Larocco, 1995). Figure 1.1 illustrates the relation among these four dimensions. These four dimensions of literacy can perhaps best be captured by the various roles or positions readers and writers inhabit as they transact with written language. There is the role of code breaker (linguistic dimension), the role of meaning maker (cognitive dimension), the role of text user and critic (sociocultural dimension), and the role of scientist and construction worker (developmental dimension). Other researchers have made similar distinctions (e.g., Gee, 1996; Luke, 1995, 1998; New London Group, 1996).

At the center of the literacy act is the cognitive dimension, the desire of the language user to explore, discover, construct, and share meaning. Even in those circumstances in which there is no intended "outside" audience, such as in the writing of a diary or the reading of a novel for pure enjoyment, there is an "inside" audience—the language users themselves. Their generation of cognitive meanings involves the employment of a variety of mental processes and strategies. Surrounding the cognitive dimension is the linguistic, the language vehicle through which these meanings are expressed. As illustrated in chapter 2, language consists of various systems, and the reader or writer must coordinate these transacting systems with the meanings being constructed.

Literacy events, however, are more than individual acts of meaning making and language use. Literacy is a social act as well. Therefore, the meaning and language that are built and used are always framed by the social identity (e.g., ethnic, cultural, gender) of the individual and the social context in which the language is being employed. Finally, encompassing the cognitive, linguistic, and sociocultural dimensions is the developmental. Each act of literacy reflects those aspects of literacy that the individual does and does not control in any given context. Potentially, development never ends, and individuals may encounter literacy events that involve using literacy in new and novel ways. These experiences offer the opportunity for additional literacy learning that results in developmental advancements. *Becoming* literate rather than *being* literate more accurately describes our ongoing relationship with written language (Leu, 2000).

DISCIPLINARY PERSPECTIVES VERSUS LITERACY DIMENSIONS

Each disciplinary perspective has contributed significantly to our understanding of literacy. Unfortunately, as previously noted, all too often these contributions have failed to consider, at least explicitly, the existence and impact of other perspectives. Each lens privileged a particular aspect of literacy for analysis and often ignored others. Stated somewhat differently, who was doing the looking and how the looking was accomplished determined what was ultimately seen. However, if each act of literacy is conceived as involving various dimensions, it is critical that literacy as a multidimensional process not be confused with disciplinary perspectives. Disciplinary perspectives frequently result in viewing reading and writing from a singular angle that may obscure an understanding of how literacy operates in the real world.

Many cognitive psychologists, for example, in an attempt to understand the operation of perception in the reading process, have frequently examined the reader's ability to identify letters and words. Individual letters or words are presented under timed conditions, and the responses of the readers are noted. Based on the responses and the time required for identification, particular understandings of the role and nature of perception in the reading process have been developed. Not surprisingly, particular features of letters and words were found to be especially critical to effective and efficient perception. Such views have resulted in bottom-up theories of perception and the reading process.

In authentic situations—the reading of real texts in the real world for real reasons—language is not stripped of its internal and external contexts. Rather, language is embedded in both a textual and situational environment that provides additional perceptual cues. An advertisement on a billboard, for example, will typically include letters and words that are framed by larger units of text, such as sentences. Although sentences are composed of letters and words, they also contain syntactic and semantic information. In addition, advertisements often incorporate other communication systems, such as illustrations, photographs, and numerals. The use of color and print size may also contribute to the message being conveyed. Finally, most readers understand the pragmatic nature of advertisements—that is, purchase this now; you need it! All of these textual and situational cues are sampled by readers as they generate meaning from print. Therefore, how the reader perceives isolated letters or words in tachistoscopic experiments may say little about how letters and words are perceived or utilized when they are embedded in broader situational and linguistic contexts (Cattell, 1885; Rumelhart, 1994). Such context-reduced research is reminiscent of the joke about a drunken man who was looking for his keys under a streetlight: He hadn't lost his keys there, but the light was good.

In contrast, a dimensional approach to literacy acknowledges the various, intertwined, and symbiotic aspects of language and the need to search for the keys where they were actually lost. When reading and writing are conceived as multidimensional in nature, the tendency to reduce literacy to, or understand literacy from, a single disciplinary perspective is avoided. The acknowledgment of the complex nature of literacy that must be viewed from multiple lenses is more than an intellectual or academic necessity; it is an instructional one as well. Such a view can serve as a foundation for literacy education and help ensure that curricula and instructional strategies begin to account for all that must be learned if proficiency in reading and writing is to be developed in our students. The creation of a continuity of experience between the school and home, as advocated by Dewey (1938), and the linking of learning in school and out, as suggested by Resnick (1987), through real-world literacy instruction for real-world literacy users is the ultimate goal of this book.

A LITERACY BELIEFS PROFILE

Before reading on, it might be helpful to first consider your current beliefs about literacy. Table 1.1 contains a literacy beliefs profile, a questionnaire that is intended to help you reflect on your current conceptions of reading and writing. I am grateful to DeFord (1985) for her early efforts at developing such profiles to examine instructional beliefs for the teaching of reading. Take a few minutes to consider each question, and mark the extent to which you agree or disagree with the assertion. If you are unsure of some of your beliefs, you can always mark number three. If possible, after you complete the profile, compare, contrast, and discuss your beliefs with others who are also reading this book. After the book has been read, you will be asked to return to the beliefs profile and mark your answers a second time. Then compare and contrast your two sets of answers and examine how your views have or have not changed.

A LITERACY STORY

A literacy story is a true event that demonstrates how literacy operates in the real world. As defined by Heath (1982a), a literacy event is "any action sequence involving one or more persons, in which the production and/or comprehension

TABLE 1.1

A Literacy Beliefs Profile

Directions: Read the following statements. Circle the response that best indicates your beliefs about literacy (reading and writing).

SD (strongly disagree)   <— 1 — 2 — 3 — 4 — 5 —>   (strongly agree) SA

	SD				SA
1. Being labeled as a "proficient" reader and writer is a subjective process.	1	2	3	4	5
2. Becoming literate may have a negative impact on the individual's sociocultural identity.	1	2	3	4	5
3. The perception of individual letters within words is a significant part of reading and writing.	1	2	3	4	5
4. Reading and writing are developed from the part to the whole: letters —> words —> sentences —> paragraphs —> stories.	1	2	3	4	5
5. A major difference between effective and ineffective readers and writers is that effective readers and writers make fewer mistakes.	1	2	3	4	5
6. The development and use of literacy is influenced as much by sociocultural demands as by the schools.	1	2	3	4	5
7. Reading and writing can be mastered and perfected.	1	2	3	4	5
8. There is a positive relationship between being literate and an individual's socioeconomic development and/or status.	1	2	3	4	5
9. Effective readers and writers initially focus on the overall meaning of what they are reading and writing rather than on correct word identification, spelling, punctuation, capitalization, and individual facts and details.	1	2	3	4	5
10. English spelling reflects the meanings of words.	1	2	3	4	5
11. What it means to be literate varies from group to group and from era to era.	1	2	3	4	5
12. Children learn literacy more quickly when their errors or mistakes are corrected.	1	2	3	4	5
13. Comprehension involves getting the author's intended meanings from the print.	1	2	3	4	5
14. A lack of print in the home is a significant reason why children have difficulty learning to read and write in school.	1	2	3	4	5
15. Writing is speech written down; reading is translating print to speech.	1	2	3	4	5

16. There is a difference between "comprehending" and "interpreting" a text.   1   2   3   4   5

17. The use of letter and sound relationships (phonics) is a significant part of reading and writing.   1   2   3   4   5

18. Literacy is learned through imitation, practice, and mastery.   1   2   3   4   5

19. Writing is a process of first "thinking it" and then "saying it"; reading is a process of first "saying it" and then "thinking it."   1   2   3   4   5

20. Learning to read and write ensures a more equitable and just society.   1   2   3   4   5

21. What a text "means" is significantly influenced and at times controlled by those in positions of power and influence.   1   2   3   4   5

22. Texts have meaning in and of themselves.   1   2   3   4   5

23. Speaking a dialect can cause problems when learning to read and write.   1   2   3   4   5

24. Becoming literate significantly changes the individual's intellectual capacities.   1   2   3   4   5

25. Individuals who are literate are likely to be more ethical and moral.   1   2   3   4   5

26. Reading and writing involve making "guesses."   1   2   3   4   5

28. It is possible to accurately determine a person's reading and writing "grade level."   1   2   3   4   5

27. The culture of the poor is a significant reason why some children have difficulty learning to read and write in school.   1   2   3   4   5

28. All texts, even fictional stories, reflect particular beliefs or ideologies.   1   2   3   4   5

29. It is usually best to slow down when encountering problems during reading and writing.   1   2   3   4   5

30. Being bilingual frequently causes difficulty when learning to read and write in English.   1   2   3   4   5

31. Being a good speller is positively related to being a good reader and writer.   1   2   3   4   5

32. Comprehension or understanding is relative.   1   2   3   4   5

33. Learning and knowing how to read and write in one context, such as in the home or in the church/mosque/synagogue/temple, supports learning and knowing how to read and write in school.   1   2   3   4   5

34. Everyone speaks a dialect.   1   2   3   4   5

(continued on next page)

TABLE 1.1 (continued)

Directions: Read the following statements. Circle the response that best indicates your beliefs about literacy (reading and writing).

SD (strongly disagree)   <— 1 — 2 — 3 — 4 — 5 —>   (strongly agree) SA

	SD				SA
35. Effective readers and writers make fewer revisions than ineffective readers and writers.	1	2	3	4	5
36. The function or purpose for reading and writing significantly influences how well someone can read or write.	1	2	3	4	5
37. It is a sign of ineffective reading and writing when the individual rereads or rewrites.	1	2	3	4	5
38. Reading and writing in English are linear, left-to-right, and top-to-bottom processes.	1	2	3	4	5
39. English spelling is determined by relating letters to the sounds which the letters represent.	1	2	3	4	5
40. The difficulty of a text can be determined by word length, word difficulty, sentence length, and number of words and sentences in the text.	1	2	3	4	5

of print plays a role" (p. 92). As has been illustrated, acts of literacy involve various dimensions: linguistic, cognitive, sociocultural, and developmental. These four dimensions are represented in the language story found in Table 1.2. The power of such stories is that they help those of us interested in literacy education to keep our focus on the use of literacy in authentic contexts. In a sense, they help us avoid reductionistic, single-discipline-based understandings of reading and writing.

The story presented in Table 1.2 concerns an initial encounter with a computer program guide that was being used to learn a new software program. Figure 1.2 contains a portion of the guide on which the story is based. This literacy story is used throughout the book to highlight the multidimensional nature of literacy. After each dimension has been discussed, the story will be analyzed from that particular dimension. In chapter 12, the story is revisited and the various dimensions are summarized and synthesized.

ABOUT THIS BOOK

This book grew out of a concern that literacy is too often viewed in reductionistic ways. One dimension, such as linguistic, or even a particular feature of a dimension, such as graphophonemics within the linguistic dimension, is highlighted and used

TABLE 1.2
A Literacy Story

Many years ago, when I first began using IBM's personal computer software program WordPerfect to write academic papers, I purchased a copy of *Microref Quick Reference Guide* (Microref Systems, 1988). Although I had no experience with WordPerfect and limited experience with computer reference guides, I did have knowledge of other IBM software programs and had been using an IBM personal computer for several years. I therefore had a basic notion of how WordPerfect might work and was able to make sense from some of the print based on this background knowledge.

At this point in the story, I must confess that I disdain reading and following directions. I avoid such contexts when possible. When avoidance is not an option, I will usually attempt to discover what needs to be done on my own, ignoring the directions or using them selectively. Or, if I can get a family member or friend to help me, I will do so. On the other hand, I tend to prefer learning in context. In this case, I wanted to learn the software program as I used it to write a paper. The purpose or function drove my engagement with the program.

As I read through the guide and attempted to use different aspects of the program to write a paper, I engaged in numerous revision (rethinking/rereading) strategies. However, there were numerous points in the *Reference Guide* that puzzled or confused me and I found rereading and rethinking to be of little help. Basically, I was unable to "read" the text.

To overcome this problem, I frequently called a professor at another university who was familiar with the program. This colleague "talked me through" certain points in the guide, explained areas of confusion, and suggested possible solutions to problems that I encountered. At times, she ignored the guide altogether and directed me to execute certain commands based on her personal knowledge of and experience with the program. As I began to learn the program, my questions changed and became more sophisticated as I moved beyond "plugging and chugging" to more advanced executions. Over time, with numerous experiences using WordPerfect to write academic papers, and with help from my colleague, I eventually became an independent user of both the *Guide* and the software program.

to define reading or writing. Such a reductionistic stance is especially damaging to elementary teachers and their students. All too often, the view finds its way into the classroom and is used to frame instructional materials, privileging particular aspects of literacy and ignoring others. This is especially true in today's educational climate where the federal government, through the No Child Left Behind legislation (United States Department of Education, 2001), is funding reading programs that are limited in their instructional scope. However, as Young (1992) reminded us in *Seven Blind Mice*, "Knowing in part may make a fine tale, but wisdom comes from seeing the whole."

My initial attempt to move beyond the telling of a fine tale was to develop and teach both an undergraduate and a graduate course on the multidimensional nature

SAVE A BLOCK OF TEXT AS A DOCUMENT

1. Position cursor at beginning or end of text to be saved as a document
2. Hold down **ALT** and press **F4** (Block)
3. Highlight block of text to be saved
4. Press **F10** (Save)
5. Type a new document name and press **RETURN**

EDITING A COLUMN OF TEXT

DELETE A COLUMN OF TEXT

1. Position cursor on first character of column to be deleted
2. Hold down **ALT** and press **F4** (Block)
3. Highlight column of text to be deleted by moving cursor horizontally and vertically
4. Hold down **CTRL** and press **F4** (Cut or Copy)
5. Press **1** (Cut/Copy Column)
6. Press **1** (Cut)

APPEND A BLOCK OF TEXT

Use this procedure to copy text to the end of an existing document.

1. Position cursor at beginning or end of text to be appended
2. Hold down **ALT** and press **F4** (Block)
3. Highlight block of text to be appended
4. Hold down **CTRL** and press **F4** (Cut or Copy)
5. Press **3** (Append)
6. Type name of existing document and press **RETURN**

MOVE A COLUMN OF TEXT

Use this procedure to move one or more columns of text or numbers defined by the following codes: Tab, Align Tab, Indent, or Hard Carriage Return. Do not use this procedure to move Newspaper or Scriptwriting columns.

1. Position cursor on first character to be moved
2. Hold down **ALT** and press **F4** (Block)
3. Highlight column of text to be moved by moving cursor horizontally and vertically
4. Hold down **CTRL** and press **F4** (Cut or Copy)
5. Press **1** (Cut/Copy Column)
6. Press **1** (Cut)
7. Position cursor on first character to follow moved text
8. To move column or block to new location, hold down **CTRL** and press **F4** (Cut or Copy)
9. Press **4** (Retrieve Column)

DELETE A BLOCK OF TEXT

1. Position cursor at beginning or end of text to be deleted
2. Hold down **ALT** and press **F4** (Block)
3. Highlight block of text to be deleted
4. Press **DEL**
5. To delete text, press **Y** (Yes)

NOTES:

WordPerfect saves up to three deletions so that you can undelete text (**F1**) if desired.

If there is no more room in memory or on disk to save a deletion, WordPerfect will give you the option to delete the block without saving the deletion.

COPY A COLUMN OF TEXT

Use this procedure to copy one or more columns of text or numbers defined by the following codes: Tab, Align Tab, Indent, or Hard Carriage Return. Do not use this procedure to copy Newspaper or Scriptwriting columns.

1. Position cursor on first character to be copied
2. Hold down **ALT** and press **F4** (Block)
3. Highlight column to be copied by moving cursor horizontally and vertically
4. Hold down **CTRL** and press **F4** (Cut or Copy)
5. Press **1** (Cut/Copy Column)
6. Press **2** (Copy)
7. Position cursor on first character to follow copied text
8. To copy column, hold down **CTRL** and press **F4** (Cut or Copy)
9. Press **4** (Retrieve Column)

FIG. 1.2. Computer program guide. From Microref Systems, Inc. (1988). *Microref quick reference guides.* Chicago, IL: Microref.

of literacy. A variety of students enrolled in the course, but many, if not most, planned to become or were elementary teachers. The response to the course was so positive and the insights gained by the students so significant that I decided a more formal presentation of the course content was warranted. Thus, the genesis of the book and its primary audience: those individuals who will become or currently are involved in literacy teaching and learning with children. The book is intended to provide these readers with conceptual knowledge about the nature of reading and writing that can serve as a base for written language instruction. Although the book is focused primarily on English literacy, research on biliteracy—reading and writing in two languages—is included. The increasing linguistic diversity in the United States has made this research all the more critical. Regardless of where one teaches, bilingual learners are sitting in our classrooms.

In writing this book, I have tried to be cognizant of the fact that most readers are not—nor will they become—linguists, psychologists, cultural theorists, or the like. I have attempted, therefore, to keep discussions on a level that will be useful to readers as they develop, implement, and evaluate literacy curricula and instruction for the students they teach. General understandings about literacy are presented, accompanied by specific examples for illustrative purposes. On the other hand, I have also attempted to be respectful of the knowledge and expertise that teachers bring to their craft and to their reading of this book, so I have tried to avoid oversimplifying complex issues or controversies in the field.

Despite the tremendous gains that have been made in our understanding of literacy during the last several decades, debate about the very nature of literacy continues. I am not neutral in this debate; in fact, I believe that neutrality is neither desirable nor possible. Therefore, my analysis and discussion of literacy reflect a particular vantage point that has emerged from researchers studying literacy within contextualized situations. Like Young (1992), I believe that various literacy "parts" can only be fully understood when they are considered within the whole. When there is disagreement in the field about a particular issue, however, I acknowledge this fact and provide a general sense of alternative perspectives.

Throughout the book, I include numerous demonstrations and "hands-on" experiences through which particular literacy concepts are introduced. Debriefings and more formal discussions of the concepts under consideration follow the demonstrations and hands-on experiences. Initially, most of the activities were developed for my interdisciplinary university courses. I have found that these experiences provide an avenue through which current beliefs about literacy can be suspended and examined, thus allowing for new insights that might contradict currently held views.

The remainder of the book is organized around the four dimensions of literacy previously introduced. So as to not isolate each dimension from the other, and fall into the same trap as disciplinary perspectives, throughout the discussion of each dimension, links are made to the previous dimensions addressed. Within the linguistic dimension, chapter 2 focuses on the nature of language, chapter 3 addresses oral and written language relationships, and chapter 4 discusses language variation. Chapters 5, 6, 7, and 8 explore the cognitive dimension of literacy, re-spectively, the constructive characteristics of perception, reading, comprehending, and writing. The sociocultural dimension of literacy is represented in chapters 9 and 10. Finally, the developmental dimension, which considers the learning of literacy and the various factors that impact the process, is discussed in chapter 11. Because the primary audience of the book is classroom teachers, chapter 12 ad-dresses the teaching and learning implications that emerge from an understanding of the multidimensional nature of reading and writing.

II

The Linguistic Dimension
of Literacy

2

The Nature of Language

Language is the vehicle or avenue through which ideas are constructed during reading and writing. Because the use of language for the generation of ideas is so deeply embedded in our everyday activities, we seldom consider the nature of language itself. We often fail to ponder the internal characteristics of written language and what must be known about these characteristics for the effective and efficient use of language to occur. However, although we may be unaware of its attributes on a conscious, explicit level, our implicit (unconscious) knowledge of language is employed every time we make meaning through print. The focus in this chapter is on the properties of language that are understood and used (at least on the implicit level) by the proficient language user when creating meaning through written discourse. Or, stated somewhat differently, what must readers and writers know about language that allows them to "crack the code" as they transact with written discourse?

Two aspects of literacy as a language process are considered. The first is the internal, physical properties of written language. Second, the impact of the situational context on the language user's understanding of these physical properties is demonstrated.

WHAT MAKES LANGUAGE LANGUAGE?

The linguistic dimension of language is concerned with the analysis of text as an object of study. Just as a connoisseur of fine arts might analyze the internal properties of a painting or musical score, a linguist focuses on the various physical properties of language itself. To be fully understood, not only must these various properties be identified and defined, but also the relation of each property to all of the others must be explained. However, before the properties of language are explored, let us take a few minutes to analyze the linguistic texts (language events) and nonlinguistic texts (nonlanguage events) illustrated in Figs. 2.1 and 2.2.

C.F.Y.

(call for you)

Date: _____

To: _____

From: _____

Subject: _____

_____
_____

The Great Big Enormous Turnip
A Russian folktale by Alexei Tolstoy

Once upon a time an old planted a
little turnip.   The old man said,
"Grow, grow, little turnip.   Grow
strong."   And the turnip grew up sweet
and strong and big and enormous.
Then one day the old man went to
pull it up.   (story continues)

Subway Rush Hour
by Langston Hughes

Mingled
breath and small
so close
mingled
black and white
so near
no room for fear

Ollie and Leroy
by Sally Johnson

One morning Ollie and Leroy
was getting ready to go to school.
Leroy, he put on one of Ollie's
socks 'cause he lost his.   Ollie say,
"Boy, give me my sock" but
Leroy wouldn't give it to him.
Leroy say, "It my sock."   But
Ollie know it wasn't 'cause it
wasn't even the same color as
Leroy.   (story continues)

RUB OUT ROACHES

!! SHOCKING NEWS FOR ROACHES !!

* no sprays   • no residues
* no chemicals   • no smells

Locally Owned and Operated

1-888-999-9999

FIG. 2.1.   Language events. The poem, "Subway Rush Hour" is from *Collected Poems by Langston Hughes*. Copyright © 1994 by the Estate of Langston Hughes. Reprinted by permission of Alfred A. Knopf, a Division of Random House Inc. British Commonwealth rights granted by Harold Ober Associates.

As you examine these examples, consider which features are present across all the language events. At the same time, consider which of these identified features are missing in the nonlanguage events.

First and foremost, language is a meaning-based system of communication. Its use involves a language user with intentions to construct meaning that ultimately is made visible through the linguistic system. Meaning is at the heart of language and its use. This characteristic, although necessary, is not sufficient for defining what

Dick
Jane
Sally
Spot
Mother   STOP
Father
Look

A, B, C, D, E, F, G, H, I, J K, L, M, N, O, P, Q, R, S, T, U, V, W, X, Y,

a. 12 x 7 + 4 x 6 - 1 =
b. 3(4 + 6) =
c. a(x + 2y) =

Directions: Circle all of the words that begin with the same sound as **can** and **come**.

a. Mother could catch Sally.
b. Dick carried cookies.
c. Dick used the cookies to call Spot to the car.

0, 1, 2, 3, 4, 5, 6, 7, 8, 9

FIG. 2.2. Nonlanguage events. From AH-CHOO by Mercer Mayer (1976). Copyright © Mercer Mayer. Used by permission of Dial Books for Young Readers, a division of Penguin Putnam Inc.

is and is not language. Artists, mathematicians, musicians, and dancers would all claim to be involved in meaning making.

A second aspect of language as a meaning-making system is that it has a dual structure. Language operates on two levels, surface and deep. Semioticians, individuals who study how meaning is generated and shared, have proposed that all meaning making involves the use of signs. Signs are the physical vehicles (e.g., sight, touch, hearing, smell) through which meanings are expressed. A sign, therefore, is something that stands for something else (Smagorinsky, 2001). This relation between the vehicle and its meaning is often referred to as the relation between the surface structure and the deep structure (Smith, 1994a, 2004). As

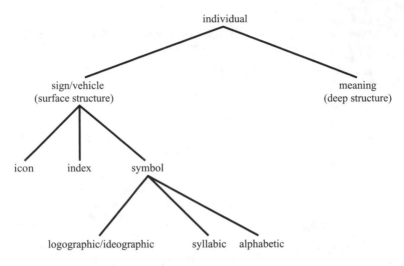

FIG. 2.3. Signs and their various expressions.

indicated in Fig. 2.3, the surface structure is another name for the physical vehicle through which meaning is conveyed. The surface structure is that aspect that can be seen, felt, heard, or smelled. The deep structure is the meaning that the vehicle is representing. The construction of meaning involves, among other things, the building of links between the surface structure and a corresponding deep structure.

Three types of signs have been identified. The first is iconic. Icons are signs in which the physical property of the surface structure resembles the meaning being conveyed. Illustrations and pictures are typically iconic in nature. They look like that for which they stand. For example, a photograph of a clock is iconic because many of its physical properties—shape, numerals, and hands—are similar to those of an actual clock. In fact, the similarity between some icons and what they represent is so strong that when shown a photograph of a clock and asked to identify what it is, most of us would quickly say, "clock," even though on a subconscious level we realize that what we are viewing is not actually a clock. Rather, it is an iconic representation of a clock. Language is not iconic because there is nothing in its nature, such as the way a word looks or sounds, that resembles what it is representing. The physical aspects—sound or visual configuration—of the word clock are unrelated to the physical characteristics of the clock on a kitchen wall.

A second kind of sign is indexical. An index is a sign that points to what is being represented. It contains physical aspects that are related to the conveyed concept. A ticking sound might be an index pointing to a clock because many clocks emit that sound. Smoke coming out of a kitchen window might be an index that points to a fire, because "where there is smoke, there is fire." Physicians make frequent use of indexical signs as they attempt to discover to what bacteria or virus a fever, rash, or headache might point. Forensic science makes use of indexical signs to determine who may have been involved in a crime to which there were no witnesses. Although an index does not physically resemble the meaning for which it stands, as does an icon, the properties of an index are related to the properties of the meaning being represented. Again, language is not indexical because there is nothing in its physical nature that indicates what it means.

The third kind of sign is symbolic; language is a symbolic sign system. A symbol is an arbitrary yet systematic correspondence between the symbol's physical properties and what it represents. There is no inherent reason why the spoken word /clock/ or the written word <clock> represents an instrument that keeps track of time. (When referring to sound categories in the language, the category is designated with the // marking; when referring to letter categories, the < > designation is used.) This fact is easily demonstrated by the various ways in which the concept of a clock are represented in different languages. However, although arbitrary, the relation is systematic. All language users within a particular discourse community must agree to accept—if only for a limited period of time or within particular contexts— the relation between the surface and deep structure once it has been established.

Language is also a rule-governed, creative, and generative system. Most instances of language use are unique; they do not represent a limited list of memorized words or sentences that are used over and over again in different combinations. Rather, through the use of rule-governed or systematic combinations, a limited number of elements—such as the 26 letters of the English alphabet or a finite number of grammatical rules—generate an infinite number of ideas and ways to express them. For the most part, knowledge of these rules is implicit (not conscious); the users of language cannot necessarily explain them or their operation even though they use them. As many teachers can attest, it is not an uncommon experience for high school or college students to have difficulty learning traditional English grammar (explicit knowledge) and yet at the same time demonstrate their implicit understanding of English syntax in their writings. Decades of research have documented this as well (e.g., Hillocks, 1986; Hillocks & Smith, 2003; Weaver, 1998). It is through the knowledge and use of these various rule-governed systems that texts are generated.

The outcome of any literacy event is typically the construction of a "text"; that is, a meaningful unit of language that is intended to communicate (de Beaugrande, 1980). Gee (1996) has defined "discourse" in a similar way: "Connected stretches of language which hang together so as to make sense to some community of people" (p. 90). It is important to note at this point that texts may also be nonlinguistic and nonsymbolic in nature. Paintings, photographs, buildings, and flags can all be texts or "configurations of signs that provide a potential for meaning" (Smagorinsky, 2001, p. 137). Even more importantly for our purposes, many texts are multimodal; they contain linguistic as well as nonlinguistic signs. The use of pictures, tables, figures, color, various font sizes and shapes are frequently part of what makes a text a text (Waller, 1996).

The multimodality of texts has been considerably enhanced with the advent of computer technology. The use of sound and video, along with the embedding of hypertexts, expands the notion of what texts are traditionally thought to be. As we

TABLE 2.1

Text and the Systems of Language

Any size unit of language that forms a unified whole. To be unified, the text must be coherent externally and internally. External coherence refers to the relationship between the text and the context of situation. A text must be relevant within a particular environment. To be internally coherent, all systems of language must be present or implied and working together.

Magazine articles, letters, stories, traffic signs, newspaper articles, advertisements, poems, novels, e-mails, shopping lists

shall see in the cognitive dimension of literacy, multimodality and hypertext computer capabilities also challenge the linear, right-to-left and top-down processing that was the norm for most written texts (Kinzer & Leander, 2003; Lankshear & Knobel, 2002; Leu, 2000; Wysocki, 2004).

As indicated in Table 2.1, according to Halliday (1973, 1974) and Halliday and Hasan (1976, 1980), a text is a linguistic unit of any size that forms a unified whole. To be unified, a text must display both external and internal coherence. To be externally coherent, a text must be situated in an appropriate context; it must be relevant to its location. A traffic sign at an intersection, a menu in a restaurant, and a children's book in a library would all be examples of a text, a linguistic unit embedded in a plausible environment.

To be internally coherent, a text must reflect, either implicitly or explicitly, the systems of language shown in Tables 2.2 to 2.15 and these systems must be working together. Even seemingly isolated words as those found on traffic signs, such as <STOP> or <YIELD>, in fact, have an implied linguistic wholeness based on the situation in which they are encountered. The command <STOP> means, "You, the driver, halt your vehicle at this point. Do not proceed until it is your turn and then look both ways before moving forward." The command <YIELD> tells the driver of the vehicle, "Be careful; the oncoming traffic has the right of way. Proceed with caution." Words on shopping lists represent a similar kind of situation.

It is these various systems—what K. Goodman (1996) termed cue systems—that readers and writers employ when interacting with written language to build meaning. Readers, or code breakers, use the cues as a blueprint or guide to construct meaning as they transact with a text. Writers, or code makers, use the cues to express the meanings they are generating. Because the systems of language are such a significant part of what makes language language—and oftentimes the prime focus of literacy instruction—a separate section in this chapter is devoted to them.

THE SYSTEMS OF LANGUAGE

The systems of language in Tables 2.2 to 2.15 represent a synthesis of ideas taken from a variety of sources that are referenced throughout the next portion of this chapter. The tables summarize the ideas to be presented, provide examples, and serve as reference points for future use. My intent here is to provide a general overview of what readers and writers know and utilize as they interact with print. No attempt has been made to make the synthesis exhaustive; nor are claims made that the various definitions presented are universally accepted by all linguists. In fact, there is a lack of consensus as to the exact nature of the systems of language and the rules that govern their operation (e.g., Graessner, Golding, & Long, 1996; Weaver & Kintsch, 1996). Although one goal of linguists is to delineate necessary and sufficient conditions for the systems that make language language, linguists readily admit that they have yet to generate all of the rules that govern these systems. Finally, although readers and writers utilize their knowledge of the systems of language to construct text, this is not to say that all systems are equally controlled by all readers and writers in all situations. Based on experiences—or lack thereof—in various communicative contexts, particular systems may be more or less controlled than others.

Pragmatic

The pragmatic system expresses the various functions, uses, and intentions that the language can serve. It governs what forms of language are appropriate in particular contexts. Just as furniture has various functions—to sit or lie on, to eat or write on, to place items in—language also serves various purposes. Proficient readers and writers have implicit knowledge of these functions and when and how to employ them in appropriate ways in particular contexts. All other systems of language are embedded within, and governed by, the pragmatics of the situation, the most powerful system. The purpose underlying the use of literacy will influence the type of text read or written, the structure of the text, its genre, the meaning and the structure of the sentences within the text, the words selected, and so on.

Teachers, because they play a significant role in structuring the context in which their students read and write, have a significant impact on the pragmatics of the situation (Kucer, 1994). When I was a junior in high school, for example, one of my favorite English teachers required her students to write in a journal on a regular basis. In evaluating our journals, she gave us two grades, one for content and one for form. Although every journal entry was evaluated for content, only particular entries received a grade for such written language conventions as spelling and punctuation. Additionally, the teacher would inform us ahead of time when an entry was to receive a form grade. I had little difficulty with content, but I was not a very proficient speller. Consequently, my form grades were rather low due to all of the "unconventional" spellings.

My response to this problem was not to become a better speller, as I am sure my teacher intended. Rather, on those days in which our entries were to be evaluated for form, I focused little attention on the content of my writing. I would select a topic that would allow me to use words that I was fairly certain I could spell

TABLE 2.2

The Pragmatic System of Language

The functions, uses, and intentions of the language user as they relate to particular contexts.

Instrumental
(I want)
Literacy used as a means of getting things; satisfying material needs.

Regulatory
(Do as I tell you/How it must be)
Literacy used to control the behaviors, feelings, or attitudes of others.

Interactional
(Me and you/Me against you)
Literacy used to interact with others; forming and maintaining personal relationships; establishing separateness.

Personal
(Here I come)
Literacy used to express individuality and uniqueness; awareness of self; pride.

Heuristic
(Tell me why)
Literacy used to explore the environment; to ask questions; to seek and test knowledge.

Imaginative
(Let's pretend)
Literacy used to create new worlds.

Informative
(I've got something to tell you)
Literacy used as a means of communicating information to someone who does not possess that information.

conventionally. If, in the process of writing, I came to a word I was unable to spell, I changed the word to one I knew how to spell, regardless of the impact on my intentions and meanings. Although these entries were rather trite in content and stilted in form, I was able to raise my grade for written language conventions.

A number of researchers have delineated various taxonomies for the functions that language can serve (K. Goodman, 1996; Halliday, 1973; Heath, 1983; Smith, 1977; Taylor & Dorsey-Gaines, 1988). Halliday's list of functions has perhaps received the most attention and is presented in Table 2.2. Regardless of which scheme is employed to describe the uses of language, what is significant is that readers and writers have an understanding of the various functions of language and the rules for their appropriate use.

Halliday (1973) proposed that the text evolved during a language event always fulfills at least one of seven functions, although in many cases multiple purposes are served. Again, because it is the language user who must link the surface structure with the deep structure, the understood function(s) of a particular text may vary from individual to individual and from situation to situation.

The instrumental, or "I want," function is the use of literacy to obtain things, to satisfy material needs. Language serves this function when we fill out an order form or make a shopping list before we go to the grocery store. It is the language of requests or demands. The regulatory, or "do as I tell you/how it must be," function is the use of literacy to control the behavior, feelings, or attitudes of others. A note to one's daughter to clean her room, laws passed by the U.S. Congress to govern human behavior, and traffic signs are examples of using literacy in a regulatory manner. Literacy used to interact with others, to form, maintain, and dissolve personal relationships, represents the interactional, or "me and you/me against you," function of language. Letters or e-mails to friends and family, many greeting cards, letters to Dear Abby or Ann Landers, and postcards sent while on vacation can be interactional in nature.

The personal, or "here I come," function is the use of literacy to express individuality or the sense of self. Autobiographies, journals, and diaries frequently express the personal function of language. The heuristic, or "tell me why," function is the use of literacy to explore the environment and world. It involves asking questions and seeking and testing knowledge. Scientists and other types of researchers often make use of this function through surveys, interviews, and the like. In contrast, the use of reading and writing to create new worlds and to leave the here and now is the imaginative, or "let's pretend," function. Reading for enjoyment and the writing of creative stories or poems are examples of the imaginative use of literacy.

The final function of language is the informative, the "I've got something to tell you" function. It is the use of literacy to communicate or discover information that is not already known. The literacy used in schools most often reflects the informative function. However, because the effective and efficient use of literacy involves the use of print for various purposes and functions, it is critical that schools provide students with a range of literacy activities so they have the opportunity to develop proficiency with all of these functions. In the final chapter, we will examine various instructional strategies (see Table 12.5) that classroom teachers might use to engage their students in the various functions that written language can serve.

As previously noted, texts can express or serve multiple functions. This multiplicity can be represented in a number of ways. In one of the more well-known examples, the book *Alice in Wonderland* by Lewis Carroll (1988), was explicitly written by the author for at least two reasons. One fulfills the imaginative function: the reader enters a fantasy world as the adventures of Alice are played out. On another level, the text serves as a critique of British society and royalty, Queen Victoria in particular. Carroll essentially used an imaginative function as a "cover" for informative purposes. This is not to imply, of course, that readers are necessarily aware of these multiple functions. It is probably the case that many readers of *Alice in Wonderland*, young or old, understand the text to be a fantasy.

A second way in which the multiplicity of functions is realized relates to the concept of stance. Stance represents the purpose that the language user brings to the discourse. Just as Carroll brought at least two stances to his writing of *Alice in Wonderland*—to tell an engaging story and to critique society—the reader brings a stance as well. This stance may or may not correspond with that of the author. The writers of weekly news magazines such as *Newsweek* or *Time* probably intend their discourse to serve informative and heuristic purposes. Readers can encounter unknown information about world and national events and also have their questions answered. However, "news junkies" also read such magazines for enjoyment and pleasure. Although not imaginative in the *Alice in Wonderland* sense, their enjoyment does take them away from the here and now. In this case, the stance of the writer and the stance of the reader may not be in complete alignment.

The various functions that texts serve in classroom settings was explored by Rosenblatt (1978, 1991a, 1991b). She argued that many commonly used texts in high school English classrooms were intended by their authors to produce "lived through" experiences or "poems" in their readers. In effect, the works were produced for aesthetic purposes and the authors intended—or hoped—that their readers would assume a similar stance. However, the stance taken by many teachers is efferent or informational in nature. The "carrying away" of facts and figures is the focus of instruction. Successful students in such instructional contexts are those who can, in effect, read against the grain of the text. Successful students assume an information-gathering stance as they interact with texts written for primarily aesthetic purposes.

A complementary view of stance was also proposed by Spiro (1977). He suggested that the stance of the reader toward a text can be understood in terms of high versus low text integrity. In a high-integrity stance, the reader's intent is to maintain the content of the discourse. Text meanings are privileged and the reader attempts to learn and recall the meanings in the exact form in which they were presented. In this situation, the reader avoids integrating the meanings of the text with what is already known about the topic. In a low-text integrity stance, the reader attempts to integrate the meanings in the text with what is known about the topic. There is not a concern for maintaining the ideas intact. Rather, the reader wants to expand and more fully develop existing knowledge with the new ideas presented by the author.

Testing in schools often encourages the reader to maintain a high-text integrity stance. Tests may require the reader to recall or "give back" the meanings in the form in which they were presented. Integrating text meanings with prior knowledge makes it difficult to discern which meanings were brought *to* the page and which meanings were generated *from* the page. An incident I experienced in graduate school may help clarify this distinction.

I was taking my first psycholinguistic class during my first semester in graduate school. I had little knowledge of the topic and was somewhat disturbed by the large number of advanced PhD students in linguistics who were also enrolled in

TABLE 2.3

The Text Type System of Language

Particular discourse forms with distinguishing features and patterns

narration, exposition, poetry, drama

TABLE 2.4

The Genre System of Language

A class of texts marked by distinctive styles, forms, or content within a text type

Novels, short stories, mysteries, folktales/fairy tales
(narration)

Research papers, directions, essays, medical reports, editorials
(exposition)

Epics, sonnets, odes, elegies
(poetry)

Tragedies, comedies, romances
(drama)

the course. They had a wealth of background in the subject and appeared to already know much of what the professor was teaching. However, when tests were given, these same students frequently received rather low grades. I found this puzzling until the professor reviewed the answers to an exam. One of the linguistic students challenged the professor on a number of answers related to questions concerning language acquisition. The student insisted that his answer was as "correct" as the professor's and cited research to support his stance. The professor replied that he was testing us not on what we brought to the class, but on what we had learned from the class. The students in linguistics were having difficulty privileging the professor's "text," whereas I had no difficulty doing so because I knew so little about the topic.

Text Type, Genre, and Text Structure

The meanings that are generated to meet an individual's purpose are displayed through various text types, genres, and text structures. These three systems of language, represented in Tables 2.3, 2.4, and 2.5, are addressed together because of the intimate relation among them. Text types—narrative, exposition, poetic, dramatic—are expressed through particular genres and text structures and reflect particular features, patterns, and content. Narratives are realized through such genres as novels, short stories, mysteries, and folktales. Research papers, newspapers, medical reports, and many textbooks are genres within the expository text type. Finally, the poetic text type can be articulated, for example, through epics,

TABLE 2.5

The Text Structure System of Language

The total organization of meanings across a text type

Temporal Order: time order

Attribution: idea development

Adversative: compare/contrast

Covariance: cause/effect

Response: problem/solution

sonnets, and odes and the dramatic type through comedy, tragedy, and romance genres. This relation between text type and genre might be compared to furniture. Chairs, a type of furniture, are of various genres: dining room and rocking chairs, chairs for reclining, highchairs for infants, and so on. Each genre reflects particular characteristics that best serve its purpose or function.

The meanings that are generated through text types and genres are expressed in a variety of corresponding structures; temporal order, adversative, response, attribution, and covariance. Figure 2.4 visually illustrates these various structures. As indicated, temporal order texts, commonly associated with narratives and dramas, involve the organization of ideas by time or when they occurred. The rules used to structure ideas in this manner are commonly referred to as a story grammar. Table 2.6 presents a story grammar by Stein and Glenn (1979; Stein & Trabasso, 1982), although numerous grammars exist (e.g., Mandler & Johnson, 1977; Rumelhart, 1975; Thorndyke, 1977). As conceived within this representation, a story consists of an explicit or implicit setting (characters, time, location) and a number of episodes. Episodes involve an event that initiates a response in the form of a goal by the protagonist and an attempt to obtain the goal. The attempt is followed by the consequence of obtaining or not obtaining the goal and the reaction of the protagonist to the consequence.

In most reader and writers, even young children, knowledge of "storiness" is one of the most well developed text structures. To a large extent, our lives or lived-through experiences are stories. Additionally, many television programs, movies, and songs reflect temporal order structures. A young child may never have been read to in the home, yet still bring a developing story grammar to school based on these other narrative experiences. As we will see in chapter 4, however, different story grammars exist within American society. Some children will bring grammars that align with the grammar used by the school whereas others may have a grammar with a rule system at variance with that found in the classroom.

Attributions involve the development of factual, conceptual, and generalizable knowledge. Typically, facts are linked to concepts and concepts are linked to generalizations. And, facts, concepts, and generalizations are usually presented by order of importance or significance. Adversatives involve the comparing and

- Time Order

  setting + episode [initiating event + internal response

  + attempt + consequence + reaction]

- Compare and Contrast

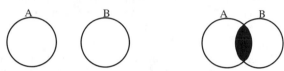

- Problem and Solution

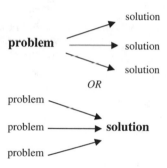

- Cause and Effect

- Idea Development

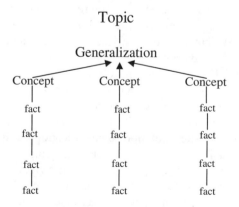

FIG. 2.4. Text structures and the systems of language.

29

TABLE 2.6

A One Episode Story Grammar

Category	Example
Setting: introduction of the main characters; may contain information about the context in which the story occurs	Once upon a time there a was a big blue fish named Albert. He lived in a big icy pond near the edge of the forest.
Episode	
Initiating event: an action or event that serves to cause a response in the main character.	One day Albert was swimming around the pond with nothing to do. Then he spotted a big juicy worm on top of the water.
Internal response: the goal of the main character	Albert knew how delicious big juicy worms tasted. He wanted to eat one for his dinner.
Attempt: an overt action to obtain the main character's the goal.	So he swam very close to eat the worm for his dinner.
Consequence: an event, action, or state that marks the attainment or nonattainment of the main character's goal.	Suddenly, Albert was pulled through the water into a boat.
Reaction: an emotion, action, or state the expresses the main character's feelings about the goal attainment or nonattainment. Or, the consequences of the goal attainment or nonattainment.	Albert felt sad. He wished that he had been more careful.

contrasting of ideas in which similarities and differences are noted. Covariance structures demonstrate how particular events occur or come into being because of other events. Finally, response structures present a problem with a number of possible solutions or, conversely, several problems that can be resolved by a single solution. Attributions, adversatives, covariances, and responses are frequently found in expository discourse.

Weaver and Kintsch (1996) have presented a slightly different yet complementary framework for the structure of attributions found in expository texts. They suggest that expositions depict three types of relations: general–particular, object–object, and object–part. General–particular relations involve the identification of characteristics, definitions, classifications, and illustrations of objects, processes, events, etc. Object–object relations compare and contrast entities, processes, events, etc. Finally, object–part relations involve an analysis of the associations and interactions between the parts and whole of objects, processes, events, etc.

At this point, a cautionary note is warranted. The characteristics assigned to each text type, genre, and structure are best understood in terms of dominance (de Beaugrande, 1984). That is, particular characteristics may permeate a text, but not completely control it. Consequently, any text may actually contain a mix of types and structures. An expository text, such as that found in the social sciences, may include the kind of time-sequenced events that typically are found in literary narrative discourses as well as information in an attributive form. A problem–solution structured scientific text may in many ways resemble the structure of temporal ordered discourse of a literary novel. Narratives, although time ordered, can also make use of covariance and response structures.

The overlap of structures can once again be compared to that of furniture. Although usually intended for different purposes, both a bed and a couch share a number of physical or structural characteristics. The dominant use of a couch is for sitting and a bed for sleeping; however, it is not uncommon for people to sleep on a couch and sit on a bed. Text types and structures, like furniture, are only predictive in nature and provide the reader or writer with an initial and general orientation toward the discourse. Finally, as the various text types, genres, and structures are considered, it is important to remember that the text type, genre, and structure employed are governed by the pragmatics of the situation. The purpose, intentions, and meanings of the language user will determine the features, patterns, and organization of the meanings constructed. Put simply, the form of the discourse follows its function.

The function–form relation is important to consider when teachers introduce students to various text types and structures. Text types, often called the modes of discourse within instructional settings, need to be embedded within contexts that require their use. Too often, students are taught how to write in the various modes without first considering why a particular mode is required. The function of the text within the communicative context is not examined. Rather, students simply learn the patterns and structures of the modes and demonstrate their knowledge when required, such as on standardized tests. If students are to be helped to use various literacy forms in the "real world," a consideration of their appropriate use in various contexts must be an essential part of the instruction.

It is with the systems of language of text types, genres, and text structures that the concept of "intertextuality" becomes particularly significant. Simply put, intertextuality represents the linguistic, conceptual, and situational links that readers build among various texts (Beach, Appleman, & Dorsey, 1994; Hartman, 1992, 1994; Hartman & Hartman, 1993). Readers and writers come to learn and make use of their intertextual knowledge because they have had numerous encounters with particular types, genres, and structures of texts. These encounters have allowed them to build an understanding of the distinguishing features of narratives and expositions (text types), for example, and the characteristics of directions as well as fairy tales (genres). Additionally, proficient language users have learned which structures, such as temporal order or attribution, typically accompany particular text types and genres. And, readers and writers know which text types, genres, and structures are most appropriate—functional—in which situations.

This interplay among text type, genre, and text structure becomes particularly important for teachers to consider as students move beyond the primary classroom. Frequently, students who have acquired the literacy "basics" in the early grades suddenly encounter difficulty with informational, disciplinary-based discourses in the upper grades (Donahue, Voelkl, Campbell, & Mazzeo, 1999; Rand Reading Study Group, 2002; Wilhelm, 1996). Depending on the age of the students, this phenomenon has been termed the "fourth grade hump" (Allington, 2001; Chall, 1983; Gee, 1999) or the "middle school hump" (Allington, 2001; Snow et al., 1991). It would appear that two factors significantly contribute to these reading difficulties. One factor concerns the nature of texts and tasks, the second the nature of instructional mediation (Carrasquillo, Kucer, & Abrams, 2004).

Literacy increasingly becomes a primary vehicle for transmitting information in the intermediate, middle, and high school (Alvermann, 2002; Alvermann & Phelps, 1998; Wells, 1995). Students encounter academic discourses and disciplinary concepts in such fields as science, mathematics, and the social sciences that go far beyond that of the more familiar and comfortable literary and personal narrative. Cognitive academic language (Cummins, 1994) demands significantly increase as the use of expository discourse becomes the norm. As the use of informational texts take on increased importance in the curriculum, the kinds of text types, genres, and structures students are asked to read and write shift as well. The well-known time order structures are accompanied by compare and contrast, problem and solution, and cause and effect organizational patterns (Kucer, Brobst, & Bolgatz, 2002; Carrasquillo, Kucer, & Abrams, 2004). These new patterns frequently contain multiple charts, figures, tables, and maps that add to processing demands. The concepts in these texts also become increasingly remote and abstract in nature. Although narratives continue to be used in the curriculum, their length increases significantly. "One sitting" readings are replaced by extended "chapter books" that are independently read across space and time (Wilhelm, 1996).

Not only do the content and linguistic nature of the texts read and written change, so too does the nature of the sentences and vocabulary. Especially in the sciences and social sciences, sentences become more complex syntactically and contain a much wider range of specialized vocabulary. Even teacher talk, which was conversational and informal in nature during the early grades, becomes more presentational and formal. The language of the teacher, impacted by the written language of the discipline, often takes on the characteristics of a lecture (Barnes & Todd, 1995; Cazden, 1988, 2001; Kutz, 1997).

This intertwining of new language structures and new concepts places new linguistic and cognitive demands on the students. Academic literacy tasks require students to analyze, synthesize, evaluate, and critique texts in ways not experienced in the elementary classroom. The specialized ways with words (Greenleaf, Schoenbach, Cziko, & Mueller, 2001) and the specialized ways of thinking within the disciplines (Greenleaf, Jimenez, & Roller, 2002) frequently cause students difficulty. What students have learned about literacy in the early grades, therefore, often will not automatically transfer to these content areas. Literacy abilities that were functional in the primary grades may suddenly become inadequate. Additionally, because the texts encountered through reading and writing increase in length, students may lack adequate "repair strategies" to help them work their way through processing difficulties. Dilemmas that students were able to ignore in shorter texts become increasingly problematic with longer stretches of discourse.

Accompanying these new disciplinary linguistic and cognitive demands is a decreased emphasis on literacy instruction. Interestingly, this shift in instructional focus from process to content occurs at the same time that reading and writing in the disciplines take on increased importance. Many teachers in the upper grades assume—or hope—that the literacy "basics" have already been taught and mastered and concentrate their instructional attention on "delivering" content. This does not mean that all reading and writing instruction ceases, but that such instruction is not typically extended into the content areas of mathematics, social sciences, and sciences (Kucer, Brobst, & Bolgatz, 2002; Carrasquillo, Kucer, & Abrams, 2004).

When literacy needs are addressed, an elementary school or remedial model is often used. Unfortunately, such instructional models are typically ineffective with older students because they fail to address their instructional needs with the language of academic literacy (Alvermann, 2002; Fielding, Schoenbach, & Jordan, 2003; Greenleaf, Schoenbach, Cziko, & Mueller, 2001; Hull & Schultz, 2001; Moje, Young, Readence, & Moore, 2000; Schoenbach, Greenleaf, Cziko, & Hurwitz, 1999). In the upper grades, the "basics" have shifted from letters and words to reading, writing, and thinking like a scientist, mathematician, or social scientist. Literacy takes on forms and purposes not previously experienced by the students. These new forms, purposes, and processing demands require that teachers show, demonstrate, and make visible to students how literacy operates within the academic disciplines (Keene & Zimmermann, 1997; Tovani, 2000). Simply telling them will not suffice (Jimenez & Gersten, 1999; Lee & Jackson, 1992). Existing literacy gaps between successful and struggling students are only exacerbated in these school contexts and continue to grow at an accelerated rate (Moore, Bean, Birdyshaw, & Rycik, 1999). Too often, the adage, "the rich get richer and the poor get poorer" is played out within the schooling context (Au, 1993; Flores, Cousin, & Diaz, 1991).

Semantic

The semantic system of language governs the meaning relations among words within the sentence. Just as texts reflect a rule-governed organization of meaning across sentences and paragraphs, sentences reflect a rule-governed organization of meaning among words. The roles assigned to the words in a sentence establish each word's relation to other words within the structure. Fillmore's (1968) case grammar is probably one of the best known descriptions of the semantic roles that can be assumed by words within a sentence. Table 2.7 illustrates the more common roles, followed by an example of each one.

TABLE 2.7
The Semantic System of Language

The meaning relationships among morphemes within the sentence

Agent
one who causes or performs an action
Jan sailed the boat.

Action
The behavior taken
Jan sailed the boat.

Object
Someone or something receiving an action
Jan sailed the boat.

Locative
Place or locus of an action or entity
Jan sailed the boat into the harbor.

Experiencer
An animate object experiencing a temporary or durative state
Jan felt hungry after the sailing.

Instrument
A force or object involved in a state of action
Jan cut her sandwich with a knife.

Goal
Desired or obtained endstate
Jan wanted a sandwich for lunch.

Entity
A person or thing having distinct or particular characteristics
The sailor was late for the race.

Possession
A relationship between an object and a possessor
That is Jan's sailboat.

Attribution
Characteristics of an entity, object, agent, or action that could not be known from its
class characteristics alone
Jan's sailboat is red and white.

State
A condition of being
Jan wants a bigger sailboat.

Beneficiary
One who is the inheritor of a relationship
Jan received a sailboat for her birthday.

TABLE 2.8

The Syntactic System of Language

The knowledge of grammatical or structural arrangements within the sentence

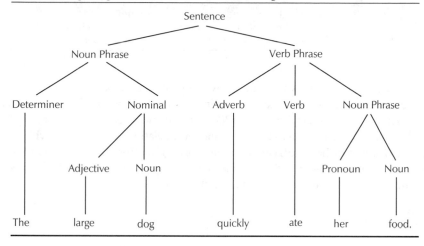

Once again, the furniture example can help illustrate the semantic relations found in sentences. A chair consists of legs that are related to the seat in that the legs provide the seat with its support. Similarly, the agent of a sentence is related to its action in that the agent is the entity that takes the initiative that causes something to occur.

Syntactic

The syntactic system of language reflects the rules that govern the grammatical arrangements of words within the sentence. As indicated in Table 2.8, a sentence is typically composed of a noun phrase and a verb phrase. A noun phrase may include a determiner (e.g., the) and a nominal composed of an adjective (e.g., large) and a noun (e.g., dog). Similarly, the verb phrase includes a verb (e.g., ate) that may be modified by an adverb (e.g., quickly). The verb phrase may also include a second noun phrase with a pronoun (e.g., her) and a noun (e.g., food). In English, determiners and adjectives precede nouns and adverbs precede verbs.

As can be readily observed, there exists an intimate relation between the semantic role and syntactic assignment of words within a sentence. Agents, for example, are frequently expressed through nouns in the subject position and actions are linked to verbs. Some theorists have suggested that young children actually learn the syntactic rules for their language through the use of the semantic system (Bruner, 1974). The infant is born or "hard-wired" with a predisposition to seek

TABLE 2.9

The Morphemic System of Language

The knowledge of wordness; the smallest meaning-bearing unit of language		
cat + s	laugh + ed	look + ing
box + er + s	run [n] er	re + search
pre + view	re + statement	un + doubt + ed + ly

out patterns and relations within the environment. The semantic system reflects the everyday actions and behaviors exhibited by those around the young child. Interactions with the environment reflect such relations as agent, action, object, and so on. As the child comes to understand these relationships, many of which are directed at him or her, a conceptual framework for interpreting the world is constructed. This framework is then mapped onto the syntactic system, which reflects an arrangement that is complementary to the semantic system.

Morphemic

Morphemes are the smallest meaning-bearing unit of language. Morphological knowledge reflects the language user's understanding of "wordness" in terms of meaning, semantic role, and syntactic category. We will more closely examine how the exact meaning of a morpheme is determined later in this chapter as well as in chapters 7, 9, and 10.

As illustrated in Table 2.9, there are two basic types of morphemes: unbound and bound. Unbound or free-standing morphemes are individual elements that can stand alone within a sentence, such as <cat>, <laugh>, <look>, and <box>. They are essentially what most of us call words. Bound morphemes are meaning-bearing units of language, such as prefixes and suffixes, that are attached to unbound morphemes. They cannot stand alone. Their attachment modifies the unbound morphemes in such things as number or syntactic category. Adding the bound morpheme <s> to the unbound morpheme <cat> changes the noun's number; the addition of the <ed> to <laugh> changes tense. Similarly, the addition of <er> to <run> changes the verb to a noun. As noted in the previous discussion, beyond their individual meanings, morphemes also play various syntactic (e.g., nouns, verbs, adjectives) and semantic roles (e.g., agents, actions, objects) within the sentence itself.

Morphemes can also convey different types of information. Content morphemes, which include nouns, verbs, and adjectives, are "informationally salient" (Gee, 1999, p. 102). They provide new substance to the text. The category of content words contain a large number of members and is constantly growing. It is easy to add new words to this category. In contrast, function words, such as determiners, pronouns, and prepositions, provide relatively less new information

TABLE 2.10

Content and Function Morphemes

A distinction between two types of information

Function Words (grammatical words)	Content Words (lexical words)
Determiners/articles (the, a, an, this, that, these, those), pronouns (he, she, their, those), prepositions (in, on, to, of), quantifiers (some, many, all, none)	Nouns (boy, girl, people, house, box), verbs (running, defeat, eating), adjectives (large, red, beautiful, wooden)
Closed categories: contain a small number of members	Open categories: contain a large number of members
New members cannot easily be added; resistant to borrowing from other languages or the invention of new words	New members can be easily added through borrowing from other languages or the invention of new words
Provide less new information, are informationally less salient	Provide new information in the text, are informationally more salient
Show how the content words relate to each other	

Adverbs (e.g., quickly, easily, strategically): often operate in a way that is midway between a function and a content word

---

to the text. Function words indicate how content words relate grammatically to one another. The function word category contains a small and relatively stable number of members. Adverbs, such as <quickly> and <easily>, usually operate in a way that is between function and content words (Gee, 1996, 1999). The characteristics of content and function words are summarized in Table 2.10.

In addition to the morphological categories of bound and unbound, and function and content, there is a third category of morphemes known as connectives or signals. These morphemes (unbound) indicate relations among ideas across sentences within a text. They both connect ideas and signal or mark these connections by their very existence. As illustrated in Table 2.11, connectives can signal such relationships as time, opposition, concession, and summary (Just & Carpenter, 1987). Readers use these signals to understand how ideas are associated across sentences and paragraphs. Similarly, writers use these morphemes to mark the relationships among their ideas.

Not surprisingly, particular text structures often reflect the use of particular connectives. The nature of the ideas within a text structure, and the relationships among these ideas, are typically signaled by the types of connective used. For example, temporal or time order text structures often make use of such morphemes as <not long after>, <now>, <before>, and <after> because these words signal time relations among events. In contrast, adversative or compare/contrast text structures make use of <however>, <but>, <as well as>, and <on the other hand> connectives

TABLE 2.11

Connective or Signal Morphemes

A special class of morphemes that indicate conceptual relationships among various ideas across the text

Connective/Signal	Indicated Relationship
Also, again, another, finally, furthermore, likewise, moreover, similarly, too	Another item in the same series
Afterwards, finally, later, on, next, after	Another item in a time series
For instance, for example, specifically	Another example or illustration of what has been said
Accordingly, as a result, consequently, hence, then, therefore, thus, so	A consequence of what has been said
In other words, that is to say, to put it differently	A restatement of what has been said
All in all, altogether, finally, in conclusion, the point it	A concluding item or summary
But, however, on the other hand, on the contrary	A statement opposing what has been said
Granted, of course, to be sure, undoubtedly	A concession to an opposing view
All the same, even though, nevertheless, nonetheless, still	The original line of argument is resuming after a concession

because they signal or make similarities and differences among ideas. Various text structures and their corresponding connectives are delineated in Table 2.12.

Orthographic

The orthographic system of language represents the rules for spelling within the language. These orthographic rules not only determine how words are spelled in a conventional sense, but also what spelling patterns are common within the language. As illustrated in Table 2.13, the letter patterns <ead>, <eet>, <qu>, <cei>, and <pho> are frequently found in English words. We can readily think of words that reflect these patterns. On the other hand, the letter sequences <qtp>, <rzf>, and <ltg> are rare in the spelling system. Thinking of words that reflect these orthographic sequences would be difficult, if not impossible.

Interestingly, writers frequently demonstrate their knowledge of the orthographic system through their unconventional—i.e., incorrect—spellings. The misspellings of both children and adults commonly reflect acceptable spelling patterns and orthographic rules, even though they may be incorrect within the particular

TABLE 2.12

The Relationship Between Connectives or Signals, Morphemes, and Text Structures

Text Structure	Typical Connective or Signal
Temporal order (time order)	Time, not long after, now, as, before, after, when
Adversative (compare/contrast)	However, but, as well as, on the other hand, not only . . . but also, either . . . or, while, although, unless, similarly, yet
Response (problem/solution)	Because, since, therefore, so that, consequently, as a result, this led
Covariance (cause/effect)	To, so that, nevertheless, thus, accordingly, if . . . then
Attribution (idea development)	To begin with, first, secondly, next, then, finally, most important, also, in fact, for instance, for example

TABLE 2.13

The Orthographic System of Language

The knowledge of spelling patterns or relationships among letters

ead;   eet;   qu;   cei;   pho   <u>but not</u>   qtp;   rzf;   ltg

word being spelled (Wilde, 1992). It is less likely that a writer will misspell a word using such uncommon sequences of letters as <qtp>, <rzf>, or <ltg> and more likely for a writer to misspell a word using such common sequences of letters such as <ead>, <eet>, <qu>, and so forth. Both the orthographic and graphophonemic system of language will be explored in more depth in the following chapter on oral–written language relationships.

Graphophonemic

The graphophonemic system expresses the rules for relating letters and sounds within the language. In English, this relation involves 26 letters (graphemes) and approximately 44 sounds (phonemes). Because English is an alphabetic language, there is a rule-governed relation between letters and sounds that is expressed through the orthographic system. However, as demonstrated in chapter 3, more than sound is involved in English spellings. As the example in Table 2.14 illustrates, teachers typically try to teach children the relation between letters and sounds through such rules as "When two vowels go walking, the first does the talking."

TABLE 2.14

The Graphophonemic System of Language

The knowledge of letter/sound relationships; relationships between letters and sounds; how twenty-six letters are related to approximately forty-four sounds

When there are two vowels side by side, the long sound of the first vowel is heard and the second vowel is usually silent

TABLE 2.15

The Graphemic System of Language

The knowledge of letter shapes and formations

A a **A a** A a A ɑ A a   <u>but not</u>   g q; b d p

Graphemic

The graphemic system expresses the rules for the formation of letters within the language. As shown in Table 2.15, each grapheme can be constituted in a variety of ways. Letters, especially when displayed in cursive, reflect a wide range of styles and formations, yet they are still judged to be the same letter. On the other hand, there are other features among letters that demonstrate less variation but represent critical features that distinguish one letter from another. In some ways, for example, the <A>s in Table 2.15 reflect as much variation as that found among <b>, <d>, and <p>. However, the differences among the <A>s are not taken to be critical; they do not represent different letters despite their variation. The differences among <b>, <d>, and <p> are critical; they do contain features that represent different letters.

Young children frequently demonstrate their understandings of critical features in their writings. It is not uncommon for the <b>, <d>, and <p> to be used interchangeably and such use is often viewed as a problem with reversals. However, perception—or the lack thereof—may not be the problem. Instead, the child is usually demonstrating an understanding of object permanency and applying it to the alphabet. For most objects in the world, regardless of the vantage point from which they are viewed, the objects remain what they are. Viewing a couch from the side, from the back, or from overhead does not change the fact that it is a couch. Position is not a critical feature in defining the nature of most objects. Young children develop this understanding of objects rather early in life and bring this knowledge to their interactions with written language. However, with print, letters (objects) do not always maintain their "letterness" when repositioned. The letter <p> is no longer a letter <p> when it is rotated in the <b> position; nor is it a <p> when repositioned as a <d>. For these letters, positioning is a critical feature and the object changes as the positioning changes.

TABLE 2.16
"The Great Big Enormous Turnip"

Once upon a time an old man planted a little turnip. The old man said, "Grow, grow, little turnip. Grow sweet. Grow, grow, little turnip. Grow strong." And the turnip grew up sweet and strong and big and enormous. Then one day the old man went to pull it up. He pulled—and pulled again. But he could not pull it up. He called the old woman. The old woman pulled the old man. The old man pulled the turnip. And they pulled—and pulled again. But they could not pull it up. So the old woman called her granddaughter. The granddaughter pulled the old woman. The old woman pulled the old man. The old man pulled the turnip. And they pulled—and pulled again. But they could not pull it up. The granddaughter called the black dog. The black dog pulled the granddaughter. The granddaughter pulled the old woman. The old woman pulled the old man. The old man pulled the turnip. And they pulled—and pulled again. But they could not pull it up. The black dog called the cat. The cat pulled the dog. The black dog pulled the granddaughter. The granddaughter pulled the old woman. The old woman pulled the old man. The old man pulled the turnip. And they pulled—and pulled again. But they could not pull it up. The cat called the mouse. The mouse pulled the cat. The cat pulled the dog. The black dog pulled the granddaughter. The granddaughter pulled the old woman. The old woman pulled the old man. The old man pulled the turnip. They pulled—and pulled again. And up came the turnip at last.

Source: Tolstoy, A. (1976). *The great big enormous turnip.* Glenview, IL: Scott Foresman.

Analyzing "The Great Big Enormous Turnip"

Now that you have a better understanding of the various systems of language, take a few minutes to read the folktale "The Great Big Enormous Turnip" (Tolstoy, 1976) found in Table 2.16. Then, using Table 2.17, identify the various systems of language.

As you no doubt experienced in trying to identify various language systems, as previously noted, the systems are not as clearly defined or as easily discerned as might be expected. For example, given what we know about the history of folktales, "The Great Big Enormous Turnip" may have originally been intended to serve an informative function; it extols the cultural virtue (and necessity) of working together to accomplish a task. The informative function might also reflect the notion that little things (e.g., the mouse) can make a big difference (e.g., it was the assistance of the mouse that accomplished the pulling up of the turnip). However, the function might also be regulatory; it commands—rather than informs—individuals in the culture to work together for the good of the group. Finally, many readers perceive the text as a "flight of fancy" serving the imaginative function.

Although the text type is clearly narrative and the genre a fairy or folk tale, the structure might be interpreted as temporal order (time order), covariance (cause–effect), or response (problem–solution). Semantically, most of the sentences begin with an agent (e.g., <man>, <woman>, <dog>, etc.), followed by an action (e.g., <pulled>), that is followed by a locative (e.g., <up>). Syntactically,

TABLE 2.17

Text Analysis of "The Great Big Enormous Turnip"

1. *Pragmatic*:	What function(s) does the text serve?
2. *Text Type*:	What text type is represented?
3. *Genre*:	What genre is represented?
4. *Text Structure*:	What organization is represented?
5. *Semantic*:	Select three different sentences and semantically classify the morphemes.
6. *Syntactic*:	Using the same sentences that were semantically analyzed, syntactically classify the morphemes.
7. *Morphemic*:	Identify three words containing one morpheme and three words containing at least two morphemes.
	Identify three function words and three content words.
	Identify two connective or signal words.
8. *Orthographic*:	Identify three different spelling patterns.
9. *Graphophonemic*:	Identify three different letter-sound patterns.
10. *Graphemic*:	Identify two shapes that represent the same letter.

the agent is expressed through a noun, the action through a verb, and the locative through an adverb. The morphemes <time>, <black>, and <mouse> contain a single morpheme, whereas <granddaughter>, <pulled>, and <planted> contain two morphemes. <Woman>, <dog>, and <old> are content words whereas <the> and <they> are function words. There are actually very few connective or signal words in the text, with such exceptions of <then>, <and>, and <but>. The spelling patterns <ed>, <ack>, and <an> are common in English, as are the letter–sound relations expressed by <m>, <b>, and <t>. Finally, both <T> and <t> represent the same grapheme in English.

CONTEXT, SITUATION, AND THE SYSTEMS OF LANGUAGE

Each system of language has been presented as if it were isolated from and unaffected by the other systems. However, as indicated in Fig. 2.5, each system is embedded within other systems. Morgan (1983) described the embedding of the various systems of language within a text as forming a web of meaning. Each system is contextualized within the others. Internally, the various systems transact and operate in a supportive and symbiotic fashion. Similarly, a text is externally embedded in a meaningful situation and impacts and is impacted by the environment in which it is located. A full understanding and use of the systems of language cannot occur unless the systems are considered within the text as well as within the situation in which they are operating.

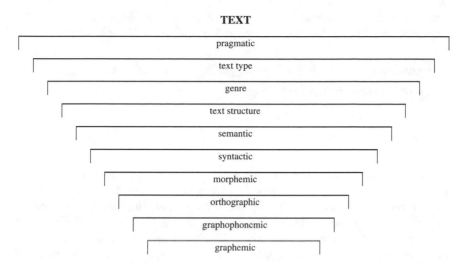

FIG. 2.5.   Internal relationships among text and the systems of language.

Internal Context

The assignment of linguistic categories to various text features often cannot be accomplished without first taking into account the linguistic context in which any particular system of language is embedded (Rumelhart, 1994). For example, the feature <1> can play various linguistic roles depending on the context in which it is found. In isolation, however, it is ambiguous. In the word <look>, for example, it is the letter <l>. In the numeral 2,341, it is the number one. The assignment of a graphemic role in many instances is not possible unless the feature is found at least within a morpheme. This is especially true when the script being analyzed is handwriting, which is much less uniform than typed manuscript.

A similar case exists with morphemes. The syntactic and semantic nature, as well as the meaning, of the words <hose>, <bank>, and <table> vary based on the sentences in which they are found. <Hose> may represent what we use to wash a car (noun); it may represent the act of spraying water (verb); or it may be the stockings worn by women (noun). <Bank> may be the raised land on the sides of a river (noun), an institution in which we deposit our money (noun), or the act of depositing money in the institution (verb). <Table> may refer to something on which we eat (noun), a grid with numbers (noun), or putting off a decision (verb). Words represent a "class" of potential morphemic, syntactic, and semantic categories and meanings determined by the linguistic context in which they are embedded.

Not only does the linguistic assignment of letters and words depend on the text in which they are found, so too do sentences. Determining the meaning of a sentence may not be possible unless the sentence is embedded within a broader linguistic context. The following sentences are ambiguous in isolation:

Flying planes can be dangerous.

Visiting professors may be tedious.

The chickens were too hot to eat.

They are eating apples.

Within a textual context, however, we would immediately know if flying planes refers to the pilot doing the flying or the planes themselves (planes can crash and harm people); we would know if the professor was doing the visiting or was being visited; we would know if the chickens were so hot that they were unable to eat or if the chickens were too hot to be eaten. Finally, in context, we would know if a group of people were eating the apples or if the apples were for eating as compared to being for cooking.

External Context

Because a text is a linguistic unit embedded within an appropriate environment, the operation of the systems of language is impacted by the situation in which they are found. The following language story illustrates this situational impact.

One early February morning when I was in graduate school, I went to the student union's cafeteria to have coffee and to study for an examination. I was one of the first individuals in the cafeteria. As I sat down, I noticed folded pieces of white cardboard with red lettering on each table. I also realized that there were no ashtrays on any of the tables. (This was before there were specific smoking and nonsmoking sections in public places or the banning of smoking altogether.) Taking my books out of my backpack, I glanced at the print on the cardboard and read, <Thank you for not smoking between 11:30 a.m. and 1:30 p.m. Monday thru Friday>. I remember thinking that it was rather strange to have nonsmoking hours but was too focused on studying to think much about it.

About an hour later, a friend of mine joined me to study. After our initial "how are you" interactions, I showed Robert the sign and asked him why smoking was prohibited between 11:30 and 1:30. He looked puzzled and responded, "It's not that you can't smoke; it's that you can't study. Those are lunch hours and they want people who need to eat to be able to locate places to sit." As indicated in Fig. 2.6, my friend was indeed correct; I had misread the sign. Although I knew the difference between the words <studying> and <smoking>, the situation had influenced my interpretation of the morphological system of language in the sentence. Therefore, a "text is never interpreted alone, but in terms of the context in which it appears" (Smagorinsky, 2001, p. 135).

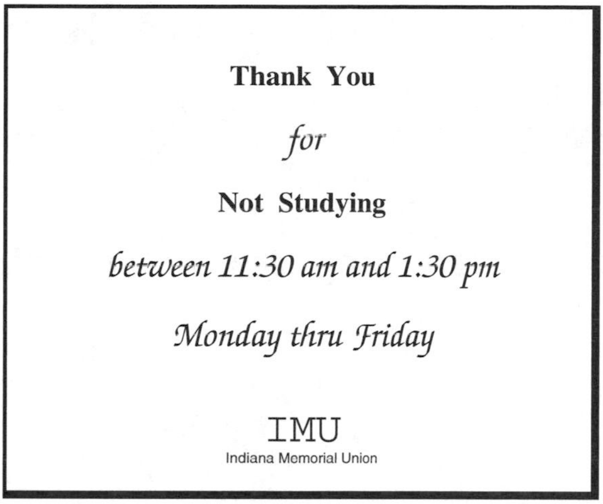

FIG. 2.6.   Thank you for not studying.

Halliday (1974) suggested that the context of the situation has a direct impact on the communicative register, which is the meaning potential that is available within a given context. The register represents the range of meanings appropriate to the situation as well as the forms available for their expression. Essentially, the register frames the meanings and systems of language that can be employed in the situation. In the previous example regarding no studying, the location — a cafeteria—the lack of ashtrays, and the folded pieces of cardboard on which the print was written influenced the meanings that I generated.

CONCLUSIONS

In this chapter, we found that the nature of language is far more complex than commonly thought. Not only is language a system for communication, but it is also a system that is symbolic. There is no direct link between the surface structure and the deep structure. Rather, links are established by human actions. Various interacting systems are also part of language. These systems range from the more global, such as pragmatics, to the more local, such as graphemes.

Oral and Written Language Relationships

Both oral and written discourse are expressions of language and therefore exhibit certain shared features, such as dual structures and rule-governed systems. Writing is not, however, as commonly believed, simply oral language expressed through print. Written language extends and builds on the oral language system but does not replicate it. Both the purposes to which written language is put and the situations in which it is framed differ from spoken language (de Beaugrande, 1984; K. Goodman & Y. Goodman, 1979; Purcell-Gates, 1989). Although at times the two expressions of language can be used interchangeably, such as a telephone call substituting for a letter, each expression is particularly useful for particular types of communication in particular circumstances. In fact, the development of written language was most likely driven by the need for a language form to meet specific situations not well served by spoken language. This difference in purpose and in context of situation impact the nature of written and spoken language and result in different internal characteristics.

In this chapter, we begin with an examination of the situational and processing demands of the two expressions of language. We then consider how these differing demands impact the very nature of the oral and written language systems. Because of the seemingly never-ending phonics debate, special attention is given to the relationship between spoken language sounds and written language letters.

THE LANGUAGE EXPRESSIONS, CONTEXT, AND PROCESSING DEMANDS

As indicated in Table 3.1, the oral and written language expressions tend to be used in different situational contexts. In general, oral language is found in here-and-now situations. There is a need or desire for immediate linguistic interchange, and the communicative event unfolds as the participants interact person-to-person with one another. The interaction is typically face-to-face unless supported by the use of such

TABLE 3.1

Oral and Written Language and the Situational Context

Oral Language	Written Language
Here and now	Over space and time
Person-to-person	Long distance audience
Immediate communication	Delayed communication
Instantly perishable; no record of the meanings exchanged	Permanent as desired; a record of the meanings exchanged

technology as the telephone. Even with technological support, there is still voice-to-voice interaction that unfolds in real time. Unless recorded in some manner, spoken language is instantly perishable. Once uttered, the language disappears. On the other hand, because it is difficult to generate and revise a number of "drafts" before speaking, it is also, consequently, difficult to "take back" something after it has been stated (Halliday, 1987). When a statement is expressed, the meanings have been exchanged and may linger long after the language has vanished.

In contrast, written language, because of its permanent nature, is especially useful when communication is to occur over space and time with a long-distance audience. The writer need not be in the presence of the reader; in fact, the reader may not yet have been born. Consequently, print allows the writer to express—as well as to share—ideas when and where desired. In addition, there is a record of the communication that has transpired. The writer is also able to draft, evaluate, and discard various ideas and their expression before they are shared with the reader. "Misspeaking" is far less common in written than in spoken discourse. Similarly, the reader is free to decide when and where the text will be read. The author may or may not be living and if living need not be in close proximity as is commonly the case in oral language. And, because of the absence of the author, the reader may use the meanings generated from written language in ways and in situational contexts not intended or anticipated by the writer.

The differences between the perishable and permanent nature of spoken and written language, respectively, have a profound impact on how each is processed by the audience. The impact is summarized in Table 3.2. Although explored in greater depth in the chapters on the cognitive dimension of literacy, a brief discussion of this impact is addressed here. An understanding of the differences in processing will contribute to an understanding of why the systems of language vary across the two language modes.

Paradoxically, the processing of oral language by the listener is to a large degree governed by the speaker. The speaker ultimately controls the production of the language and the speed at which it is delivered. Because in most instances oral language is instantly perishable, it is processed by the listener in a rather linear manner. The listener is unable to return to previous spoken segments of language

TABLE 3.2
Processing Demands in Oral and Written Language

Oral Language	Written Language
Speaker controlled	Reader controlled
Reprocessing: listener must ask for clarification or repetition	Reprocessing: reader can reread and/or rethink at anytime
Linear	Recursive
More demands on attention	Fewer demands on attention
More demands on memory	Fewer demands on memory

and reprocess them if a meaningful interpretation of an utterance was unattainable. Repetition of the language must be requested and granted if reprocessing is to occur. Listeners frequently attempt to influence the production of oral language, especially in conversational contexts, by providing the speaker with feedback. Listeners may reiterate what they believe was uttered, or ask for clarification and even repetition. In turn, speakers are typically considerate of their audiences. There may be contexts, however, in which this type of interaction is not possible, such as when listening to speeches or when numerous individuals are involved in the communicative event. Finally, the speed with which spoken language disappears requires greater attention by the listener. Because reprocessing may not always be possible, the listener must take care to attend to what is being said and to remember previous ideas to which subsequent unfolding meanings may be linked.

The reader, in contrast, has a great deal more control when interacting with written discourse. Within particular cognitive constraints, the reader can determine the speed at which a written text is processed due to the permanent nature of print. Rereading and rethinking can occur at any time, making reading much more recursive in nature than listening. Because the reader is able to return to previous portions of the text or even skip ahead, there are fewer demands on attention and memory. If the reader's mind wanders or if particular ideas in a text are forgotten, the reader can simply return to those portions of the discourse that have been problematic and reprocess the print.

These differences in processing demands between oral and written language account for many of the significant differences found between the two language modes. However, an additional factor that must also be taken into consideration when examining the internal differences between oral and written language is the degree to which the discourse is planned (Chafe & Danielewicz, 1987; Danielewicz, 1984). Too often, spontaneous oral discourse, such as dinner conversation, is compared with planned written discourse, such as a newspaper article. In these comparisons, the differences between oral and written language tend to be exaggerated. A more adequate understanding of the relation between spoken and written discourse requires that the forethought given to the discourse being constructed be taken into account.

TABLE 3.3

Planned and Unplanned Discourse

< —— *Unplanned Discourse* —————— *Planned Discourse* —— >	
Discourse that reflects less forethought and organizational preparation.	Discourse that reflects more forethought and organizational preparation.

Examples

Oral	*Written*	*Oral*	*Written*
Table conversations	Personal letters	Lectures	Academic articles
Party conversations	Electronic mail	Speeches	Newspaper articles

The degree to which discourse is planned reflects the extent to which the speaker or writer is able to consider, reflect on, organize, and revise the meanings to be conveyed. Forethought is the critical element. As indicated in Table 3.3, unplanned discourse tends to be relatively spontaneous and continually open to shifts in topic, focus, and dominance of ideas and participants. During dinner conversations, for example, the content of the language may shift from one topic to another, and various speakers and ideas may hold sway at different points in time. It may be difficult for a speaker to plan, even when desired, what is to be said; the conversation often times moves too quickly to allow for such considerations. The writing of a letter to a friend may also reflect a similar lack of planning. Often, the focus of such letters is on updating the friend on particular life events or to fulfill a social obligation related to "Yes, I owe you a letter and haven't forgotten that you exist." The use of electronic mail on the Internet makes spontaneous writing even more convenient. Even a casual examination of the linguistic features of many electronic mail interactions documents the relatively spontaneous nature of this form of communication. Typographical errors, misspellings, sentence fragments, and incorrect punctuation are not uncommon. Additionally, the use of such abbreviations as <pls> for <please>, <btw> for <by the way>, and such iconic representations as :) for a smiling face would be unlikely to make their way into more planned discourse.

Planned discourse, on the other hand, allows the language user more of an opportunity to consider and reconsider the meanings to be conveyed, regardless of the linguistic mode utilized. A speech or a classroom lecture affords the time for forethought as does the writing of an article for publication. The communicator has the opportunity beforehand to draft and redraft what is to be "said." What is interesting, however, in the case of planned spoken discourse is the degree to which print often plays a role. It is not uncommon for written notes to be produced and utilized when giving a classroom lecture or a speech at a conference. Such notes serve as a framework for and a reminder of those ideas that the speaker intends to address. The key to effective communication in such situations is the ability of the speaker to maintain the structure and characteristics of spoken language. This is no easy task; many of us have had the experience of attempting to understand written discourse that is being read aloud. Although oral language is the vehicle, the speech is actually little more than spoken written discourse. In such situations, the listener is disadvantaged in at least two ways. Requests for clarification, possible in face-to-face spoken language encounters, are difficult. Additionally, the ability of the listener to reprocess the language at will is denied. Essentially, the listener is put in the most difficult situation possible: having to make sense of a written text within the contextual constraints of a spoken language situation.

The mix of oral and spoken discourse cited in the previous example serves as a reminder that the two language modes are not always easily distinguished or as dichotomous in nature as is often conceived. Spoken and written discourse are not unified and unconnected language systems (Chafe & Danielewicz, 1987; Halliday, 1987). The use of such forms of computer mediated communication (CMC) as chat rooms and instant messaging further blurs the distinction between oral and written discourse (McNeal, 2003). On the one hand, the situational context may be similar to oral language in that communication unfolds in the here and now and is person-to-person (or at least computer-to-computer). Like oral language, communication can be immediate and both parties are able to request clarification as necessary. Planning, although possible, delays the online interactive nature of the communicative process. On the other hand, some forms of CMC are permanent in that messages can be saved and/or printed. Additionally, readers are able to reprocess texts on the screen even if they are not printed.

A more useful conceptualization of the two modes might place them on a continuum, with mixed uses a frequent phenomenon, especially when the discourse is planned. Gee (1996) also cautions us to consider the cultural practices that are involved in the use of oral and written language. These cultural practices may impact the features that are displayed in the two language modes as much as the modes themselves. The interaction between literacy and cultural practices will be explored in chapter 9 when we turn our attention to the sociocultural dimension of written language.

ORAL AND WRITTEN LANGUAGE DISTINCTIONS

Even with consideration of the role of forethought in language production and the mixture of spoken and written language use, there exist a number of emblematic differences in the systems of the two discourse modes (Chafe & Danielewicz, 1987; Danielewicz, 1984; de Beaugrande, 1984; Halliday, 1987; Smith, 1994a, 2004). These differences exist regardless of the degree to which the discourse is planned, although the similarities in the modes increase as the degree to which they share contextual and processing constraints increase. Table 3.4 represents the internal characteristics of the two modes.

TABLE 3.4

Oral and Written Language Distinctions

System of Language	Oral Language	Written Language
Pragmatic	Can serve all functions	Especially useful for the informational function
Text type	Especially useful for narratives and poetry	Especially useful for exposition
Genre	Especially useful for short stories, folk/fairy tales, and "notes"	Especially useful for research papers, novels, and longer texts
Text structure	Especially useful for time-ordered structures	Especially useful for attribution
Semantic	Less conceptually dense; chaining of ideas across sentences	Greater conceptual density; packing or embedding of more information into each sentence
	Less words per sentence	More words per sentence
	More redundant; more repeating of ideas	Less redundant; more elaboration rather than repeating of ideas
Syntactic	Less embedding of dependent clauses and phrases	More embedding of dependent clauses and phrases within the sentence
	More use of the standard subject-verb-object pattern	Less use of the standard subject-verb-object pattern
Morphemic	Less varied vocabulary	More varied vocabulary
	Less use of technical terms	More use of technical terms
	Less use of nominalizations and adjectives	More use of nominalizations and adjectives
Phonological Orthographic Grapho-phonemic	Rule-governed sound patterns	Rule-governed spelling patterns based on both sound and meaning
	Variable pronunciations	Standardized spelling
Graphemic	Ear/sound	Eye/letter
	Approximately 44 sounds	26 letters

In general, both language modes can and do serve all functions of language. However, because of the relatively permanent nature of print, written language is especially useful for the informational function as conveyed in expository discourse using an attribution structure. The writers of more lengthy texts found in such genres as research papers, novels, textbooks, and the like can more fully develop their ideas without fear that readers will fail to understand or remember the information. Readers can always return to previously processed discourse and reread when necessary.

Returning to the discourse is not usually possible with spoken language. To overcome this constraint, the narrative text type is commonly used in oral discourse when there is a need to convey information. Witness the use of time-ordered Biblical and folktale narratives to express the beliefs of particular communities. Although now in written form, many of these narratives were originally expressed and handed down from generation to generation through spoken language. Because time-ordered structures and the relations expressed within these structures are so salient—we live these structures on a daily basis—they are easily understood and memorable over time. Listeners can recall the content by accessing the time-ordered structure as a mnemonic device for remembering. Poetry, although recorded in written form, is usually intended to be read aloud. Both the sounds and meanings of poetic language are intended to impact the listener's aesthetic and cognitive experience.

Semantically, written discourse has a tendency to be conceptually more dense than oral language. More information and words are packed into the sentence, although there is less redundancy—i.e., the repetition of ideas. Writers feel less of an obligation to reiterate their meanings, knowing that readers are able to control their processing and reprocessing of the discourse. The packing of information into the sentence results, syntactically, in more embedding of dependent clauses and phrases within a sentence. Again, readers can typically cope with such syntactic disruptions because they can easily link, for example, the subject, verb, and object by rereading if necessary. Similarly, writers feel less of a responsibility to use the standard subject–verb–object pattern because of the control that readers have during text processing.

On the other hand, the fleeting nature of spoken discourse results in sentences that are less conceptually dense. Instead, ideas are chained across sentences in oral language. This chaining or repetition of meanings results in discourse that is more redundant and sentences that are shorter in nature. Dependent clauses and phrases are less frequent in spoken language, and speakers tend to make greater use of the subject–verb–object pattern.

Morphologically, written discourse reflects a more varied vocabulary and makes use of more technical terms. Writers are able to spend the time necessary for the selection of words to vary their discourse. Additionally, there is a greater use of nominalization (e.g., making a verb into a noun, such as <runner> from <running>) and the use of adjectives. In spoken language, vocabulary and the use of technical terms is relatively more constrained, as is the use of nominalization and adjectives.

THE LINK AMONG LETTERS, SOUNDS, AND SPELLING

The following discussion of the relation between spoken and written discourse addresses both the orthographic and graphophonemic systems of language. The phonological system (rule-governed sound patterns) found in spoken language is, by necessity, also included. In the discussion of the nature of language in chapter 2, the idea that humans express meanings through three kinds of signs—icons, indexes, and symbols—was addressed (see Fig. 2.3). It was noted that language is a symbolic sign system because there is an arbitrary yet systematic relation between the language's surface structure and deep structure. As represented in Fig. 2.3, there are three basic avenues through which language as a symbol system can express meanings: logographic (sometimes termed ideographic), syllabic, and alphabetic. In each of these three systems, there exists a different kind of relation between the written sign and spoken language. Because of this variation, it is necessary to address the spoken–written relation of the orthographic and graphophonemic systems together.

In logographic languages, such as Chinese, each written character represents an idea or morpheme(s) in the language. Generally speaking, the characters are not fully phonetically marked and linked to the sounds in the spoken language system (Ho & Bryant, 1997). Historically, it is believed that logographs evolved from written signs that were more iconic in nature. Hieroglyphic-like characters that visually resembled their meanings were stylized over the centuries, such that the characters moved away from an iconic to a more symbolic representation.

This relation among character, meaning, and sound is similar to the numeral system in which a number, such as 5, stands for a concept and not for the spoken sounds in the word /five/. Mathematicians around the world, speaking various languages, have different morphemes for the number 5, yet they link the 5 to the same idea or concept. They share the same mathematical language and concepts although they do not share the same linguistic language. The result of this relation is that mathematicians can communicate with one another through the numeral system even though they may not be able to communicate through their respective linguistic systems.

Similarly, the primary link of the Chinese written logographic system is to meaning, rather than exclusively to sound. This relation allows the Chinese, who speak various languages, at least on the phonemic level, to utilize the same written language system for communication. Two individuals may be unable to interact verbally with one another, yet they are able to communicate through a shared written language.

In syllabic languages, the relation between written and spoken language is quite different. In Japanese, which makes use of a syllabary in its writing

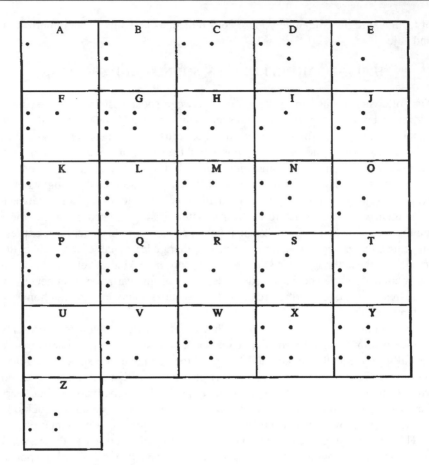

FIG. 3.1.   The Braille alphabet.

system—although logographics are utilized as well—each individual sign represents a syllable in spoken language. Whereas in English a group of signs (letters)
often constitutes a syllable, such as the three letters <ble> representing the second
syllable in the word <table>, a syllabic writing system uses a single character to
represent the syllable.

In alphabetic writing systems, the individual letters are loosely related to the
basic sounds (phonemes) of the spoken language. To a large extent, English and
other European languages employ an alphabetic written sign system. Even Braille,
the written language system for the blind, is alphabetic in nature (see Fig. 3.1). In
English, the 26 letters of the alphabet are related in a rule-governed fashion to the
approximately 44 sounds of the spoken language. The challenge facing alphabetic
languages is that there are typically far more individual sounds in the spoken

TABLE 3.5

Variations in Letter–Sound Relations in English

---

* One letter represents several different sounds.
  <c> — >   /cat/
            /ice/

* One group of letters represents several different sounds.
  <gh> — >   /rough/   <ph> — >   /telephone/
             /through/   /haphazard/
             /ghost/   /shepherd/

* One sound is represented by several different individual letters.
  /j/ — >   <gem>
              <jeep>

* One sound is represented by individual as well as groups of letters.
  /f/ — >   <telephone>
              <fun>

* One sound is represented by a group of letters.
  /ch/ — >   <choice>   /e/ — >   <eat>
  /th/ — >   <the>   /t/ — >   <butter>

---

language that must be systematically linked to a much more limited number of letters. A rule system for the linking of letters and sounds must account for this discrepancy. Consider for a moment the variations found in the relation between letters and sounds in English that are illustrated in Table 3.5.

Several attempts at generating a rule system that accounts for letter–sound relations in English are particularly noteworthy and revealing. Berdiansky, Cronnel, and Koehler (1969) examined the letter–sound relations in 6,092 one- and two-syllable words in the comprehension vocabularies of 6- to 9-year-old children. Comprehension vocabulary was defined as words the children understood when used in typical spoken language contexts. This language corpus was a subset of the approximately 9,000 words that most children this age are capable of comprehending. The remaining 3,000 or so words were more than two syllables in length and deemed to be too complex for the analysis undertaken.

In attempting to generate rules for the relations of the 6,092 words, the researchers immediately encountered the problem of deciding what was a rule and what was an exception. If a rule was required to account for every instance of a particular letter–sound relation represented in the corpus, with few if any exceptions, a tremendous number of rules were required. For example, a common phonic rule taught to children is that "when two vowels go walking" (e.g., <read>), "the first vowel does the talking." Therefore, in the written word <read>, the <e> represents a long sound and the letter <a> is not heard. However, in some contexts, the word <read> is pronounced /red/, an exception to the rule. Numerous other exceptions to this rule exist, such as <chief>, <thief>, and <said>. On the other

TABLE 3.6

Letter–Sound Relationships

	Consonants	Vowels	Total
Letter-Sound Correspondences	83	128	211
Rules	60	106	166
Exceptions	23	22	45

hand, if fewer rules were generated, a large number of exceptions existed. These exceptions become, in fact, additional rules to be learned. There exists a symbiotic relation between rules and exceptions; attempts to limit one result in an increase in the other.

Ultimately, the researchers decided that each rule needed to account for a particular letter–sound relation in at least 10 words from the corpus. Table 3.6, modified from F. Smith (1994a), summarizes the major findings of this research. In the corpus of 6,092 one- and two-syllable words, 211 letter–sound relations were found (83 for the consonants, 128 for the vowels). A total of 166 rules existed (60 for the consonants, 106 for the vowels), each of which represented at least 10 instances of the given letter–sound correspondence. Accompanying these rules were 45 exceptions (23 consonants, 22 vowels).

As is readily apparent, any attempt to teach or learn all of the rules and exceptions as the sole basis for reading and spelling development would be difficult at best. What is also interesting is that the rule-governed nature of the letters in the English alphabet varies across consonants and vowels. Letter consonants are much more consistent in the sounds they represent, whereas letter vowels are far are more variable. This accounts for the much greater number of letter–sound correspondences found with the vowels as well as the greater number of rules necessary to account for these correspondences.

In a classic second study examining the relation between letters and sounds, Clymer (1996) identified 45 phonic rules or generalizations that were taught to children in four basal readers. Clymer's intent was to discover the degree to which the phonic generalizations taught to children were useful (i.e., they supported the child in correctly pronouncing unrecognized words). Remarkably, in his review of the basal series, Clymer found that there was a lack of consensus among publishers as to which generalizations were to be taught; generalizations that were common across the four basal readers were minimal.

After the generalizations were identified, Clymer (1996) developed a word list that included all of the words introduced in the four basals as well as the words from the Gates Reading Vocabulary for the Primary Grades. The list contained 2,600 words. Each generalization was then applied to all of the words in the list that were relevant to the generalization. For example, the first generalization stated that when two vowels are side by side, the first vowel "says its name" and the second vowel is silent. All words in the word list containing two adjacent vowels were located and the generalization was applied to each word's pronunciation. The degree to which the generalization generated the correct pronunciation was computed as a percentage and labeled the "percent of utility." The findings of this study are presented in Table 3.7.

As the findings demonstrate, a significant number of the phonic generalizations taught to children fail to apply. Further compounding the issue is that many generalizations fail to account for a variety of English dialects. Even when the generalization can be applied, it may lead to a pronunciation that is at variance from the reader. In such cases, the child may apply the generalization correctly, yet still fail to recognize the word. Clymer (1996) concluded by noting that if the criterion of 75% application is set to determine the usefulness of any generalization, only 18 are helpful: 5, 8, 10, 16, 20, 21, 22, 23, 25, 28, 29, 30, 31, 32, 40, 41, 44, and 45. This research was largely corroborated by Emans (1967) and Bailey (1967).

Recently, Johnston (2001) has taken another look at portions of Clymer's (1996) research. She examined two letter-sound generalizations related to vowel combinations: 1) "when two vowels go walking, the first does the talking," and 2) the "final e" generalization in which the preceding vowel is long if followed by a consonant and a silent <e>. Johnston selected vowel combinations for her study because consonants are much more regular and are more easily learned by young children. Also, as she noted, of the 45 generalizations analyzed by Clymer, 10 involved consonants and 9 of these consonants had a utility of at least 95%.

Rather than rely on basal readers, as did Clymer (1996), Johnston (2001) selected 3,000 most frequently used words from *The American Heritage Word Frequency Book* (Carroll, Davies, & Richman, 1971). These words were identified from a range of reading materials used in grades three to nine. Words with vowel combinations, such as <ay>, <ee>, and <ow> were then categorized by letter combination and by a rule for how the combination was pronounced. Therefore, rather than treating vowel combinations as one general category, as did Clymer, Johnston developed subcategories for each vowel combination. These subcategories included two vowels that represent one sound, two vowels that represent two possible sounds, and vowel pairs that represent three or more sounds. Table 3.8 represents the findings of this analysis.

According to Johnston (2001), five vowel pairs that represent one long sound are worth teaching because of their high degree of regularity: <ay>, <oa>, <ee>, <ai>, <ey>. Additionally, although they do not represent a long vowel sound, she recommended that the vowel combinations of <aw>, <oy>, <oi>, and <au> should be taught because of their regularity.

Johnston (2001) also subcategorized words by specific vowels that contained a vowel-consonant-final and silent <e> combination, as in <cake> and <stove>. She found, as illustrated in Table 3.9, the <a_e>, <i_e>, and <u_e> arrangements to

TABLE 3.7

The Utility of 45 Phonic Generalizations

Generalization[a]	No. of Words Confirming	No. of Exceptions	Percent of Utility
1. When there are two vowels side by side, the long sound of the first one is heard and the second is usually silent.	309 (bead)[b]	377 (chief)[b]	45
2. When a vowel is in the middle of a one-syllable word, the vowel is short.	408	249	62
Middle letter	191 (dress)	84 (scold)	69
One of the middle two letters in a word of four letters	191 (rest)	135 (told)	59
One vowel within a word of more than four letters	26 (splash)	30 (fight)	46
3. If the only vowel letter is at the end of a word, the letter usually stands for a long sound.	23 (he)	8 (to)	74
4. When there are two vowels, one of which is final e, the first vowel is long and the e is silent.	180 (bone)	108 (done)	63
5. The r gives the preceding vowel a sound that is neither long nor short.[a]	484 (horn)	134 (wire)	78
6. The first vowel is usually long and the second silent in the digraphs ai, ea, oa, and ui.	179	92	66
ai	43 (nail)	24 (said)	64
ea	101 (bead)	51 (head)	66
oa	34 (boat)	1 (cupboard)	97
ui	1 (suit)	16 (build)	6
7. In the phonogram ie, the i is silent and the e has a long sound.	8 (field)	39 (friend)	17
8. Words having double e usually have a long e sound.[a]	85 (seem)	2 (been)	98
9. When words end with silent e, the preceding a or i is long.	164 (cake)	108 (have)	60
10. In ay the y is silent and gives a its long sound.[a]	36 (play)	10 (always)	78
11. When the letter i is followed by the letters gh, the i usually stands for its long sound and the gh is silent.	22 (high)	9 (neighbor)	71

#	Rule			
12.	When a follows w in a word, it usually has the sound a has in was.	15 (watch)	32 (swan)	32
13.	When e is followed by w, the vowel sound is the same as represented by oo.	9 (blew)	17 (sew)	35
14.	The two letters ow make the long o sound.	50 (own)	35 (down)	59
15.	W is sometimes a vowel and follows the vowel digraph rule.	50 (crow)	75 (threw)	40
16.	When y is the final letter in a word, it usually has a vowel sound.[a]	169 (dry)	32 (tray)	84
17.	When y is used as a vowel in words, it sometimes has the sound of long i.	29 (fly)	170 (funny)	15
18.	The letter a has the same sound (i) when followed by l, w, and u.	61 (all)	65 (canal)	48
19.	When a is followed by r and final e, we expect to hear the sound heard in care.[a]	9 (dare)	1 (are)	90
20.	When c and h are next to each other, they make only one sound.[a]	103 (peach)	0	100
21.	Ch is usually pronounced as it is in kitchen, catch, and chair, not like s.[a]	99 (catch)	5 (machine)	95
22.	When c is followed by e or i, the sound of s is likely to be heard.[a]	66 (cent)	3 (ocean)	96
23.	When the letter c is followed by o or a the sound of k is likely to be heard.[a]	143 (camp)	0	100
24.	The letter g often has a sound similar to that of j in jump when it precedes the letter i or e.	49 (engine)	28 (give)	64
25.	When gh is seen in a word, gh is silent.[a]	30 (fight)	0	100
26.	When a word begins in kn, the k is silent.	10 (knife)	0	100
27.	When a word begins with wr, the w is silent.	8 (write)	0	100
28.	When two of the same consonants are side by side only one is heard.[a]	334 (carry)	3 (suggest)	99
29.	When a word ends in ck, it has the same last sound as in look.[a]	46 (brick)	0	100
30.	In most two-syllable words, the first syllable is accented.[a]	828 (famous)	143 (polite)	85
31.	If a, in, re, ex, de, or be is the first syllable in a word, it is usually unaccented.[a]	86 (belong)	13 (insect)	87
32.	In most two-syllable words that end in a consonant followed by y, the first syllable is accented and the last is unaccented.[a]	101 (baby)	4 (supply)	96
33.	One vowel letter in an accented syllable has its short sound.	547 (city)	356 (lady)	61

(continued on next page)

TABLE 3.7 (continued)

Generalization[a]	No. of Words Confirming	No. of Exceptions	Percent of Utility
34. When y or ey is seen in the last syllable that is not accented, the long sound of e is heard.	0	157 (baby)	0
35. When ture is the final syllable in a word, it is unaccented.	4 (picture)	0	100
36. When tion is the final syllable in a words, it is unaccented.	5 (station)	0	100
37. In many two- and three-syllable words, the final e lengthens the vowel in the last syllable.	52 (invite)	62 (gasoline)	46
38. If the first vowel sounds in a word is followed by two consonants, the first syllable usually ends with the first of the two consonants.	404 (bullet)	159 (singer)	72
39. If the first vowel sound in a word is followed by a single consonant, that consonant usually begins the second syllable.	190 (over)	237 (oven)	44
40. If the last syllable of a word ends in le, the consonant preceding the le usually begins the last syllable.[a]	62 (tumble)	2 (buckle)	97
41. When the first vowel element in a word is followed by th, ch, or sh, these symbols are not broken when the word is divided into syllables and may go with either the first or second syllable.[a]	30 (dishes)	0	100
42. In a word of more than one syllable, the letter v usually goes with the preceding vowel to form a syllable.	53 (cover)	20 (clover)	73
43. When a word has only one vowel letter, the vowel sound is likely to be short.	433 (hid)	322 (kind)	57
44. When there is one e in a word that ends in a consonant, the e usually has a short sound.[a]	85 (leg)	27 (blew)	76
45. When the last syllable is the sound r, it is unaccented.[a]	188 (butter)	9 (appear)	95

[a]Generalizations were found "useful" according to the criteria.
[b]Words in parentheses are examples—either of words that conform to or are exceptions, depending on the column.

TABLE 3.8
Vowel Pairs Regularity

Pair One Sound	Number	Percentage	Example
ay	38	96.4	play
oa	16	95	coat
ee	70	95.9	feet
ai	76	75	rain
ey	9	77	monkey
aw	11	100	saw
oy	8	100	boy
oi	14	100	join
au	19	78.9	cause
Two Sounds Alternative			
ow	74	68	snow
		31.9	how
ew	16	88.3	blew
		18.7	view
oo	52	50	boot
		40.4	book
ei	12	50	eight
		25	either
Three or More Sounds			
ea	177	49.6	seat
		16.7	head
		14.3	fear
ou	188	43.2	out
		17.8	touch
		7	your
ie	55	49	field
		27.2	tied
oe	9	44.4	toes
		33.3	shoe
		22.2	does

be fairly regular. It is worth noting, however, that even with the regularity found in these vowel pairs and final <c> subcategories, only a single sound is being addressed within a word and that these words are largely single syllabic in nature.

From a less academic perspective, Merriam (1984) in her poem "One, Two, Three—Gough!" nicely illustrated the apparent confusion within the graphophonemic system of English.

TABLE 3.9

Patterns for Final e

Vowel Pattern	Number of Words	Percentage of Regularity	Example
a_e	130	77.7	cake
e_e	31	16.6	these
i_e	128	74.2	five, fire
o_e	89	58.4	stove, more
u_e	26	76.9	rule, refuse

"One, Two, Three—Gough!"
> To make some bread you must have dough,
>   Isn't that sough?
> If the sky is clear all through,
>   Is the color of it blough?
> When is the time to put your hand to the plough?
>   Nough!
> The handle on the pump near the trough
>   Nearly fell ought.
> Bullies sound rough and tough enough,
>   But you can often call their blough. (p. 120)

This variability between letters and sounds in English, in contrast to the more consistent relation found in such languages as Spanish, has led many educators to lament the English spelling system. Some have even called for a new or modified alphabet to solve the numerous orthographic irregularities in English (Venesky, 1980). The irregularity of English spelling, however, may not be as irregular as it appears if we move beyond a strictly alphabetic analysis of the language. Or, as suggested by Templeton and Morris (2000), if we are able to break "through the sound barrier" (p. 528) when considering how English words are represented in written language.

Two columns of words are found in Table 3.10. The first column consists of homophones, words that sound alike but that in this case are spelled differently. In oral language, if these words were said in isolation, it would be difficult to know which particular word was being spoken. In the second column are words that contain identical parts. These parts represent different sounds but are spelled the same. For example, the <s> in <dogs>, <cats>, and <horses> makes three distinct sounds: /z/, /s/, and /uz/; the <g> in <sign> is silent but is heard in the word <signature>. Take a few minutes to analyze the two lists of words. Try to generate a spelling rule for the difference in spelling for words that sound alike (Group 1) and the continuity of spelling for word parts that sound different (Group 2).

If you were able to generate a spelling rule for each column, you may have discovered that the relation between letters and sounds in English orthography is not based solely on the alphabetic principle. Meaning also plays a critical role. The

TABLE 3.10

Examining English Orthographic Patterns

Group One	Group Two
feat — feet	walked — hugged
threw — through	sign — signature
tail — tale	except — exception
sea — see	medicine — medical
principle — principal	equate — equation
bare — bear	critical — criticize
their — there — they're	hymn — hymnal
I — eye	bomb — bombard
to — too — two	solemn — solemnity
night — knight	autumn — autumnal
hour — our	music — musician
son — sun	logic — logician
blue — blew	resign — resignation
main — mane	photograph — photographer
rain — reign	paradigm — paradigmatic
brake — break	muscle — muscular
rowed — rode — road	
meet — meat	
no — know	
new — knew	
wrap — rap	
wring — ring	
write — right	

Orthographic Rule

Group One	Group Two

words in the first column are spelled differently even though they have identical pronunciations because of the influence of meaning. The words in the first column are different morphemes and represent different meanings. Consequently, their spelling represents not so much a link with spoken language as it does a link to meaning. Spelling in English marks meaning as much as it marks sound. The general rule in English is that when words sound alike but have different meanings, the words are spelled differently. Put another way, English orthography, when

FIG. 3.2.   The relationship among sound, meaning, and spelling.

possible, accommodates meaning rather than sound (C. Chomsky, 1970; Strauss 2001, 2003; Wolf & Kennedy, 2003).

On the other hand, when there are elements of meaning that are shared by various words, the tendency of the English language is to maintain a shared spelling. The <s> is pronounced differently in <dogs>, <cats>, and <horses>, yet it is spelled the same way because <s> at the end of nouns typically signifies plurality. Similarly, the <g> in <sign> may not be heard, yet it is included because of the semantic relation between <sign> and <signature>, in which the <g> is pronounced. A second general rule in English is that when parts of words are related semantically, the spelling is the same for these parts even when the sound varies.

Given the spelling–meaning–sound relations represented in English, readers need not necessarily go through sound to access word meaning. In fact, overreliance on sound may actually inhibit the reader's ability to understand. In the phrases <eye sea too feat> versus <I see two feet> and <the cross-eyed bear> versus <the cross I'd

bare>, spelling, not sound, indicates the meaning being represented. Interestingly, as indicated in Fig. 3.2, advertisers, newspaper editors, and cartoonists have long been aware of the relation among spelling, meaning, and sound. The advertisement <Sea What Makes Us Famous> is for a restaurant specializing in seafood, and <Sacks of University Heights> promotes a resale clothing store in San Diego. Similarly, the cartoonist John Long word-plays with the Three Stooges in <The three stewges>, and the newspaper headline <French have the Gaul to take on EuroDisney> reflects the ancient name for France and the Celts who lived there.

The use of a spelling system that is not exclusively based on sound has another advantage: It assures that regardless of what dialect one speaks, the spelling will be the same. Some dialects distinguish between /pin/ and /pen/ (i.e., they are homophones); others do not. Some dialects pronounce /oil/ and /all/ in the same way; other dialects do not. Given the English spelling system, the pairs of morphemes are spelled differently, even though in some speech communities one would need to use context to distinguish which word was being used. In a sense, this relation is similar to the Chinese language. The Chinese use the same written language system, although various regions in the country speak a language that is incomprehensible to speakers in other regions. English speakers use the same written language system although they speak different dialects.

A LITTLE HISTORY ON THE DEVELOPMENT OF THE ENGLISH SPELLING SYSTEM

How meaning came to operate in the English spelling system is an interesting story. Originally, according to Templeton (1992), the spelling system was almost exclusively alphabetic in nature. In Old English (450–1066), individual letters represented individual sounds and each letter within a word tended to stand for a sound; that is, there were no "silent" letters. At this time, the Romans introduced to England an alphabet that was based on Latin.

Between 1066 and 1500 (Middle English), letter–sound relations became more complex. Much of the variability depicted in Table 3.5 (e.g., different letters representing the same sound, a single letter representing different sounds) came into being at this time. Perhaps the most significant change was that groups of letters rather than only a single letter also came to denote a single sound. This change was primarily due to the growing influence of the French language within the European context in general and on the English in particular (Hodges, 2000).

The printing press was introduced at this time and brought with it the notion of a standardized spelling. Previously, scribes used a variety of spellings for the same word; even Shakespeare spelled his name several different ways. In fact, in some quarters, the mark of a learned individual was the number of different ways in which the person was able to spell his or her name. The London dialect was used as the basis for determining which pronunciations were to be represented in print. Initially, many of the early printers were from Germany and Holland

and not proficient speakers of English. Due to their lack of proficiency, printers inadvertently introduced peculiar spellings based on what they thought they heard being spoken. For example, the spoken /yottee/ was spelled as <yacht>. Attempts at reforming the spelling system at this time further distanced the spoken and printed word. Reformers wanted English print to look more like French or Latin. Therefore, such written words as <dette> came to be spelled <debt>. It was also at this time that silent letters began to appear, such as in the word <bite>. Due to a shift in pronunciation, the final /e/ was no longer pronounced, but it was retained in spelling.

Finally, during what is known as the early period of Modern English (1500–1700), English orthography was impacted by scientific and geographical discoveries. These discoveries were labeled and described using Greek and Latin vocabulary and word elements that contributed to the meaning dimension of the spelling system. It was also during this time, owing largely to the increased use of the printing press and the dramatic increase in the availability of reading materials, that spelling continued to become increasingly standardized. Finally, the development of dictionaries both in England and the United States further stabilized the English orthography. By the end of the 17th century, the spelling system as we currently know it was largely established (Hodges, 2000). Today, English spelling is considered to be historically phonetic. Words are spelled approximately the way they were 500 years ago. However, the spoken language has changed so much that a speaker today would be unable to understand a speaker from an earlier period.

Many of the same forces that led to the standardization of our spelling system also impacted punctuation. The printing press in particular promoted the uniformed use of punctuation. Initially, however, early writing systems often failed to mark word and sentence boundaries by the use of space or punctuation. In fact, writing was primarily intended to be read aloud and it was the responsibility of the reader to determine where words and sentences began and ended. Interestingly, punctuation is usually the last convention of written language to be standardized. Even then, it is a relatively unstable system. Both within and across languages, there is significant variation in the use of punctuation among language users. The use of commas and apostrophes are particularly open to variation (Hodges, 2000).

CONCLUSIONS

In this chapter, we found that although language can be expressed in both spoken and written modes, print is not speech written down. Rather, written language builds on and extends spoken language. The use of each language mode is impacted by the context of situation as well as processing demands. Finally, the relationships between letters and sounds in English are complex, although not random. The spelling system reflects meaning as well as sound.

4

Language Variation

The issue of within-language variation (i.e., dialects) has been and continues to be an emotional one for many Americans. The national furor over Ebonics simply brought to the surface issues and feelings that continue to bubble and brew in the nation's subconscious. Therefore, before embarking on an examination of language variation, it might be helpful to briefly review the characteristics of language and the relation between oral and written language. These understandings will help us take a more thoughtful look at what are inherent properties of language—variation and change.

As previously discussed, language is a generative system of communication that has a dual structure: surface and deep. This dual structure is symbolic in that there is nothing in the surface structure that indicates what is being represented in the deep structure. Although the relation between surface and deep structures is arbitrary, it is also systematic. That is, there are rules that govern how the various systems of language operate and interact with one another. It is the individual, using his or her implicit knowledge of these rules, that links the surface structure to deep structure.

Additionally, it has been shown that there is not a one-to-one correspondence between spoken and written language. Writing is not simply speech written down. Although there are times when the two language modes share many internal characteristics, especially when the context and purpose for the communication are similar, there also exist significant differences. Consequently, written language does not fully reflect any individual's spoken language patterns.

With this in mind, the remainder of this chapter examines the nature of language variation, how this variation came to be, and the influence of variation on the reading and writing processes. Although "variation" and "dialect" are used interchangeably, variation is employed as the preferred term. The reason for this decision is that for many individuals, the term dialect refers to a substandard form or the incorrect use of the language by "other people." As will be shown, all language variations are linguistically as well as cognitively equal and all individuals, including the writer and readers of this book, speak a dialect.

WHAT IS LANGUAGE VARIATION?

A commonly held view of language—in this case, English—might be illustrated as follows:

   Standard English   +   Dialect 1 + Dialect 2 + Dialect 3 + etc.

   (The way it should be.)   (The wrong way.)

In this view, speakers of standard English use the language appropriately—they know the correct rules—and speakers of dialects use the language inappropriately—they lack knowledge of the correct rules. However, as first shown by Labov (1970, 1972) over three decades ago, nonstandard forms of English are systems of communication that reflect a deep and surface structure. These forms are as rule-governed and internally logical as standard forms and can effectively express concepts and propositions (LeMoine, 2001; Wolfram, Adger, & Christian, 1999). Linguistically, dialects are simply differences in the way that the systems of language are represented within a particular language or discourse community (Farr, 1991). The nonstandard language rules that govern the various systems such as pragmatics, syntax, and morphology vary from the rules that govern standard forms, but they are rule-governed nonetheless.

Although the rules for the systems of language vary across dialects, within any particular language there are more commonalities among the dialects than there are differences. For the most part, dialects are mutually comprehensible among people speaking the same language and do not represent separate, distinct language systems (Delpit, 1990; K. Goodman & Buck, 1997; Perry & Delpit, 1998; Sims, 1982). Rather than being viewed as deviant, deficient, or substandard, dialects can be more accurately understood as representing variations on a theme, with the theme being the language itself. This view of language might be illustrated as follows:

   ENGLISH = Variation 1 + Variation 2 + Variation 3 + etc.

From this perspective, there is no one English language that currently or historically exists or existed in a pure, unadulterated form, one uncontaminated by the uneducated or misinformed masses. Linguistically, there is not one right and many wrong ways, or several right ways and several wrong ways for using the language. Languages by their very nature are not uniform (Wolfram, Adger, & Christian, 1999) and the English language is more accurately understood to be the sum total of all of its dialects or variations. All dialects in their totality make up what is known as English, and all language users, even speakers of the standard form, speak a dialect. Additionally, what is known as standard English is, in fact, not a single form. Rather, standard English is actually a collection of socially preferred dialects (Delpit & Dowdy, 2002; Farr & Daniels, 1986; Wolfram, Adger, & Christian, 1999). Therefore, standard English in the southern region of the United States varies from the New England standard, which in turn varies from the standard in the Midwest.

This is not to deny that particular variations of English have more status or power than others. In fact, standard English might more accurately be termed Power English because it reflects the language used by the dominant groups in U.S. society. As is demonstrated in the section on the sociocultural dimension of literacy, all dialects are not held to be of equal value or worth by our society. A wide range of judgments (e.g., ethnicity, socioeconomic status, educational background, intelligence, and morality, to name but a few) are made about an individual based on his or her language use. These judgments, however, are not grounded on linguistic or psycholinguistic data. To a large extent, such judgments reflect the privileged position of the evaluator within a variety of sociocultural contexts (Stubbs, 2002).

Although there are numerous spoken dialects within any language, there is a single written language system that is functional across spoken dialects. Our written language system does not fully reflect any individual's or group's spoken language for, as has already been demonstrated, written language is more than a transcription of speech in a visible form. Additionally, written language is a conservative system that is more resistant to change than spoken language. This most likely is due to the permanent nature of writing and the ease with which it can be revised and made to correspond or conform to a standard form. The result of this phenomenon is that as spoken language continues to change and evolve over time, there is not a parallel change in written language, which thus lags behind.

Before reading on, take a look at the various dialect examples in Table 4.1 that were generated from readers and writers of all ages. The examples have been categorized by the system of language represented, and they come from a number of sources, both published (e.g., Allen & Watson, 1976; Delpit, 1990; K. Goodman, 1977; K. Goodman & Buck, 1997; Sims, 1982; Whiteman, 1981) and unpublished. Compare and contrast the "standard" form with the dialectal form. What relation do you see emerging among the various types of dialects and their standard forms?

The most significant feature of dialect use in reading and writing is that its use does not change the meaning of the text. This is because dialects typically only represent variations in the surface structure of the written discourse. These differences in surface structure representations mirror differences in the rules for the various systems of language. The meaning or underlying deep structure representation, however, is maintained. This functionality of the written language system across a range of spoken dialects results in individuals being able to communicate through a shared written discourse regardless of the variation of their spoken language.

TABLE 4.1
Examples of Language Variation

System of Language	Examples
Text structure	Topic associating narratives for topic centered, temporal ordered narratives
Syntactic	Look for looked call for called help for helped thing for things work for works was for were is for are likeded for like helpeded for helped goed for went he'd be talking for he'd been talking he don't for he doesn't John be going for John was going that ain't no cup for that isn't a cup none of us never for none of us ever do it quick for do it quickly
Morphemic	Pop for soda hotcakes for pancakes headlights for headlamps greens for salad faucet for spigot bag for sack skillet for frying pan family for kin couch for sofa for davenport
Orthographic	Behaviour for behavior colour for color flavour for flavor
Graphophonemic	All for oil da for the sku for school wif for with gonna for going to brefis for breakfast laybairy for library axed for asked asst for asked pitchur for picture idear for idea lot bub for light bulb amond for almond cot for caught
Graphemic	A a **A a** A a A ɑ

What is important to note about these dialect features is that they are being labeled as such from a standard form perspective. For example, I am judging the writer's use of the word <kin> for <family> as demonstrating the influence of dialect on the writing process. However, the writer might just as easily judge my use of <family> for <kin> as being dialect driven, and she would be correct.

The most common text structure for narratives within the European American language community is time ordered. As discussed earlier, such structures are topic centered and contain at least one episode with an initiating event, internal response, attempt, and consequence. The episode and its internal components are presented in a linear, time-sequenced fashion. However, Michaels (1981; Michaels & Cazden, 1986), discovered that some urban African American students had a narrative style that they termed as topic associating. In these narratives, various events related to the topic were developed, shifting scenes were common, and the overall discourse lacked a strict adherence to time order. Unfortunately, as noted by Gee (1990), when given these narratives to evaluate, European American teachers often found them to be "rambling and confused" (p. xvi). Teachers attributed the inability of these students to tell a story as a reason for the poor literacy development among many African American students. In contrast, the African American teachers found the same stories to be well structured and comprehensible. These teachers evaluated the students who told these stories as bright and capable.

A common syntactic dialectal feature found in the reading and writing of certain speech communities is the dropping of such inflectional endings as <ed> and <s>. The lack of explicit marking of tense and number does not mean, as has been asserted by some, that the language community lacks an understanding of these concepts. The reader and writer are fully aware of the past, present, and future as well as the fact that nouns can vary in quantity; these concepts are simply not explicitly marked on the syntactic or morphological level. Instead, context is used for such marking. The dropping of the adverbial ending <ly>, as in <Do it quick> for <Do it quickly>, is even more typical. This omission of the <ly> occurs not only with readers and writers within a particular dialect, but also across dialects, including individuals who speak the standard form of the language.

The use of multiple negation, as in the example, <that ain't no cup>, is often seen to be evidence for the view that nonstandard forms of English are illogical. The reasoning appears to be that two negatives equal a positive; therefore, the sentence is actually asserting <that is a cup>. However, mathematical reasoning is not applicable to the rules for English syntax. In fact, at one time, the use of multiple negation was the only way certain negative statements could be made in Old and Middle English. Currently, standard dialects in French and Spanish make use of double negatives (Wolfram, Adger, & Christian, 1999).

A particularly interesting syntactic variation is the use of the "bare" helping verb <be> among some African Americans. Rather than reading <he'd been talking>, the reader substitutes <he'd be talking>. Similarly, instead of reading <John was going>, the reader says <John be going>. In both examples, the same general meaning is conveyed; that is, someone had been talking or going somewhere. Also, in both examples, a systematic and logical syntactic rule system has generated the miscues. However, the use of <be> has also been found to have an additional meaning.

As documented by Gee (1996) and Rickford (in Johnson, 1998), the use of <be> rather than <is> also marks distinctions in time and frequency. An event may be of limited duration at a particular point in time or may be ongoing, habitual, and extended in nature. In <he'd be talking>, the reader is indicating an understanding that the talk had been frequent or ongoing rather than limited in duration. Therefore, within this variation of English, someone who <be talking> represents an individual who had been talking continuously or for some time. Similarly, when the reader says <John be going>, we know that his movement is of some duration or a frequent occurrence. Interestingly, Gee noted that this use of <be> to mark ongoing or repeated events is a rather recent innovation within this particular dialect. Additionally, it tends to be used among younger African Americans.

The morphological system is often not recognized as a system that reflects dialectal features. The variation in word usage is simply viewed as a matter of personal choice. Some individuals call carbonated beverages /pop/, whereas others use the term /soda/. These choices, however, reflect rule-governed language use by particular communities and are dialectal in nature. Midwesterners typically use the word /pop/, and Easterners and Westerners are more likely to use /soda/. Similarly, my grandmother called the long piece of furniture in her living room a /davenport/, I call it a /couch/, and many younger people call it a /sofa/. Communities can exist in time as well as in place. Perhaps one reason many people do not consider morphological differences to be dialectal in nature is that this variation is not viewed with the same negativity as saying /don't/ for /doesn't/ or /he'd be talking/ for /he's been talking/.

Spelling is usually conceived as being one of the more highly conventionalized systems of language, and to a large degree this is the case. However, even within a language's orthography, there are dialect variations. The British spell the ending sound found in such words as /behavior/, /color/, and /flavor/ with an <our>, as compared to the American use of <or>.

Pronunciations, sometimes commonly referred to as accents, reflected in the graphophonemic system are also rule-governed and can vary from community to community. The most well-known examples are speech communities that do and do not distinguish between the pronunciation of <pin> and <pen> or <oil> and <all>. A lesser known example is the word <almond>. Several years ago, I was working with a school district in the San Joaquin Valley in central California. The district was situated in a large farming community where grapes and almonds were grown. When the teachers talked about /almonds/, the /a/ was pronounced as in /ape/ and the /l/ was silent. At first, I was confused as to what was being discussed, but eventually was able to use context to discover that the teachers were talking about the nut and not saying /amen/!

Many teachers are extremely sensitive to children's use of nonstandard pronunciations of certain words when reading. One that they find particularly troublesome is the use of /axed/ for /asked/ by some students, notably African American students. Unrecognized by many European Americans is the fact that they themselves may fail to pronounce /asked/ in a standard way. A speech coach in New York City frequently works with television newscasters; typically, her clients are middle-class European Americans who speak, for the most part, standard English. The newscasters are referred to her by their employers because of a failure to pronounce particular words in an acceptable manner. One of the most common is /asked/ which is pronounced as /asst/. The newscasters are unaware of their use of this nonstandard pronunciation and may at first have difficulty even hearing how they actually say the word (Jacobs, 1997).

Finally, even graphemes reflect variations. The <a> can be represented in various ways, as illustrated in Table 4.1. The print fonts available on my computer range from Chicago, through New York, to Mishawaka, and beyond.

CAUSES OF LANGUAGE VARIATION

Variation is an inherent part of language and its use. In part, this variation is due to the very nature of language itself. The rules that govern the systems of language are human constructions, developed across space and time to fit the needs of the community. These rules are not, as commonly thought, static structures that must be as they are, impermeable to change or modification. As the needs and experiences of the community evolve, so too does the community's language.

The previous discussion concerning the change in the English spelling system serves as one example of language change. As the British increasingly came in contact with the French language and culture, or as scientific discoveries impacted the British experience, the orthography was adapted to accommodate these encounters. Similarly, as the British colonial empire was expanded throughout the world, new experiences, ideas, and languages led to new forms of expression within English.

More significantly, the potential for language change emerges whenever a group of individuals associates and communicates more frequently or significantly among themselves than with individuals from other groups. These communications tend to be substantial ones in that they reflect particular experiences that bond the individuals into a community. In general, "people who share important cultural, social, and regional characteristics typically speak similarly, and people who differ in such characteristics usually differ in language or dialect as well" (Wolfram, Adger, & Christian, 1999, p. 1). As already noted, the basis for this bonding and within-group interaction may be age or geography. It may also be based on occupation, social class, ethnicity, and gender. Interestingly, according to Wolfram, Adger, and Christian, regional dialects tend to be distinguished by differences in pronunciation, such as /pin/ and /pen/ and vocabulary, such as /pop/ and /soda/.

Social dialects, in addition to pronunciation and vocabulary variations, also reflect grammatical differences, such as /he don't/ and /he doesn't/.

Dialects, therefore, are not the result of verbal deficits that in turn are reflective of cognitive deficits. Rather, they result from group membership and isolation in some form from other groups within the society. Stated somewhat differently, dialects reflect both internal ties and external distances. Disturbingly, Labov and Harris (1983) found that the shared linguistic features of the English spoken by middle-class European Americans and working-class African Americans have actually decreased since Labov's earlier dialect research (Labov, 1970, 1972). They attributed this increasing divergence to an increase in social and economic segregation within U.S. society.

The nature of dialects and the reasons for their existence is important not just from a linguistic perspective, but from an educational perspective as well. Distar, an emergent literacy curriculum, is perhaps the best example of what occurs in educational settings when an understanding of language variation is lacking or viewed from a deficit perspective (Bereiter & Engelman, 1966; Engelman & Carnine, 1982). Originally developed for urban African American children, Distar was based on the premise that these children lacked language: not just a lack of standard English, but also a lack of a fully formed linguistic system. Essentially, African American children were viewed as having a verbal deficit. This belief led to a second belief. In general, all children develop spoken language unless they have severe cognitive limitations. If African American students lacked language, it was quite natural to assume that this was due to some type of cognitive impairment: the students must have cognitive deficits as well; otherwise they would have developed spoken language.

LANGUAGE VARIATION AND THE READING AND WRITING PROCESSES

The degree to which an individual's spoken dialect impacts the reading and writing process is a contested one. Contributing to this dispute is the limitation of much of the existing research in this area (K. Goodman & Buck, 1997; Hall & Guthrie, 1980; Sims, 1982). Consequently, a number of issues must be taken into account when the dialect research is considered. The first is the population used to investigate the issue. All too frequently, dialect and literacy research has focused on African Americans. Although all Americans speak a dialect, with some exceptions (e.g., Purcell-Gates, 2002), African Americans are disproportionately studied. Confounding this problem, researchers have not always been consistent in their definitions of "speakers of Black dialect." Some have simply assumed that all African Americans speak a nonstandard form of English. Linguistic analyses of what dialect the population being researched actually speaks are frequently not conducted. The result is that the language data collected may have been generated from both standard and nonstandard speakers of English.

The second limitation is that researchers have used varied definitions and measurements of reading and writing. In reading, some researchers have asked comprehension questions, some have used cloze techniques, some have focused on vocabulary, and others have used recall procedures. Similarly, writing has been assessed through analytic procedures (e.g., grammar, vocabulary use) and holistic measures.

Perhaps one of the most significant limitations is that much of the dialect research assumes a priori that evidence of the use of nonstandard English in reading or writing is automatically evidence of interference. Rather than investigating the exact nature of the impact, researchers simply assume that the impact is negative. This problem is compounded by the very nature of the literacy tasks used to examine the effects of dialect and the contrived, laboratory-like conditions under which the data are collected. Many of the tasks fail to reflect contexts in which language is used in natural or authentic ways. Given these methodological problems, the findings of this research are often inconclusive and conflicting.

Keeping in mind these limitations, Table 4.2 summarizes much of the research on the interaction of nonstandard dialects with the reading and writing processes (Allen & Watson, 1976; Burke, 1973; Delpit, 1990; K. Goodman, 1977; K. Goodman & Buck, 1997; Sims, 1982; Whiteman, 1981; Wolfram, Adger, & Christian, 1999). In general, the findings indicate that all readers and writers show the influence of their oral language when interacting with print, a fact already demonstrated in Table 4.1. As also demonstrated, in general, spoken forms of English—standard or nonstandard—do not interfere with an individual's ability to generate meaning through written discourse. Both readers and writers shift their use of dialect in the direction of the standard form when engaged in written discourse. In fact, readers and writers do not use most of the dialectal features found in their spoken language. Speakers of nonstandard dialects at the very least have receptive control over standard English. Even though they may speak a nonstandard form of the language, they can readily understand the standard form. More important, as speakers of all forms of English increase their literacy proficiency, the impact of their spoken language on their written language decreases (Wilde, 1992). A personal example might help clarify this point.

When I was in high school, we typically read several novels each semester in my English classes. Although I usually enjoyed the literature, when it came to reading Mark Twain's *Huckleberry Finn*, I balked. I did not particularly appreciate slapstick humor, had initially experienced difficulty with the various dialects used, and therefore avoided engaging with the text. The night before the test on the novel, I found myself in the position of having done little of the reading. Deciding that the time had finally come to tackle Twain, I started reading the novel late in the evening. By the morning, I had completed the novel and in the process had actually come to enjoy it. More important, as I read the text, I began to understand the various dialects used by the characters; I had developed receptive control of nonstandard forms of English. My experience is similar to what occurs with

TABLE 4.2

Research Summary on the Influence of Oral Dialect on the Reading
and Writing Processes

Reading	*Writing*
Readers shift their use of dialect when reading aloud. This dialect more closely approximates the standard dialect than does their oral language dialect.	Writers shift their use of dialect when writing. This dialect more closely approximates the standard dialect than does their oral language dialect.
Readers make miscues that shift from one dialect to another; this shift happens in both directions.	Speakers of a nonstandard dialect do not use in their writing most of the features found in their oral language.
There is a lack of consistency in the use of linguistic features from the oral language dialect in reading. Readers vary from sentence to sentence in their use of oral language features.	The few features from the speakers of nonstandard dialects that are used in their writing are used frequently, e.g.: • tendency to omit inflectional endings: plural <s>, past tense <ed>, possessive <s> • absence of <is> and <are>: She so calm and look so at ease; They trying to get away from the fire.
Most dialect miscues are graphophonemic in nature, i.e., pronunciation.	There are features found in the oral language of speakers of nonstandard dialects that are rarely found in their written language: • use of multiple negation: He can't do nothin' about it • use of ain't • use of be: Sometimes my ears be itchin.
No important difference in reading can be attributed to dialect. Dialect has not been found to interfere with reading comprehension.	As writing proficiency increases, the influence of spoken dialect features decreases.
Speakers of a nonstandard dialect show receptive control over the power dialect. They are able to accommodate their reading to the styles of written English.	
As reading proficiency increases, the influence of spoken dialect features decreases.	

speakers of nonstandard dialects. They are surrounded by standard language forms (e.g., radio, television, movies, print materials) and learn to control these forms even when they are not spoken.

This phenomenon is similar to what occurs when speakers of American English view British comedies. Initially, the British dialect, usually morphemes, may cause some confusion. Referents may not always be easily identified. Even here, the referents may not always be dialectal in nature, but rather indicators of shared national or cultural experiences, or a style of humor, unknown to most Americans. However, as the continued popularity of these shows on PBS indicates, the viewer can usually understand the general ideas being expressed and over time readily learns many of the British English morphemes.

As this example clearly demonstrates, American viewers are not only capable of learning and comprehending features of the British dialect, but they are also disposed to do so. In other circumstances, this may not be the case. Speakers of the standard dialect, especially when in positions of power, such as employers and teachers, may be unwilling to adapt to nonstandard forms of the language. That is, they may be reluctant to make linguistic adjustments so as to comprehend what is being conveyed by speakers of nonstandard English (Wolfram, Adger, & Christian, 1999). On the other hand, speakers of nonstandard forms typically have less difficulty understanding standard forms. Their relatively lower social and economic status frequently means that their very survival depends on understanding the standard forms spoken by those in positions of power.

As indicated in Table 4.2, when reading, the individual typically shifts from the nonstandard to the standard form and back again (Sims, 1976). There is a lack of consistency in the application of the features of the oral language from sentence to sentence. When the impact of the spoken dialect on reading miscues is analyzed, most tend to be graphophonemic or pronunciation in nature. Even more interesting is the research that has examined the use of dialectal readers (i.e., stories written in the readers' own nonstandard dialect). When interacting with such discourse, the reader continues to shift back and forth between standard and nonstandard forms. Readers standardize nonstandard forms and change standard forms to nonstandard forms. In both cases, the miscues were high quality in nature; that is, they maintained the meaning of the author while changing the surface structure of the text. Most significant, dialect did not negatively impact the reader's comprehension of what was read. Sims provided the following examples.

Nonstandard English to Standard English:

Text: Ollie say, "Boy, give me my sock."

Reader: Ollie said, "Boy, give me my sock."

Text: . . . and it start to bleeding.

Reader: . . . and it started to bleed.

Text: . . . and the people . . . gets mad.

Reader: . . . and the people . . . get mad.

Standard English to Nonstandard English:

Text: Ollie pointed to Leroy.

Reader: Ollie point to Leroy.

Text: Ollie said, "Leroy, give me my sock."

Reader: Ollie say, "Leroy, give me my sock." (p. 130)

This translation from one dialect to another occurs even when a speaker of one standard form of English is reading a second standard form of the language (Allen & Watson, 1976). In this case, an adult who speaks standard American English is reading the text "Poison" (R. Dahl, 1974), which is written in standard British English.

British text: It must have been around midnight when I drove home, and as I approached the gates of the bungalow, I switched off the head lamps of the car so the beam wouldn't swing in through the window of the side bedroom and wake Harry Pope.

American reader: It must have been around midnight when I drove home. As I approached the gate of the bungalow I switched off the headlights of the car so the beams wouldn't swing in through the window of the side bedroom and wake Harry Pope.

The American reader's dialect causes <gates> to be changed to <gate>, <head-lamps> to <headlights>, and <beam> to <beams>. In the United States, we tend to think of there being a single gate to a house, especially a smaller house, which the author's use of <bungalow> would imply. We also call the lights on the front of a car <headlights> rather than <headlamps>. Because a car has two headlights, there are two beams.

What is so interesting about these American English dialect miscues is their immediate acceptance by the university students I teach. They argue that these miscues simply reflect different ways of expressing the same idea and that the American version is as adequate as the British version. However, when they encounter the previously discussed nonstandard dialectal miscues in Table 4.1, suddenly there is a problem. These readers do not speak the language correctly and are in need of basic grammar instruction. Of course, the effect of dialect in the two examples

TABLE 4.3

The Day My Parents Moved

One day about nine months ago, my mother and father had to move because of being laid off at Delco Remy in Anderson, Indiana. They had to move to Oklahoma to get a job because there were more jobs opening there and their were good chances of getting hired.

My feeling were that I didn't want them to leave because I would be missing them a lot while I was in college at Indiana University and when I got to go home on the weekends in Anderson I would think about getting to see them but I wouldn't see them because they were not there. Me and my sister **she stay** with my grandparents in Anderson were very sad when they left. We wanted them to stay very much.

My grandparents feelings about them having to move to Oklahoma to work. They were disappointed because **they family** was very close and it seemed like something like this would never happen. They were not especially happy about it in no certain ways. But right now **my grandparent are** like a mother and father to me and my sister and we are very close.

Their feeling my parents were that they had to think a lot about moving or not but it was the money because they could **have went** when they were first laid off. They also were not happy about it along with us. They didn't want to go but it was something they had to do and to challenge it. Moving to Oklahoma was a task because of moving a lot of furniture, loading it onto a truck, making a terrible thirteen hour trip, and unloading the truck of furniture. Myself I have been to Oklahoma twice and my sister four times, and my grandparents once.

The overall effect not getting to see them everyday like we use to like old times and them not getting to see us with the family. We love them a lot or better even more. We have to face it. It was something they had to do. But, **I am kinded glad**, because they have their jobs. My mother works in a bank and she is a part-time hair dresser and my father works at Delco Remy there. The most important thing is that they are making money again.

---

is identical; the readers have simply translated the texts into more familiar language forms without impacting the meaning. However, given the low status of the nonstandard dialects, the students immediately view such miscues as "wrong."

The impact on writing of nonstandard dialects is similar to that of reading. Writers shift their use of dialect to the standard form and do not employ most of the features found in their oral language. Those that are used, however, are used frequently. These writers tend to omit inflectional word endings and delete <is> and <are>. However, as will be seen, the omission of these inflectional endings may be related as much to writing proficiency as to dialect. On the other hand, there are dialectal features commonly found in spoken discourse that rarely occur in written language. Use of multiple negations, such as <that ain't no cup>, and the bare helping verb <be>, previously discussed, are fairly uncommon.

Often, teachers confuse the use of nonstandard English in student written discourse with a lack of proficiency with the writing process itself. The essay in Table 4.3 was written by Rick, an African American student enrolled in a college freshman composition course that I taught. The writing assignment required students to discuss a personal experience that had significantly impacted their lives. When I share this essay with teachers, they often respond that this student's nonstandard dialect is interfering with his ability to write well. It certainly is true that the student makes use of a number of common dialectal features, some of which have been underlined and boldfaced. There is the omission of the inflectional ending <s> in the words <opening>, <feeling>, <staying>, and <grandparent>. However, the student is not consistent: He uses the <s> inflectional ending with <feeling> the second time the word is used and then drops it once again in the third use of the word. Rick also adds inflectional endings, as in <there were more jobs opening> and in <I am kinded glad>. Additionally, he uses <they> for <their> when talking about the family being close and states that <they could have went> rather than <they could have gone>.

Even with the use of these nonstandard dialectal features, the basic meanings that Rick is attempting to convey are actually fairly accessible. We know that his parents were forced to look for work in Oklahoma, that the move took its toll on the family, and that the move was necessary and in some ways for the best. In addition, Rick's overall structure is clear; he uses a parallel form to discuss how he, his grandparents, and his parents felt about the move. Although the teachers "blame" dialect for the difficulty they experience in reading the essay, I think the student's lack of experience with expressing ideas in writing is the real issue here. Rick had done very little writing before entering the university and was struggling to find the appropriate language forms through which to convey his ideas. Even if we were to standardize all of the dialectal features used, the manner in which Rick expresses his ideas would still cause the reader some difficulty. Similar observations about such writers were made by Shaughnessy (1977).

Another factor not commonly discussed that impacts the use of dialect is stress. Many individuals who are bidialectal—they speak a "home" dialect as well as the standard school dialect—are able to proficiently use two language forms in the appropriate contexts. When they encounter stressful situations that require the use of standard English, however, the influence of the nonstandard form may become evident. I once had an African American graduate student, Linda, who spoke both nonstandard and standard English, although in class she exclusively spoke and wrote her assignments in the standard form. In our class discussions about the linguistic and cognitive equality of all forms of English, Linda was adamant about the need to suppress the nonstandard dialect of African American students. Her argument was that to "make it" in U.S. society, these students needed to learn standard English. This view was so strong that she often had great difficulty acknowledging the parity of all dialects, while at the same time acknowledging the need for the students to learn standard English.

Interestingly, on the midterm examination, Linda used a number of nonstandard language forms in her essays. I was rather surprised to see this, given her previous and exclusive use of standard English and her feelings about nonstandard language forms. In private, I asked Linda if she was aware that she had done this. She said she was not. She then rather sheepishly smiled and said that this sometimes happened in her writing when she was under stress and time constraints.

Wilde (1992) reviewed much of the research examining the impact of non-standard dialects on the spelling of elementary school children (e.g., Groff, 1978; Kligman, Cronnel, & Verna, 1972; O'Neal & Trabasso, 1976). Research indicates a moderate effect of dialect on spelling in the early grades. In the spelling of African American children who spoke a nonstandard dialect, the effects were typically found in the deletion of the past tense marker <ed>. With time, however, this moderate effect decreased and was found to largely disappear by the fifth grade. That is, literacy proficiency lessens the impact of dialect. Such moderate effects should not be surprising given what we know about the relation between spoken and written language. Writing is not the simple translation of sound into print. The systems of language for oral and written language vary on many levels, including the orthographic. Even young children demonstrate their knowledge of this difference in their spelling.

Wilde (1992) also noted that virtually all of the discussion of the impact of dialect on spelling refers to speakers of less prestigious forms. Little consideration has been given to the impact of prestigious dialects, such as Bostonian Brahmin English in which /park/ is pronounced as /pahk/, on reading and writing. The lack of research about speakers of more prestigious dialects is most likely due to their high levels of literacy attainment. For speakers of less prestigious dialects, lower levels of literacy development have often been attributed to their oral language patterns. However, as is shown in the next section of this chapter, there are alternative explanations for this phenomenon.

THE IMPACT OF VARIOUS FORMS OF SPOKEN ENGLISH ON LITERACY DEVELOPMENT

There is little debate that literacy is unevenly distributed in the U.S. society. Although this distribution is often analyzed at the individual level (e.g., Sarah can read better than Michael), much of this variation among individuals can be attributed to the group(s) to which they belong. It is widely acknowledged, for example, that literacy abilities are highly correlated with socioeconomic status. The higher the status of the group to which the individual belongs, the better the individual's literacy abilities tend to be. Similarly, the variation of English spoken can in many cases be a fairly accurate predictor of how well a group will read and write. Groups speaking a nonstandard form of English frequently have lower literacy abilities than those groups speaking a more prestigious form.

Traditionally, these low rates of literacy attainment have been attributed to, among other things, dialect. The use of nonstandard forms of English is perceived as interfering with and therefore inhibiting reading and writing development. As documented, however, written language reflects no individual's spoken language and, in general, dialect has not been found to interfere with the making of meaning through written discourse. Rather, literacy attainment is highly correlated with economic status. Not surprisingly, those groups with high economic status tend to speak a standard form of English. We must therefore search for causes other than dialect for literacy learning difficulties experienced by particular groups in our society. This search takes us to what I call "outside-in" and "inside-out" factors, which are briefly addressed. A fuller discussion of these and other factors and their impact on literacy learning and use are developed in greater detail in chapters 9 and 10.

Outside-in factors are focused on how schools in general, and teachers in particular, respond to the use of nonstandard dialects in the classroom setting. As Sims (1976) and Delpit (1995; Perry & Delpit, 1998) have noted, the dialect of some African Americans is of low prestige within U.S. society. In fact, some even question whether or not the dialect is a form of language at all. Consequently, its use is stigmatized as a signal of membership in a low-status group. Schools, embedded as they are within the wider culture, may reflect these views. All too often, this view results in the perception that dialect-speaking students are less capable and consequently that they will learn less (Purcell-Gates, 2002; Ladson-Billings, 2002). Two examples illustrate such perceptions within schooling contexts.

In the capacity of a school district consultant, I was working with a group of teachers in analyzing the characteristics of coherence, those linguistic elements that make a text "hang together." I distributed two sets of student writing: one that had been determined through a previous analysis to be highly coherent and a second that had been deemed highly incoherent. The texts had been written by college students who spoke a nonstandard form of English. Rick's personal experience narrative, discussed earlier, was included in the analysis. The teachers were asked to read through the two sets of texts and to list those characteristics that added to and detracted from coherence. Interestingly, the teachers were initially unable to complete the task. They were so upset by the students' use of nonstandard forms that they saw no difference between the two groups of texts. Student use of dialect made all the texts unacceptable, regardless of what other qualities they may have contained. It was only after a great deal of discussion that the teachers were able to analyze the texts as originally intended.

Such a stance towards nonstandard forms was more recently made evident in a teacher education literacy class that I was teaching. We were reading and learning about dialects and their impact on literacy development. One particular mathematics teacher was having great difficulty understanding the nature of dialects because she was so adamantly opposed to the use of nonstandard forms in school contexts. At one point, the teacher shared the fact that most of her students spoke a nonstandard form of English. However, she refused to allow her students to talk in class unless they exclusively used standard forms. This, of course, resulted in very few of her students talking or even engaging with the course content. In a sense, students were denied access to mathematical concepts because they spoke a form of English not acceptable to the teacher. In this case, the students may indeed have learned less, but it was due to the stance of their teacher, not their dialect. Although these are only two examples, and personal experiences at that, I suspect that such bias is far more commonplace than we would like to believe.

In addition to lowering teacher expectations, student use of dialect may also result in teachers who overcorrect the surface level features of language and ignore the deep structure. Although Rick used a number of nonstandard features in his writing, his difficulties are far more significant than dialect. During oral reading, teachers may correct miscues that reflect a change in the way that something is expressed, but not a change in or disruption of meaning. For example, in one first-grade classroom, a child read <He goed home> for <He went home>. Although the shift from <went> to <goed> is simply a syntactic and morphological substitution that causes no change in the deep structure, the teacher insisted that the sentence be read as it was written. The result of this type of response to dialect may be students who think that reading and writing are not expressions of language and that their own spoken linguistic facility is of no relevance when engaging with written language. In fact, given such responses, it may actually interfere.

Finally, if the instructional focus is on eradicating the use of dialect in student reading and writing, the literacy curricula implemented may lack quality literature. There may be the assumption that the students are incapable of reading such stories because they have yet to master standard language forms. In these contexts, literacy instruction is reduced to its lowest level as students are taught standard pronunciations, morphology, and syntax. Meaning making and comprehension, the ultimate goals of engaging with written language, may receive little instructional time and attention.

Inside-out factors focus on the response of the students to the norms and values of the dominant culture. Schools, as sociopolitical systems, reflect dominant culture values and represent in a very real way the agenda of those in positions of power. Research indicates that in the early grades, students who speak a nonstandard form of the language begin to acquire standard English as they progress through the grades. This acquisition is demonstrated in both their spoken and written language. As they mature, however, they also begin to develop a more explicit awareness of their own sociocultural identity and the relation of their home community's language forms to those of the dominant culture. Additionally, they learn about societal power relationships and the status of their own community within the broader society.

This growing awareness often results in students who perceive the school's attempts to change their language forms as a rejection of themselves and their communities. These attempts come to be viewed as acts of oppression. The example of the mathematics teacher might serve as an example of such rejection. Language, as one of the most intimate reflections of self and community, significantly "marks" the individual's and group's place in the world. Therefore, students may feel that the acquisition of standard English ultimately represents a rejection of their home community. Many unwilling students come to see success in school and the use of standard English as taking on "White ways." As observed by Kohl (1994), "To agree to learn from a stranger who does not respect your integrity causes a major loss of self. The only alternative is to not-learn and reject their world" (p. 134). These students actually begin to resist even those features of standard English they have learned. Their school language begins to reflect the forms they originally brought to the school in the earlier grades.

Resistance, however, can occur even among young children. Piestrup (1973) examined first-grade teachers' responses to the dialect pronunciations of their African American students. When teachers consistently "corrected" the use of nonstandard forms, the children's use of these forms actually increased. In those classrooms where teachers did not engage in such correcting behavior, the children grew in their development and use of standard forms. As noted by Erickson (1987) and Pease-Alvarez and Vasquez (1994), mutual trust is sacrificed when teachers and children are in such linguistic conflicts. The result is that students may become either passively or actively resistant.

Parents may also contribute to their children's resistance to learning standard forms of English. Ogbu (1999) found that African American parents, when interviewed, were resolute in their belief that the schools needed to teach their children to speak standard English. Some parents even expressed stereotypical and negative views towards their own language use. When their children used standard forms in the home context, however, or in some instances even attempted to correct the nonstandard forms of the adults around them, the parents accused them of "puttin' on" (p. 171). They interpreted their children's use of the standard form as claiming to be superior to other African Americans.

Ogbu (1999) also documented that many students did have the ability to use standard forms of English in the classroom when they desired to do so. Students were in effect bidialectal and able to modify their language forms as the situation required. I am reminded of a group of California African American physicians who used standard English when talking with their European American patients. When relaxing in other contexts, such as at lunch or in the clinic's "break room," they comfortably shifted to another, nonstandard form of English. Smith (2002) has argued that such code switching is best developed by giving students linguistic choice in the classroom, allowing home and school dialects to co-exist.

Another response is known as reproduction theory (McDermott, 1987, 1995). Reproduction theory might, in some respects, be considered to be both an outside-in and an inside-out analysis of the failure of some students to become literate. In reproduction theory, the teaching and learning in the classroom can be viewed as scenes from a play. All participants—students as well as teachers—have roles to play. The participants' roles are assigned by the larger culture and economic marketplace. The schools, in effect, are there to maintain the status quo and protect the privileges and perceived entitlements of those who benefit the most from the way in which the system is constructed. As such, there must necessarily be winners and losers for the system to work. The acting out of these school roles reproduces or replicates the successes and failures found in society.

Groups that have been assigned the role of teacher are to act and behave in ways that will ensure that some students will ultimately be unsuccessful in becoming proficient readers and writers. Likewise, the script for some students compels them to act and behave in ways that will contribute to their failures as readers and writers. For the most part, the roles and scripts the participants play in the classroom are not conscious. Neither teachers nor students have an explicit awareness of what they are doing. The result, however, is that teachers fail to effectively teach reading and writing and students fail to learn what is necessary to become effective readers and writers, at least within the school context.

CONCLUSIONS

Variation is part and parcel of language. Because language reflects the experiences of individuals and the social groups to which they hold membership, it is only natural that these varied experiences will find expression in language. Such variations—or dialects—are not distinct, unique languages, but rather are all part of the same language system. In general, dialects are mutually comprehensible. Written language tends to demonstrate less variation and reflects the dialect of no particular group. Although speakers of nonprestigious forms of English may, as a group, experience difficulties with literacy, the form itself is not the source of the difficulty. Rather, factors such as poverty, racism, and lack of acceptance of nonstandard language forms are more likely the source of the problem.

REVISITING WHAT MAKES LANGUAGE LANGUAGE

In the beginning of chapter 2, you were asked to examine language and nonlanguage events as a way to begin thinking about the linguistic characteristics of language. Now that you have a fuller understanding of this dimension, return to Figures 2.1 and 2.2 and reconsider the differences between the language and nonlanguage events. Hopefully, your reexamination will lead you to some of the following conclusions.

In Figure 2.1, each event communicates, has a dual symbolic structure, and contains, either implicitly or explicitly, the various systems of language. The events are contextualized and reflect both internal and external coherence. Although particular language systems, as in <Ollie and Leroy>, may be nonstandard in nature, they are nonetheless rule-governed and systematic.

There are various reasons why the events in Figure 2.2 are considered to be nonlanguage. The column of words, the alphabet, and the <STOP> contain some of the systems of language but lack others. Internal coherence is not present. Similarly, the column of words, the alphabet, and the <STOP> are not framed by or embedded within a situation or environment. They lack external coherence.

The phonic exercise is limited linguistically because the focus is on one particular system of language (graphophonemic) to the exclusion of all others. Although forms of communication, the mathematical equation, the partial traffic sign, the illustration from a Mercer Mayer wordless picture book, and the musical score are not linguistic languages. The illustration and the No U-Turn sign are icons rather than symbols and the equation and the score do not reflect the systems of language, either implicitly or explicitly.

THE LINGUISTIC DIMENSION OF THE LITERACY STORY

To conclude our examination of the linguistic dimension of literacy, let's return to the literacy story and the computer program manual, the *Microref Quick Reference*

TABLE 4.4
The Linguistic Dimensions of a Computer Program Guide

System of Language	Computer Program Guide Analysis
Pragmatic	Regulatory: the guide is intended to provide directions for the use of the software program
	Informative: through providing directions, the guide is also informing the user as to what can be accomplished through the use of the software program
Text type	Exposition: provides the user with factual and conceptual information
Genre	Directions that begin with an overview of when to use a particular procedure followed by the steps to be taken; also use of icons which represent keys on the computer key board
Text structure	Attribution: presents factual and conceptual information that is focused on various topics
	Temporal order: although not a time ordered story, the information is sequenced in terms of which particular commands must be executed in which particular order so as to accomplish a particular task
Semantic	Many of the sentences have an implied agent (the user) + an action to be executed on the keyboard + a locative that places the action at a particular location on the keyboard and/or the computer screen; absence of attribution
Syntactic	Many of the sentences have an implied subject (the user) in the first noun phrase + a verb; absence of adjectives and adverbs
Morphemic	Use and repetition of technical terms related to the computer keyboard and word processing: cursor, position, hold, down, press, delete, column, text; use of numerals as connectives to indicate time sequence

Guide (Microref Systems Inc., 1988), that were presented in chapter 1 (Table 1.2 and Fig. 1.2). As mentioned at the start of that chapter, linguists are interested in the text as an object of study. Linguistically, what can be said about the "text" in Fig. 1.2? Or, from the reader's perspective, what must be known, at least implicitly, about language in order to "crack the code?" Table 4.4 sets forth some of the significant characteristics of various systems of language that are reflected in this example of written language.

As a manual for how to use a software program, the function of the text might be considered regulatory. As the reader of the guide, I wanted to be told how to use WordPerfect. Additionally, through learning how to execute particular commands to accomplish particular tasks, I also learned new things that the program would allow me to do. The text came to serve an informative function as well. The previous software program that I had used did not allow the formation of columns, and I had never considered the need to construct them. The *Microref Quick Reference Guide*, however, explained how to format columns, and I quickly came to see the usefulness of columns in my writing.

The text type displayed is exposition and it makes use of an attribution structure. There are also temporal order characteristics to the structure in that the commands must be performed in a particular sequence. The genre is that of directions, and as is typical with such texts, there is a lack of development. The directions are stated in a simple and straightforward manner with little or no elaboration. To support the reader in understanding these directions, the use of icons and numerals are interspersed with symbols. Reference to the <return> and the <4> keys, for example, are embedded in black boxes to represent the keys on the computer keyboard. The sentences frequently have an implied agent in the initial noun phrase, followed by a verb in which the actions to be taken are set forth. Adjectives and adverbs are absent. It was just this lack of elaboration and sparse sentence development, a common characteristic of the genre of directions, that caused my initial difficulties in using the guide. Finally, morphologically, the dialect of "computerese" is present in the use and repetition of such technical terms as <block>, < ALT>, and <cursor>. Connectives—words that help a text "hang together"—are replaced with the use of numerals to indicate time sequences.

III

The Cognitive Dimension
of Literacy

5

The Constructive Nature of Perception

At this point in the book, you hopefully have developed a fuller understanding of the nature of written discourse and the various systems of language that make up a text. An examination of the cognitive dimension of literacy moves us from a focus on the written discourse and "cracking the code" to an examination of the individual who is transacting with the print and making meaning. Essentially, a cognitive discussion of literacy focuses on the mental processes, strategies, or procedures the individual engages to construct meaning. Because in the construction of meaning there is a transaction between a mind (cognition) and a text (linguistic), this chapter can best be conceived of as a psycholinguistic extension of the previous chapters.

PERCEPTUAL EXPERIMENTS

To enable you to better understand perception and its role in the reading process, the first part of this chapter engages you in a series of experiments. In Table 5.1— don't look at it just yet—eight lines of print are presented. Cover all of the lines of print with a piece of paper or your hand. Then, briefly glance—for about one second—at the first line of print, cover it once again, and write down everything you saw. Move to the second line and do the same thing; continue until all eight lines of print have been looked at.

Now that you have glanced at each line of print and recorded what you saw, for each line write down the total number of letters that you recorded. For line seven, each group of marks (e.g., = /, *&) constitutes an individual letter. If you look at the total number of letters perceived across the various lines of print, you should see a remarkable difference in the numbers. Part of this may be due to acclimation to the experiment or failure to examine each line for the same amount of time. In addition, some lines have more letters than others. However, something else is also going on here. Examine the lines of print and the number of letters perceived

TABLE 5.1

Perception and Lines of Print

1. BOY   HORSE   DESK   GRASS   COFFEE

2. JKG   YZX   PDU   MVB   DFQ

3. WASHINGTON   D. C.   IS   THE   CAPATAL   OF   THE   UNITED   STATES.

4. THR   ING   HOM   ERS   STR   ION

5. LAPIZ   Y   PAPEL   GATOS   Y   PERROS

6. D   J   E   K   G   I   T   L   G   O   Q   M   C   N   X

7. =/   *&   @#   =−   !∼   _)   #%   +^   ($

8. BACON   AND   EGGS   ICE   CREAM   AND   CAKE

one more time and see if you can determine why you were able to read more on some lines than others.

We can use our knowledge of the systems of language discussed in the previous chapters to begin to explain the differences in your perception. My guess is, for example, that you were able to perceive more in line three than in lines two, six, or seven. As illustrated in Table 5.2, there are more or fewer systems of language present in each of these lines of print. Consequently, as more or fewer systems are made available, the reader is able to perceive more or less. If you are able to read Spanish, line five contained numerous systems of language. On the other hand, if you are monoliterate in English, very few systems were accessible. Typically, biliterate readers of English and Spanish perceive more on line five than do English monoliterates. Therefore, one characteristic of perception, which is an intimate part of the reading process, is that *what* is being read influences *how* it is read.

In addition, in line three, did you notice the misspelling of <capital>? In my university class, when I flash this line of print on an overhead projector, most students fail to perceive the misspelling and write the word as it is conventionally spelled. I happened on the power of misspelling a word in one of the lines of print when I was teaching my first university literacy methods class. At the time, rather than use the sentence about the capital of the United States, I used a line from a popular commercial jingle: <It takes two hands to handle a Whopper>. The jingle was part of an advertising campaign and was constantly seen on television and billboards and heard on the radio.

As the class and I debriefed and discussed why we perceived more on some lines than others, one student continued to insist that she had seen every letter on every line. When I shared the Whopper line, another student in class asked how

TABLE 5.2
Perception and the Systems of Language

Line	Available Systems
1. BOY HORSE DESK GRASS COFFEE	Graphemes Graphophonemics Orthographics Morphemes
2. JKG YZX PDU MVB DFQ	Graphemes Graphophonemics
3. WASHINGTON D.C. IS THE CAPATAL OF THE UNITED STATES.	Graphemes Graphophonemics Orthographics Morphemes Syntax Semantics Pragmatics
4. THR ING HOM ERS STR ION	Graphemes Graphophonemics Orthographics Morphemes
5. LAPIZ Y PAPEL GATOS Y PERROS	Graphemes Graphophonemics Orthographics Morphemes Partial syntax Partial semantics
6. DJEKGITLGOQ MCNX	Graphemes Graphophonemics
7. =/ *& @# =− !~ _) #% +^ (\$	Graphemes
8. BACON AND EGGS ICE CREAM AND CAKE	Graphemes Graphophonemics Orthographics Morphemes Partial syntax Partial semantics

the student had spelled <Whopper>. The student responded, "Just like it's spelled, w-h-o-p-p-e-r." The second student quickly replied, "But that is not the way it is spelled on the transparency. Dr. Kucer has spelled it w-h-o-o-p-e-r! You must not have actually seen every letter." I remember thinking to myself, "Sometimes being a poor speller has its advantages!"

These two examples of misperception are similar to what happens when we proofread our own writing. It is not uncommon for typographical errors to go unnoticed. In such instances, all of the systems of language are available, yet there is still misperception. To avoid this problem, many professional proofreaders actually "read" from bottom to top and from right to left to better perceive what is actually on the page. Why this inability to read what is on the page? To begin to answer this question, it is necessary to look at more traditional as well as current understandings of perception.

Traditionally, our view of perception was similar to that of a vacuum cleaner sweeping up dirt on a carpet. Whatever the vacuum cleaner—or eye—went over was put into a bag—or the brain. Cognitively speaking, perception was conceived as a one-way process in which the print was recorded by the eye, similar to a photograph, and then processed by the brain. Not only was this described perceptual process one way in nature, it was also rather passive. The eye did little more than record the information available and the brain's role was to simply process whatever it was provided. In a sense, as illustrated here, the print environment largely determined what was perceived.

print —> eye —> brain —> meaning

More recently, however, perception has come to be understood in more dynamic and constructive ways. In this understanding, the eye and brain are much more actively and transactively involved in information processing. Under the direction of the brain, the eye selectively picks up relevant information from the print environment. What is selected is determined by both the print available and what the brain determines is important or relevant. Then, based on the print selected and contributions by the brain, meaning is constructed. In the previous example concerning Washington, DC, the misspelling of <capital> may have been misperceived because the brain knows the correct spelling and simply overrode what the eye had selected. Or, as we see next, the letter <a> may have been ignored altogether.

Smith (1994a, 2004) explained perception as involving an interaction between visual and nonvisual memory. Smith suggested that rather than a one-way and passive process as described previously, perception is a very active and constructive process in which nonvisual information—the brain—influences what visual information—the print—is selected by the eye. The relation between visual and nonvisual information is a reciprocal one. The more the brain knows, the less information the eye needs to select; the eye is required to pick up only information that is unknown to the brain. The brain therefore fills in the gaps that the eye creates. Figure 5.1, adapted from Smith, illustrates this process. Although perception and reading are the focus here, comprehension has also been included in the figure. As I show in the following chapter, much of what we know about perception and reading is relevant to comprehension as well.

In the next three experiments—Tables 5.3, 5.4, and 5.5—the beginning of a short story is shared. However, in each table, various letters in the story have been omitted. Read the story found in the three tables, and monitor how difficult or easy it is to predict the words that contain deleted letters.

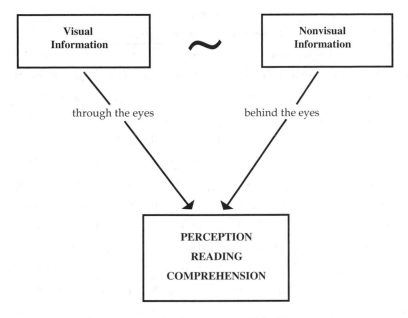

FIG. 5.1.   Visual and nonvisual information. Modified from Smith (1994a). *Understanding Reading* (p. 102). Hillsdale, NJ: Lawrence Erlbaum Associates.

TABLE 5.3
Perception and Beginning Letters

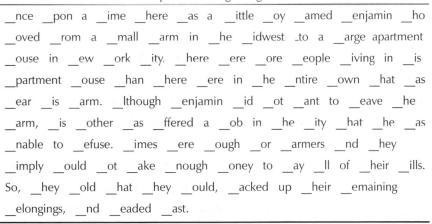

_nce	_pon a	_ime	_here	_as a	_ittle	_oy	_amed	_enjamin	_ho

_nce _pon a _ime _here _as a _ittle _oy _amed _enjamin _ho
_oved _rom a _mall _arm in _he _idwest _to a _arge apartment
_ouse in _ew _ork _ity. _here _ere _ore _eople _iving in _is
_partment _ouse _han _here _ere in _he _ntire _own _hat _as
_ear _is _arm. _lthough _enjamin _id _ot _ant to _eave _he
_arm, _is _other _as _ffered a _ob in _he _ity _hat _he _as
_nable to _efuse. _imes _ere _ough _or _armers _nd _hey
_imply _ould _ot _ake _nough _oney to _ay _ll of _heir _ills.
So, _hey _old _hat _hey _ould, _acked up _heir _emaining
_elongings, _nd _eaded _ast.

Similar to the experiment with the eight lines of print, you most likely found certain tables easier to read than others. Some of this difference is due to the fact that as you began to understand the story, it became progressively easier to predict what was going to happen next. You essentially had more nonvisual information to guide your reading. Also contributing to this variance is the fact that certain

TABLE 5.4

Perception and Middle Letters

T_e lit_le b_y w_s sho_ked wh_n he fi_st s_w t_e apar_ment th_t h_s mo_her h_d ren_ed dur_ng o_e of h_r vis_ts to N_w Yo_k Ci_y. T_e apar_ment w_s on t_e fi_th fl_or a_d t_e s_n co_ld on_y occasi_nally be se_n thr_ugh t_e liv_ng ro_m win_ows. T_e apar_ment w_s ve_y sm_ll, at le_st wh_n comp_red to the_r fa_m ho_se. The_e w_s a ve_y ti_y kit_hen wi_h no win_ow a_d it w_s t_o sm_ll to e_t in. Th_y h_d to p_t the_r kit_hen ta_le in t_e liv_ng ro_m. Alth_ugh th_s see_ed rat_er o_d to t_e b_y, th_s w_s a fai_ly com_on thi_g peo_le d_d in t_e Ci_y. T_e bathr_om w_s ju_t ab_ut lar_e eno_gh to tu_n aro_nd in, b_t d_d ha_e a win_ow. Benj_min's bed_oom w_s actu_lly lar_er th_n t_e liv_ng ro_m whi_h w_s unfor_unate sin_e th_t w_s wh_re h_s mot_er h_d to sle_p. Benj_min wond_red wh_t w_s so gr_at abo_t h_s mot_er's n_w j_b th_t ma_e th_m ha_e to li_e in su_h condi_ions.

TABLE 5.5

Perception and Ending Letters

Benjami_ an_ hi_ mothe_ wer_ luck_, howeve_, to be livin_ in an elevato_ buildin_ sinc_ man_ of th_ othe_ building_ on thei_ bloc_ di_ no_ hav_ elevator_. Benjami_ especiall_ learne_ to appreciat_ th_ elevato_ whe_ he an_ hi_ mothe_ ha_ to carr_ grocerie_ bac_ fro_ th_ grocer_ stor_. On th_ far_, th_ bo_ though_, we ha_ a c_r in which_ to carr_ grocerie_. The_ als_ ha_ a doo_ ma_ wh_ too_ package_ an_ mad_ sur_ uninvite_ guest_ di_ no_ invad_ thei_ privac_. Howeve_, sinc_ the_ di_ no_ reall_ kno_ anyon_ in th_ Cit_, surpris_ visitor_ wer_ unlikel_. In fac_, Benjami_ woul_ hav_ enjoye_ an_ visito_ sinc_ he wa_ rathe_ lonel_.

TABLE 5.6
Perception and Vowels

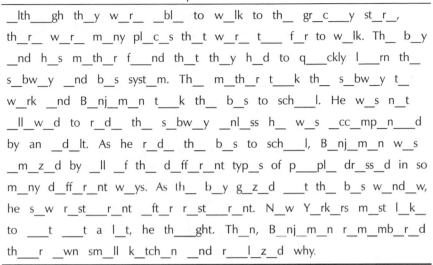

_lth___gh th_y w__r__ __bl__ to w__lk to th__ gr__c___y st__r__,
th__r__ w__r__ m__ny pl__c_s th__t w__r__ t___ f__r to w__lk. Th__ b__y
__nd h__s m__th__r f___nd th__t th__y h__d to q___ckly l___rn th__
s__bw__y __nd b__s syst__m. Th__ m__th__r t___k th__ s__bw__y t__
w__rk __nd B__nj__m__n t___k th__ b__s to sch___l. He w__s n__t
__ll w__d to r__d__ th__ s__bw__y __nl__ss h__ w__s __cc__mp__n___d
by an __d__lt. As he r__d__ th__ b__s to sch___l, B__nj__m__n w__s
__m__z__d by __ll __f th__ d__ff__r__nt typ_s of p___pl__ dr__ss__d in so
m__ny d__ff__r__nt w__ys. As th__ b__y g__z__d ___t th__ b__s w__nd__w,
he s__w r__st___r__nt __ft__r r__st___r__nt. N__w Y__rk__rs m__st l__k__
to ___t ___t a l__t, he th___ght. Th__n, B__nj__m__n r__m__mb__r__d
th___r __wn sm__ll k__tch__n __nd r___l__z__d why.

parts of words are easier to "guess" than others, or some parts of words are more salient or important than others. Typically, the beginning letters in a word are more important than the middle or ending letters. Initial letters are more difficult to predict from context and when missing, reading tends to be more problematic than when middle or ending letters are absent.

Ending letters tend to be the second most important letters in a word. Their absence also can cause difficulty when reading, but usually not to the same degree as when beginning letters are omitted. Middle letters are the least salient and often have minimal impact on perception when they are deleted. In a sense, this means that when perceiving, or reading, not all letters are created equal; some letters are more important to process than others. It was not by chance that when I misspelled <capital>, I selected the middle part of the word. I knew that you would be much less likely to perceive the misspelling in this position than if I had selected a beginning or ending letter. Interestingly, Wilde (1992) found that when young children misspell words, they misspell the middle letters more frequently than the beginning or the ending letters. Because beginning and ending letters are more salient or more likely to be perceived by the reader, children tend to first learn to conventionally spell these parts of words

In Tables 5.6 and 5.7, the story continues. Once again, particular letters have been omitted throughout the story. Read the next two parts and again monitor the degree of difficulty experienced.

The omission of the vowels in Table 5.6 tends to be much less disruptive than the lack of consonants in Table 5.7. In fact, it is doubtful that you were able to

TABLE 5.7

Perception and Consonants

___e _o_ _i_e _i_ _e_ ____oo_. ___e _ea__e_ __a_
_a__, e____u_ia__i_, a__ _a_e _i_ _ee_ _e__o_e_.
_a__ of ___e __u_e____ in _i_ ___a__ _e_e ___o_
o___e_ _ou___ie_ a__ ___o_e _a__ _i__e_e___
_a___ua_e_. __e_ _e_e __ie____, _o_e_e_, a__ __ie_
to _a_e _i_ _ee_ _o__o_a_e in _i_ _e_
_u___ou__i___. At _i____ _e__a_i_ _a_ _i__i_u____
u__e__a_i_ a__ of ___e_i__e_e_ _a_e___, _u_
_oo_ __e to u_e____ a__ ___a_ __e __u_e___ _e_e
_a_i__. In _a__, __e_ _o___i_ __a_ he a_o_ _a_ an
a___e__, he _u___ _ou____' _ea_ it! _e__a_i_
_ui_____ _a_e a_e___ _ie___ at ____oo_, a____ou___
___e _o_ _i_e_ _oo_a_ a_a_ to _i_i_ a_e_ ____ool.

read much of the story when the consonants were missing. These two experiments once again inform us about the inequality among letters when reading. Returning to the misspelling of <capital>, I elected to misspell the vowel rather than the consonant because I knew that this would be less disruptive to the reading process. It is interesting to note that written Arabic and Hebrew for adults typically omits the vowels (Elster, 2003). The reader is able to predict the word from context, using both the available consonants and the wider framework of the discourse. Wilde (1992) found that children tend to correctly spell the consonants in words and experience more difficulty with the vowels. This developmental pattern will be explored in more depth in chapter 11.

The previous experiments remind me of the word game, Probe, that I played when I was an elementary teacher. In the game, each player decides on a word that is then spelled out with individual letter cards. The cards are placed face down on the table and each player takes a turn asking an opponent if his or her word contains a particular letter. If the word contains the letter, the card is turned face up. Although words frequently involve the same letter in different positions, only one card must be revealed. The questioner continues to ask about particular letters until the response is negative—the word does not contain a particular letter—or until a prediction as to what the word might be is made.

As I quickly discovered when first learning to play the game, predicting letters and ultimately the word is based on the kinds of letters and their positions in

TABLE 5.8

Perception and Tops of Letters

Une of Benjamin's favorite things to do was to go to

Central Park. The Park reminded him of his previous life on

the farm, with all of the trees and grass. Their apartment

was only a few blocks from the Park and Benjamin was

constantly asking his mother to take him of to let him go

by himself. His mother did not feel comfortable with

Benjamin going to the Park alone and insisted that he only

go there with her. On the farm, he was able to go out and

play alone whenever he wanted. Benjamin wasn't use to

having to be escorted everywhere he went by his mother.

the word. Asking about consonants rather than vowels and focusing on word beginnings and endings usually resulted in faster and more accurate predictions.

The final part of the story is presented in Tables 5.8 and 5.9. Read each table and monitor your reading.

As you no doubt discovered, the tops of letters provide more useful information than the bottoms. According to Weaver (2002), approximately twice as many letters contain parts that are above rather than below an imaginary line dividing them into tops and bottoms.

The contribution of the reader's knowledge of the systems of language to the act of perception is demonstrated whenever one has an eye examination by an optometrist or ophthalmologist. During these examinations, the Snellen eye chart or its equivalent is frequently used. Lines of print are presented, and the patient is asked to "read" what is written. As indicated in Table 5.10, very few systems of language are presented; graphemes and graphophonemics are often the largest systems available. This is because the doctor is testing for visual acuity, not perception. The doctor wants to determine the visual clarity of the letters. Allowing the patient to use what is known about the systems of language interferes with an acuity test and becomes, instead, a test of perception or reading.

The power of the systems of language and the reader's desire to use his or her background knowledge cannot be overemphasized. Figure 5.2 contains a highway sign designating the location of a state university in Southern California. On close examination, it is apparent that the word <state> has been misspelled. This

TABLE 5.9

Perception and Bottoms of Letters

For the first time in his life, Benjamin and his mother began to visit museums and see Broadway shows. Benjamin was overwhelmed by the size of the museums and all that was in them. Until moving to New York City, Benjamin's main form of entertainment had been the television. Now he was able to visit art and history museums on the weekends. He was able to see dancers, singers, and actors and actresses on stage. Although Benjamin missed many things that farm life had to offer, he was slowly beginning to like his new home.

TABLE 5.10

Snellen Eye Chart

T   E

P V L

H C O E

H P D N L

D V H T L U

E V O U C T Y

P C Y L H N D V

FIG. 5.2.   Cal Steta University.

misspelling was captured in a photograph that was published in a local newspaper. Of course, there was the usual public response about poor spelling and state workers who did not take their jobs seriously. However, from a perceptual point of view, perhaps poor spelling had little if anything to do with the gaffe. It most likely was the case that the "writer" of the sign did, in fact, know how to spell <state> but simply placed the letters in the wrong order. In this instance, what we have is not so much a misspelling as a miswriting; that is, the writer knew how to spell the word but simply wrote it incorrectly. The various individuals who must have seen the sign before it was erected along the highway also were certainly able to read and write the word <state>. They simply did not perceive what was actually written because they knew what the sign was supposed to say. This constructive nature of perception is also the reason many lawyers would prefer to have no eyewitnesses to the scene of an accident or crime rather than two. Agreement as to what actually occurred between two or more witnesses is notoriously difficult to obtain.

The constructive nature of perception has also been demonstrated with biliterate readers. In a series of intriguing studies (Kolers, 1969, 1973), French–English proficient biliterates read passages in which both languages were used. Initially, the passage began in a single language and was then interspersed with the other language. Kolers found that the readers' comprehension was unaffected by the mixed language passages. As the passages were read aloud, it was common for the readers to translate words to the other language. This translation usually occurred at transition points, where a string of words written in one language suddenly switched to the second language. When interviewed, readers typically were unaware that the passages had been in two languages or that they had translated from one language to the other. Kolers (1973) argued that this occurred because readers "were treating words in terms of their meanings rather than in terms of their appearance on the page" (p. 48).

In all of the previous experiments, perception was influenced by visual and nonvisual information, between what was known and what was presented. In the following section, these two sources of information are more fully developed.

THE SYSTEMS OF LANGUAGE, MEMORY, AND PERCEPTION

As we have seen, the transaction of two sources of information—visual and nonvisual—allows perception to be both selective and constructive. Readers pick up the most salient or informative visual cues (what was termed surface structure in previous chapters) based on the text itself and available linguistic and conceptual background knowledge. Pickup is not from the smallest system of language to the largest but rather involves a sampling of a variety of language cues, with the more global cues (e.g., pragmatics, text structure, semantics) significantly influencing the more local cues (e.g., graphemes, graphophonemics, morphology). This process is thought to involve both short-term and long-term memory systems. Nonvisual information consists of these two systems.

Traditionally, as previously addressed, the two memories were viewed as operating in a linear and noninteractive manner. (See Fig. 5.3.) In this commonsense understanding of perception, print is the driving force in the process and involves a linear, part-to-whole movement of information. The eye's responsibility is to take in the available print, beginning with the smallest system of language. The print is placed into short-term memory (STM), where it is processed from letters into words, etc., made meaningful, and then put into long-term memory (LTM).

We now know, however, that it is misleading to see information as entering from one direction only. As illustrated in Fig. 5.4, not only is there an interplay between visual and nonvisual information, but there is also communication between STM and LTM. Each memory system makes use of information contained in the other. Additionally, when the eye picks up print, it samples from a variety of language cues. As we saw in chapter 2 on the nature of language and in this chapter with the misspelling of <capatal>, the sampling of various systems of language is necessary because it is often difficult to interpret lower systems without first interpreting those that are more global. This phenomenon requires that the eye purposefully seeks information on such things as text type and structure as it picks up information about graphemes and morphemes.

Facilitating the selection of information on a variety of language levels is the transaction between STM and LTM (Smith, 1994a, 2004). As illustrated in Table 5.11, STM contains whatever print the reader is attending to at the moment.

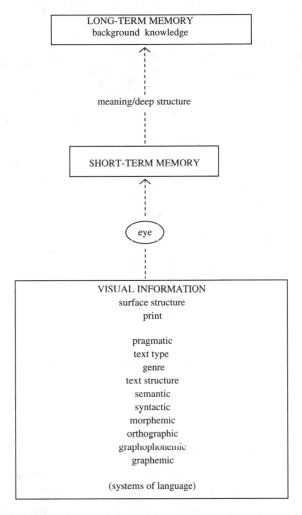

FIG. 5.3. A traditional view of the interaction among the systems of language, memory, and perception.

In general, its capacity is limited, usually to about seven unrelated bits of information per second. (It is not by chance that telephone numbers contain seven digits.) If reading were a letter-by-letter process, and if the average length of a word were seven letters, the reader would be able to process approximately 60 words per minute. However, on average, most readers can process 200 to 400 words per minute, depending on the particular text being read, purpose, and context (Adams & Bruck, 1995; Just & Carpenter, 1987; Smith, 1994a, 2004; Stanovich, 1996; Weaver, 2002).

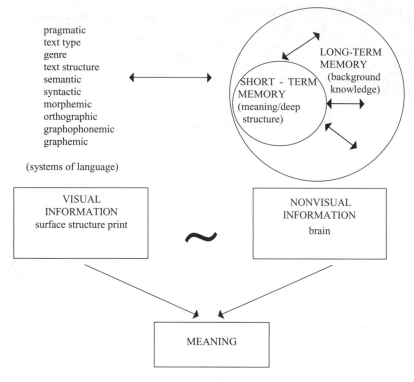

FIG. 5.4. A transactional view of the relationship among the systems of language, memory, and perception.

TABLE 5.11
Characteristics of Short-Term and Long-Term Memory

Characteristic	Short-Term Memory (Working Memory)	Long-Term Memory (Permanent Memory)
Capacity	Limited (contains whatever the individual is attending to at the moment)	Practically unlimited (contains the individual's conceptual and linguistic knowledge of the world)
Persistence	Very brief (information is lost if attention is diverted)	Practically unlimited (information is stored indefinitely)
Retrieval	Immediate (information is the current focus of attention)	Depends on organization (must tap into the information structure)
Pick-up	Very fast (information is engaged whenever it becomes the focus of attention)	Relatively slow (information must be processed)

Information can remain in STM only for a very brief time unless it is rehearsed. When attention is diverted, the information is lost. This is why if you are rehearsing or repeating a telephone number as you walk to the telephone and someone calls your name, the number is often lost. This loss of information is termed "masking" by cognitive psychologists; the new information placed into STM covers up or replaces what is already there.

Although the capacity and persistence of STM is limited, retrieving information from it is very easy. Whatever happens to be the focus of attention at the time is immediately available. Additionally, it is also relatively easy to put information into this system. All you need to do is attend to—pick up—the information and it is immediately available. Of course, knowing or deciding what information to give attention can be problematic in certain contexts. The use of computer technology, with its various modalities and hyperlinks, offers the reader myriad sites to attend. Information is plentiful, but attention is always scarce (Lankshear & Knobel (2002).

The nature of LTM is far different from that of STM. LTM contains the individual's knowledge of the world, both conceptual and linguistic. This information, often called schemata, is structured and interrelated much like that found in an encyclopedia (Rumelhart, 1980). As far as we know, the capacity of LTM is relatively unlimited, as long as the individual is able to move the information from STM into LTM. It also appears that once information is stored, it remains indefinitely. The difficulty, however, is in locating the information or remembering it. Remembering or recall is usually most successful when one has linked the information to a salient knowledge structure that can be easily tapped into.

In contrast to STM, in which information can be placed at a relatively fast rate, storing information in LTM is rather slow. It is estimated that it can take 4 to 5 seconds per idea before storage occurs. The process operates most effectively and efficiently when the information can be made meaningful (i.e., translating the surface structure into a deep structure) when it is within STM and then linked to existing structures of knowledge in LTM.

VISUAL PROCESSING AND MEMORY

It should come as no surprise that the eye does not move smoothly across the line of print during the reading process. We already know that the information the eye picks up is selective, with some letters providing more information than others. In fact, rather than a smooth sweep, the eye actually jumps along. This jumping movement, called a saccade (a French word that means "jerk"), moves the eye forward (a progression) as well as backward (a regression). In general, there is little difference in the types of saccades between children and adults. On average, children have one regression for every four progressions; adults have one regression for every six progressions.

During its movement, the eye is functionally blind; it picks up no new information. Rather, information is selected only when the eye comes to rest or fixates. It is estimated that fixations occupy from 90% to 95% of the eye's time during reading. Interestingly, fixations tend to focus on the first third of a word, the place where the most useful information is located (Just & Carpenter, 1987). Information is selected only once during a fixation and the information picked up wipes out or replaces the information in STM from the previous fixation. Although there exists variability in processing, the average duration of a fixation is one fourth of a second long. Proficient readers typically process one word per fixation and five or more words per second (Adams, 1990; Adams & Bruck, 1995; Rayner, 1997). Both fixations that result from forward and backward movements provide the eye with useful information to place in STM.

In a review and synthesis of eye movement studies, Rayner (1997) found that readers fixated on between 70% and 80% of the words in a text. The majority of content words (adjectives, nouns, verbs) receive a direct fixation and many function words (conjunctions, articles, prepositions) are focused on as well. More specifically, other researchers discovered that over 80% percent of the content words were fixated on and approximately 40% of the function words (Just & Carpenter, 1987; Smith, 1994a, 2004). Additionally, longer words were more likely to receive a fixation than shorter words (Stanovich, 1996). It would appear that just as all letters are not created equal, so too is the case with words.

Linguistically, we can explain the differences in what types of words receive or fail to receive fixations. As illustrated in chapter 2, content words—e.g., nouns, verbs, adjectives—are informationally salient; they provide new substance to the text. Because content words contain a large number of members, they are, in a sense, less predictable for the reader. On the other hand, function words—e.g., determiners, pronouns, prepositions—indicate how content words relate grammatically to one another. As such, they provide relatively less new information to the text. Because function words contain fewer members, they are also more predictable (Gee, 1999). Given these differences in information saliency as well as linguistic predictability, it is not surprising that readers tend to fixate more on content rather than function words. Content words represent core meanings and are not as easily anticipated.

The length of the word is a primary factor in determining where fixations occur (Rayner, 1997). If the fixated-on word is relatively short or predictable, information about the next word in the text may be gathered and processed. When such processing is possible, the fixation duration is usually increased and the subsequent word may be skipped altogether. In these circumstances, although the word has not received a fixation, it is presumed to have been processed. Just and Carpenter (1987) have suggested that there is a tendency for more letters to the right of the fixation to be processed than to the left. According to Rayner (1997), the perceptual span for vision in general extends 14 or 15 characters to the right of the fixation. However, the perceptual span for effective word identification is quite small and tends not to exceed seven to eight letter spaces. Additionally, it is at the center of the fixation that acuity is sharpest and letters most easily perceived. Acuity outside of this region drops off markedly, as does letter identification.

The size of the word identification span, however, is not static and there is both between- and within-reader variation. Additionally, the written discourse itself impacts perception. If words are short, the reader may be able to identify several in a single fixation. Or, if the fixated word is highly predictable—function words, for example, are more predictable than content words—the reader may also acquire information from the next word in the text. On the other hand, if the fixated word is unexpectedly difficult to process, little information may be obtained about the upcoming word.

Finally, the number of fixations required to process a text is also variable. When the content or linguistic nature of the text is demanding, fixations occur more frequently. Under these conditions, a single word may require a longer or even an additional fixation in order for identification to occur. Saccade lengths—the span between fixations—may decrease and the frequency of regressions increase (Just & Carpenter, 1987; Rayner, 1997; Rayner & Pollatsek, 1989).

Similar to saccades, the number of fixations per second does not vary to any great extent between children and adults. Children have on average three fixations per second and adults have about four fixations per second. This fixation rate stabilizes around the fourth grade (Smith, 1994a). However, poor readers tend to produce many more fixations—both forward and backward—than those who are proficient. Additionally, difficult texts result in more and longer regressions among all readers. Because processing takes time, there can be little improvement in reading by increasing the rate at which saccades and fixations are made. Reading cannot be accelerated by simply moving along faster. This is why research on "speed reading" has consistently found that attempts to significantly increase the rate at which a text is processed usually result in a corresponding decrease in comprehension (Just & Carpenter, 1987).

The real key to the difference in processing between beginning and advanced or poor and good readers is the amount of information that can be identified in a single fixation. For children, it takes about 100 to 200 fixations to read 100 words, about one to two fixations per word. On the other hand, adults can read 100 words with 90 to 100 fixations or one fixation per word.

Children or less proficient readers have what Smith (1994a, 2004) termed tunnel vision. The narrow width of their fixations results in their picking up less information than proficient readers. Such narrow fixations require the reader to engage in many more fixations than proficient readers to read the same amount of information. Frequently, tunnel vision also interferes with the comprehension process. Similar to a funnel into which too much water is poured too quickly, STM becomes overwhelmed with bits and pieces of discourse. The reader is unable to make sense of the contents in STM because not enough information is available. At the same time, the reader is unable and/or unwilling to supplement the information picked up with information from LTM.

It is important to note that there is a general consensus concerning the basic nature of the memory systems, saccades, and fixations. There is, however, a fundamental disagreement over the extent to which print is accessed and processed. The role of context and background knowledge in perception is also contested. These differences will be addressed in the following chapter on the reading process.

"A PIN FOR DAN" AND "THE GREAT BIG ENORMOUS TURNIP"

To better understand the role of perception in the reading process, the readings of two stories are examined: "A Pin for Dan" (Fries, Fries, Wilson, & Rudolph, 1966) and "The Great Big Enormous Turnip" (Tolstoy, 1976; see Kucer, 1985b). The "reading levels" of both texts were analyzed using the Spache (1978) readability formula. In determining text difficulty, the Spache formula calculates the number of words and sentences, word difficulty, and average sentence length. "A Pin for Dan" (PFD) has 55 words, 10 sentences (including the title), 4 difficult words, and an average sentence length of 5.5 words. "The Great Big Enormous Turnip" (GBET) contains 281 words, 44 sentences, 4 difficult words, and an average sentence length of 6.4 words. Except for length, both stories are highly similar, with an average readability level of 2.0. This means that PFD and GBET can be read, with instructional support, by students who are reading at the second-grade level.

A third-grade student, Reader A, read PFD, and a third-grade student, Reader B, read GBET. The texts were read aloud and no assistance was provided when the reader encountered "things" that were not known. The readings were audio recorded and the miscues were marked. The two stories with marked miscues are presented in Tables 5.12 and 5.13. For those unfamiliar with miscue analysis, the circled C with a line indicates a corrected miscue; the line illustrates at what point the reader went back to correct and the length of the regression. Words omitted are circled; words inserted are indicated by a ^. Repetition of words is underlined and marked with a circled R. Partial attempts at pronouncing words are coded with the sound(s) uttered followed by a —. Take a moment to examine the miscues of Reader A and Reader B. Which reader do you think demonstrates the most effective and efficient reading strategies? Why?

Even a casual examination of the two stories most likely finds Reader B to be a far better reader than Reader A. A more formal analysis of the miscues supports this observation. After all miscues were marked, each sentence was analyzed in terms of its semantic acceptability. The question was asked: Does the sentence as finally read make sense, regardless of whether or not the miscues changed the author's intended meaning? Because a primary goal of a reader is to generate meaning, such an analysis gives insight into the reader's attempt to make meaning

TABLE 5.12

In-Process Reading Behaviors of Reader A

001   Ⓒ   from Ⓓ
      "A | Pin For Dan"

002   A man had a | tin pin.

003   Ⓒ ② Ⓡ ③   ④
                    of   cup
      It's a | pin for a | cap.

004   Ⓒ   Dan Ⓒ   ⑥
                  wind
      Can | Dad | win it for Dan?

005   ⑦
      Dad (wins) the pin.

006   Ⓒ   ⑧
      | The pin is (in) a bag.

      For Dan

007   Ⓒ In ⑨   Ⓒ
                           t-
      | On the bag is a | tag.

008   ⑩ 2 fists
              1. first   cup Ⓡⓜ
      The pin fits on Dan's cap.

009   Ⓒ   ⑪
          D-   ed   cup Ⓡⓜ
      | Dad pins it on the cap.

010   The pin is Dan's pin.

TABLE 5.13
In-Process Reading Behaviors of Reader B

001 ① "The Great Big Enormous Turnip"

② out ↯upon ③ ④ ©t-
002 Once upon a time an old man planted a little turnip. The old man

© li- ©t- ⑤set
003 said, Grow, grow, little turnip. Grow sweet. Grow, grow, little

©st- ©gro- ⑥strong ⑦st-
004 turnip. Grow strong." And the turnip up grew up sweet and strong and

⑧ Ⓡ
005 big and enormous. Then one day the old man went to pull it up. He

⑨ ↯agen
006 pulled--and pulled again. But he could not pull it up. He called

©o-
007 the old woman. The old woman pulled the old man. The old man

008 pulled the turnip. And they pulled--and pulled again. But they

009 could not pull it up. So the old woman called her granddaughter.

010 The granddaughter pulled the old woman. The old woman pulled the

011 old man. The old man pulled the turnip. And they pulled--and

⑩
012 pulled again. But they could not pull it up. The granddaughter

013 called the black dog. The black dog pulled the granddaughter. The

014 granddaughter pulled the old woman. The old woman pulled the old

015 man. The old man pulled the turnip. And they pulled--and pulled

016 again. But they could not pull it up. The black dog called the cat. The

110

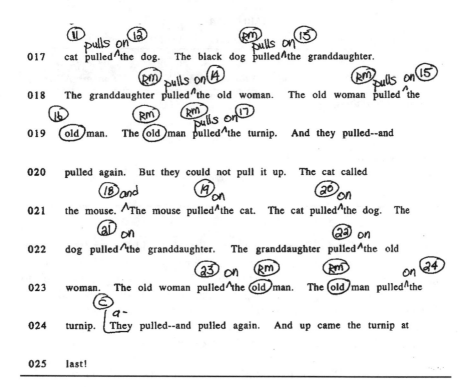

017   cat pulled^the dog.   The black dog pulled^the granddaughter.

018   The granddaughter pulled^the old woman.   The old woman pulled^the

019   old man.   The old man pulled^the turnip.   And they pulled--and

020   pulled again.   But they could not pull it up.   The cat called

021   the mouse. ^The mouse pulled^the cat.   The cat pulled^the dog.   The

022   dog pulled^the granddaughter.   The granddaughter pulled^the old

023   woman.   The old woman pulled^the old man.   The old man pulled^the

024   turnip.   They pulled--and pulled again.   And up came the turnip at

025   last!

when transacting with print. The sentences as finally read were also evaluated in terms of meaning change. This question was asked: Does the sentence as finally read change the author's intended meaning? Not only is reading a meaning-seeking process, it also is a process in which the reader attempts to understand the intentions of the author.

The impact of the miscues on sentence meaning in the two stories is represented in Table 5.14. This analysis indicates that Reader A and Reader B demonstrated differing abilities in their construction of meaning from the two texts. In PFD, 30% of the sentences lack meaning; the miscues in the sentences in lines 003, 005, and 008 disrupt the semantic acceptability of the three structures. Similarly, in the reading of PFD, 40% of the miscues disrupt the author's intended meaning (lines 003, 005, 008, 009). The reader believes that the pin is for a cup, is unaware that Dad wins the pin, and misses the idea that the pin fits on Dan's cap.

In contrast, the miscues in GBET result in semantically unacceptable sentences only 9% of the time. These sentences are in lines 002, 003, 004, 005, and 006. Similarly, the reader's miscues changed the author's basic message in 19% of the sentences (lines 002, 003, 004, 005, 006, 019, 023). However, in five of these sentences (lines 005, 006, 018, 023, 024), the meaning change is relatively minor.

TABLE 5.14

Evaluation of Miscues for Semantic Acceptability and Meaning Change

	A Pin for Dan	The Great Big Enormous Turnip
Semantic Acceptability		
Yes	70%	91%
No	30%	9%
Meaning Change		
Yes	40%	19%
No	60%	81%

There are additional differences between Reader A and Reader B. Although Reader B initially produced a nonsense word for <again> (line 006), when the reader encounters <again> later in the text (lines 008, 012, 016, 020), she is able to successfully read it. Also, after reading <old man> several times (lines 002, 005, 007, 011, 014, 015), the reader simply chooses to omit <old> when it refers to the man (lines 019, 023), although she does not do this when <old> relates to the woman (lines 007, 009, 010, 014, 018, 022, 023). Interestingly, in discussing the story after the reading, Reader B described the man as being old.

The reader of GBET also made editorial changes in the text, essentially changing the surface structure but maintaining the deep structure. Beginning on line 017, she changes the tense from past to present and begins to insert <on> in this structure every time it is encountered. Reader B also decides to link the two sentences on line 021 with <and>, something the author might have elected to do when writing the text. These miscues, however, are not simply misreadings; the reader has successfully read these structures previously in the text. Rather, the miscues reflect her recognition that the text contains familiar language patterns.

It is evident that the readings of the two texts are markedly different and, therefore, it is tempting to evaluate Reader B as superior to Reader A. However, Reader A and Reader B just happen to be the same child, Susan. How can this be, given that both texts are on the same readability level? We can return to our previous discussion concerning the systems of language and perception to help us understand this phenomenon.

Although both texts are similar when analyzed from a readability perspective—number of words and sentences, difficult words, average sentence length—they are quite different in other linguistic aspects. In fact, the very nature of readability formulas may explain the differences in the readings of Susan. Most readability formulas are word based; the difficulty of any piece is largely determined by the number of words in the passage that are predicted to be difficult for the reader. Such formulas ignore a variety of influences that contribute to text difficulty. For one thing, they fail to adequately consider the syntactic complexity of the sentences in a text, which is not always determined by the number of words per sentence. A simple sentence may be longer than a complex one if several adjectives or adverbs are used, although it may not be more difficult to read. Miscue research (Allen & Watson, 1976) has consistently found that elementary students are able to read complex sentences when a number of factors are present: (a) grammatical function of words and their meanings are familiar, (b) phrases are familiar, (c) phrases are in a predictable order both within and between sentences, and (d) word order is predictable.

In addition to ignoring syntactic complexity, readability formulas fail to consider whether the author's language patterns are similar or parallel to those of the reader. Students may initially experience difficulty when encountering texts using syntactic structures that differ from their own, regardless of the length of the sentences. There also appears to be an implicit assumption underlying many readability formulas that conceptual difficulty is based primarily on what kinds of words are used in a passage. The more difficult the words—sometimes determined by the number of syllables—the more difficult the text is predicted to be. However, a reader may know or be taught all of the significant words and still experience reading difficulty. As we will discover in chapter 7, this is because most words have multiple meanings, or at least multiple shades of meaning. Only through the use of context can the particular meaning of a word be determined. This requires the reader to look beyond the word or even sentence level when attempting to make sense of any word.

Even if the reader should happen to know all of the words in a passage and can handle the syntactic complexity of the sentences, there is still no guarantee that the text will be an "easy" one to read. A text is more than a series of words or sentences strung together. Rather, written language consists of a complex hierarchy of interrelated ideas or chunks of meaning that form a unified whole. As such, it consists of a variety of interrelated and embedded systems (e.g., pragmatics, text type, semantics, graphophonemics) as illustrated in Figure 2.5. Our perception or identification of each system is influenced by the other systems in which any particular system is embedded. Comprehension of text involves the pulling together and relating of these ideas so that a coherent semantic structure is formed. As with the meanings of most words, each chunk of text only has meaning and makes sense in relation to all the other chunks in the text. Simple word and sentence counts cannot hope to capture the complexity of the ideas an author is attempting to convey; nor can these counts adequately predict a reader's ability to build a unified whole from any particular piece of reading material.

The conceptual background knowledge of the reader also impacts perception and the identification of each language system. Perception, as we can clearly see, is influenced by the text being processed and by the individual doing the

TABLE 5.15

Comparison of Texts From a Predictability Perspective

Predictable Component	A Pin for Dan	The Great Big Enormous Turnip
Graphophonemics	Frequent use of <i> and <a> in various combinations: <an>, <ag>, and <in>	Words are selected based on the intentions of the author and meanings to be conveyed
Language	Constrained sentences because of an attempt to limit words to those containing the short <i> and <a>	Varied and natural language patterns selected to convey the author's intentions and meanings
Textual	Not a complete story; requires a great deal of inferencing to link all elements of the story into a coherent whole	Repetitive and cumulative structure; each episode builds upon and extends the previous episode; a coherent story
Picture/print relationship	One picture; extends the print	Pictures are parallel or redundant with the print; the pictures "tell" the story
Author/reader background relationships	Little relationship; uncommon for boys to wear pins on their caps	A folk tale; a genre experienced by many children
Overall predictability	Unpredictable	Highly predictable

processing. As readers construct meaning, they sample the print and predict the author's message using a variety of language cues. K. Goodman (1967) referred to this process as a psycholinguistic guessing game.

Rhodes (1979a, 1979b, 1981), among others, suggested that the concept of predictability might serve as a more valid framework for understanding the transaction between a reader and a text. In contrast to word-focused readability formulas, the predictability of a text is judged in terms of (a) the use of natural language patterns; (b) the match between the reader's language and the author's language; (c) the use of repetitive or cumulative syntactic, semantic, or episodic sequences; (d) the match or redundancy between the print and the pictures; and (e) the relation between the conceptual background of the reader and the text. Using this criteria as a guide, the varying degrees of predictability in PFD and GBET are illustrated in Table 5.15.

As can be readily observed, the two stories are radically different from a predictability perspective. PFD focuses solely on graphophonemic predictability. Forty percent of the words in the passage contain one of three letter–sound patterns: <an>, <ag>, or <in>. The frequent use of these letters and sounds permeates the text, results in rather stilted sentences, and limits the degree to which other aspects of the story can be predictable. When teachers are asked to read this story aloud, they frequently comment that PFD reminds them of a tongue twister.

The lack of predictability on the textual level in PFD is particularly noticeable. There are numerous gaps in the story line that require a great deal of inferencing on the part of the reader if all events in the story are to be related. The reader is never quite sure, for example, where the story is taking place or who the man is. How Dad wins the pin, why the pin is in a bag, or how Dan's name happens to be on the tag are not explained. The one inference the reader could easily make because of the previous events in the story is stated explicitly in the text: <The pin is Dan's pin> (line 010). The sole picture in the story, the tag, requires yet another inference on the part of the reader. To fully understand the text and the picture, the reader must relate <On the bag is a tag> (line 007) to the picture of the tag with Dan's name on it.

In many ways, PFD violates what Tierney and LaZansky (1980) called the contractual agreement between readers and writers: As readers and writers attempt to communicate with one another, they have certain rights and responsibilities "which define what is allowable vis-à-vis the role of each in relation to the text" (p. 2). One critical responsibility of the writer within this contract is to produce an informative text that provides the reader with enough information so that countless numbers of inferences need not be made. When the writer fails to fulfill this part of the contract, meaning is sacrificed. PFD violates just this aspect of the reader–writer contract. The writer of the text is inconsiderate in not supplying the reader with all of the information necessary for a complete understanding of the story.

Perhaps even more inconsiderate is the purpose or pragmatics of the text. If one asks the question, "What was the author trying to teach the reader through the text?," an answer is not readily forthcoming because the primary function of the text is to teach the reader particular letter–sound combinations. Such a focus results in the formation of a story that is created from a bottom-to-top use of the systems of language, a violation of how most texts are generated.

Finally, the relation between the story content and the reader's background is probably limited at best. Although most children certainly understand the concept of winning, the notion of a pin for a boy's cap may be foreign to them. Most important, PFD fails to reflect the types of stories many children encounter at home before entering school. Taylor and Dorsey-Gaines (1988) and Teale (1984), among others, documented the frequency with which parents share stories with their preschool children and its effect on initial literacy development. It is difficult to imagine that stories such as PFD would have found their way into most homes.

In contrast, GBET is predictable on several levels, although not on the graphophonemic level. The author has made no attempt to limit the use of certain sounds and letters. Instead, the text contains a variety of graphophonemic relations, and its language patterns reflect those of oral language. In fact, most stories such as GBET (i.e., folktales) were originally shared within the community through the use of spoken language. Only later did they come to be preserved in written discourse.

Textually, there is a repetitive and cumulative story line in GBET. Each episode in the story repeats and builds on the previous language patterns and events in the text. Structurally, each episode might be depicted as:

1. An attempt is made to pull up the turnip.
2. The attempt fails.
3. The last character to lend a hand seeks assistance.
4. The next character found to help is always smaller.
5. Once again, they all attempt to pull up the turnip, each character pulling the character which sought its help.

Although it is not possible to show the illustrations that accompany the story line in GBET, the illustrations do in fact tell the story. When children are asked to "read" the story using only the pictures, the story they tell almost always parallels the story conveyed by the print. The folktale characteristics in GBET also add to its predictability. Many children experience this genre through story reading in the home, watching television, or in kindergarten and first grade. Finally, if we consider why the author might have written the story, such themes as "working together, people can accomplish things that cannot be accomplished individually" or "little things can make a big difference" readily come to mind. The writer was driven by pragmatics or purpose in the development of the story, not the repeated use of particular sound–letter relations.

A common educational belief is that "shorter is easier." The readings of Susan, as well as what we know about perception itself, clearly challenge this belief. The limited length alone of PFD probably guaranteed that Susan's miscues would disrupt to a greater degree the overall meaning of the story than they would in a text the length of GBET. As can easily be seen, length may actually support the perceptual and reading process rather than inhibit it.

As we will see in the following chapter, readers attempt to process the language in the biggest chunks possible. The size of the chunks is impacted by the reader's focus, available nonvisual information, as well as the text itself. The material can "tell" the reader in very direct ways what linguistic elements are the most significant and what strategies to use. As noted by Spencer (1988), texts teach what readers learn. Simons and Ammon (1989) similarly documented the counterproductive impact of such controlled texts—what they termed "primerese"—on young readers. It is interesting to note, however, that the use of "decodable" texts—texts with constrained letter–sound patterns—have found their way back into many beginning reading programs. Susan's processing of the decodable text, "A Pin for Dan," should prompt us to consider whether such texts actually support readers and their development (Allington & Woodside-Jiron, 1998; Cunningham, 2000).

CONCLUSIONS

Human beings are typically discriminating in their transactions with the world. There is simply too much information available for everything to be selected and processed. Transaction with print is no different. Readers actively select some print for analysis and supplement the information selected with background knowledge. Based on this visual and nonvisual information, an understanding of the text is constructed. Given this reciprocal relation between reader and text, the effectiveness and efficiency of perception will fluctuate as the relation between reader and text varies.

6

The Reading Process

In chapter 5, the role of perception in the reading process was considered. In contrast to what is commonly believed, we found perception to be a selective and constructive act. In this chapter, we expand our view of the reading process and explore the mental processes, strategies, and procedures in which the individual engages to construct meaning through print. We begin with a look at the factors that impact the reader–text–writer transaction. This examination is followed by a theory and model of the reading process and a look at proficient and less proficient readers.

FACTORS INFLUENCING THE READER–TEXT–WRITER TRANSACTION

There are a number of variables that influence the transaction among reader, text, and writer (see Table 6.1). Some factors, such as the systems of language, have already been fully developed in previous chapters. Other factors, such as background knowledge, are addressed in more depth in chapter 7. Of particular importance here, however, is the fact that these factors are involved in a relationship between two individuals, the reader and the author, via written discourse. As the nature of these factors vary, so too will the relationship and communication between the reader and writer.

Too often, when text processing problems are experienced, responsibility is given to only one of the two participants. If a child experiences difficulty reading a story, for example, the teacher may hold the reader accountable for the problem. The child is thought not to have developed proficiency with the strategies that are necessary for successfully generating meaning from the text, or the teacher may feel that the student has not been adequately prepared for the reading. In contrast, if the teacher encounters difficulty reading a student paper, the writer is often held responsible. In this case, it is the author who is thought not to have

TABLE 6.1

Factors Influencing the Reader–Text–Writer Transaction

READER <—> TEXT <—> WRITER

Systems of language	Systems of language
Availability of, and flexibility with, the reading strategies	Availability of, and flexibility with, the writing strategies
Background knowledge	Background knowledge
Purpose for the reading	Purpose for the writing
Ability and willingness to assimilate and/or accommodate during reading	Ability and willingness to assimilate and/or accommodate during writing

developed proficiency with the strategies that are necessary for successfully generating text meanings. In both these examples, it may indeed be the case that only one individual—reader or writer—is the source of the problem. However, it may just as likely be that the other party involved in the transaction has responsibility as well. Because communication is a two-way process, it is necessary to examine the contributions of both individuals to any meaning-making event.

Systems of Language

As has already been demonstrated, the relationship between the reader's language and the writer's language influences the ease with which a text can be processed. Potentially, shared language systems can more easily produce shared understandings. It is important to remember, however, that a similarity in reader–writer language does not necessarily result in fewer miscues, only miscues that tend to be more meaningful within the context of the discourse. In fact, as Susan so clearly demonstrated in chapter 5, miscues may actually increase as the reader becomes familiar with the text's language and meaning. The reader may come to feel comfortable translating the author's preferred way of expressing an idea to the reader's preferred way, while at the same time maintaining the author's meaning.

The same influence is found in writing as well. When generating a text for an audience that shares the author's language variation, the writer need not spend inordinate amounts of time and cognitive energy selecting language forms that will be readily comprehensible to the reader. Rather, linguistic structures commonly used by the writer can be accessed and employed with less difficulty and effort.

Strategies

A second factor that influences a reader's and writer's transaction with print is the strategies available to the language user and his or her flexibility in employing them. Strategies represent those cognitive processes or behaviors that the individual engages so as to create meaning through written discourse. Readers and writers, for example, predict meanings when transacting with print. As reading or writing proceeds, these anticipated meanings are monitored and evaluated in light of subsequent and future meanings. Strategies for the most part operate in a transactive and parallel manner. That is, more than one strategy may occur at any given moment and these strategies need not operate in a particular sequence.

Background Knowledge

Not only do readers and writers bring their language to the printed page, conceptual knowledge is brought as well. There exists a symbiotic relationship between the knowledge conveyed through a text by the author and the knowledge conveyed through a text by the reader. In general, the more the reader's and author's backgrounds parallel one another, the smoother the construction of meaning is likely to be. For the reader, background knowledge impacts both the quality of the miscues and how a text is ultimately understood. In fact, background knowledge related to the content of a text has been found to have an overriding influence on the reading process, whether in traditional print form (Alexander & Jetton, 2000; Tierney & Pearson, 1994) or in hypertext processing (Lawless, et al., 2003). Similarly, for the writer, background knowledge impacts his or her ability to manipulate and translate ideas into written language. If I am writing about a personal experience, accessing and using this knowledge will be relatively easy. Both the meanings and their organization are already ordered in a time-sequenced structure. However, if the writing task calls for synthesizing information that is not already cognitively integrated in my mind, I am likely to encounter more processing difficulties as I put pen to paper.

The relationship of the reader's and writer's backgrounds is more than an issue of amount or quantity. Knowledge has a number of additional qualities that influence the literacy processes. The organization of the knowledge and its depth or extensiveness must be taken into account. The general or specific nature of the knowledge and its interconnectedness with other knowledge structures also have to be considered. Finally, the flexibility of the reader or writer in using existing knowledge to build new knowledge through assimilation and accommodation will have a significant impact on reading and writing. These various qualities of background knowledge are explored throughout the following chapter on comprehension and in chapter 8 on the writing process.

Purpose

Language users do not initiate an engagement with a text without a reason or purpose. These intentions or goals, which are realized through the formation and implementation of plans, may change or evolve as the text is developed. Nonetheless, intentions drive reading and writing acts. As noted in chapter 2 on the nature of language, Halliday (1973) delineated various functions that language can serve. A reader or writer might engage the printed word for an instrumental purpose, to satisfy or obtain material needs; or the purpose may be to explore the environment, to ask questions and seek knowledge; or the language user may engage with written discourse to leave the here and now and enter into a new world. These purposes have a direct and significant impact on how and what meanings are ultimately constructed through written discourse.

Assimilation and Accommodation

As meaning is constructed, it is not uncommon for the reader and writer to be changed cognitively. What the language user knows when the transaction with print terminates may be qualitatively and quantitatively different from what he or she knew when the transaction was initiated. Both readers and writers build knowledge through two basic processes of learning: assimilation and accommodation. In some instances, the meanings constructed through print fit within the knowledge structures of the reader or writer; a cognitive congruency exists between the individual and the information. Therefore, the addition of information to LTM results in an elaboration or extension of existing knowledge structures. The new knowledge is simply added to, or assimilated into, what is already known. In this top-down process, the meanings fit within existing cognitive frameworks.

There are also instances when the information to be generated through print will not easily fit into the language user's available cognitive structures. The reader may lack the knowledge to make sense of the information presented; or, the writer, through the very act of writing, may discover new meanings or insights that create disequilibrium with existing knowledge structures. For the information to be understood by the reader or writer, a restructuring or accommodation of what is known is required. This bottom-up process results in a modified cognitive framework from which the reader or writer is then able to assimilate the meanings under construction. In general and to varying degrees, both assimilation and accommodation occur during reading and writing.

The impact of assimilation and accommodation is most noticeable when students encounter ideas that conflict with their worldviews. During the teaching of a graduate course on literacy development, I assigned my students an article about the constructive nature of language learning. The author of the article contrasted the commonsense notion of language learning (i.e., imitation and reinforcement) with a constructivist perspective (i.e., rule generation, testing, and modification). During class discussion of the article, many students failed to understand that the author was explicitly rejecting a behavioristic view of language learning. Their view of language development as a process whereby young children mimic the language of their parents was so strong that it blinded them to the perspective presented by the author. Rather than accommodate this new view, students "forced" the information into their existing cognitive structures.

Given the impact of language, strategies, background, purpose, and assimilation and accommodation on discourse processing, the notion of reading and writing as monolithic abilities becomes untenable. All acts of literacy are not equal. Reading and writing do not consist of a set of subskills that can be easily isolated, practiced, mastered, and then used with the same degree of proficiency or facility from one text to the next. Rather, language performance changes as the relevant factors impinging on the literacy process change. As conditions and contexts vary, so too will the process and the product of the literacy event.

It is important to note that the previous discussion was largely focused on "traditional" texts. That is, texts printed on paper. However, computer technology and the texts the reader is able to access through the World Wide Web, for example, are increasingly becoming a standard form of reading. Frequently, these texts contain hyperlinks to additional texts written by additional authors. In such circumstances, the notion of text is expanded (Kinzer & Leander, 2003) and the relationship between the reader and the writer is no longer a static one. Rather, the relationship is variable and dynamic as the reader moves from one hypertext to the next.

WHAT DO THEORIES AND MODELS HAVE TO DO WITH TEACHING READING AND WRITING?

Before examining what transpires when an individual puts eye to print, a brief introduction to theories and models is necessary. This provides a framework for what can and cannot be expected from a reading theory and model. Even more importantly, this examination helps demonstrate how theories and models are relevant to teachers as they promote literacy development in their students.

Simply put, a theory is an explanation of a particular phenomenon that captures its critical elements or factors and their transactions. More than a description of the phenomenon's surface structure, a theory attempts to explain its deep structure. These explanations are working hypotheses that highlight significant factors and relationships, while at the same time ignoring those factors and relationships that are only peripherally related to the phenomenon. Theories, therefore, disregard idiosyncratic behaviors, focusing instead on behaviors that are common across contexts. Given a complex phenomenon, theories help us perceive more effectively through a process of selective attention as they attempt to represent and organize relevant data (D'Angelo, 1975; de Beaugrande, 1980; Harste & Burke, 1978). In the case of reading, a theory identifies the common processes and strategies used by efficient and effective readers to make meaning through print. Additionally, a reading theory sets forth various factors, such as background knowledge and purpose, and their impact on the reader's use of the identified processes and strategies.

A model, in contrast to a theory, is a nonlinguistic representation of the key factors and their interrelationships in a theory. In many respects, a model is an illustration or icon of the phenomenon. A model of the reading process, therefore, illustrates the strategies and processes involved, the factors influencing these processes, and the interplay among them.

It is commonly assumed that classroom teachers are at best uninterested and at worst hostile to theory. Teachers, it is said, are practitioners, more concerned about what to do on Monday than about philosophical issues. However, theories, even those which are unexamined, can and do have a direct influence on classroom instruction. As Steiner (1978) noted, theories serve three functions. First, they allow for a greater understanding of a phenomenon. Teachers need and want to understand how the reading process operates. In my own elementary school teaching, I can remember being frustrated teaching young children to read. Although I was able to understand and follow the instructions in the basal reader, I never fully understood why I was engaging the students in particular activities. This was especially the case when introducing my students to reading skills that I did not know myself. However, rather than questioning the usefulness of these skills, I simply assumed that I was deficient in some way as a reader. This confusion was largely due to my lack of understanding concerning how the reading process operated and what the children needed to learn to successfully engage in the process.

Additionally, Steiner (1978) proposed that theories allow for the generation of predictions concerning the phenomenon. A theory of reading allows the teacher to anticipate how well students might be able to process and understand a particular text. When I gave Susan the two stories, "A Pin for Dan" (Fries et al., 1966) and "The Great Big Enormous Turnip" (Tolstoy, 1976), to read, I knew beforehand what miscue patterns I would most likely observe. My understanding of the reading process, the student, and the texts allowed me to predict Susan's processing behaviors prior to the actual acts of reading.

Finally, an understanding of theory allows us to influence the phenomenon itself. For teachers, this means they can promote literacy development in their students by the types of reading materials selected or the kinds of instructional support provided before, during, and after reading is initiated. By changing the text for Susan, I was able to influence the strategies she used and the systems of language on which she focused. As can readily be observed, the ability of theory to help teachers understand, predict, and influence their students' transactions with print demonstrates the relevance of theory to classroom settings.

A THEORY AND MODEL OF THE READING PROCESS

In this section, a theory and model of the reading process is presented and discussed. The theory and model of reading (Fig. 6.1) has been adapted from Kucer (1985a, 1987, 1989b; see also Tierney & Shanahan, 1996). The theory and model is also used in chapter 8 on the writing process so that links between the two modes of discourse production can be developed. For both reading and writing, five features are addressed: knowledge search, context, goals and plans, strategies, and evolving text.

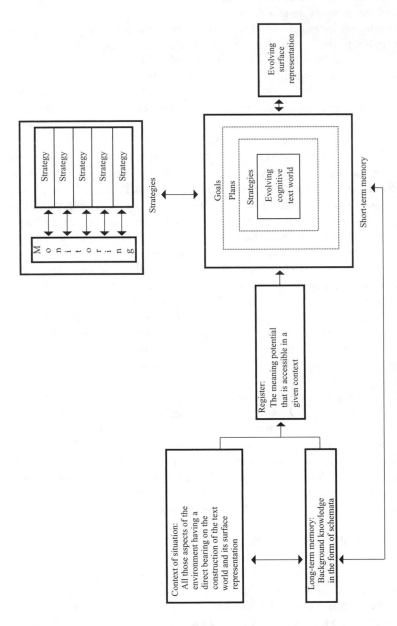

FIG. 6.1.   A model of the reading and writing processes. From Kucer, S. B. (1985a). The making of meaning: Reading and writing as parallel processes (p. 320). *Written Communication, 2,* 317–336.

Knowledge Search

Perhaps the most appropriate place to begin a discussion of the reading process is with the quest for meaning that permeates all language use. When reading is initiated, the language user searches for background knowledge relevant to the communicative situation. Background knowledge, stored in LTM, is represented in what cognitive scientists have termed schemata, "the building blocks of cognition" (Rumelhart, 1980, p. 33). Simply defined, schemata are complex structures of information that represent the individual's past encounters with the world. They contain the reader's knowledge of objects, situations, and events, as well as knowledge of processes, such as reading, washing clothes, or home buying.

As discussed more fully in the following chapter on comprehension and in chapters 9 and 10, all knowledge is implicitly or explicitly culturally coded. Because we operate within a variety of social contexts and assume a variety of social roles or identities, our lives are permeated and influenced by cultural markings (Ferdman, 1990). In fact, "it is not possible to think, act, [and mean] independent of culture" (Smagorinsky, 2001, p. 146). Our experiences with and knowledge of objects, situations, events, and processes are always culturally based. The discussion of cultural knowledge, therefore, is interwoven with the discussion of knowledge in general so as to avoid the danger of separating culture from experience.

There is a similar danger in separating cognitive knowledge from affective knowledge. As Eisner (1994) noted, this distinction between cognition and affect can result in "practical mischief"; that is, schools too often value the cognitive over the affective and focus on what students know rather than what students feel. In reality, there can be neither affect without cognition nor cognition without affect. To have feelings is to have a reaction to something that is known, to an idea. Likewise, to know something always entails accompanying feelings. Even the lack of feelings is, in effect, an affective response to something known.

Schemata might best be conceptualized as cognitive maps. On such maps, each location represents a concept or idea, with the roads from one location to the next signifying conceptual linkages. The number of linkages among concepts indicates the degree of their interrelatedness. Potentially, each concept in a knowledge structure can be related to all other concepts if the individual is capable of building roads from one location to another. Smith (1975) suggested that organization is the key to adding information to and retrieving information from schemata.

Maps can also represent information on a variety of levels of specificity—from world maps to national maps to city maps, and so on. Similarly, schemata contain both global and local information that is hierarchically arranged. The schema highest in the hierarchy represents knowledge in its most global and abstract form. Those that are embedded and lower in the structure contain information of a more specific nature. The reader's knowledge of the various systems of language is one such example of how this embedding might operate, with pragmatics serving as the overarching concept within which other systems such as text structure, semantics, and morphology are embedded (see Figure 2.5 for an illustration of this embedding).

As the individual searches available background knowledge, he or she evaluates its relevance and appropriateness. For the reader, the background must support the construction of a plausible interpretation for the print being encountered. During the process of reading, as new information is encountered, the reader continually evaluates the background knowledge being used to support an understanding of the text. Readers, however, do not construct their understandings only from what is already known. They also utilize meanings and relationships that have been discovered through their engagements with the text. Simply by reading, readers come to see what was not previously seen.

Under many literacy conditions, the location of appropriate background knowledge can be a major obstacle for the reader. If the relevant information is not readily available, an extensive search will become necessary. If the information is not available in a usable form, accommodations may be necessary. Van Dijk and Kintsch (1983) proposed that in most cases, available schemata will not fit the requirements of the reader. Rather, the schemata "provide a basis or a background for comprehension, but no more" (p. 304).

As we have seen with Susan, as readers increase their background knowledge during the very process of reading, their miscues become more meaningful. This relation between background and the quality of miscues was also explored by Rousch (1976). He studied the quality of the miscues made by two groups of fourth graders who had the same reading and intellectual ability. One group, however, had extensive conceptual awareness of the content in the text to be read; the second group had little prior knowledge. In analyzing the students' miscues, Rousch found that the group with the most background knowledge produced miscues that were more syntactically and semantically acceptable and had higher retelling (comprehension) scores. Simply by manipulating the relation between the background of the reader and the background of the author, Rousch was able to impact the ability of the children to effectively and efficiently process and understand text.

The impact of background knowledge on the reading process—and writing as well—has been one reason why many educators have advocated the use of thematic units in the classroom (Kucer et al., 1995; Richards & McKenna, 2003; Silva & Delgado-Larocco, 1993; Silva & Kucer, 1997). In such units, there is a continual building up of linguistic and conceptual knowledge related to the topic under study. As this knowledge is developed, students come to more effectively manage the reading and writing processes. A similar kind of building up of knowledge can also occur through the use of hyperlinks which can offer "readers a more vivid and rounded sense" (Lankshear & Knobel, 2002, p. 30) of the topic. In a third-grade bilingual classroom in which I recently worked, there was a student, Elvis, who demonstrated great difficulty speaking, reading, and writing in English. He was reluctant to enter into class discussions, and during the first months of school, he attempted to avoid many of the activities presented by the teacher. In November, the children decided that they wanted to explore a theme on amphibians and reptiles. Suddenly, Elvis became one of the more proficient English language users in the class. He actively contributed to class discussions and eagerly engaged in the literacy activities related to the topic. The teacher and I were astonished at this unexpected transformation and asked Elvis about his interest in participating. He proudly informed us that he was an "expert" on the topic and had several pet amphibians and reptiles at home.

The Contextual Dependency of Reading

If, as has been suggested, reading is an act of meaning making, it is necessary to begin to account for the impetus that drives this act and causes a reader to initiate a conversation with a text. In a sense, we must begin to account for the contextual dependency of literacy. Such an accounting is necessary because reading does not evolve within a communicative vacuum, devoid of situational and cultural supports and restrictions. Rather, acts of reading are functionally based and arise from a transaction between the language user and the context of the situation. The context of a situation, as defined by Halliday (1974), consists of all aspects of the environment that have a direct bearing on the construction of meaning. This includes such things as the person doing the reading, the subject matter, the role that the text is playing within the situation, and any other participants in the communicative event.

Through a transaction between reader and context, a meaning potential—what Halliday (1974) called a register—is realized. The register defines the range of meanings and structures typically associated with a particular setting. Consequently, the register places parameters on which meanings and forms are most accessible during the reading process. By narrowing the available semantic and structural options, the register supports the reader in predicting those configurations of meaning that are likely to be encountered in any communicative setting. Furthermore, it provides the necessary framework within which the relevance and appropriateness of the reader's linguistic and conceptual background knowledge for the given setting can be judged. Therefore, the meanings generated must not only be internally coherent (i.e., cohere in and of themselves); they must be externally coherent as well. They must fit within the environment in which they evolve. This intimate relationship between knowledge and context means that the reader is never using background information with complete freedom. Rather, the availability of knowledge is not only cognitively dependent, but situationally dependent as well. The knowledge available varies from situation to situation.

Sankoff (1980) proposed a probabilistic model of language processing to account for this relation between background knowledge and context. He argued that in any language situation, the meanings and structures produced are not so much dependent on one's "competence" as a reader as they are produced relative to the social context itself. As situations and perceptions change, so too will the knowledge available. This phenomenon occurs because in different contexts, different patterns of schemata are activated. Knowledge is defined as a fluid construct, rather than a fixed entity, that is capable of changing from situation to situation (Nejad, 1980). Researchers have found that what is recalled from a reading is greatly influenced by the situation in which the text is read (Carey, Harste, & Smith, 1981; Pichert & Anderson, 1977; Smagorinsky, 2001). This impact of context on understanding is further developed in the forthcoming chapter on comprehension.

For all that has been said about the environment and register, it must not be forgotten that these are not "givens" for the reader. They are not objective entities in and of themselves, outside of and separate from the language user. Each context is defined by the particular reader's experiences within the culture and by his or her past encounters with similar situations. Grounded in these experiences and the knowledge that they have engendered, readers will selectively attend to certain elements of the context of situation while systematically ignoring others.

Because of differing experiences, different individuals may come to characterize, define, and interpret the same context in various ways. Each characterization results in the production of unique meaning potentials. This in turn affords the reader unique options and choices and may result in unique understandings. Although there is no situation that the individual faces that does not to a certain extent prescribe the meanings to be engaged, the range of options and meanings available is governed by the background knowledge of the reader. As we will see in the chapters on literacy as a social practice and the authority of written discourse, the individual's background knowledge is significantly impacted by his or her various social identities.

Goals and Plans: Reading as an Intentional Act

As with most human behavior, reading is a goal-directed and purposeful process. The context of a situation not only sets parameters on the range of meanings and structures to be encountered, but it also serves as the very impetus for transacting with written discourse. The meanings ultimately realized in any given situation are the product of an internal response by the individual toward a communicative goal. The language user brings his or her intentions to the literacy event. Although the background knowledge available for text processing is constrained by the context and the resulting register, the knowledge that is actually used for constructing meaning is determined by the reader's intentions.

The outcome of any goal is that of a problem: how is the goal to be fulfilled or realized? Because all texts are not read for the same reason or in the same way, the reader must decide, sometimes consciously and sometimes unconsciously, what must be done for the goal to be attained. This results in a tentative plan of action that represents the language user's determination to act in a particular fashion. Plans are designed to take the language user from where he or she is at the present moment to where he or she wants to be—the goal—at the conclusion of reading.

Therefore, plans and their corresponding goals give directionality to reading. They serve as a control mechanism, guiding the reader down particular pathways and helping the reader avoid others in the search for meaning.

The purpose of the reader has a direct impact on discourse processing because readers vary their interactions with written discourse based on their intentions. If the reader is seeking a specific piece of information, scanning may be initiated. In such cases, the reader ignores much of the print, focusing attention only on that information being sought. Reading a recipe to find the amount of an ingredient or to determine cooking time and temperature would engage the reader in scanning. Skimming is employed when the reader is seeking a general understanding of the text. It is not uncommon for the morning newspaper to be skimmed when one is pressed for time before going to work. The reader's purpose is simply to get a "feel" for what has happened in the world, with the hope of a closer reading later. Such a close reading is usually initiated when a fuller, more detailed understanding of a text is desired. If the purpose is to recall the information in a text—rather than simply to fully understand it—the reader may need to reprocess the text several times and engage in recall attempts. Finally, the need to memorize will repeatedly focus the reader's attention on the surface level of the discourse. Proficient readers are flexible in the way they process a text based on their goals and plans. They vary their reading to fit their needs. Less proficient readers, on the other hand, tend to exhibit less flexibility and process all texts in a similar manner, regardless of the purpose of the reading.

A personal experience illustrates the relationship among goals, plans, and processing, and their changing nature in reading. A number of years ago, I was involved in teaching a graduate reading disabilities course. I had assigned my students an article on the role that STM plays in the reading process and planned to discuss the topic the following week. Having read extensively in this area, my initial reading goal was simply to acquaint myself with the manner in which the author addressed the subject. Because I did not anticipate encountering a great deal of new information, my plan was to quickly skim the text, looking for specifics that I might include in my upcoming lecture. In essence, I planned to assimilate the new information to further extend my current understanding of STM.

Once I began reading, however, I discovered that the author was addressing the topic in a rather unique manner. My initial prediction that the author would share my understanding of the role of memory in the reading process did not appear to be totally accurate. In a sense, there was a mismatch between my background knowledge and the author's. Being a flexible reader, I set aside my initial goal for reading and replaced it with such alternatives as: What exactly does this author believe about the memory system? Do the author's beliefs make sense based on what I presently know about the issue? What accommodations do I need to make in my own understanding of the role of memory in the reading process to comprehend the author's meanings? It was only through meeting these new goals that I was able to return to my initial reason for reading the text. Such a change in goals also

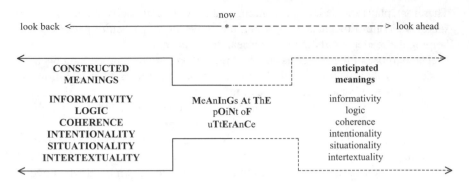

FIG. 6.2.   Continuity building in reading and writing. From Kucer, S. B. (1989b).
Reading a text: Does the author make a difference? (p. 162). In B. Lawson,
S. Ryan, and W. R. Winterowd (Eds.), *Encountering student texts: Interpretive
issues in reading student writing*. Urbana, IL: NCTE.

required that I modify my initial plans. Rather than quickly skimming the text, my
new goal required a far more detailed and in-depth reading.

In a more general sense, the goal of any reader is to build what has been termed
continuity (de Beaugrande, 1980, 1984; Kucer, 1989b). As illustrated in Figure 6.2,
continuity involves a number of characteristics. These characteristics guide the
evaluation of constructed meanings as well as those meanings that are anticipated
or predicted. The first two characteristics of continuity are informativity and logic.
The ideas presented must convey understandable or comprehensible information.
They must be meaningful in and of themselves. In addition, ideas must be logical or
reasonable; the ideas must conform or correspond to what the reader knows about
the world in general and about the topic in particular. In judging informativity and
logic, the reader relies on an external source: his or her background knowledge.

As already demonstrated, meanings must be internally coherent as well
(Halliday, 1974; van Dijk, 1980; van Dijk & Kintsch, 1983). Each idea should
be conceptually linked to those around it and also relate, at least indirectly, to all
other meanings in the text. The meanings generated by the reader must form a
unified and noncontradictory whole. Van den Broek and Kremer (2000) suggest
that one way in which readers build coherence is by being particularly sensitive to
referential and causal or logical relations throughout a text. Referential relations
refer to objects, people, and events that are repeated throughout the text. Readers
must remember that these entities have been referenced earlier in their reading.
That is, readers must remember that the entities have been previously addressed
in some manner and are being returned to at this point in the text. Causal relations
indicate how different events or facts impact one another. In our previous discussion of story grammar in chapter 2, we know that seeing the worm caused the fish,
Albert, to attempt to eat it.

With computer technologies, coherence takes on expanded forms. The use of
sound, video, and hypertexts requires that the reader understand the conceptual

relationship among these various sign systems and the text being processed (Kinzer & Leander, 2003). These sign systems and links offer the potential for additional or expanded readings and may actually decenter the initial text being processed.

Intentionality is the fourth characteristic by which continuity is judged. Reading is a functional process; it is used to accomplish "acts" in the world. As such, reading is always goal- and plan-oriented (Bruce, 1980; Meyer, 1982; Pratt, 1977). If the meanings generated are to be acceptable, they must reflect the purpose that drives the reader.

Directly related to the characteristic of intentionality is that of situationality. Goals and plans, as we have seen, do not emerge in a vacuum but rather are situationally based. It is a communicative context that first provides the impetus for the individual to engage in the reading act. In fact, Halliday (1973, 1974; Halliday & Hasan, 1980) and Brandt (1990) proposed that the meanings in any text always contain elements of the context from which they were generated; the context is embodied in the discourse produced. The meanings, therefore, must be relevant to the current or a recoverable situation.

Finally, the continuity of the meanings generated is evaluated in terms of intertextuality. Just as meanings must relate to a relevant situation, so too must they relate to previously encountered texts (Bazerman, 2004; de Beaugrande, 1980; Hartman, 1992; Hartman & Hartman, 1993). As we saw in the chapter on the nature of language, no world of meaning stands alone, and both its content and form will display features found in other texts. The meanings must be linked to existing text types and genres, such as narration or exposition and, respectively, short stories or research articles. In addition, they must reflect an organizational pattern, such as time order, antecedent–consequent, or comparison–contrast, that is acceptable within a particular text type (Meyer, 1982). A number of studies have explored the supporting role in which experiences with particular types of written discourse in one context impact and sustain subsequent encounters with similar discourse in other contexts (DeFord, 1981; Eckhoff, 1983).

Reading Strategies

Strategies are information processing procedures that operate within STM. Strategies, driven by print, background, and purpose, guide the reader's transaction with print and the construction of meaning. Using the print and background knowledge, strategies allow the reader to build a deep structure from the surface structure of the written discourse. Those meanings constructed within STM are ultimately stored in LTM.

Before continuing the discussion of reading strategies, it would be helpful to first examine your own reading behavior. As a proficient reader, your own transactions with print can serve as a framework and guide for understanding what readers do in general. The left hand column in Table 6.2 contains a short story modified from Y. Goodman and Burke (1980). Read the story, and monitor your cognitive actions.

TABLE 6.2

Reading Demonstration

The Boys	*Reading Behaviors and Reasons*
The boys had been out all day long looking for game. Their arrows were nearly gone and some of the boys had broken the strings on their bows. So, they decided to stop hunting and sat down to rest under a large oak tree by a cool stream. Over at the edge of the wood they saw their friend, Henry, making a bow to a little girl with a bow in her hair who was walking down the road. She had tears in her dirty dress and also tears in her eyes. The girl gave Henry a note which he brought over to the group of young hunters. Read to the boys, it caused great excitement. After a minute but rapid examination of their weapons, they ran down to the valley. Does were standing at the edge of the lake, making an excellent target. The boys watched for a minute, and then began to shoot.	

Note. Adapted from Y. Goodman and Burke (1980).

In the right hand column, jot down your reading behaviors and why you engaged in these behaviors.

In reading "The Boys," you may have engaged in some or all of the following behaviors. When you encountered the second <bow> in the text, you may have predicted a noun and the morpheme that means an object from which to shoot arrows. This meaningful prediction was based on the fact that <bow> was used earlier in the text that had the boys hunting with <bows and arrows>. However, as you read on, monitoring and evaluating the sensibility of your predictions and attempting to integrate meanings across sentences, you discovered that this prediction did not make sense in the context of <to a small girl>. At this point, you may have engaged in a variety of revision behaviors. You may have stopped reading, returned to reread the sentence, and changed your prediction; or you may have stopped reading and mentally rethought and changed your prediction; or you may have decided to continue reading to see if your prediction would ultimately make sense. Similarly, you may have mispredicted when encountering other homographs (i.e., words that are spelled alike but that are pronounced differently and have different meanings) in the story: <tears>, <read>, <minute>, and <does>.

After making a number of mispredictions, you may have also changed the manner in which the text was read. Many readers initially think that this short story will be relatively easy reading and anticipate few difficulties. However, as readers encounter various homographs, they realize that a closer monitoring of their meanings is warranted and they vary their reading of the text accordingly. Readers may slow their reading, and become more cautious in their predictions, hoping to avoid the time and effort demanded when predictions must be revised. On the otherhand, some readers may decide to actually speed up their reading. They quickly skim the text to discover what is to be encountered. Then, based on this general understanding, they return for a closer reading.

Although a demonstration, your processing of "The Boys" highlights a number of strategies that are part of the reading process. Drawing from a variety of sources (e.g., de Beaugrande, 1980; K. Goodman, 1996; Just & Carpenter, 1987; Kucer, 1989a, 1995; Kucer & Tuten, 2003; Rumelhart, 1994; Smith, 1994a, 2004; Weaver, 2002), Table 6.3 formally identifies and defines these strategies. It is worth repeating here that these strategies are never mastered or perfected. As texts, contexts, and purposes change, so too will the ability of the reader to manage the process.

Evolving Cognitive Text World

As the reader puts eye to print, a mental world of meaning is constructed within STM and stored in LTM. Using the various strategies, the reader builds a web of meaning (deep structure) from the print (surface structure). Throughout the creation of this evolving "new text" (Smagorinsky, 2001, p. 134), the meanings are continually monitored, evaluated, and updated—revised—as necessary. Meanings, consequently, are provisional in nature.

The evolving world of meaning serves a variety of functions for the reader. First, as we have seen, previously constructed meanings support the reader in selecting and sampling the print and in forming predicted language and meanings. This orienting function also allows the reader to evaluate the degree to which new meanings cohere with past meanings and to make adjustments as required. In the case of Susan, for example, her developing understanding that there was a repetitive and cumulative pattern in "The Great Big Enormous Turnip" (Tolstoy, 1976) allowed her to accurately predict the word <again> the second time it was encountered in the text. Therefore, as noted by Smith (1994a, 2004), as the world of meaning evolves, the reader relies less on the surface structure (visual information) and more on the deep structure (nonvisual information) that has been constructed.

AN EXAMINATION OF PROFICIENT
AND NONPROFICIENT READERS

Now that you have a better understanding of reading and the factors that influence the process, it would be useful to examine the behaviors of proficient and less proficient readers. Most teachers listen to their students read on a regular basis. All too often, however, their analysis of student reading is quantitative rather than qualitative; that is, the number of words "missed" are calculated but not the impact

TABLE 6.3

Reading Strategies and Processes

---

1. Generates and organizes major ideas and concepts. Readers understand that the ideas in a text can be ordered in terms of their significance. They know that all ideas are not of equal importance. Readers attempt to get the "big picture" and look for generalizations and concepts and their corresponding or supporting facts and details.

2. Develops and supports generalizations and concepts with details and particulars. Readers develop and link details and facts to major ideas and concepts. Generalizations are linked to concepts and facts; facts and concepts are linked to generalizations.

3. Organizes or integrates meanings across the text into a logical and coherent whole. Readers pull ideas together so that they form a unified and noncontradictory whole. Facts and details are linked to major ideas, concepts, or generalizations. Major ideas are related to supporting evidence and supporting evidence is related to major ideas.

4. Samples and selects visual information from the available print. Readers selectively pick up only that print which is necessary for the formulation of meaning. Word beginnings and endings, consonants, and tops of letters typically provide the most useful information. In many cases, much of the print is ignored.

5. Uses a variety of linguistic cues. Readers use a variety of cues or kinds of information to make meaning from what they are reading. Readers select from a range of systems of language: pragmatic, text type, text structure, genre, semantic, syntax, morphology, orthography, graphophonemic, grapheme.

6. Uses a variety of text aids—e.g., pictures, charts, graphs, subheadings, and multimodal technologies. In addition to the use of linguistic cues,

readers utilize text aids. They realize that text aids have been used by authors to facilitate, extend, highlight, and organize text meanings.

7. Uses relevant linguistic and conceptual background knowledge. In order to generate meaning, readers make use of relevant linguistic and conceptual background knowledge. Readers bring their knowledge of their world and language to the text in order to make meaning from the print. It is through the use of this knowledge that readers are able to determine whether or not what they have read sounds like language, makes sense, and meets their purpose.

8. Makes meaningful predictions. Readers make meaningful predictions based on what has been previously read, the visual information sampled and selected, and their background knowledge.

9. Monitors and evaluates the meanings generated. Readers continually assess the meanings generated. They ask themselves: "Does this sound like language?" "Does this make sense?" "Does this meet my purpose or intention?"

10. Revises when meaning is lost or purposes are not realized. Readers change their predictions or meanings when they answer "no" to the questions: "Does this sound like language?" "Does this make sense?" "Does this meet my purpose or intention?"

11. Utilizes a variety of strategies when revising. When revision is initiated, readers utilize a variety of strategies that are appropriate to what is being read. Readers may: stop reading and rethink what has been read, reread previous portions of the text, read ahead to gather more information, read on to see if there is a need to revise, form a tentative prediction and read on to see if it makes sense, ignore it, seek assistance from an outside source (e.g. dictionary, encyclopedia, another reader), stop reading, use text aids, substitute a different meaning, sound it out.

12. Generates inferences or goes beyond the information given. Writers do not make all meanings explicit in their texts. Rather, they expect readers to be able to go beyond the information given and make unstated connections on their own. Readers generate inferences by building links between their prior knowledge and the information generated from the text.

13. Reflects on, and responds and reacts to, what is being read. Reading is an affective as well as a cognitive process. Meanings generated elicit personal reflections, responses, and reactions from the reader. Readers argue, affirm, talk to, laugh, or cry at the meanings that the author is conveying.

14. Varies the manner in which texts are read based on different purposes. Readers do not process all texts in the same way. Rather, they vary their reading depending on their purposes, such as to locate specific details, to find the general idea of the text, to understand the entire text, to remember the text, to memorize the text. How a recipe is read to discover what ingredients need to be purchased differs from the reading of a mystery for enjoyment, and both differ from how one reads directions to assemble a bicycle.

---

of these miscues on meaning. Also, the miscues are usually attributed to a lack of graphophonemic or word recognition skills. The impact of other systems of language, meaning, and context may not be considered.

Tables 6.4 and 6.5 contain miscues made by proficient and less proficient readers at a variety of grade levels. These miscues have been taken from a number of sources, both published (e.g., Allen & Watson, 1976; Cambourne & Rousch, 1979; K. Goodman, 1977; Kucer & Tuten, 2003; Sims, 1982) and unpublished. Take a few moments to read through and analyze the patterns of miscues in the two tables. As you read, keep in mind the impact that the miscues have on meaning and the degree to which the reader relies on various systems of language, especially the use of graphophonemics.

An examination of the proficient reading behaviors in Table 6.4 demonstrates the overwhelming concern of effective and efficient readers with meaning. In general, most of their miscues make sense within the context of the sentence. Reader One, for example, substituted <aspirin> for <oxygen> (a noun for a noun that makes sense within the sentence), formed a contraction out of <does not>, and changed the tense of the verb <pet>.

Both Readers Two and Five used their dialects to change the surface structure of the text being read. Reader Two changed the verb <went> to <goed> and omitted the <ed> on <land>. Similarly, Reader Five omitted the <s> on <gate>, changed <headlamps> to <headlights>, and added an <s> to <beam>. Although we may feel more comfortable with the dialectal miscues of Reader Five than those of Reader Two, the same linguistic and cognitive processes and products are involved in both readings; that is, the syntactic and semantic acceptability and integrity of the discourse is maintained. Our discomfort most likely stems from sociocultural reasons and the status of various dialects. This issue was examined in the previous chapter on language variation.

The consistent miscuing of <basketball> for <baseball> by Reader Four is particularly interesting and revealing. It demonstrates that proficient readers monitor and evaluate the meanings they generate. Every sentence in the story "Bill Evers and the Tigers" (Bank Street College of Education, 1965) containing the word

TABLE 6.4

Miscues Made by Proficient Readers

Reader One

a) Let's try giving Claribel some ~~oxygen~~ aspirin.

b) I can't hear her heart ~~a~~ ~~beat~~ . ~~it~~ But that does not prove ~~doesn't~~ she's dead.

c) He would whistle ~~to~~ for his canary and ~~pet~~ pat his dog.

Reader Two

a) He ~~went~~ goed home.

b) The spaceship land(ed) right in front of his house.

Reader Three

a) And then CRASH-BANG, |a ~~bear~~ deer --a big black bear--came into the forest. ©

b) |And when he ~~was~~ saw not hungry, the bear went out of the forest with a © crash and bang. CRASH-BANG.

Reader Four

Note: every sentence from the text containing the word <baseball> is shown.

a) The boys on the Tiger's ~~baseball~~ basketball team were excited.

b) Bill Evers, the ~~baseball~~ basketball star, was in town.

c) They wanted him to write his name on a ~~baseball~~ basketball.

d) Ben felt funny about calling a ~~baseball~~ basketball star.

e) I'm on the Tigers ~~baseball~~ basketball team.

basketball
ba-

f) He wanted to show the boys how to play better baseball. Then, just
when Bill Evers was showing Ben the right way to hold his bat, [reader
stops and looks at the previous page] a newspaper man came in. Bill
Evers wrote his name on the baseball.

Reader Five

a) It must have been around midnight when I drove home, and as I
   lights
   approached the gates of the bungalow I switched off the headlamps of
   S   *int-*
   the car so the beam wouldn't swing in through the window of the side
   bedroom and wake Harry Pope.
   It had
b) "What is it, Harry?"

   leaning   *touching*
c) "Listen, Harry," I said, and leaned forward and touched his shoulder.
   "We've got to be quick."

d) "Come on now, quickly, tell me where it bit you."
   laying
e) He was lying there very still and tense as though he was holding on to
   himself hard because of sharp pain.

   was
f) "Who's been bitten?" The question came so sharply it was like a small
   explosion in my ear.

<baseball> is represented in Table 6.4. Although not readily apparent until the
author tells the reader that <Bill Evers was showing Ben the right way to hold
his bat>, there were no textual cues other than graphophonemics to indicate that
<basketball> was not an acceptable prediction. However, because the reader was
monitoring the text for meaning, when he encountered the word <bat>, he realized that his prediction of <basketball> suddenly no longer made sense. When he
subsequently encountered <baseball>, he read it as the author intended. It should
not come as a surprise that Reader Four was from Indiana, a state with a passion
for basketball and without a major league baseball team.

   Reader Three demonstrated a similar kind of monitoring, but within the sentence
itself. The reader initially predicted <deer> for <bear>. However, after correctly

reading <a big black bear> within the same structure, the reader returned and changed <deer> to <bear>. Although deer are big, they usually are not black. Similarly, the reader substituted <saw> for <was> (a verb for a verb that makes sense up to that point in the sentence), read the following word <not>, and immediately returned to correct the miscue. In both cases, it is the meaning following the miscue that told the reader that meaning was lost and that correction strategies were warranted. In a sense, the text itself gave the reader feedback about the meaningfulness of the predictions.

TABLE 6.5

Miscues Made by Less Proficient Readers

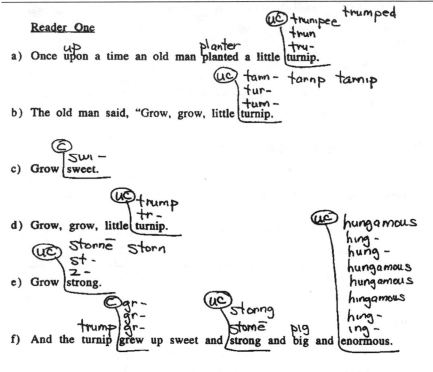

g) **Then one day the old man went to pull it up. He pulled--and pulled**

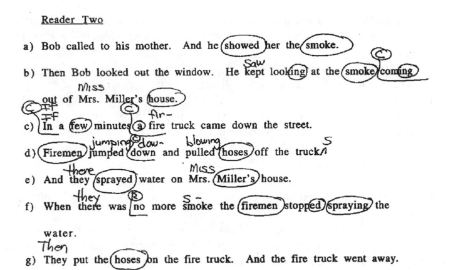

Reader Two

a) Bob called to his mother. And he showed her the smoke.

b) Then Bob looked out the window. He kept looking at the smoke coming
out of Mrs. Miller's house.

c) In a few minutes a fire truck came down the street.

d) Firemen jumped down and pulled hoses off the truck.

e) And they sprayed water on Mrs. Miller's house.

f) When there was no more smoke the firemen stopped spraying the
water.

g) They put the hoses on the fire truck. And the fire truck went away.

Reader Three's behavior also helps to more adequately account for and explain what many teachers refer to as reversals. Graphically speaking, the <d> in <dear> is a reversal of the <b> in <bear> and <saw> is a reversal for <was>. However, we know that readers use more than graphemes when they read. Other systems of language and background knowledge are also used. If the words that precede <bear> and <was> are examined, we see that the prediction of <deer> and <saw> make sense. The substitutions are based, therefore, not only on graphophonemics but also on the use of previous sentence syntax and semantics. The substitutions are not reversals but logical predictions based on the preceding context in which the words are found. As previously noted, it is the subsequent context following each miscue that tells the reader in very direct ways that the substitutions are unacceptable. It is just this moderate use of graphophonemics, along with the use of other systems of language and monitoring for meaning, that characterizes proficient readers.

Before taking a look at the less proficient readers, it is worth noting that these proficient readers were only able to demonstrate the range of their abilities because they were provided the opportunity to read whole texts in an uninterrupted manner. That is, they read long pieces of connected discourse with no assistance or interference from the researchers. If the researcher had prompted a correction for every miscue the reader made, it would have been impossible to know if the reader was able to use context and monitor for meaning because the researcher would have assumed that role. Additionally, it is important to remember that we are examining patterns rather than instances of reading behavior. No one miscue can be used to assess the proficiency of any particular reader. Rather, it is the profile of miscues across a text that distinguishes effective and efficient readers from those who are struggling.

Unfortunately, many readers, especially those who are struggling, are not provided with opportunities to develop the full range of strategies and self-monitoring abilities that are required for effective and efficient reading. Teachers frequently monitor for their students and enter into the reading process by supplying the student with the miscued words or with phonic strategies. The teacher provides the feedback rather than the text. However, Allington (1983) found that when teachers are silent and allow students to read the text without intervention, the students begin to use more effective reading strategies and become sensitive to the use of context. Rather than the process breaking down, the students actually improved their reading of the text.

The miscues of the two less proficient readers shown in Table 6.5 reflect a far different use of language cues. In general, struggling readers over-rely on the use of graphophonemics, underutilize context, and have difficulty monitoring for meaning (K. Goodman, 1996; Paris, Wasik, & Turner, 1996). This focus on letters and sounds is demonstrated by the fact that most of their substitution miscues are high in graphic and sound similarity. For example, Reader One's substitution of <planter> for <planted> and Reader Two's substitution of <then> for <they> in Table 6.5 visually and auditorily resemble the target word in the text.

Although both of these substitutions violate the syntax and semantics of the sentence, neither reader made an attempt to correct them. To a certain extent, this is because less effective and efficient readers fail to monitor for meaning and often have not developed strategies for correcting violations to the integrity of written discourse. Whereas the proficient readers illustrated in Table 6.4 engaged read-on or reread strategies to help them correct meaning-violating miscues, less proficient readers too often rely on sounding out strategies. When Reader One came to the word <enormous>, for example, she attempted to sound it out eight times. In fact, all of the substitution miscues in the sentence are highly similar in graphics and sound. In general, Reader One's miscues are either nonsense words that make little sense in and of themselves or are real words that do not make sense in the context of the sentence.

In contrast to Reader One, who attempted to sound out most unrecognized words, Reader Two's strategy was to simply skip most words that were not instantly pronounceable. It is almost as if the reader is reading from a series of flash cards with a single word printed on each card. Context is largely ignored.

When working with readers who are overly concerned with graphics and sound, the use of Reading Strategy Wall Charts can be effective in promoting the development and use of a wider range of strategies (Kucer, 1995). During one academic year, Kucer and the classroom teacher, Cecilia Silva, introduced various strategies for overcoming unrecognized words to a class of third grade bilingual students. As each strategy was introduced and experienced by the students, or when students

TABLE 6.6

Reading Strategy Wall Chart

READING STRATEGY WALL CHART

When reading and you come to something that you do not know, you can:

1. Stop reading → think about it → make a guess → read on to see if the guess makes sense.

2. Stop reading → reread the previous sentence(s) or paragraph(s) → make a guess → continue reading to see if the guess makes sense.

3. Skip it → read on to get more information → return and make a guess → continue reading to see if the guess makes sense.

4. Skip it → read on to see if what you do not understand is important to know → return and make a guess if it is important; do not return if it is not important.

5. Put something in that makes sense → read on to see if it fits with the rest of the text.

6. Stop reading → look at the pictures, charts, graphs, etc. → make a guess → read on to see if the guess makes sense.

7. Sound it out (focus on initial and final letters, consonants, known words within the word, meaningful word parts) → read on to see if the guess makes sense.

8. Stop reading → talk with a friend about what you do not understand → return and continue reading.

9. Stop reading → look in a glossary, dictionary, encyclopedia, or related books on the topic → return and continue reading.

10. Read the text with a friend.

11. Stop reading.

---

discovered a strategy on their own, the teacher wrote the strategy on a large piece of chart paper. The Wall Chart was hung in the front of the room and students were encouraged to use the various strategies listed when they encountered unrecognized words. In the spring of the year, when most of the strategies had been introduced or discovered by the students, the teacher typed the list on $8\frac{1}{2}''$ by $11''$ paper and gave copies to student for each reference. Table 6.6 illustrates how the chart appeared at the end of the year.

Not only do less proficient readers overutilize graphophonemics and have difficulty making use of context, they also believe that each word must be read correctly. The substitution of <couldn't> for <could not> is the best miscue made by Reader One. It modifies the surface structure of the text but has no impact on meaning. However, because Reader One assumed that good readers read exactly what is on the page, she corrected, or overcorrected, the miscue. The miscue is considered overcorrected because there is no need to correct it; the miscue does not change the meaning of the sentence (Y. Goodman, Watson, & Burke, 1987).

TABLE 6.7

Summary of Proficient and Less Proficient Reading Behaviors

Proficient Reading Behaviors	Less Proficient Reading Behaviors
Attempt to make what is read sound like language and make sense	Attempt to identify all of the words correctly
Monitor what is read for sense and coherence	Monitor what is read for correct letter/sound and word identification
Build meaning using the text, their purpose, and their background	Build meaning by attempting to identifying the letters and words correctly
Utilize a variety of strategies when meaning breaks down: reread, rethink, read on and return if necessary, substitute, skip it, sound out, seek assistance, use text aids (pictures, graphs, charts), ignore it, stop reading	Utilize a limited range of strategies when meaning breaks down: sound out, skip it
Selectively sample the print; use a mixture of visual (print) and nonvisual (background) information	Utilize most of the visual (print) information
Use and integrate a variety of systems of language to create meaning	Rely heavily on graphemes, graphophonemics, and morphemes
Vary the manner in which texts are read based on purpose	Read all texts in a similar manner regardless of purpose
Typically correct one in three miscues	Typically correct one in twenty miscues
Attempt to correct miscues that effect meaning	Attempt to correct miscues that fail to resemble the word
"Chunk" what is read	Letter-by-letter processing results in tunnel vision

According to Smith (1994a, 2004), the result of an over reliance on graphophonemics is tunnel vision. STM is filled with letters and sounds, resulting in a loss of meaning. The reader is unable to understand what is being read because other systems of language are ignored. Rather than selecting visual cues from various systems, the reader attempts to process every letter. Proficient readers, however, are selective in the cues employed. They chunk the language processed, using the most informative language cues and appropriate background knowledge. Table 6.7 summarizes much of what has been said about proficient and less proficient readers.

BILITERATE READERS

Reading in two languages is becoming an increasingly common phenomenon in the United States. Regardless of where teachers work, they are encountering students who are bilingual as well as biliterate. Biliterate students are not engaged in altogether different processes when reading in two languages. However, there are a number of factors that are unique to this population, and understanding how these factors impact the reading process can help teachers promote the literacy development of bilingual students in their classrooms.

By its very nature, the bilingual population is extremely varied. Bernhardt (2000) has noted that second language reading is "a diverse, complicated, and frustrating landscape to traverse, let alone explain or predict" (p. 791). This variation manifests itself in such things as whether or not students first learn to read in their home language (other than English) and then learn to read in the language of the school (English) or whether they first learn to read in English and only later learn the written form of their home language. There is also the issue of whether their home language is maintained at school as the English language is introduced or if the school language becomes a substitute for the home language. Additionally, the degree of oral proficiency in both the first and second language impacts the literacy processes. According to Bernhardt, two critical variables in second language literacy are the degree to which the first language has been developed in oral and written form as well as the linguistic similarity between the two languages.

To address all the possible variations, unfortunately, is beyond the scope of this chapter and this book. The focus here is on comparing and contrasting the cognitive processes used when individuals are proficient readers—efficient and effective—in their home (first) language and in the English (second) language. However, because of the varied circumstances and experiences encountered by bilingual students, care needs to be taken not to over-generalize the findings from the biliteracy research.

In general, there is a positive and supportive relationship between the processes and strategies used in the first and second languages (Allen, 1991; Buck, 1977; Carrasquillo, Kucer, & Abrams, 2004; Fitzgerald, 1995; Jimenez, Garcia, & Pearson, 1995, 1996; Weber, 1996). Individuals who are proficient in two written language systems are frequently able to successfully employ strategies used in the first language for use in the second language. In both languages, readers monitor their processing through such metacognitive procedures as evaluating, revising (e.g., rereading, reading on, substituting), and predicting upcoming meanings and structures. Biliterates make inferences, draw conclusions, and ask questions. In English as well as in the home language, readers draw on their background knowledge of content and the systems of language to make sense of the ideas being encountered. Vocabulary items that are similar in both languages—cognates—such as the Spanish word "producto" for the English word "product," are also relied on in the making of meaning. Except for the use of cognates, proficient biliterate readers employ the same basic strategies discussed in Tables 6.3 and 6.6.

Interestingly, not only do biliterates employ similar strategies in the two languages, but they frequently have a unitary view of reading. According to Jimenez et al. (1996), biliterate students typically discuss their reading processes and learning to read in a first and second language as two sides of the same coin. As stated by one student in their research, "There aren't really any differences [between reading in English and Spanish]; I mean they're both based on the same thing, how you understand it, how you read it, how you take it, and how you evaluate it and all that" (p. 99). Others have made similar observations (e.g., Cummins, 1988, 1991; D. Freeman & Y. Freeman, 1994).

There are similarities in reading in two languages, but some consistent differences are also evident. Biliterates may translate—code switch—from one language to the other, and this translation occurs in both directions. Occasionally, miscues made in English can be attributed to the use of syntactic knowledge of the first language. The reader may predict a word order that reflects the language with which the reader is most comfortable. This is especially the case when the reader has a strong spoken command of the first language and less of a command of the second. However, as readers develop oral proficiency in the second language, they typically develop increased reading fluency in the second language as well (Bernhardt, 2000).

Although readers successfully employ a wealth of available strategies when reading in both languages, the extent to which monitoring and revision strategies are necessary may vary. It is not uncommon for biliterates to encounter unknown vocabulary more frequently than monolinguals. Like proficient monolinguals, proficient biliterate readers are able to apply various strategies to determine the meanings of these words. However, the repeated need to engage these revision strategies may impact the degree to which the reader is able to comprehend the text. The cognitive energy required to make such repairs may limit the attention the reader is able to apply to understanding the overall meaning of the text. This is in contrast to monolingual readers who typically encounter fewer unknown words and therefore may find it less necessary to engage in revision.

The need for additional monitoring and revision is not language specific, however. The content and structure of the text, as well as opportunities to read in the language under consideration, determine the need to monitor and repair, not whether the text is in the reader's first or second language. It is not uncommon for the biliterate reader's first oral and written language to be one other than English. However, if the school setting does not honor and maintain the reader's home language, and if academic subjects are encountered largely in English, monitoring and repair may be more frequent in the child's home language than in English.

Interestingly, in her review of the research on biliterates, Fitzgerald (1995) found that regardless of the language being read, unfamiliar content had a more significant impact on the biliterate reader than unfamiliar text structure. Weber (1996), Allen (1991), and K. Goodman and Y. Goodman (1978) reported similar findings concerning the relationship between background and linguistic knowledge more generally. As previously noted, background knowledge tends to "trump" or have a dominating influence on the reading process. More importantly, Weber also found that it was through direct experience with the concepts at hand, rather than simply through the introduction of vocabulary words, that biliterate readers can be provided with the necessary background knowledge to effectively process the English written discourse.

Similar patterns are found when proficient bilingual students reading in English are compared and contrasted with proficient monolingual students reading in English. Both groups engage metacognitive strategies and monitor for meaning. They generate inferences, recall superordinate ideas, and focus more on content than on function words. At times, however, the bilingual readers did not use context as effectively as monolingual readers and monitored their comprehension more slowly. These differences, however, may be developmental; that is, with time and experience, the bilingual students will come to use context as effectively as the monolingual readers. More importantly, they will be proficient in reading two languages rather than one.

READING: AN ALTERNATE VIEW

Throughout this chapter, reading is depicted as a selective and constructive process. The reader is envisioned as an active participant in the construction of meaning, picking up only the most salient linguistic cues and ignoring others. Through the use of background knowledge, the previous text processed, and the print selected, the reader actively builds a prediction or hypothesis for the written discourse encountered. This perspective, what I am terming the selective sampling view, however, represents only one of two predominant perspectives in the literacy field. Although it is beyond the intent and scope of this book to present multiple perspectives within each of the various dimensions of literacy, a brief overview is given of an alternative understanding, what I am calling the dense processing view, of the reading process. Table 6.8 summarizes the key areas of contention between these two perspectives which are compared and contrasted in the following discussion.

Disputes over the nature of the reading process have a long history in the psychological literature (e.g., Cattel, 1885, Gough, 1972; Huey, 1968/1908). However, the use of computer-controlled display screens, video cameras, and eye tracking technology have produced reading data that was previously unavailable. Drawing upon this data, a number of researchers have recently claimed, and with a degree of scientific certitude not previously seen in the field, that "the convergence of basic research on the reading process . . . is so strong" that it has led to a "Grand Synthesis" (Stanovich, 1998, p. 44). To a large extent, this synthesis is centered on the understandings that (a) "skillful readers virtually process each individual letter of every word" (Adams & Bruck, 1995, p. 7), (b) the processing of individual letters and words is largely automatic and obligatory, (c) the processing of individual letters and words is not impacted by other language systems, i.e., the surrounding linguistic context, or background knowledge, and (d) that struggling readers rely on the systems of language and background knowledge as a compensatory strategy due to poorly developed word recognition—graphophonemic—skills.

TABLE 6.8

Dense Processing Versus Selective Sampling in Reading

Dense Processing	Selective Sampling
Fixations	
Most of the visual array (print) is processed	Print is selectively sampled and the brain utilizes strategies to limit the amount of perceptual information it uses to just that which is necessary
Automaticity	
Words are recognized almost instantly and involve relatively little cognitive attention and resources	Words are recognized as quickly as they are due to use of the previous context and selective sampling
Obligatory—readers identify words regardless of intentions or focus of attention	Dense processing causes tunnel vision—the inability to process and make sense of the graphics put into working memory
Automaticity times vary depending on word length and how frequently the word is used in written language	
Context	
Expectations and predictions are not factors in word identification	Word identification is influenced by background knowledge and the higher-ordered systems of language (context) as well as by graphics
Word identification is encapsulated, i.e., not impacted by background knowledge or higher-ordered systems of language (context), which frees cognitive resources for comprehension	
Context only supports accurate prediction of upcoming words 20–35% of the time	
Use of context takes time and effort, thereby making processing of print less efficient and effective	
Proficient and Nonproficient Readers	
Poor readers rely on context because they lack word recognition skills; use of context is a compensatory strategy	Poor readers lack the ability to effectively and efficiently make use of previous context upon which to form tentative hypothesis as to what any given word might be
	Poor readers are unable to select word parts or letters within a word that will provide the most useful information for word identification

Advocates of dense processing argue that reading, at least initially, is print driven and that most of the visual array is processed. Reading, rather than being a psycholinguistic guessing game in which vision is incidental, involves the processing of virtually every letter and word on the page. In fact, readers are said to be reluctant to predict upcoming words through the use of context and background knowledge; they prefer to process words letter by letter. This reluctance is probably due to the fact that context does not provide enough information to support the formulation of accurate predictions. In general, these researchers argue that the use of context can only support accurate word predictions approximately 25% of the time. Therefore, word recognition through letter identification is the foundation of the reading process.

As letters are perceived, they are clustered into familiar spelling patterns and frequently recoded into sound (phonological recoding). According to Stanovich (1998), the issue of recoding is not one of if, but of how much; recoding is obligatory and readers identify words regardless of their intentions or focus of attention. The degree to which recoding occurs before a word is recognized (i.e., phonological mediation) is related to the frequency of the word and the spelling patterns involved. Low-frequency words containing less common spelling patterns tend to be recoded more fully than do high-frequency words with more common spelling patterns. For example, <made> is a high-frequency word commonly encountered in written discourse. Additionally, the consonant–vowel–consonant–silent <e> sequence is predictable within English orthography. Therefore, there would be less phonological recoding for <made> than <sword>, which is less frequent as well as phonologically less predictable.

Given the requirement that each letter must be processed, it might be thought that STM would have difficulty holding all of this information for the duration necessary. Depending on the particular word, the capacity of STM might be reached before word identification has occurred, or a subsequent fixation might replace its content before processing had been completed. However, the limitations of STM and the immediate manner in which readers recognize most words suggest that some degree of automaticity has been developed. That is, the speed of reading, given the dense processing in which readers engage, is largely possible due to the fact that words are recognized almost instantly (Adams & Bruck, 1995; Just & Carpenter, 1987; Stanovich, 1996). Although word recognition does involve some cognitive attention and resources, it is a relatively effortless process for skilled readers. In contrast to other processes, however, such as comprehension, which involve the allocation of attention and memory, the automatic process of word recognition is relatively undemanding of cognitive resources (Walczyk, 2000).

Automaticity becomes possible through the overlearning of letter and spelling patterns based on the readers' multiple encounters with written language. Readers build and store in memory orthographic patterns and common letter combinations that reflect the interconnectedness among letters within the language. The relations between letters and sounds have become so well learned that fewer cognitive resources are required for word identification. This allows the reader the time and cognitive capacity to construct an interpretation for the clause or sentence in which the words are embedded. However, as is the case with phonological recoding, automaticity is a question of degree, not an either–or proposition.

According to Stanovich (1996), expectations and predictions are not primary factors in word identification and feature extraction from words is not impacted by higher-ordered systems of language or world knowledge. This situation, termed information encapsulation, has two advantages for readers. First, it allows the print to be processed without distortion—i.e., readers perceive what is actually written. Distortions or misreadings are less likely because information outside of the word does not penetrate processing mechanisms. Secondly, it allows readers to process the print as efficiently as they do. Readers need not closely monitor the accuracy of the words identified because of possible influences from outside sources of information. Encapsulation largely prevents such influences or encroachments from occurring. Readers are able to use their freed cognitive resources to develop an understanding of the words and sentences that have been processed (Adams, 1990). It is at this point in the process—i.e., after words have been identified—that the use of context becomes critical and useful (Kintsch, 1998).

The ability of the reader to quickly and effortlessly map letters to sounds to words through phonological recoding is perceived as critical to effective and efficient reading. Word recognition accounts for much of the variance in reading ability, and poor readers demonstrate poor letter and word attack skills. In contrast to the previous analysis of miscues made by proficient and less proficient readers, within this view it is the less efficient and less effective readers who rely on context because of poor word identification skills. In fact, the use of context is a compensatory strategy that is only utilized when there are deficits in lexical accessing (West, Stanovich, & Cunningham, 1995). That is, proficient readers rely on their knowledge of words to identify them whereas less proficient readers rely on context because of word recognition deficiencies. These attempts by poor readers to use context to aid in the identification of words, however, are largely unsuccessful. Skillful readers are only able to correctly predict upcoming words based on context between 20% and 35% of the time (Adams & Bruck, 1995; Pressley, 1998; Stanovich, 1996). Additionally, the use of context upon which to base predictions takes time and effort, thereby making the processing of print less efficient as well as less effective. This is why as word recognition abilities increase, the use of background knowledge and higher-ordered systems of language decrease (Stanovich, 1996, 2000). Proficient readers can ignore context because they have no difficulty identifying words on the printed page.

As has already been discussed in this as well as in the previous chapter, K. Goodman (1993, 1993, 1996), Smith (1994a, 2004), and Kucer and Tuten (2003) among others, have argued that readers selectively "pick" from the graphic display. Not all available print is processed; rather, the brain selects just that which is necessary for the construction of meaning. In fact, the brain actually utilizes "strategies to limit the amount of perceptual information it uses to just enough for making sense of the print and confirming its predictions. "Perception is what you *think* you see" (Goodman, 1996, p. 40). Proficient readers also utilize the syntactic and semantic environment within which any word is embedded upon which to build their perceptions (Rumelhart, 1994). Word identification is not so much encapsulated as it is impacted and facilitated by the various systems of language and the background knowledge of the reader.

Krashen (1999), in an analysis and evaluation of eye fixation research, has argued that these studies themselves indicate selective sampling on the part of readers. He notes that Just and Carpenter (1987) acknowledge in their own research that 60% of content words and 20% of function words may not receive a fixation. Given the difference in linguistic predictability between these two types of words, as discussed in the previous chapter on perception, it is not surprising that readers tend to fixate more on content rather than function words. Content words are not as easily anticipated and are more informationally salient.

Research by Ehrlich and Rayner (1981) and Zola (1984), according to Krashen (1999), also reveals that as words become more predictable from context, fixation duration is reduced. Readers need not fully sample the visual display because of the previous context. "Rather, the reader needs to note enough of the word to confirm what it is" (Krashen, 1999, p. 6). Variability in fixation frequency and duration, perceptual span, and words receiving a fixation, therefore, are due not only to the particular word itself, but to the previous context that allows selective sampling to occur. Processing speeds are only possible because readers are capable of making use of the previous text as well as the target word itself upon which to build their predictions, not because of automaticity.

Finally, dense processing may actually cause readers to struggle rather than facilitate their interactions with print. Struggling readers have not developed those processing strategies that allow them to selectively sample the print. They lack the ability to effectively and efficiently make use of previous context upon which to form tentative hypotheses as to what any given word might be. Struggling readers are unable to use previous story and sentence meaning as well as sentence syntax to both narrow or restrict the upcoming possibilities and to base predictions. Additionally, they are unable to select those word parts or letters within the word that will provide the most useful information for word identification (Goodman, 1996; Smith, 1994a, 2004; Weaver, 2002). This view is in marked contrast to those of such previously referenced researchers as Adams and Bruck (1995) and Stanovich (1998), who cite the lack of developed word recognition skills as the reason less proficient readers are forced to rely on context.

It is unlikely that the "reading wars" will be settled anytime soon. Nor is it anticipated that a consensus will be reached, with each camp conceding a little to reach a compromise. Each paradigm utilizes different research models, collecting, analyzing, and interpreting data in radically different ways. As is readily apparent, given that there is very little overlap between these two views, fruitful discussions between advocates of each perspective become increasingly difficult.

CONCLUSIONS

In this chapter, we have examined the role of the language user as meaning maker. Rather than passively "taking in" whatever the author has to offer, readers actively select and construct meaning as they work their way through a text. In many ways, this construction of meaning is similar to that of a scientist engaged in an experiment. The reader samples the data (print), constructs a tentative understanding (prediction) based on the data selected and background knowledge, tests (monitors) the hypothesis as more data are gathered, and revises when necessary. Effective and efficient readers sample from a wide range of systems of language, whereas less proficient readers tend to focus on the lower level systems (graphophonemics and morphology). What is ultimately comprehended depends on such factors as the reader's background, purpose, context, and the content of the text. It is in the following chapter that the role of background knowledge is more extensively addressed.

Understanding Written Discourse

This chapter extends our understanding of the reading process by highlighting the act of text comprehension. The goal of any reader is to understand the text being encountered, and there are a number of cognitive factors that impact how a text is ultimately understood. We begin with an examination of the nature and role of background knowledge on meaning making. We then shift our attention to the relationship between vocabulary knowledge and comprehension. The chapter concludes with a discussion of context, meaning, and recall. Once again, I present a series of demonstrations to help you more fully discern what is involved in the process of constructing meaning when the reader puts eye to print.

THE NATURE AND ROLE OF BACKGROUND KNOWLEDGE IN UNDERSTANDING

In Table 7.1, a short story about a character named Pat is presented in four parts. This story has been adapted from R. Anderson, Reynolds, Schallert, and Goetz (1977). On the lefthand side of a piece of paper, number from one to four. If possible, do this activity with a friend so that you can compare and contrast your responses to the story. Now, cover all but the first part of the text. Read the first part and write a one- or two-sentence interpretation of what is happening. Don't just write what was said; rather, write about what you think is *happening* in the story. Support your interpretation using information from the story. Uncover and read the second part. Does your initial understanding still make sense? If it does, support it with additional information from the story. If your interpretation no longer is viable, generate and support a new one. Using this procedure, continue throughout the four parts of the story. If doing this activity with a partner, after you finish reading all four parts, share all of your interpretations and the reasons for each.

If your responses are like those of other readers (see Table 7.2), you discovered a number of things about the process of comprehending. One aspect of

TABLE 7.1

Pat

1. Pat slowly got up from the mat, planning the escape. Pat hesitated a moment and thought. Things were not going well.

2. What was most bothersome was being held, especially since the charge had been weak. Pat considered the present situation.

3. Pat was aware that it was because of the early roughness that the penalty had been so severe—much too severe from Pat's point of view. The situation was becoming frustrating; the pressure had been grinding for too long. Pat was being ridden unmercifully.

4. Pat was getting angry now and felt it was time to make the move. Success or failure would depend on what Pat did in the next few seconds.

Note. Adapted from R. Anderson, Reynolds, Schallert, and Goetz (1977).

TABLE 7.2

Interpretations of Pat

Prediction		Support
1.		1.
	Wrestler	On the mat; planning escape
	Prisoner	Planning escape; mat; not going well
	Pet	Escape; not going well; gets up from the mat
2.		2.
	Wrestler	Being held; lock; timing
	Prisoner	Being held; charge; lock; timing; charge was weak
	Pet	Plan to escape
3.		3.
	Wrestler	Penalty; roughness; pressure; ridden
	Prisoner	Early roughness; pressure; ridden; penalty
	Pet	Early roughness; penalty
4.		4.
	Wrestler	Make a move; success or failure; timing
	Prisoner	Angry; success or failure; time to make move;
	Pet	Time to make move

comprehension2 is that the prior experiences of the reader exert a powerful influence on how a text is ultimately understood. Many individuals who never considered that this story might be about a wrestling match have little knowledge of the sport. For these readers, wrestling was never an option. However, as demonstrated in Table 7.2, readers can use the same words in a text to generate very different interpretations. The word <penalty> , for example, was used to support a wrestler, prisoner, and pet interpretation.

One of the more interesting interpretations I have encountered had Pat as a horse who was being "broken" for riding. Although I had used the text numerous times, this interpretation was a first. When I asked the students to support their interpretation, many stated that they had grown up on ranches and that breaking horses was a common event in such contexts. When one considers that I was teaching at the University of Wyoming, this student response is not all that surprising. Since moving from Wyoming, I have never again encountered this understanding.

What is also noteworthy about the process of comprehension is that the reader's background also influences the saliency or prominence of the ideas in the text. Readers who predict that Pat is a prisoner attempting to escape often downplay the statement <Pat was being ridden unmercifully>. They either tend to generate an understanding that the prison guards or other prisoners were "hassling" Pat or acknowledge that they were not quite sure what to make of the statement. On the other hand, readers who see Pat as a wrestler understand the statement to mean that Pat's opponent is in control of the match.

In considering the impact of prior experiences on the comprehending process, I am reminded of a student named Jeanette. As part of an interdisciplinary literacy class I was teaching, Jeanette and other members of the class were to audiotape their reading and retelling of the short story "Poison" (R. Dahl, 1974). When analyzing her retelling in light of what had actually been stated in the text, Jeanette noted the impact of her nursing career. She changed the statement that the main character was <lying on the bed> to he <was supine in his bed>, <serum> was changed to <antivenin>, <tubing> to <tourniquet>, and <snake> to <viper>. In discussing these changes, Jeanette noted that she was unaware that she had made them until she reread the text and realized that her many years in nursing had impacted her retelling.

In reading about Pat, you probably also made a number of changes to your predictions as you encountered new information. A critical aspect of the comprehending process is that the building of meaning is predictive and hypothetical; it involves constant monitoring and updating of predictions. The reader is building a world of meaning partially based on the print encountered and must be sensitive to subsequent meanings that may require modification—accommodation—of this world. Readers, therefore, must be flexible in their interpretations and allow new information to impact their tentative understandings.

Although Pat is the name of the individual in the story, Pat, in fact, has undergone a number of transformations over the years. In the original research, Pat's name actually was Rocky. However, after the release of the popular movie *Rocky*, most students gave a wrestling match as their interpretation. I changed Rocky to Richard and continued to use this name for a number of years. Then, I began to wonder what would occur if a more gender-neutral name, such as Pat, were used.

Interestingly, the name change had little impact on student predictions. Most students—male and female alike—tended to view the protagonist of the text as a male, regardless of the name used. In fact, students frequently insisted that the pronoun <he> was used until they were given the opportunity to reexamine the story. When asked to support this gender interpretation, students relied on stereotypical knowledge. Most prisoners and wrestlers are men, they asserted, and the degree of physical activity in the story makes them think of male rather than female behavior. This use of stereotypical behavior, however, can also be used to interpret Pat as a female as well. Recently, a student shared that he thought Pat was a woman because the character was so "emotional," as signified by the use of the words <bothersome>, <frustrating>, and <angry>. Regardless of interpretation, comprehension always involves the use of prototypical knowledge that reflects "'normal' events in a simplified world" (Gee, 1996, p. 78).

Steffensen, Joag-Dev, and Anderson (1979) investigated the impact of such cultural experiences on comprehension. Individuals from the United States and India read and recalled two passages, one about an American wedding and the other about an Indian wedding. There are significant differences between American and Indian matrimonial costumes. American weddings tend to provide the occasion for an elaborate ritual and highlight the bride's family. In contrast, Indian weddings often involve issues of social status and financial interests and the groom's family is dominant. The researchers discovered that when a cultural congruence existed between the individual and the text, readers read more rapidly, recalled greater amounts of information, produced more culturally appropriate elaborations, and generated fewer culturally based distortions.

In the Pat demonstration, the content of background knowledge has been the primary focus. This content represents the individual's knowledge of and experiences with events, objects, and situations. There is an additional kind or form of knowledge, however, that also impacts comprehension: knowledge of processes, procedures, or strategies. Process knowledge is action oriented and makes use of content knowledge when it operates. For example, home builders make use of their knowledge of the nature or characteristics of houses (content knowledge) as well as their knowledge of how houses are constructed (process knowledge). Similarly, readers draw upon their knowledge of the subject being read about (content knowledge) as well as their knowledge of the reading strategies (process knowledge).

R. Anderson, Spiro, and Anderson (1978) explored the interaction between process and content knowledge in a study in which individuals were given two stories to read. One story was about dining at a restaurant, and the second concerned grocery shopping. When asked to give an unaided recall after each story was read, readers did far better in the restaurant story. Not only did they remember more of the content, but they also maintained the order of food and drink consumed. Interestingly, the same food and drink were mentioned in both stories. However, because most individuals have what the researchers term a more articulated, or more organized, script for the process of eating in restaurants than shopping for groceries, they were better able to recall the restaurant story.

Although not noted by the researchers, the very way in which food is organized in many grocery stores contributes to less articulated scripts. Grocers want consumers to traverse as much of the store as possible. They know that even if a shopper plans to buy only one or two items, additional items are more likely to be

TABLE 7.3

The Procedure

The procedure is actually quite simple. First you arrange things into different groups. Of course, one pile may be sufficient depending on how much there is to do. If you have to go somewhere else due to a lack of facilities, that is the next step, otherwise, you are pretty well set. It is important not to overdo things. That is, it is better to do too few things at once than too many. In the short run this may not seem important, but complications can easily arise. A mistake can be expensive as well. At first, the whole procedure will seem complicated. Soon, however, it will become just another facet of life. It is difficult to foresee any end to the necessity for this task in the immediate future, but then one never can tell. After the procedure is completed, one arranges the materials into different groups again. Then they can be put into their appropriate places. Eventually, they will be used once more and the whole cycle will then have to be repeated. However, that is part of life.

Note. From Bransford and Johnson (1973).

purchased the more the shopper walks around the store. Grocery stores, therefore, are often arranged in such a manner that consumers encounter as many items as possible as they move from aisle to aisle.

Now that you have discovered a number of principles that govern comprehension, read the story contained in Table 7.3 (Bransford & Johnson, 1973). When you finish reading, write a one- or two-sentence interpretation of what the story is about.

Most readers finish the text knowing little more than they did when they started. Not only do they have difficulty remembering all of the steps in what is perceived as a rather complicated procedure; they also fail to recognize the procedure itself. In the previous demonstration, the nature of the reader's background played a critical role in how Pat was understood. In this demonstration, many readers initially believe it is a lack of background knowledge that is causing them difficulty. However, this is actually an example of the reader having the appropriate background (clothes washing) but being incapable of using it. The author fails to provide the necessary cues for the reader to access the relevant knowledge. Therefore, if comprehension is to occur, writers must help readers link their prior experiences and the ideas in the text.

Although only a demonstration, the difficulty you may have experienced in comprehending the clothes washing story is all too common for students (Rumelhart, 1984). This is especially true when they read in the content areas. Writers of social science and science texts may fail to help students build a relation between what they know and the information being presented. Dewey (1938) believed this inability to access relevant background knowledge occurred because schools taught information in an isolated manner, making it difficult for students to connect ideas to one another and to what they already knew.

According to Gee (1996), humans, including readers, "try to understand something new in terms of how it resembles something old. We attempt to see the new

"Farming on the Mountainside"

Early mountain farmers in many parts of the world studied their
environment.   As they looked around, they saw raised, level plows, or
natural terraces (ter ' isez), on mountainsides.   A terrace, jutting out from
the mountain, caught soil and water that would otherwise run down the
slope.   Here plants grow better than on steep land.

Sometimes people like to have a place on their house where they can
sit outside when the weather is nice.   We call this part of the house a porch
or terrace.   It is a flat place where we can set our chairs.

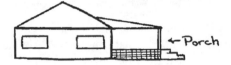

Sometimes we dig a flat place into the side of a mountain.   Then we
can plant food on these flat places.

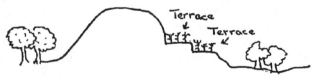

We call the flat places in the mountain a terrace.

FIG. 7.1.   Terracing.

thing as a type" (p. 71). Burke (1976), among others (e.g., Ortony, 1980; Siegel,
1995), suggested that one way to promote such bridge building between the known
and unknown is through the use of metaphoric teaching. She told of working with
a young child who was to read a chapter from a social studies text. In the chapter,
there was a short paragraph about mountainside terracing (see Fig. 7.1). The student was unable to read or recognize the word <terrace> and appeared to lack an
understanding of the concept. In many ways, the text for this student was similar
to the procedures text. The student, however, actually had the background knowledge required for understanding, but the author simply failed to provide an avenue
through which the knowledge could be accessed. In an attempt to help the student
locate relevant background knowledge, Burke quickly drew two pictures—one of
a house with a porch and one of a terrace on a mountainside—and wrote a short

paragraph to accompany the illustrations. She gave the student the text and the student read it aloud, recognizing both the word <terrace> and understanding its meaning.

Burke (1976) said that she had not anticipated that the student would recognize the word in this new context; however, she was not surprised by the student's ability to understand the concept the word represented. She realized that most children know about porches, have seen them, and have likely sat on them. Her text simply drew on these experiences and linked them to a concept that had similar characteristics. When both teaching and assessing student comprehension, teachers should consider to what extent texts support students in drawing on their prior experiences of the world.

WORD KNOWLEDGE AND COMPREHENSION

In the next demonstration, you need to know the meaning of the words listed in Table 7.4. By "know," I do not necessarily mean that you must be able to produce a dictionary-like definition; rather, I mean knowing in the sense that you would be able to understand the word if it were encountered in context. If there are words in the table that are foreign to you, take a few moments to look them up in the dictionary.

TABLE 7.4

Word List

Addition	Equivalent	Variance
Provide	Or	Nonspecific
Encountered	Suspected	Polynomial
Application	Represented	Transformations
To	A	Dummy
An	Square	Curvilinear
This	Predictor	By
The	Linearity	Providing
One-Way	In	Important
And	Interval	Later
Discrete	As	Results
With	Regression	Analysis
Variables	Can	When
Tested	Be	Directly
Deviation	From	Can
Linear		

TABLE 7.5

Regression With Dummy Variables

In addition to providing an equivalent to a one-way analysis of variance, regression with dummy variables can provide an important alternative to polynomial regression, or square root and logarithmic transformations, when nonspecific curvilinear relationships are encountered or suspected. In this latter application, an interval predictor variable with discrete values can be directly represented by dummy variables. As in the case of polynomial regression, the significance of the deviation from linearity can be tested by comparing the results of linear regression with the results of dummy regression.

Note. From Glass and Stanley (1970).

Once you are familiar with the words, read the text (Glass & Stanley, 1970) in Table 7.5, which is entirely made up of these words. When you finish, jot down the ideas that you remember and understand.

Unless you have a well-developed working knowledge of statistics, you probably found "knowing" the words to be of little help in understanding the text. Although it is a long-standing U.S. educational tradition to teach children vocabulary words before they are encountered in a story (Nagy & Scott, 2000), the impact of such instruction is inconclusive (Ruddell, 1994). This is most likely the case because words have multiple meanings or at least shades of meaning (R. Anderson & Nagy, 1996; R. Anderson & Shifrin, 1980). Word meanings shift and slide depending on the context in which they are embedded, as do the ideas to which they refer (Labov, 1973). Further complicating the issue is the fact that the "context is not really something that can be seen and heard, it is actually something people make assumptions about" (Gee, 1996, p. 75).

Jenkins, Pany, and Schreck (1978) conducted one of the few studies to actually examine the impact of vocabulary instruction on the comprehension of connected discourse as measured through unaided retellings. One group of fourth graders was taught the meanings of vocabulary words before they read a text, whereas a second group received no instruction. To measure the effects of instruction on student comprehension, students were asked to read and retell a story in which the vocabulary words were embedded and to answer vocabulary-focused comprehension questions. The researchers found that teaching vocabulary had a direct positive effect on sentence comprehension and vocabulary-focused questions. However, it had no overall impact on the comprehension of connected discourse as measured through story retellings.

The general ineffectiveness of teaching word meanings on comprehension should not come as a surprise. As noted in chapter 2, words or morphemes often represent concepts. Concepts cannot easily be represented by dictionary definitions, which is what vocabulary instruction often provides the reader (Nagy & Scott, 2000). Rather, conceptual knowledge typically represents webs of meanings—what were termed schemata in the previous chapter—similar to those found in an

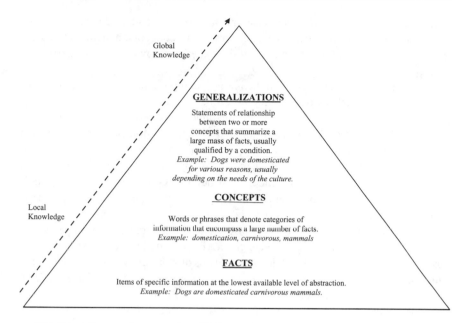

GENERALIZATIONS

Statements of relationship
between two or more
concepts that summarize a
large mass of facts, usually
qualified by a condition.
*Example: Dogs were domesticated
for various reasons, usually
depending on the needs of the culture.*

CONCEPTS

Words or phrases that denote categories of
information that encompass a large number of facts.
Example: domestication, carnivorous, mammals

FACTS

Items of specific information at the lowest available level of abstraction.
Example: Dogs are domesticated carnivorous mammals.

Global
Knowledge

Local
Knowledge

FIG. 7.2.   Forms of content knowledge.

encyclopedia. The concept <dog>, for example, is defined in my dictionary as a "domesticated carnivorous mammal"; this is not a very extensive definition. In my encyclopedia, however, <dog> is given twenty pages of discussion, addressing such issues as the body of a dog, kinds of dogs, choosing a dog, and the history of dogs; this is a much more expansive representation of the concept. Knowing a concept and its corresponding linguistic expression, therefore, can represent different degrees of depth and width of information (Baumann, Kame'enui, & Ash, 2003). Concepts with depth are extensive in their development, whereas concepts with width are those that are interconnected with other concepts. Both of these characteristics of knowledge impact the degree to which a word is understood or "known."

Figure 7.2 illustrates various "levels" of content knowledge and their interrelationship (Banks, 1991, 1993; Kucer, Silva, & Delgado-Larocco, 1995; Silva & Delgado-Larocco, 1993; Silva & Kucer, 1997). Facts are the lowest or narrowest level of content knowledge and represent specific pieces of information. That dogs are domesticated carnivorous mammals is a fact. Concepts, as we have seen, embody a large number of facts. Domestication, carnivorous, and mammals are all concepts. While it is possible to "give" students a fact, a concept or web of meaning is usually developed through multiple experiences with the concept in various contexts. Generalizations are the most global forms of knowledge that indicate a relationship among two or more concepts and that summarize a large number of facts. That dogs were domesticated for various reasons, usually depending on the needs of the culture, is a generalization. Similar to concepts, generalizations develop over space and time through multiple experiences with various interrelated concepts.

The relation between word knowledge and comprehension is further complicated by the fact that words in a text are embedded within other systems of language. As represented in Figure 2.5, the surrounding systems impact the meaning of any individual morpheme. Additionally, comprehension involves more than the simple accumulation or "adding up" of individual word meanings. Rather, readers must understand the context in which any word is "nested" (Baumann, Kame'enui, & Ash, 2003). The reader must build links between and among individual words—i.e., concepts—and the other systems of language represented in the text.

As already observed, the reader's prior knowledge significantly impacts text comprehension. This prior knowledge cannot be provided through a short discussion of word meanings. Rather, "deep, rich levels of word knowledge are needed in order to affect text comprehension" (Baumann, Kame'enui, & Ash, 2003, p. 778). In order to develop these levels of knowledge, readers must have varied experiences with the concepts in varied linguistic contexts. As noted in the previous chapter, this is one reason the use of thematic or inquiry units have become so popular in elementary classrooms. Through multiple encounters with the generalizations, concepts, and facts related to the topic, students build a fuller and richer understanding of the language that is used to explore the ideas in the theme. Deep and rich levels of word knowledge can also be developed through the use of hypermedia and hypertext reading. When information is presented in multiple modalities, such as through print, visuals, and sound, the content is more memorable and more easily comprehended (Kamil, Intrator, Kim, 2000). The reading of learners with little background, or reading longer and more difficult texts, is facilitated because the information is presented in a variety of modalities.

When considering the learning of vocabulary, teachers must first determine exactly what it is that students need to learn. At least three types of learning are possible. First, it may be the case that the word is part of the student's speaking and/or listening vocabulary but is unrecognized in print. For example, the child may use the word /dog/ in oral conversation and/or recognize the word when spoken by others. Second, the child may understand the concept that a word represents but not know the word—i.e. its name—for the concept. This frequently occurs when a child is learning English as a second language. I know of a young immigrant child from southeast Asia who called a fan a "wind machine." She clearly understood what a fan did, but she simply lacked the English label. Finally, it may be the case that the child lacks both an understanding of the concept and its linguistic referent. When working with children, it is important that teachers distinguish what it means when the child is said to "lack the vocabulary" necessary to comprehend a particular text.

TABLE 7.6

The Two Boys Ran

The two boys ran until they came to the driveway. "See, I told you today was good for skipping school," said Mark. "Mom is never home on Thursday," he added. Tall hedges hid the house from the road so the pair strolled across the finely landscaped yard. "I never knew your place was so big," said Pete. "Yeah, but it's nicer now than it used to be since Dad had the new stone siding put on and added the fireplace."

There were front and back doors and a side door that led to the garage which was empty except for three parked 10-speed bikes. They went in the side door, Mark explaining that it was always open in case his younger sisters got home earlier than their mother.

Pete wanted to see the house so Mark started with the living room. It, like the rest of the downstairs, was newly painted. Mark turned on the stereo, the noise of which worried Pete. "Don't worry, the nearest house is a quarter of a mile away," Mark shouted. Pete felt more comfortable observing that no houses could be seen in any direction beyond the huge yard.

The dining room, with all the china, silver, and cut glass, was no place to play so the boys moved into the kitchen where they made sandwiches. Mark said they wouldn't go to the basement because it had been damp and musty ever since the new plumbing had been installed.

"This is where my Dad keeps his famous paintings and his coin collection," Mark said as they peered into the den. Mark bragged that he could get spending money whenever he needed it since he'd discovered that his Dad kept a lot in the desk drawer.

There were three upstairs bedrooms. Marked showed Pete his mother's closet which was filled with furs and the locked box which held her jewels. His sisters' room was uninteresting except for the color TV which Mark carried to his room. Mark bragged that the bathroom in the hall was his since one had been added to his sisters' room for their use. The big highlight in his room, though, was a leak in the ceiling where the old roof had finally rotted.

Note. From Pichert and Anderson (1977).

CONTEXT, MEANING, AND RECALL

It is not uncommon for teachers to tell their students to "read for the most important ideas" or to ask their students to identify the main ideas of a story. In the passage presented in Table 7.6 you are to read the text three times, each with a different purpose. First, read the text simply to understand what is going on. When finished, jot down the most important ideas or information. Now, read it a second time, using the perspective of a burglar, and again write down the most important ideas. Finally, read the text as a home buyer and record the most relevant information.

If you compare and contrast the information listed from the three perspectives, you will probably find different information listed for each. The home buyer perspective focused your attention on attributes that did or did not appeal to the type of residence you value. The privacy of the house, multiple bathrooms, three bedrooms,

TABLE 7.7
The Rocket

A great black and yellow V-2 rocket stood in a New Mexico desert. Empty, it weighted five tons. For fuel it carried eight tons of alcohol and liquid oxygen.

Everything was ready. Scientists and generals withdrew to some distance and crouched behind earth mounds. Two red flares rose as a signal to fire the rocket.

With a great roar and burst of flame, the giant rocket rose slowly and then faster and faster. Behind it trailed sixty feet of yellow flame. Soon the flame looked like a yellow star. In a few seconds, it was too high to be seen, but radar tracked it as it sped upward to 3,000 m.p.h.

A few minutes after it was fired, the pilot of a watching plane saw it return at a speed of 2,400 m.p.h. and plunged into earth forty miles from the starting point.

Note. From de Beaugrande (1980).

and den may have been appealing. On the other hand, the damp basement as a result of the new plumbing may have caused you concern. As a burglar, the coins, jewels, and dining room contents would have been of interest. If you are similar to my students, when you read the text simply to comprehend, you probably listed information that was represented in both the home buyer and burglar perspectives.

As discovered by Pichert and Anderson (1977), the developers of the story, the significance of any idea in a text is influenced by the perspective from which the text is read. The purpose of the reader impacts which ideas are seen as the most important or salient, which ideas are most likely to be recalled, and their order. Perspective, therefore, results in all text meanings not being created equal. Consequently, the author does not solely determine the importance of ideas; readers have a say as well.

This discussion of purpose should remind you of the pragmatics discussion in chapter 2. The pragmatic system of language, which is impacted by the context of the situation and the resulting register, reflects the language user's stance toward the discourse being encountered. As noted, Rosenblatt (1978) discussed this concept in terms of efferent and aesthetic reading, whereas Spiro (1977) addressed stance in terms of high and low text integrity. In an intriguing follow-up study using the Rocky text, Carey et al. (1981) had students read the story in two very different contexts. The first had students enrolled in a physical education class sitting on mats when they read the story. The second group read the text as part of a course in education. Not surprisingly, the students sitting on the mats tended to understand Rocky to be a wrestler rather than a prisoner. The very location of the text caused students to call forth particular background knowledge that impacted how the text was ultimately understood. No text is interpreted in isolation, but rather "in terms of the context in which it appears" (Smagorinsky, 2001, p. 135) and can take on different meanings in different contexts.

In our last demonstration for this chapter, read "The Rocket" (de Beaugrande, 1980) given in Table 7.7. Read the text so that you can remember its content. When finished reading, put this book away and come back to it at least one hour later.

TABLE 7.8

Retelling Taxonomy

Category	Definition
Match	The idea expressed in the retelling matches an idea in the text. The surface structure may be different, but the deep structure is the same.
Substitution	The idea expressed in the retelling is a substitution for an idea in the text. A substitution represents a modification of an idea expressed in the text that is semantically acceptable.
Addition	The idea expressed in the retelling is not found in the text but is semantically acceptable. An addition may represent implicit text meanings or an inference which is feasible.
Summary	At least two separate ideas in the text are condensed into one general idea in the retelling.
Conflict	The idea expressed in the retelling contradicts an idea expressed in the text.
Rearrangement	The order of the ideas and their interrelationships expressed in the retelling are at variance with the order of the ideas and their interrelationships expressed in the text.
Deletion	The idea expressed in the text is not expressed in the retelling.

Now that some time has lapsed since you read "The Rocket," write down everything you can recall from the story without looking back at the text. When finished, use Table 7.8 to classify each idea recalled or forgotten into one of the seven categories. To accomplish this, you will need to compare and contrast what you remembered with the actual text shown in Table 7.7. This retelling taxonomy was developed by Kucer and Silva (1996, 1999a,b), through an analysis of numerous retellings from a variety of readers.

If you are like most readers, the ideas you recalled did not always match those in the text. In fact, your retelling most likely represents a transformation of what was read. Rosenblatt (1978) characterized this transformation as a "new event." By this Rosenblatt meant that the meanings that are "carried away" from a text are a synthesis of the meanings brought to the page by the author and the reader. Indeed, some of the meanings may match those of the author, some may be modifications, and others may represent entirely new ideas.

From a transactional perspective, it is not always possible to determine which retold ideas came from the reader and which came from the author; rather, there is a merger or synthesis of ideas from both participants. If this view is correct, it might be more appropriate to evaluate a reader's comprehension as one might evaluate a piece of writing. The ideas comprehended would be judged not against what was read, but as a new text or a new event. In fact, Irwin and Mitchell (1983) developed a holistic assessment for evaluating retellings that looks amazingly like an instrument to be used as a holistic writing rubric.

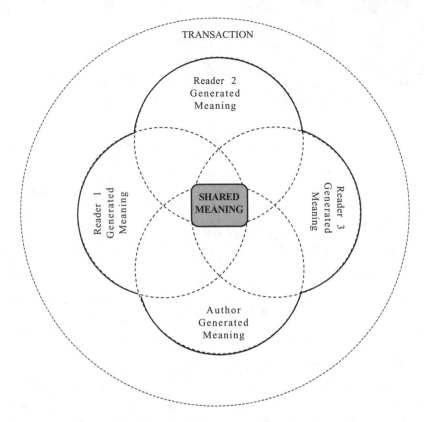

FIG. 7.3. Comprehension as transaction.

Although we might think that, in general, readers and writers have a shared understanding of what a text "says," this sharing of meaning may not always be as extensive as we might think. In one study (Kucer, 1983a, 1983b), university professors and graduate students were asked to read five different compositions written by college freshmen. These texts were fairly short, usually two to three typed (double-spaced) pages long. After reading each text, readers wrote a three- to five-sentence summary. The summaries were then analyzed for the degree to which readers shared understandings as expressed in their summaries. Interestingly, the highest degree to which readers shared meanings on any text was 51%. The lowest was 25%. On average, shared meanings accounted for 37% of the ideas expressed in the summaries.

As illustrated in Fig. 7.3, a transactional view of comprehension sees variance in readers' understandings as a natural part of the comprehending process. Different readers understand the same text in radically different ways and these ways may not always match those of the author. The notion of any text containing

TABLE 7.9

Principles of Comprehending

1. Recall is more likely for those ideas in the text that match the reader's world knowledge.
2. Recall is more likely for those ideas in the text that are part of a routine or normal pattern of behavior or events.
3. Ideas in the text are changed or altered to produce a better match with world knowledge.
4. Ideas in the text are confused when they are closely related in world knowledge.
5. Ideas in the text that are only incidental to its meaning are easily forgotten.
6. Inferences made during reading often cannot be distinguished from those ideas that are explicitly stated in the text.

its own autonomous meaning independent of a reader and a context is therefore suspect. Of course, this makes problematic the common instructional practice of asking students to answer comprehension questions as a means of assessing their understanding of a text. As we have seen, a reader may fully understand a text, but understand it differently than the person asking the questions.

Based on this variability in text comprehension between and among readers and writers, the question, "Where *is* the meaning?" might be asked. This question is particularly important because many of us may not typically experience such variability in comprehension. However, as we will see in chapter 10, there are noncognitive factors that often produce more shared meanings than occurred in many of the demonstrations in this chapter.

In summarizing the relationship among reader, text, and author, de Beaugrande (1980) developed a number of comprehension principles, listed in Table 7.9. In analyzing the relationship between your comprehension of "The Rocket" and the actual text, you probably can identify examples for many of these principles. De Beaugrande found, for example, that for the first principle, many readers recalled the scientists more than the generals. He suggested that this is because most news accounts of the space program emphasized science over the military. The idea that routines might be easily recalled as expressed in the second principle is not surprising. We know from the discussion of narrative structure that so-called story grammars exert a powerful influence on our understanding of our world. We reside in narrative lives, and it is not surprising that we would use this structure to help us understand temporally ordered discourse.

The idea that readers modify text meanings to more closely reflect their own experiences was documented in Jeanette's retelling of "Poison" (R. Dahl, 1974). She changed numerous words to match her experiences as a registered nurse. Similarly, de Beaugrande (1980) found that readers of "The Rocket" changed earth mounds to sand dunes—the setting was a desert—or to concrete bunkers. Readers do not just change meanings; they also fail to recall them. Ideas that are not central to the text are easily forgotten. When remembering is examined over time, most readers tend to reduce what is recalled to a summary (van Dijk, 1980). Finally, it has long been known that inferences made by readers frequently cannot be distinguished from those ideas that are explicitly stated. The previous discussion of readers believing that Pat was male because of the alleged use of the pronoun <he> in the text is an example of this phenomenon.

CONCLUSIONS

This chapter elaborated on both the role and nature of background knowledge in the construction of meaning through the process of reading. We found that the reader's knowledge reflects various characteristics, such as form (content and process), organization, and extensiveness, and that these characteristics significantly impact how a text is understood. We also discovered that the purpose of reading plays a primary role in what ideas in a text are recalled and deemed to be significant. Finally, we found that comprehension is a transactional event. Different readers may understand the same text in a variety of ways.

8

The Writing Process

In this chapter, we explore the cognitive dimension of the writing process. Like readers, writers are impacted by a number of factors, and it is by a revisiting of these factors that this chapter begins. Following this brief review, the process of writing is explored and the behaviors of proficient and less proficient writers are analyzed. The chapter concludes with a look at the cognitive interrelations between reading and writing as well as a cognitive discussion of the language story first presented in chapter 1.

REVISITING THE READER–TEXT–WRITER TRANSACTION

As noted in the previous chapter (see Table 6.1), a number of factors influence the reader–text–writer transaction: systems of language, strategies, background knowledge, purpose, and assimilation and accommodation. Because these factors have already been addressed for both reading and writing, my focus here is examining the impact of these factors on several writing samples.

The first writing sample comes from a first grader and was collected by Sowers (1979). In her study of writing development in young children, Sowers observed students in a first-grade classroom over nine months. During this time period, she found the children producing two kinds of discourse: attribute and action-sequence. Attribute writing, according to Sowers, was a simple listing of the author's feelings toward a certain person or thing. Similar to what might occur during brainstorming, it followed no particular chronological order and required limited planning on the part of the child. Sarah, one of the children in the study, produced the following attribute text. In this example, she demonstrates clear control over the syntactic and semantic systems of language.

Me and Chipper.

Me and Chipper have lots of fun.

We have fun.

I love Chipper so much.

I won't stop loving Chipper.

It is fun.

Sarah's control over these language systems changes radically, however, when she attempted to produce action-sequence stories. Action-sequence writing involves the formation of a narrative with several events and reflects the child's growing development of a story grammar. This mode of discourse placed a cognitive strain on the writing process for Sarah. It required her to plan ahead and to present the meanings in a chronological order, tasks not called for in attribute writing. As the following sentences from action-sequence texts indicate, the result of these demands is a loss of control of the syntactic and semantic systems.

He made naughty.

I was sad. I have nothing to cry what eating this turkey.

He got home just in time to watch his favorite program and lamp.

The villain is fighting on Ann from hunting cause Ann is a girl.

Such variability in the writing process is evident in more proficient writers as well. In a semester-long university composition class, the ability of students to control the coherence of their texts under varying conditions was examined (Kucer, 1983a, 1983b, 1986). During the semester, students wrote essays on five different topics: misuse of power, a personal experience, schooling, a self-selected subject, and discrimination. The texts required the use of different knowledge sources, were written for a variety of purposes, and reflected diverse text types and structures.

As expected, the differing constraints on the writers influenced their ability to control text coherence. Interestingly, this influence impacted the most proficient as well as the least proficient writers in the class. It was certainly the case that, on average, the proficient writers more frequently demonstrated control over coherence than those writers who were struggling. However, the degree of variability in the control of coherence across the five texts was almost identical between the most proficient and the least proficient writers in the class. It was not uncommon for a writer, regardless of ability, to demonstrate considerable control over coherence on one text and yet in the very next writing activity lose control of this process. There were situations for all writers in which coherence unraveled. Graves (1983) and a number of other researchers (e.g., Britton, Burgess, Martin, McLeod, & Rosen, 1975; Clay, 1975; de Beaugrande, 1980) have also documented the impact of various factors on the control of the writing process. As these studies indicate, it is no longer tenable to view writing as a monolithic process, one uniformly controlled from one situation to the next. Rather, writing ability varies as the demands of the writing task vary.

A THEORY AND MODEL OF THE WRITING PROCESS

Traditionally, writing has been conceived as a linear, step-by-step process. The task of the writer is to first "think it" and then "say it." As illustrated in Fig. 8.1, planning is the first step in the process. During this stage, the writer rehearses what is to be said. The topic is selected, the audience considered, and the length of the text determined. Additionally, the author spends time gathering his or her thoughts and attempts to make sense of the experience that is to be addressed. Following planning, pen is put to paper—or fingers to computer keyboard—and the writer transfers ideas into language. As language is selected, both the style and tone of the language are considered. Finally, once ideas have been displayed on the page, revision is initiated as an end of the line repair. It is only after a written draft exists that revision occurs (Sommers, 1994).

Currently, as illustrated in the reading and writing model in Fig. 6.1, we understand writing to be much more transactive and recursive in nature (e.g., Flower & Hayes, 1981; Hayes, 2000). As indicated by the two-way arrows in the figure, each element in the process both informs and is informed by the other elements. The strategies, for example, are not only influenced by the writer's goals and plans, but they can also impact goals and plans. Or, as the surface text is evolved, the writer may discover new meanings not originally anticipated. This discovery in turn may lead to a modification of the writer's background knowledge and a new understanding of the context of the situation. As was the case for the discussion of the reading process, five features from the model are addressed: knowledge search, context, goals and plans, strategies, and evolving text.

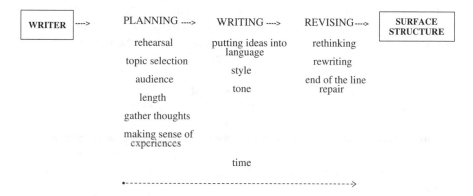

FIG. 8.1. A stage view of the writing process.

Knowledge Search

When writing is initiated, the language user engages in an ongoing search for available and relevant background knowledge stored in long-term memory. Potential ideas and meanings are placed in short-term memory which, as is the case when reading, plays a central role in the writing process (Hayes, 2000). Within short-term memory, this knowledge is explored and evaluated as to whether it will ultimately serve the writer's purpose and goals in the particular communicative situation.

As indicated in the previous chapter, often the knowledge available is not in the form required for the communicative demands. In such cases, the writer may need to reorganize the knowledge and build links from one knowledge structure to another. Just this sort of knowledge reorganization was investigated by Langer (1984). She examined the relation between the structure and content of background knowledge, the requirements of the writing task, and the resulting control of the writing process. Two groups of high school writers were used in the research. One group had extensive knowledge about the writing topic, but this knowledge was not well organized or structured. In contrast, the second group's knowledge was less extensive but far more organized. Both groups of students were asked to write two essays, one that required them to reiterate facts and to elaborate on a given idea (e.g., write an essay on your version of a utopian society) and one that involved the comparing and contrasting of information (e.g., write an essay comparing and contrasting city and frontier life).

An evaluation of the essays found that control of the writing process was significantly impacted by the relationship between the organization of background knowledge and the demands of the writing task. Students with extensive although less structured knowledge tended to produce better essays on topics that required them to set forth what they knew about the topic. The unavailability of organized knowledge had little impact on their writing because organization was not a critical dimension for this particular task. This might be compared to Sarah's attribute writing previously discussed. However, when manipulation of background knowledge was demanded, such as in a compare-and-contrast essay, organization became a critical factor. Students with well-organized knowledge controlled the writing process best under these conditions. Once again, Sarah experienced similar demands when she attempted to write action-sequence texts.

It is through this mismatch between task and background—and the resulting search process and cognitive restructuring (i.e., accommodation)—that writers frequently encounter meanings and relations not originally anticipated or considered. The discovery of meaning and writing as a tool for learning, therefore, is as central to the composing process as writing to convey already known information (Murray, 1978).

The writing sample in Table 8.1 illustrates the discoveries that can occur as writers explore their ideas about a particular topic. The writer, a college freshman

TABLE 8.1
Exploring and Discovering Knowledge

Start 1:	Seeing and hearing is something beautiful and strange to an infant.
Start 2:	To an infant seeing and hearing is something beautiful and strange to infl
Start 3:	I agree that seeing and hearing is something beautiful and strange to an infant. An infant hears a strange sound such as the working mother, he than acc
Start 4:	I agree that the child is more sensitive to beauty because it's all so new to him and he apprec
Start 5:	The main point is that a child is more sensitive to beauty than their parents because it's the child an infant can only express its feeling the reactions
Start 6:	I agree a child is more sensitive to seeing and hearing than his parents because it's all so new to him and more appreciate. His
Start 7:	I agree that seeing and hearing have a different quality for infants than grownups because when infants become aware of a sound and can associate it with the object, he is identifying and the parent acknowledges this.
Start 8:	I agree and disagree that seeing and hearing have a different quality for infants than for grownups because to see and hear for infants it's all so new and more appreciate, but I also feel that a child's parents appreciate the sharing.
Start 9:	I disagree. I feel that it has the same quality to
Start 10:	I disagree. I feel that seeing and hearing has the same quality to both infants and parents. Hearing and seeing is such a great quality to infants and parents and they both appreciate. Just because there aren't that many painters or musicians around doesn't mean that infants are most sensitive to beautiful than their parents.

at City College in New York City, is responding to this prompt: "Who is more sensitive to their environment or world, children or adults?" For ease of reading, misspellings and grammatical errors have been eliminated. Shaughnessy (1977) cited the writing to illustrate the disintegration of a writer during the composing process. On closer analysis, however, it is apparent that the writer, in fact, is undergoing a transformation in stance toward the topic. We, as readers, are privy to this discovery through the artifacts left behind from the revision process. Initially, the writer takes the position that infants are more sensitive to the world (Start 4). As the text evolves, however, he moves to the position that both adults and infants are sensitive, just in different ways (Start 7 and 8). Finally, the writer decides that infants and adults may be equally sensitive to their environments (Start 9).

As teachers work with their students to promote writing development, it is important that they consider the nature of the writing task and the search for and manipulation of information that may be required. The intent of such consideration is not to avoid writing situations in which students are required to accommodate their experiences to the task at hand. In fact, students need to learn that writing has the power to change their views of the world and to use writing to see beyond what they currently know. Rather, consideration is given so that teachers can provide their students with the necessary mediational structures and assist students in working their way through the process. When the students with the less organized knowledge in Langer's (1984) study were asked to compare and contrast urban and frontier life, for example, they might have been provided with a T-chart. In the first column of the chart, students would brainstorm ways in which life was similar. In the second column, they would brainstorm how life was different in urban and frontier settings. The contents of the chart would then be used by the students to structure and write their essays.

The Contextual Dependency of Writing

The context of situation or environment in which a piece of writing evolves has a direct impact on the function, content, and form of the text that is ultimately written. Working within the understood context, the author considers the purpose or role of the text within the situation and asks such questions as, "What is this text expected to do within this context? Is the text to inform, entertain, or convince? What knowledge is appropriate for this situation?" The author also inquires, "Who is my audience? Are the intended readers personally known or a generality based on such characteristics as occupation, interest, or ethnicity?" And, "Are they hostile or sympathetic to the ideas I want to express?" In a very real sense, it is the context of situation that activates the author's search for relevant background knowledge that was previously discussed.

As was also found to be the case with reading, the interaction between the individual and the environment determines the register within which the writer operates. The register frames the range or configuration of meanings and their linguistic expression which the writer views as being appropriate within a particular setting. The writer, therefore, is never selecting and expressing ideas and language with complete freedom. The writer is always constrained by the situation as well as his or her prior knowledge.

With all that has been said about contexts and registers, it must not be forgotten that they are not objective entities. Contexts and registers do not exist outside of, or separate from, the writer. Rather, each is actively defined by the writer based on his or her past experiences with similar situations. Precisely because of differing experiences, different writers may characterize, define, or interpret the same context in differing ways.

Frequently, students are conceived as lacking control of basic meaning making writing strategies in school contexts. In truth, it may be the case that these students are defining or understanding the particular writing context or writing genre in ways that differ or even contrast those of the teacher. Instructionally, these students need to become familiar and experienced with writing in such situations. They need to be explicitly made aware of the demands and expectations associated with particular writing circumstances. Such explicit knowledge is becoming increasingly important as students encounter standardized and high-stakes tests on a regular basis (Santman, 2002; Wolf & Wolf, 2002). We will return to the issue of context, genre, and literacy use when examining the sociocultural dimension of literacy.

Goals and Plans: Writing as an Intentional Act

As indicated in chapter 6, in a general sense, the goal of the language user, be it a reader or writer, is to build continuity (de Beaugrande, 1980, 1984; Kucer, 1989b; see Fig. 6.2). The ideas presented must be informative and logical, both to the author and the intended readers. In addition, meanings must also be internally coherent and conceptually linked to form a unified and noncontradictory whole. Because informative, logical, and coherent texts are planned to impact someone in some manner, writers also consider if their intentions or goals are being realized in the discourse. Finally, continuity of the meanings generated is evaluated in terms of intertextuality. The written discourse produced should relate to a class of previously encountered and culturally normed texts. Revisions, when initiated by the writer, are typically in response to failures to realize particular aspects of continuity.

In many cases, these various goals, and their accompanying subgoals, interact and at times even compete with one another. Writers may, for example, desire to demonstrate their expertise with the content to their audience, yet need to limit the length of the text due to situational constraints. At the same time, writers want to avoid the impression that they are arrogant or "know it alls." Writers also want to achieve a well-organized text but not to the extent that it becomes too predictable and trite. Writers frequently face the challenge of balancing these goals as they maneuver themselves through the writing process (Hayes, 2000; Smith, 1994b).

Perhaps one of the most critical goals of the writer is to build internal coherence on a global level. As writers evolve their discourse, they attempt to work out the general semantic framework within which their more local or specific meanings can be developed and attached. Unlike a rigid outline, these global frameworks are often ill-defined when writing is initiated. Additionally, they are flexible structures and easily change and evolve as the discourse itself unfolds. Nonetheless, such semantic frameworks provide an orienting function and structure for writers, propelling them down certain pathways and helping them avoid those that may be less productive.

In a fascinating study, Atwell (1980) examined the impact of global coherence on the writing process. University students—proficient and less proficient—were assigned an essay topic. After students had produced several pages of discourse, they were asked to continue writing with pens that contained no ink. This meant that although they were able to return to what had been written previously, the students were unable to read any of the new discourse produced. The writing paper, however, had a carbon backing that allowed the researcher to examine both the visible and the subsequent invisible writing at a later point in time.

An analysis of the finished texts indicated that the "blind" writing had a more significant impact on the less proficient writers than on those who were more proficient. The texts by the less proficient writers essentially fell apart once the writers were unable to see what they were composing. Coherence on both a global and local level was virtually nonexistent. For the better writers, however, the blind writing had a much less significant impact. They were able to maintain a high degree of coherence under both conditions. Atwell (1980) speculated that the reason for this difference is that proficient writers had a global idea about what they wanted to say by the time they were asked to write under blind conditions. They used these global ideas as a source for the generation of more specific ideas and to maintain the coherence of their texts. In contrast, the struggling writers moved from sentence to sentence, with little concern for the overall structure of what they were saying. Each subsequent sentence was an extension of the previous but failed to advance the writer towards more general ideas.

Writers reach their goals by developing a series of plans. Plans take the writer from where he or she is presently to where the writer wishes to be when composing is finished—that is, the goals are realized. In planning this chapter, for example, which occurred both before and during its writing, I considered what ideas were to be addressed and their potential order. Even before writing was initiated, I knew that I needed to begin the chapter with a revisiting of the reader–text–writer transaction that was first introduced in the chapter on reading. I also planned to address the same five features as in the reading process so as to build links between the two acts of meaning making. It was not until I was well into writing this chapter, however, that I suddenly realized that the concept of "writer's block" needed to be included. I struggled over where in the text to address the issue. It was only after embedding the discussion in several different parts of the chapter that I decided writer's block would be introduced in the section that addressed proficient and struggling writers.

In summary, it is important to remember that the plans utilized by writers to reach their goals propel them into the process. Plans generate rather than restrict options. Therefore, by their very nature, plans are flexible, multidimensional, and open to information—feedback—from the text itself or the situational context (Rose, 1994). If a plan fails to advance the writer toward the goal, it is modified, rejected, or replaced as necessary. Plans, like goals, are always provisional and hypothetical in nature and continue to evolve during the writing process.

As noted in previous chapters, it is important to be mindful that readers will have their own goals and plans that may not align with those of the author. This is especially the case with the use of the Internet, web pages, and hyperlinks. Readers may not follow the physical and mental paths or hypertext environments laid out by the author (Kinzer & Leander, 2003).

Writing Strategies

As illustrated in Fig. 6.1, embedded within the writer's goals and plans are the composing strategies. Strategies are those cognitive procedures employed by the writer to construct and display meanings in a written form (Flower & Hayes, 1981; F. Smith, 1994b). As previously discussed and illustrated in Fig. 6.1, a number of strategies can operate at the same time and their employment is recursive. Writers shuttle back and forth in their use of the strategies. Revision—deletion, addition, synthesis, reordering, refocusing—and the editing of such surface-level features as spelling and punctuation can occur at any point in the process. The actual writing can also serve as a form of prewriting in that it provokes the discovery of new meanings to add to the text. Or, the writer may evaluate past or future meanings as current meanings are being transcribed onto the page. Therefore, the operation of the strategies is reciprocal in that each strategy informs, and is informed by, the others. Table 8.2 sets forth significant strategies that writers engage as they generate written discourse.

Despite the fact that writing is such a dynamic, transactive, and recursive process, it is interesting to note that much writing instruction—even that labeled as "process" oriented—continues to reflect a stage view of writing. Students first brainstorm or web the ideas they might use in their writing (planning). Using their web of ideas, students then draft their meanings (writing). Finally, in small groups or with the teacher, students share and conference about their drafts, receive feedback, and make changes (revision). Oftentimes, students are forced to go through this "process" even when it ultimately interferes with their generation of meanings (F. Smith, 1983a,b).

Labbo, Hoffman, and Roser (1995) tell the story of how an exceptionally talented elementary teacher unintentionally made writing more difficult for her students by insisting that they follow the "process." Because of her focus on the steps in the process, the teacher tended to be more concerned about what she wanted to teach rather than what the child was attempting to do. In one lesson, the teacher introduced the concept of brainstorming writing topics. She then insisted that a student brainstorm writing topics even though the child already knew what he wanted to write about. As the child's comments make clear, this actually interfered with his writing.

> I just didn't want to do it. I didn't want to do a story because it was too hard to keep doing the stuff, you know, the other stuff I needed to do before I could do my story (p. 166).

Similarly, during writing conferences the teacher asked various content-oriented questions about a draft that the student had shared. It is clear that the teacher's intentions were to show genuine interest in the student's story and to help him improve it through a series of revisions. However, the student clearly articulated

TABLE 8.2

Writing Strategies and Processes

1. Generate and organize generalizations and concepts. Writers give attention to the major ideas that they want to convey. Generalizations and concepts are developed and organized. This does not mean that the major ideas are necessarily known before writing is initiated, just that the writer is constantly attempting to discover a larger framework into which meanings can be arranged.

2. Expand, extend, and elaborate generalizations and concepts. Writers fully develop their major ideas through supporting details. Generalizations and concepts are elaborated upon and extended so that they are understandable to the reader.

3. Organize or integrate meanings across the text into a logical and coherent whole. Writers pull ideas together so that they form a unified and noncontradictory whole. Facts and details are linked to major ideas, concepts, or generalizations. Major ideas are related to supporting evidence and supporting evidence is related to major ideas.

4. Use a variety of linguistic cues. Writers use a variety of systems of language through which to express their ideas. They know that their texts must conform to the established rules for the various systems: pragmatic, text type, text structure, genre, semantic, syntax, morphology, orthography, graphophonemic, grapheme.

5. Use a variety of text aids—for example, pictures, charts, graphs, subheadings, and multimodal technologies—to mark their meanings. In addition to the use of linguistic cues, writers utilize text aids to facilitate, extend, highlight, and organize text meanings.

6. Use relevant linguistic and conceptual background knowledge. In order to generate meaning, writers make use of relevant linguistic and conceptual background knowledge. Writers bring their knowledge of their world and language to the text in order to make meaning through print. It is through the use of this knowledge that writers are able to determine whether or not what they have written sounds like language, makes sense, and meets their purpose.

7. Predict/plan future meanings based on what has been written. Writers anticipate upcoming meanings based on their purpose, what has been written, and their background knowledge. Previous meanings both support and constrain future meanings.

8. Monitor and evaluate the meanings generated. Writers continually assess the meanings generated. They ask themselves: "Does this sound like language?" "Does this make sense?" "Does this meet my purpose or intention?"

9. Revise when meaning is lost or purposes are not realized. Writers change their predictions or meanings when they answer "no" to the questions: "Does this sound like language?" "Does this make sense?" "Does this meet my purpose or intention?"

10. Utilize a variety of strategies when revising. When revision is initiated, writers utilize a variety of strategies that are appropriate to what is being written. Information may be deleted, added, or substituted. Ideas may be synthesized or reordered. Or, information may be refocused to highlight particular ideas over others.

11. Use a variety of strategies when encountering "blocks." Writers utilize various strategies when they do not know what to write next or have difficulty expressing an idea. They may: brainstorm possible ideas and jot them down, reread what has been written, skip to a part that they know what will be written and return later, write it as best they can and return later, write it several different ways, write whatever comes to mind, talk it over with someone, read other texts to get ideas, or stop writing and return later.

12. Use writing to explore ideas and to discover new meanings. Writers explore their ideas and discover new meanings when they interact with print. Rather than simply writing what is already known, they use writing to investigate their thoughts and come to understand what was not previously understood.

13. Reflect on, and respond and react to, what is being written. Writing is an affective as well as a cognitive process. Meanings generated elicit personal reflections, responses, and reactions from the writer. The writer argues, affirms, talks to, laughs, or cries at the meanings being conveyed.

14. Vary the manner in which texts are written based on different purposes, intentions, or audiences. Writers do not process all texts in the same way. Rather, writers vary their writing so as to meet their needs, such as to remember particular information, to update a friend about a personal experience, or to share ideas with an audience which is not personally known. How a shopping list is written varies from that of a friendly letter, and both differ from a newspaper article.

15. Edit—the revision of spelling, punctuation, capitalization, penmanship—after meanings and purpose are met. Writers are not unconcerned with the surface structure of their texts. However, they usually wait until meanings and purposes have been met before conventions become the focus. Because revisions to meanings frequently result in the changing of words, sentences, and paragraphs, it usually is not worth the writer's time and energy to be overly concerned with conventions too early in the process.

his belief that the questions were not helping him accomplish what *he* wanted to achieve.

> What she was asking me ... mostly wasn't what I wanted. But I needed to answer her. I had to think real, real fast. So, I just made some stuff up, but I just don't like it (Labbo, Hoffman, & Roser, 1995, p. 167).

These two vignettes bring to mind a cartoon that a colleague recently shared with me. In the cartoon, a student is talking with the teacher about her struggles with writing. The student notes that she is attempting to write about what she knows—a common instructional maxim—but that all she knows is the writing workshop! I think the cartoon unfortunately captures our all too frequent fetish with methods (Bartolome, 1994) at the expense of the learner.

Although the focus here has been on the teacher's instruction, in all likelihood the teacher learned many of these process strategies from teacher educators like myself. Too often in our attempts to help students manage the writing process, we take the process from them. If strategy instruction is to be effective, it must provide students with a range of options from which they can draw when needed. Brainstorming, for example, can certainly serve as an effective strategy when we are searching for ideas about which we can write. So too can consulting various reference materials, published stories, and talking with friends and family. Similarly, talking with others about a draft can lead to significant improvements if these "others" try to help us to carry out what we want to accomplish. Also effective, however, is putting the draft aside and coming back to it later. The point here is that our instruction should open rather than constrain possibilities for our students (Glasswell, Parr, & McNaughton, 2003; Kucer, 1995, 1998).

Comparable cautions apply to the use of computer technology for promoting writing as well. Many factors impact the relationship among author, computer, composing, and the final product (Farnan & Dahl, 2003) and care should be taken when generalizing about the impact of computers on writing (Leu, 2000; Reinking & Bridwell-Bowels, 1996). In some cases, the quality as well as the quantity of computer-based writing has been found to be higher than writing by hand (Kamil et al., 2000). Daiute (2000) suggested that computers can reduce the burdens on short-term memory through the use of the thesaurus for word alternatives as well as spell check and the ease of correction. Such technology allows writers to focus their energies on generating and organizing ideas. Revision procedures, however, need to be demonstrated to the students; otherwise they may not occur. Daiute found that younger writers frequently simply added new information to the end of the text, rather than embedding the information where it made most sense. The same phenomenon has been found to occur when students write by hand (Kucer, 1995).

In order to illustrate the dynamic transactions that actually occur during the writing process, a number of these transactions are briefly discussed through the use of a draft by a proficient adult writer (see Table 8.3). The writer is addressing the question, "Who is more sensitive to their environment or world, children or adults?" As previously noted, this writing prompt was developed by Shaughnessy (1977) as she worked with struggling writers at City College in New York City. In this case, the author has written the text on the left side of the page and recorded her thought processes on the right. Each thought process is numbered for ease of reference.

In examining the behaviors of the writer, it is interesting to note when ideas were accessed during the process. The writer indicates that she immediately began thinking about the topic and her stance when the assignment was given (1, 2). She drew from her background relevant knowledge and brainstormed and recorded how both children and adults are sensitive to their worlds (3). The writer then used this list not only to decide who is more sensitive, but also to guide her actual engagement with the process (7). The list provided a framework into which she could arrange her meanings. However, ideas are not only discovered before writing is initiated; they also are encountered throughout the drafting of the text (5, 8). Some of these potential ideas were recorded in the margins of the text (12) and their appropriateness evaluated.

As well as assessing the relevance of potential meanings, the writer also monitored the meanings that had been generated in print. She reread portions of her

TABLE 8.3

A Look Into the Writing Process

Text	Writing Behavior and Reasons
	(1) I began thinking about the topic as soon as the assignment was given.
	(2) I think about the topic when I go to sleep, walk to the subway, or when I'm at work.
	(3) I made a list of how children are sensitive and adults are sensitive. I found children to be the more powerful argument based on my list.
When asked the question who is more sensitive to their world, children or adults, I was a bit stumped. However, after careful contemplation, I believe children are more sensitive to the world around them for several reasons, mainly because of their innocence.	
Children are innocent. They go through their world without any judgements because they haven't learned any yet.	(4) As I begin writing I reread what I have written to see if it makes sense.
They are young and view their world without any judgements that adults have.	(5) As I write new thoughts about the subject form in my mind that I consider using.
For example, often you won't hear a child describe another person using race as a characteristic.	(6) In the middle of writing I stop and think of other words to add.
They will say he has brown hair or wears glasses or is funny but seldom will they say he is white or black. Once a student of mine couldn't find	(7) As I'm writing the draft I check over my list.
If they do use skin color to describe a person they use color words that are a lot more descriptive than white and black.	(8) One thought led to another—jogged a memory.

(continued on next page)

TABLE 8.3 (continued)

Text	Writing Behavior and Reasons
For example, a student of mine couldn't find her swim instructor at swim lessons. I asked her to describe the person to me. I asked her questions like if the instructor was male or female, dark hair or light hair, and when I asked about skin color she told me he was pink. Well, it ended up that he was absent that day but anyway she used descriptive adjectives other than using the generalized race words black or white. He wasn't part of a group. He was pink.	(9) I go back over my text and edit.
Another reason I feel children are more sensitive to the world around them is that they are very curious and are always asking questions.	(10) Reread my data to see where I left off.
And they don't hold back. They ask about what they see and they are honest in giving answers.	(11) Combined two ideas together in one paragraph.
They tell you if they don't like something children let you know about it. It is not because they aren't sensitive to their environment in the way that means they don't respect it, but the fact that they are aware of what's around them so honestly is indication that they are in fact are sensitive to their environment.	(12) I write notes in margin about the text.
	(13) This previous section doesn't make a whole lot of sense but I know what I want to say—work on this to make it clear.

I feel children are more sensitive than adults because sometimes adults are so focused in their own little world that they are not aware of who all that is going on around them except for the part that pertains to them. Children are active and are curious to take in all that is around them. They are eager to explore and this makes them more sensitive to their environment. Adult's aren't often eager to explore because they are usually concerned with what is immediately around them.

When asked the question whether adults or children are more sensitive to their environment I feel children are I feel because of their innocence, curiosity, and honesty make them so much more aware of the world around them.

They live freely and eagerly exploring all that's around them rather than focusing on things that immediately pertain to them.

(14) Write everything down first—work on flow, sequence, clarity later.

(15) I write notes in margin.

(16) Work on conclusion to make it stronger.

181

essay to see if they made sense (4) and realized that a previous section of text was in need of revision (13). At certain points, the writer decided to delay revision. She knows what she wants to say but not necessarily how to say it (13) and "write[s] everything down first" (14). Later, she plans to return and make the necessary revisions. Although editing is part of the process (9), it is clear that the writer is first attempting to get the meanings right with herself before worrying about the surface structure (Flower, 1979). Finally, the writer reread not only to assess her ideas; rereading was also employed to reorient herself in relation to the text (10) as well as for editing purposes (9).

Evolving Cognitive Text World and Surface Structure

As with reading, writing involves the generation of an "in-head" world of meaning, the deep structure of ideas constructed in the writer's mind. Accompanying and paralleling this meaning is the surface structure, the marks the writer puts on the page. In the best of all possible worlds, there is a one-to-one correspondence between the cognitive text and the surface structure; that is, what the writer desires to articulate is actually represented in the written language on the page. However, it is this very attempt to align the deep and surface structures that writers often find challenging. What the writer wants or intends to say may not be captured by what is actually stated. That is, a disruption or discontinuity exists between intention and reality. We saw this phenomenon with the proficient writer who knew what she wanted to say but also knew that she had not been successful in articulating it (13).

The disruption between surface and deep structures can be as simple as writing the wrong word or letter for what was intended. More frequently, the tension derives from the writer not having full control over the ideas—content, form, or both— to be expressed or from encountering difficulty finding the appropriate language with which to articulate the ideas. Further complicating this relationship between surface and deep structure is the fact that by attempting to gain control over the ideas to be expressed or by articulating meaning through language, new ideas may be unearthed. This process of discovery does not mean, however, that writers do not attempt to generate a global framework of meaning into which their ideas can be embedded. It simply means that writing involves more than extending the previous sentence and that this global framework is constantly being modified and updated as necessary.

One way in which writers monitor and evaluate the degree of alignment between their intentions, cognitive meanings, and the surface level text is through the process of reading. The reading of the written text produced so far serves as an orienting device, providing writers with feedback as to where they have been and where they might be going. In a very real sense, the evolving text becomes part of the context of situation. It shapes the options available to the writer and places constraints on those meanings and structures that subsequently may find expression.

Because the writer is attempting to produce a text that reflects continuity (i.e., informativity, logic, coherence, intentionality, situationality, intertextuality), new ideas that are discovered through the process of reading must either fit within the established discourse or summon forth revisions. Revisions may involve the text constructed so far, the text that is anticipated, or both. A common response of writers to the need to revise is through the use of notes that document necessary changes. Interestingly, the focus of these notes may vary depending on the mode of composing. Writers who are composing with pencil and paper have been found to make more elaborate revision notes. They frequently used lines, arrows, and other graphics to highlight the structure and organization of the text. In contrast, the notes of writers composing on computers tended to be linguistic in nature and focused on content (Haas, 1991). Haas also found that it was easier for writers to maintain coherence in hand-written drafts than on computer screens. The author was able to more easily look from page to page to evaluate if the text "hung together." On the computer screen, it was more difficult to move from page to page and writers had to print their drafts in order to get a sense of the overall coherence of their texts. Potentially, such alterations—whether by hand or on screen—may continue almost endlessly as the writer attempts to get meanings right with himself or herself and with the audience. As noted by Pearson (1989), however, we usually never really finish a text; rather, we just simply decide to stop.

AN EXAMINATION OF PROFICIENT
AND NONPROFICIENT WRITERS

At this point in our discussion, it would be useful to examine the in-process behaviors of proficient and less proficient writers. In contrast to reading, teachers rarely observe their students as they write. Teacher understanding of writing tends to be product-oriented, and evaluation occurs after student engagement with the process is complete. The evaluation of written products through the use of such measures as holistic and analytical assessments is certainly a valuable component of teaching and learning. However, just as valuable is a consideration of how the product came to be, a consideration of the processes in which the writer engaged to produce the written artifact.

Tables 8.4 and 8.5 contain the writings and reflections of two intermediate elementary students, Crystal and LaSonja, respectively. The first is that of a fairly proficient writer; the second represents a writer who is struggling. The topics were selected by the students and as each composed, her unfolding text was videotaped. After the initial draft was complete, the video was played for the student. The tape was stopped at each point where the writer had paused or engaged in some sort of revision, such as crossing out a word or rereading a portion of the text. The student was then asked to discuss why she had paused or engaged in the revision. Read through each table and compare and contrast the in-process behaviors of the two writers.

TABLE 8.4

The Writing Behaviors of a Proficient Writer

Text	Behavior and Reasons
Space	
A long time ago in the year (1) 1900 a family from earth went to space. They were a very nice and healthy family. They stayed there (2) until the year (3) 1957. They were there a long time. ~~Ther~~ (4) Their names were Janet, (5) Bob, Lisa, (6) Michael. (7) I went along with them also. While we were there we changed. All of the girls (8) ~~I~~ had only one eye and a happy face. (9) And all the men had two eyes and a sad face. They saw this big machine. They didn't know what it was. So they went to some of the people there. They told him it was a machine that do lots of things. (10) It lets you see down to earth~~,~~. (11) It gives you food (12) and water. "What about clothes?" (13) said Lisa. The man said, "We ~~dow~~ (14) don't wear clothes." (15) (16) We ate and drank water and visited our new ~~fu~~ (17) friends. We discovered new things in space. (18) Then we were ready to go. (19) Then it was the year 1957. ~~Whe~~ (20) We got home in the year (21) 1960. ~~We were still our~~ (22) We changed back to ourselves. Everything looked the same. We went to our house and rested.	(1) "A long time ago" didn't make sense to her when related to the year 1900 but she didn't want to start over. (2) Forgot how to spell "until." (3) Wasn't sure what year to choose. Almost put 1976 but wanted something before she was born. (4) Started to write "there" when she wanted the possessive "their." (5) Couldn't think of a boy's name. (6) Was trying to think of another boy's name. (7) Was thinking of what she, as a character in the story, should do; whether she should go along with them in space or not. (8) Started to put "change" but wanted to put how they had changed. (9) Stopped to think how she was going to include the machine in the story. (10) Stopped to think of possible things the machine could do. (11) Stopped to think of what the machine could do and crossed out the comma because she wanted to put "it" and you can't put "it" after a comma. Also stated that she was making a lot of mistakes in her writing. (12) Wanted to think of more things the machine could do but couldn't think of anything else. (13) Was thinking of who said the quote. (14) Started to misspell "don't." (15) Went back and put in quotation marks because the man was talking. (16) Stopped but did not know why. (17) Started to misspell "friends." (18) Stopped to decide if the family should discover more things, talk some more, or go home. (19) Went back and read the beginning of her story to find out in what year they left for home so she could be consistent.

We were happy to see everybody. (23)

Then we went to bed.

(20) Wanted to put "we" but began to write "when."
(21) Stopped to decide what year they would arrive home.
(22) Began to put "they hadn't changed during their travels" but they had changed because they were older.
(23) Didn't know what she was going to say next.

As their reflections make clear, there are significant differences between the in-process behaviors of these two writers. The more proficient writer had as her primary focus the generation and organization of meaning. Approximately 70% of her pauses are due to her concern with ideas and their development. For example, she paused to consider the behavior of a character (7), the possible things the machine might do (10), and whether the family should discover more things or go home (18). The writer also sought to build coherence among the ideas expressed; she wanted her ideas to make sense in relation to one another. At (19), she returned to the beginning of her story so that she would be consistent in the dates used. Similarly, she realized or discovered that the characters changed during the course of their travels, if only because they are older (22).

What is also apparent is the fluidity of the text being evolved. The writer perceived her story as malleable and open to change as she discovered new meanings and insights. She initially selected the date 1976 but reconsidered because she wanted to use a time before she was born (3). She also started to write "change" and discovered that what she really wanted to discuss was how the characters changed (8). For this student, writing is clearly not a think it–say it process. Rather, a more accurate description of writing is a think about it–reflect and (re)consider–try it out process.

Interestingly, the revisions expressed at (3) and (8) never saw the light of day in the text. That is, they are not revisions that involved the surface structure, but rather they are internal to the writer. Many of the writer's ideas are expressed, evaluated, and revised cognitively. In fact, this type of revision occurs constantly throughout the writing of the text, and there may be as much internal revision as external revision. The acknowledgment of these invisible revisions is important because it they are internal to the writer. Many of the writer's ideas are expressed, evaluated, and revised cognitively. In fact, this type of revision occurs constantly throughout the writing of the text, and there may be as much internal revision as external revision. The acknowledgment of these invisible revisions is important because it is common to hear teachers express distress at the lack of revision in their students' writing. This may be true; however, there may also be revisions that are invisible to the eye but occur just the same.

TABLE 8.5

The Writing Behaviors of a Less Proficient Writer

Text	Behavior and Reasons
Hi. My name is LaSonja. (1) I'm in the 6th grade. I'm 11 years old. (2) I will be 12 (3) on Jan. 27. (4) I live at 10231 John (5) Jay Dr. in (6) apartment (7) and I like coming to summer school and I (8) like being with ~~Seve~~ (9) a lot of people (10) (11) and sometimes I like (12) to read books or writing stories and alot (13) (14) of things. (15) Some holidays me and my family go to Gary (16) for the ho (17) lidays. (18) ~~an~~ (19) I'm from ~~Wha~~ (20) Washington D.C.	(1) Was thinking of something to write. (2) Was thinking of something to write. (3) Was thinking about whether she should put the date and stuff. (4) Was thinking of something to write. (5) Stopped and thought she had messed up because she had written "John" in manuscript rather than cursive. (6) Did not know why she stopped. (7) Was thinking of something to write. (8) Was thinking of something to write. (9) Wrote "Seve" for "Steve" but wasn't sure how to spell it so she changed it to "people." (10) Messed up the "e" in "people." (11) Was thinking of something to write. (12) Did not know why she stopped. (13) Almost made a "t" after the "a" in "alot." (14) Did not know why she stopped. (15) Was thinking of something to write. (16) Was thinking about whether to put down "for the holidays." Decided to put it down. (17) Almost put an "a" after the "h." (18) Was thinking of what she had written previously and where she was from. Then put down the period. (19) Started to write "and" but changed it because it wouldn't have sounded right. (20) Made a mistake; spelled "Washington" wrong.

Although meaning was the first priority for this writer, she was not oblivious to or unconcerned with the surface structure of written language conventions. Approximately 30% of her pauses were due to conventions. In her second pause, for example, she considered how to spell <until>. She also realized her need to spell the possessive <their> (4) and began to write <we> rather than <when> (20). In general, however, these surface-level concerns did not interfere with her access to ideas or overwhelm the student as she wrote. In fact, only two of her pauses (16, 23) engaged the writer in a general search for ideas.

The behaviors of the less proficient writer are almost opposite those of the proficient writer. Only 18% of the pauses reflect a focus on meaning and its organization. At (3), for example, the writer considered whether to put the date in her story; later in the text, she thought about including <home for the holidays> (16). The writer also focused on text coherence as she reflected on what had been previously written in light of her desire to include where she is from (18). At (19), she revised because what she had started to write would not have sounded right.

The remainder of her pauses, however, primarily concern the surface structure (41%) or meaning searches (41%); for this writer, the two are intimately related. Throughout the process, the writer continually stopped because she was unsure how to spell particular words (9, 20) or because she miswrote them (5, 10, 13, 17). The impact of this focus is to block the writer's access to ideas, and she constantly stopped to "think about something to write" (1, 2, 4, 7, 8, 11, 15). Given what we know about STM and LTM, such blocks are not surprising. The writer essentially experienced tunnel vision. The flow of semantic information between the two memory systems is blocked because STM is filled with spelling patterns and graphemes.

Regardless of their proficiency, both writers had almost the same number of pauses: 23 for the proficient writer and 20 for the less proficient writer. However, the lengths of the two texts are significantly different. The proficient writer used her pauses to propel her forward in the generation and development of ideas, whereas the pauses of the less proficient writer halted the production of meaning.

The nature of the topics selected by the two writers provides further insights into their differing behaviors. It might have been predicted that the development of an original story would result in more searches for meanings than the "retelling" of a personal experience. An original story requires the generation and organization of new meanings and relationships. The cognitive demands are considerable, and the writer may need to stop frequently to consider "something to write." In contrast, in the retelling of a personal experience, the writer simply lays out in print meanings and relationships that already exist cognitively. However, even existing experiences may be unavailable or difficult to draw on if the focus of the writer is on written language conventions.

Table 8.6 summarizes the characteristics of proficient and less proficient writers. When considering the behaviors of struggling writers, it is important to note that they are not, in fact, "beginning writers." Although frequently described as such,

TABLE 8.6

Summary of Proficient and Less Proficient Writing Behaviors

Proficient Writers	*Less Proficient Writers*
Focus on the generation and elaboration of ideas	Focus on correct spelling, word choice, and syntax
Monitor what is written for sense and coherence	Monitor what is written for correct spelling, word choice, and syntax
Utilize a variety of strategies when meaning breaks down: reread, rethink, rewrite, write on and return if necessary, substitute, seek assistance, ignore it, stop writing	Utilize a limited range of strategies when meaning breaks down: sound out, seek assistance, stop writing
View writing as a process of generating, exploring, discovering, and revising meaning	View writing as a think it → say it process
Use and integrate a variety of systems of language to create meaning	Utilize a limited number of systems of language—graphemes, orthography, morphology
Vary the manner in which texts are written based on purpose	Write all texts in a similar manner regardless of purpose
Initial revisions primarily focus on meaning and organization; focus on surface level revision only after the generation of a substantial amount of discourse	Primarily focus on surface level revisions which are initiated before much discourse has been generated
"Chunk" ideas for writing	Letter-by-letter processing results in tunnel vision

this characterization is less than accurate. Cognitively and linguistically, less capable writers are vastly different from those students having their initial encounters with the written mode of language. As clearly indicated by LaSonja, a struggling writer, the problems encountered by less proficient writers frequently find their roots in the type of stance these writers take toward text (Atwell, 1980; Faigley & Witte, 1981; Flower, 1979; Hayes, 2000; Perl, 1979; Pianko, 1979; Rose, 1994; Sawkins, 1970). That is, their writing is dominated by a concern for conventions and for extending the previous sentence.

In addition, language users who frequently experience writer's block tend to operate from rigid plans and rules (Rose, 1994; F. Smith, 1994b). As indicated in Table 8.7, "blockers" commonly lack flexibility in their negotiations with the writing process and their text. If it is believed that there must be three or more points to an essay, for example, these writers have difficulty adapting or moving beyond the rule when it is not appropriate to the communicative setting. In many ways, less proficient writers have a stage view of the process and attempt to keep things neat

TABLE 8.7

The Nature of Writer's Block

Blockers	Nonblockers
Beginning is everything; can't move on until the beginning is "just right"	Rules are more flexible, less absolute
Rigid rules; e.g., three or more points to an essay or a five-paragraph essay	Rules free up rather than constrict the writing process
Too many rules that at times may be contradictory	Reject rules that are not sensible or conflict with their writing experiences
Outlines are too detailed and complex; impossible to follow	Use general plans that can be easily modified; plans provide a supportive framework within which to work
Become trapped inside their organizational plan	Writers with the least precise rules and plans have the least trouble composing
Unable to generate alternatives when something does not work or when they encounter a problem	Able to generate alternatives when something does not work or when they encounter a problem
A staged, step-by-step view of the writing process	Fluid, multidirectional view of the writing process; a back and forth process
Premature editing before a substantial amount has been written	

and tidy as they work their way through a text. In contrast, "nonblockers" utilize rules as a support system to help them to realize their intentions or goals. On the occasions when the rules are ineffective, they are able to generate alternatives and to keep the process moving. These writers understand composing to be a multidirectional and fluid process.

In considering the rigid use of rules, I am reminded of the comments of a freshman composition coordinator at a large private university. In working with freshman writers over a number of years, she discovered that one of the most persistent and difficult beliefs and behaviors to change was their conception of the nature of an essay. These students had been taught that an essay should have five paragraphs. First, there was an introductory paragraph that sets forth the thesis of the author. This was followed by three supporting examples, or paragraphs. The fifth and final paragraph was a conclusion.

In the chapter on the reading process, the use of Reading Strategy Wall Charts was discussed as a way of helping readers work their way through reading blocks. Similarly, the use of Writing Strategy Wall Charts and Spelling Strategy Wall Charts can be beneficial for students who experience writing blocks. In the same third grade bilingual classroom introduced previously, the classroom teacher and I developed a series of strategies for supporting students in working their way through writing and spelling difficulties (Kucer, 1995). Students were encouraged

TABLE 8.8

Writing Strategy Wall Chart

When writing and you come to a place where you do not know what to write next or have difficulty writing down your idea, you can:

1. Brainstorm possible ideas and jot them down on paper. Select one of the ideas and try it out.
2. Reread what you have written so far and see if an idea comes to mind.
3. Skip ahead to a part that you know what you will write about. Come back to the problem later.
4. Write it as best you can and return later to make it better.
5. Write it several different ways and choose the one that you like the best.
6. Write whatever comes into your mind.
7. Talk about it/conference with a friend.
8. Read other texts to get some new ideas.
9. Stop writing for a while and come back to it later.

TABLE 8.9

Spelling Strategy Wall Chart

When writing and you come to a word that you do not know how to spell, you can:

1. Think of "small words" that are in the word and write these first.
2. Write the word several different ways and choose the one that looks the best.
3. Write the letters that you know are in the word.
4. Write the first and last letters of the word. Put a line for the letters that go in the middle of the word.
5. Draw a line for the word.
6. Think of other words that are related to the word you want to spell, such as medical for the word medicine or musician for music.
7. Ask a friend.
8. Look it up in the dictionary or do a computer spell check.
9. Sound it out.

to use the various strategies whenever they experienced difficulty getting their ideas on paper. At the end of the year, the Writing and Spelling Wall Charts looked like those in Tables 8.8 and 8.9.

In contrast to the narrow focus of struggling writers, more proficient writers focus on the "big picture" and the filling in of details. This is not to say, however, that more capable writers know what will be said before writing is initiated. Quite the contrary; they use writing to explore and discover their ideas. What sets them apart from less proficient writers is their concern for finding a larger semantic structure within which to work. Such writers are less likely to experience blocks because their plans and rules are much more fluid. Rather than narrowing the options, plans and rules actually free up the writing process.

This difference in focus of proficient and less proficient writers is even evident in the use of rereading in the writing process (Atwell, 1980). More proficient writers tend to reread large "chunks" of what has been written. The rereading of multiple sentences and paragraphs propels the writer into the discourse and supports the writer in planning, executing, and editing the text. In contrast, struggling writers tend to focus on the surface structure violations and frequently do not venture beyond the sentence as a unit of analysis when rereading.

COGNITIVE INTERRELATIONSHIPS BETWEEN
THE READING AND WRITING PROCESSES

It has been commonly assumed that reading and writing are simply inverse or opposite communicative events. As illustrated in Fig. 8.2, reading is viewed as a decoding process. Readers passively take in or abstract the author's meaning from the page. Given the passivity of the reader, relatively few linguistic or cognitive resources are drawn on. Perhaps the most active aspect of reading is the fact that readers increase their background knowledge through what is learned from the text being processed. Finally, the role of context in which the reading occurs is thought to be of little importance. Reading a short story for pleasure, for a university course, or as part of a book club is all the same.

In contrast, writers are perceived as more actively engaged in the construction of meaning. Their meanings are encoded into print through the use of various cognitive resources. Writers express their background knowledge through print rather than build it. Because of the role of the audience, writers are keenly aware of the context and purpose for their written texts.

As has been demonstrated throughout the cognitive examination of literacy, and as illustrated in Fig. 8.3, a more accurate depiction of the relationship between reading and writing is that of parallel or complementary processes. Readers and writers are, in fact, both intensely engaged in the searching for, and the integrating of, meaning (Kucer, 1985a, 1987; Tierney & Shanahan, 1996). In both processes, "meaning is continually in a state of becoming" (Langer & Flihan, 2000, p. 118).

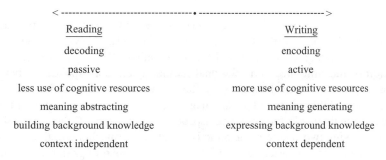

Reading	Writing
decoding	encoding
passive	active
less use of cognitive resources	more use of cognitive resources
meaning abstracting	meaning generating
building background knowledge	expressing background knowledge
context independent	context dependent

FIG. 8.2. Reading and writing as opposite processes.

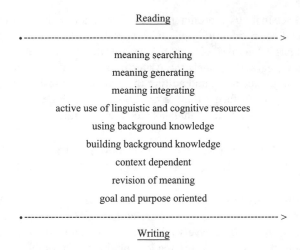

Reading

meaning searching

meaning generating

meaning integrating

active use of linguistic and cognitive resources

using background knowledge

building background knowledge

context dependent

revision of meaning

goal and purpose oriented

Writing

FIG. 8.3.   Reading and writing as parallel processes.

This state of becoming involves not only the active use of prior knowledge, but the construction of knowledge as well. Cognitively, both readers and writers can be changed through their transactions with print. Revision, commonly thought as central to the writing process, is also evident during reading. As discussed previously, readers monitor their processing of print and engage in such revision strategies as reflecting, rereading, and reading on and returning, when meaning is disrupted.

Finally, although not typically perceived as such, readers as well as writers are impacted by context and purpose. As we saw with the homebuyer–burglar demonstration in Table 7.6, the context and purpose significantly impact the meanings generated by the reader. Both readers and writers are cognizant of for whom and for what text meanings are constructed. When we turn our attention to the developmental dimension of literacy, we will see how the linguistic and cognitive similarities between the two processes support and enhance literacy learning.

CONCLUSIONS

To a large extent, the cognitive dimension of literacy involves the mind transacting with written discourse. In this transaction, both LTM and STM systems, perception, and various strategies are employed for the creation of meaning. Impacting the creation of meaning are such relational factors as the correspondence between the background of the reader and that of the writer, or the correspondence between the language of the reader and the language of the writer. In a sense, it is within the mind that the linguistic and cognitive aspects of literacy meet. However, as shown in the following two chapters, the mind is not alone on an island. Rather, the mind is embedded within a variety of social groups, and these groups impact the nature of literacy.

THE COGNITIVE DIMENSION OF THE LITERACY STORY

We now return our attention to the literacy story presented in Table 1.2 and Fig. 1.2 earlier in this book. At this point in our analysis, we want to understand what occurred cognitively as I attempted to understand and use the information contained in the *Microref Quick Reference Guide* (Microref Systems Inc., 1988). The object of study here is the mind as it interacts with the text and makes meaning. As indicated in the story, I did have experience with using IBM software programs; however, I had never used WordPerfect and had limited experience with computer guides. Therefore, my background was helpful only to the extent that WordPerfect paralleled that of other programs with which I was familiar. Unfortunately, there was little overlap between my prior knowledge and the information presented in the guide. Additionally, I tend to dislike and therefore avoid reading and following directions. Typically, I rely on accompanying pictures or illustrations and attempt to override or avoid the directions as much as possible. Such reading behavior of procedural texts—that is, instructions—is more common than we might like to think (Bovair & Kieras, 1996).

All of these factors were brought to bear as I read the guide. Because my purpose for reading was to use WordPerfect to write an academic paper (i.e., there was a need to understand, recall, and use the information), I attempted to engage in a close reading of the text. Perceptually, this meant that I "picked up" as much print as possible and read more slowly than I might in other contexts with other texts.

This close reading was reinforced by the linguistic dimension in that directions typically do not develop or elaborate on the procedures presented. Rather, each step is intended to provide just that amount of information necessary for the reader to complete the task and then to proceed to the subsequent step. The strategy of reading on when something is not understood is far less likely to be effective with directions than with a short story or a history text. If Step 2 is not understood, for example, it is most likely that Step 3, even if understood, cannot be successfully executed because it depends on the previous step having been accomplished. Additionally, the idea of simply skipping a step not understood is much more problematic than skipping a sentence or two in a short story. In directions, all subsequent steps are predicated on having successfully implemented the previous steps. Typically, a single sentence within a story does not have that much impact.

Because of my lack of background knowledge and the limited strategies that I was able to employ (e.g., skip it, read on and return), I had little success in generating meaning from the text. Reading blocks were frequent, and tunnel vision, the overloading of STM, was my constant companion as I struggled to understand how to use the program. I eventually had to abandon my own internal resources and sought help from an outside source, a more knowledgeable and experienced colleague.

IV

The Sociocultural Dimension of Literacy

9

Understanding Literacy as Social Practices

In the previous chapters on the linguistic and cognitive dimensions of literacy, the focus was on the text—code breaker, and the mind—meaning maker. To a significant extent, we found that both the linguistic and the cognitive dimensions are defined or framed by commonalities or universals. Within any language, a common set of rules governs the operation of the various systems and guides the linguistic forms that texts can take on. Language users within a discourse community have a shared understanding of these rules and are guided by them as texts are encountered or "cracked." Similarly, language users employ common mental processes and strategies as they construct meanings within a particular written form. The linguistic and cognitive dimensions of literacy, therefore, tend to highlight that which is the same across and among texts, readers, and writers. This is not to say that variation is not part of these dimensions. Variations in the systems of language—dialects—and variations in how texts are constructed based on the language user's purpose and background were addressed. However, these are variations on a theme rather than entirely new songs.

Limiting our understanding of literacy to the linguistic and cognitive dimensions, however, is to overlook the social dimension of written language. It "situates literacy in the individual person, rather than in the society of which that person is a member. As such, it obscures the multiple ways in which reading, writing, and language interrelate with the workings of power and desire in social life" (Gee, 1990, p. 27). Literacy comes to be perceived as a set of autonomous, universal features and abilities divorced from use in the world (Baron, 1992, 1997; Elster, 2003; Scribner & Cole, 1981; Street, 1984).

A sociocultural examination of literacy shifts our attention from decontextualized texts, skills, and individuals to literacy events, literacy practices, and literacy performances. Literacy becomes literacies and discourse becomes d/Discourses (Gee, 1996, 1999). As discussed earlier, a literacy event is any instance of human action that involves the use of print (Harste, Woodward, & Burke, 1984; Heath,

1982a, 1982b). Literacy practices are repeated or patterned literacy events or oc-currences within a particular community or social group (Reder, 1994; Scribner & Cole, 1981). Finally, literacy performances reflect the acting out of identity through literacy events and practices (Blackburn, 2003; Elster, 2003). Reading and writing, therefore, are not simply individual acts of thought and language, but also patterned social acts of the group. Literacy occurs not simply because an individual possesses and applies the necessary linguistic and cognitive strategies and processes, but also because group membership requires it (Devine, 1994). Luke (1995, 1998), in fact, has argued that there are no private acts of literacy, only social ones. Therefore, the way in which literacy is used or performed by the participants within a particular social configuration (i.e., literacy practices) reflects the very nature of the group and the group's position within the society.

The intent in this chapter and the next is to understand both texts and literacy users within the social world. In particular, I examine the nature of literacy events, practices, and performances used by various social groups to mediate their interac-tions with the world as well as how various social groups use literacy to produce, consume, maintain, and control knowledge. In this chapter, the nature of literacy practices of social groups is examined—that is, the individual as text user. In the chapter to follow, the focus is on power, authority, and written discourse—that is, the individual as text critic. A word of caution, however, is warranted before we continue.

Many advocates of a sociocultural view of literacy have tended to dismiss the linguistic and cognitive dimensions of literacy. In what might be considered at times to be a rather reductionistic stance, the group becomes the primary if not the exclusive domain of study. As Fig. 1.1 illustrated, the conceptual framework being employed in this book views the group as only one dimension of literacy. Although the group is powerful in nature, care must be taken not to substitute one limited understanding of literacy for another. Literacy events, practices, and performances may vary from group to group, but the linguistic and cognitive dimensions are very much part and parcel of these varied uses of literacy.

EXAMINING OUR OWN LITERACY PRACTICES

In attempting to understand literacy events, practices, and performances within a sociocultural perspective, there is often the tendency to focus on how "others" use literacy. These others are identified by their culture, socioeconomic status, gender, or any number of characteristics that are perceived as being distinct and different. Although not intended, such study of others may privilege the viewers' position as normative and blinds them to the sociocultural basis for their own literacy behaviors. This is especially true when the observers are from dominant groups in American society: European Americans, men, or the middle class. Dominant groups too often perceive their own behaviors and beliefs as the way it's "supposed to be," as unbiased, objective, universal, or at least as "American." The behaviors and beliefs of outsiders, on the other hand, are seen as multicultural, ethnic, or

TABLE 9.1

Types and Uses of Literacy

Type	Definition	Examples
Daily Living	Literacy activities that relate to ordinary family life, including obtaining food, maintaining shelter and health, finances, shopping, paying bills, caring for the children	Shopping lists, bills and checks, budgets
Entertainment or Recreational	Literacy activities that relate to passing the time in an enjoyable or interesting manner	Television guides, theater listings and reviews, magazines, newspapers, books
Spiritual	Literacy activities related to worship or metaphysical endeavors	Hymnals, bulletins and newsletters, scripture reading, order of the service guidelines
Work-related	Literacy activities related to one's place of employment	Office memorandums, order forms, applications
Social-interactional	Literacy activities related to written communication with friends or relatives; literacy used to build and maintain social relationships	Friendly letters, e-mail, greeting cards
Educational	Literacy activities related to increasing one's knowledge	Textbooks, reports and papers, "how to" materials, school forms
News-related	Literacy activities to gain information about local, state, regional, national, or world events or third parties	Newspapers and news magazines, flyers and bulletins
Archival-related	Literacy activities related to materials that are saved and referred to when necessary	Report cards, birth certificates, paid bills, insurance policies, telephone numbers, leases

hyphenated (e.g., African American, Asian American). This is quite similar to speakers of the power form of the language perceiving others as speaking a dialect but not themselves.

To avoid this blindness, we begin this chapter with an examination of our own literacy practices. Take a moment and list the last ten significant interactions that you have had with print. These interactions may involve reading, writing, or both. Significance should be determined by the importance of the activity to you, not by the duration of the literacy event. After listing the events, determine the primary purpose(s) for each. Table 9.1 contains a list of possible purposes that has been

TABLE 9.2
Group Membership and Social Identity

Culture: The individual's perceived view of the behaviors, values, norms, and ways of knowing that are appropriate to his or her ethnic group together with the value and affect that are attached to these features

Socioeconomic Status/Class: Lower, middle, upper; working class; professional class; blue collar, white collar

Gender: The ways in which masculinity and femininity are constructed, shaped, and expressed in society

Organizations: Volunteer membership in various groups, e.g., political, social clubs, sports teams, educational, professional/occupational, etc.

Occupation: Place of work; white collar, blue collar

Religion: Membership in a group focused on spiritual growth and development

Psychological Groups: Cognitive identification with a particular group, such as yuppie, buppie, guppie, jock, nerd, brain, school boy/girl

Nationality: The status of belonging to a nation by birth or naturalization

Family: Membership in a group based on lineage, legal relationships, and/or mutual affection and intimacy

Age: Membership in a group based on chronological time, e.g., infants, children, adolescents, middle aged, elderly

Sexual Orientation: Physical and/or emotional attraction to a particular sex, e.g., gay, lesbian, straight, bisexual

synthesized from a number of studies in this area (A. Anderson & Stokes, 1984; Heath, 1983; Taylor & Dorsey-Gaines, 1988). Feel free to add your own purposes if the ones listed do not address some of your literacy activities.

After you have identified the purpose(s) for each literacy activity, consider what social group membership impacted or caused your use of print in this manner. Various social groups are identified and defined in Table 9.2. These social groups have been taken, for the most part, from Ferdman (1990). As we will shortly see, however, both the identification and definition of identities operate on contested terrain and identities frequently intersect. With this in mind, you may include additional groups or modify definitions as necessary.

As I was writing this chapter, I also listed ten significant literacy events, their purpose, and the influence of various social groups. This list, identified as the literacy events of a professor, is shown in Table 9.3. In addition, I asked an artist to do the same. Table 9.4 illustrates her literacy events. To better compare and contrast the use of literacy by these two individuals, their events are summarized in Table 9.5. The *P's* represent my own use of literacy; the *A's* are those of the artist. Before reading on, compare and contrast your own literacy use with those represented in Tables 9.3, 9.4, and 9.5.

TABLE 9.3

Significant Literacy Events of a Professor

Literacy Event	Purpose	Social Group
1. Reading a brochure on how to use my frequent flyer mileage for a trip to California	Entertainment or recreational	Socioeconomic status/ class Family
2. Reading articles related to the sociocultural dimension of literacy	Work-related educational	Occupation
3. Reading a road map, road signs, ferry schedules, on a vacation to Nantucket	Entertainment or recreational	Socioeconomic status/class
4. Reading church bulletin, mass program, hymns, and chants	Spiritual	Religion culture
5. Preparing class syllabi, reviewing articles for use in course reading packets, planning activities for the first week of classes	Work-related educational	Occupation
6. Reading a book about the history of New York City	Entertainment or recreational educational	Psychological groups
7. Writing a proposal with a colleague for the Penn Ethnography Conference	Work-related educational	Occupation
0. Reading and evaluating American Educational Research Association conference proposals	Work-related educational	Occupation Organizations
9. Reading the New York Times in the morning before going to work	News-related Entertainment or recreational	Socioeconomic status/class Psychological groups
10. Reading and responding to e-mail	Work-related social-interactional	Occupation Organizations family

If we return to the literacy events and practices of the professor and the artist, we can readily discern various configurations in their use of literacy and the impact of various social groups on this use. In Table 9.5, the total row at the bottom of the table summarizes the various purposes to which literacy was put. The professor's significant literacy events tended to be for entertainment, work, and educational purposes. As indicated in Table 9.3, the relation between work and education is a symbiotic one; each supports and enhances the other. For

TABLE 9.4

Significant Literacy Events of an Artist

Literacy Event	Purpose	Social Group
1. Reading a book about the Hmong	Entertainment or recreational	Culture Occupation
2. Reading the art section of the *New York Times*	Entertainment or recreational Educational	Occupation
3. Reading the food section of the *New York Times*	Daily living or educational	Culture
4. Reading a fashion magazine	Daily living entertainment or recreational social-interactional	Gender
5. Reading essays and interviews on visual artists	Work-related educational	Occupation
6. Reading the culture section of the *Village Voice*	Entertainment or recreational social-interactional	Culture
7. Reading the class enrollment form	Work-related	Occupation
8. Reading *New Yorker* articles about President Clinton	News-related social-interactional	Gender Nationality
9. Reading the book, *Art in America*	Entertainment or recreational Educational	Occupation Nationality
10. Reading an article on how to set up an arc lamp	Work-related educational	Occupation

example, preparing class syllabi is a work-related use of literacy. However, the very process of planning a course involves reading, writing, and thinking about various issues related to course content. This planning in turn frequently results in new knowledge and therefore becomes an educational experience in and of itself. Similarly, the reading of a book on the history of New York City was done for enjoyment but was educational as well. It is also informative to note the infrequent use of literacy for particular purposes. Literacy was only occasionally employed for spiritual, social-interactional, and news-related purposes and was not viewed as significant in daily living, sexual orientation, or for archival purposes.

For the artist, literacy also served noteworthy entertainment and educational functions. Because the artist was an adjunct faculty member at a local university, the similarity between the artist's and professor's use of literacy for educational purposes is not all that surprising; both share membership in a particular community (i.e., a university). However, in contrast to the professor, the artist did not always link her educational literacy experiences to the workplace. Interestingly, the artist

TABLE 9.5

The Interaction Between Literacy Use and Social Identity: Two Language Users

Social Identity	Purpose							
	Daily Living	Entertainment or Recreational	Spiritual	Work-Related	Social	Educational	News-Related	Total
Culture	A: 1	A: 2	P: 1		A: 1	A: 1		P: 1 / A: 5
Class		P: 3			A: 1		P: 1	P: 4 / A: 0
Gender	A: 1	A: 1			A: 2		A: 1	P: 0 / A: 5
Organizations				P: 2		P: 1		P: 3 / A: 0
Occupation		A: 3		P: 5 / A: 3		P: 4 / A: 4		P: 9 / A: 10
Religion			P: 1					P: 1 / A: 0
Psychological Groups		P: 2				P: 1	P: 1	P: 4 / A: 0
Nationality		A: 1			A: 1	A: 1	A: 1	P: 0 / A: 4
Family		P: 1			P: 1			P: 2 / A: 0
Total	**P: 0 / A: 2**	**P: 6 / A: 7**	**P: 2 / A: 0**	**P: 7 / A: 3**	**P: 1 / A: 4**	**P: 6 / A: 6**	**P: 2 / A: 2**	

Note. P represents professor; A represents artist.

said that she viewed her teaching at the university as her "job" and her artistic endeavors in her studio as her "work." This distinction between job and work was not made by the professor, who frequently saw his educational and work-related activities as intimately related and part of the same fabric. Other similarities between the artist and professor were their use of print for news-related purposes and their lack of print-based activities for archival functions.

In contrast to the professor, however, the artist made significant use of literacy for social-interactional purposes. In particular, she commented that one reason she read articles on current cultural and political events was because she knew they would be topics of discussion among her friends. Also in contrast to the professor, the artist had no significant literacy events related to spirituality and only two events serving daily living purposes. Additionally, whereas the professor's significant literacy events involved both reading and writing, the artist's were exclusively reading.

Although the variation in literacy use is evident between these two individuals, the differential impact of social groups to which they belong is even more apparent. The righthand column in Table 9.5 indicates the total number of times that a particular social group interacted with a use of print. The professor viewed his use of literacy as being significantly influenced by class and occupation. His frequent use of literacy for entertainment and recreational purposes was class related—he had the economic means to finance such activities—and print used for work and educational functions was based on his university occupation. Even the professor's employment of print related to his membership in various organizations was work related, as in reading conference proposals for the American Educational Research Association. Finally, as a recent California transplant to the East coast, the professor was interested in becoming a "New Yorker" and gaining a psychological orientation toward living and working in the city. This influenced his reading of the book about the history of New York City for entertainment and educational purposes, as well as his reading of the *New York Times*.

Except for the significant impact of her occupation, the artist saw herself as being influenced by memberships in very different groups. As a woman, she was particularly interested in the Clinton–Lewinsky incident. The artist noted that she had frequently discussed the topic with her female friends. Gender also influenced the artist's reading of fashion magazines and again served as a topic of discussion with her female friends. In contrast to the professor, the artist viewed her culture— Slavic American—as influencing her reading about the Hmong, the food section of the *New York Times*, and the culture section of the *Village Voice*. The artist's strong identification with her ethnicity served as a lens when she read about other cultures. She also noted her awareness of her nationality as a factor when reading about the Clinton–Lewinsky incident and the book *Art in America*. Finally, although reading a book about the Hmong was seemingly unrelated to her creative endeavors, the artist discussed how the text impacted her thinking by providing potential ideas for artistic expression.

Although the previous discussion was based on an informal self-assessment of literacy practices, it does demonstrate both the shared as well as different identities and literacy behaviors of two individuals. What follows is a more formal discussion of the issue and an examination of several studies that have explored the impact of identity on literacy practices, both function and form.

GROUP MEMBERSHIPS AND SOCIAL IDENTITIES

By our very nature, we are social beings; or, as Vygotsky (1978) observed, our minds are embedded within society. As previously demonstrated, inherent in our "beingness" is membership in various social groups. F. Smith (1988) referred to such membership as belonging to clubs. We all belong, for example, to cultural, socioeconomic, and family groups. We may be part of religious organizations and possibly hold memberships in various psychological groups, such as being a New Yorker. According to Ferdman (1990), our social identity consists of the totality of the various groups, many of which are represented in Table 9.2, of which we are members.

Each social group or community has its own set of guidelines for what is required to be a member in good standing. Put another way, membership has its price as well as its privileges. The group attempts to socialize—directly or indirectly, consciously or unconsciously—the individual into thinking and behaving in particular ways that are appropriate to the group's view of itself and its relationship with the broader society. These guidelines impact the individual's beliefs and behaviors, and they frame his or her interpretations of and interactions with others. The knowledge, values, and behaviors that an individual comes to reflect, therefore, are not simply the products of his or her own unique and independent psychological interactions with the world. They also are the products of interactions and experiences with the various significant social groups of which the individual is a member, as well as the groups' interactions and experiences with other groups in the world. It is for this reason that these various social groups have often been labeled as interpretive communities.

Because the individual belongs to a number of social networks—identities intersect—he or she typically has multiple frameworks for behaving and for constructing and understanding experiences. Madison Avenue advertisers have long known about such group identification. Their various "ad campaigns" often are focused on selling products and services to particular groups. Similarly, on television, the Lifetime station labels itself as "television for women" and programs its shows accordingly. Additionally, it is these very attempts at "selling" to particular groups that can also, in turn, mold the actual identities of these groups. These cultural texts reflect as well as create cultural norms.

It is important to remember that group ideologies may not be conscious or always explicitly stated to and by group members. In fact, it is just this lack of explicitness that makes these social frameworks and group norms so powerful;

often, the group's members are unaware of the source of their beliefs and behaviors. This is especially the case when the individual belongs to the society's dominant group(s). Because the beliefs of dominant groups so permeate society and because the individual may so seldom encounter alternative perspectives, he or she may come to view these beliefs not as socially constructed, but rather as normative or universal.

The values of any particular group do not, however, impact the individual's beliefs and behaviors in a straightforward, unilinear manner, nor are group values necessarily deterministic. The frameworks employed for transacting with or understanding any event are influenced by the event itself, the context in which the event evolves, and the frameworks privileged or favored by the individual within a particular setting. For example, an Eastern European-American Catholic woman belongs to at least the following groups: cultural (Slavic American), gender (female), religious (Catholic), and national (United States). Her views on such issues as abortion, state funding of religious schools, or the use of armed intervention by the United States in Middle Eastern conflicts may require her to privilege particular beliefs over others when there is a lack of congruence among group ideologies.

Identity, therefore, is dynamic, often context specific in nature, and constituted by numerous fuzzy borders between and among the various social groups in which the individual has membership (D. Hoffman, 1996). As observed by McDermott (1995), identities are hammered out on a daily and ongoing basis as the individual encounters the world. Identities and their corresponding behaviors are not predetermined but rather are actively constructed in social relationships (Buckingham & Sefton-Green, 1994). Similarly, not all individuals within a social group are identical in their beliefs and actions. No community is a monolith, and its members will differ to varying degrees in beliefs and actions. Because no community is an island unto itself, any individual may hold membership in numerous clubs, and at times there will be competition among the beliefs of these various social configurations.

Finally, social groups themselves are dynamic and evolving in nature. As any group's experiences with the world change, so too may the group's understanding of itself and the world. In fact, the way any nondominant group is perceived by and acted on by the dominant group—and the way the nondominant group has come to deal with such perceptions and behaviors—becomes part of the understandings of both groups (Reder, 1994). Therefore, in most cases, group identification provides an orienting framework for the individual's beliefs and behaviors, not a straitjacket. Table 9.6 summarizes the previous discussion concerning the nature of identity.

MULTIPLE LITERACIES, IDENTITIES, AND SOCIAL PRACTICES

Literacy practices are one expression of the knowledge, values, and behaviors of any group. Each group "has rules for socially interacting and sharing knowledge in literacy events" (Heath, 1982b, p. 50). Social groups sponsor or subsidize particular configurations of written language use and deny others (Brandt, 1998,

TABLE 9.6

The Nature of Social Identity

- Social identities serve as an orientation/lens for behaving and understanding.
- Social identities serve as a potential orientation; potentially variable, potentially context-dependent, potentially flexible.
- There can be as many differences within groups as there are between groups.
- Social identities can vary across space and time; may be contradictory and inconsistent.
- Social identities are "hammered out" and negotiated on an ongoing basis; identity is on the borderline and in process.
- We all belong to various social groups.
- We may privilege one group—social identity—over another within certain contexts or may consistently privilege one group over the others.

2001). Demonstrations of, and engagements with, sanctioned forms of literacy envelop the individual's interactions with the group. With time, experience, and apprenticeship, the literacy practices of any individual come to reflect group norms and values. That is, the individual's literacy behaviors or performances express the literacy practices of the various social groups of which the individual is a member. The individual's identities are constructed "within these discourses, and such constructions offer membership in communities that involve ways of believing, valuing, and speaking" (Rogers, 2002, p. 252).

As previously discussed, the individual typically holds membership in multiple groups or interpretative communities that is, has multiple social identities. Because these various memberships are accompanied by various literacy forms and functions, the individual may possess multiple literacies as well. The manner in which a nurse is required to use literacy as he cares for patients in a hospital, for example, differs significantly from the way he uses literacy as a member of an Evangelical Christian church. And, both literacies differ from that required to negotiate a home equity loan. Therefore, "literacy is not literacy is not literacy" (Hull & Schultz, 2001, p. 583), but varies in nature depending on the circumstances. The degree to which the individual is able to successfully negotiate the use of various literacies in these various contexts reflects group memberships, or the lack thereof, and the degree to which these multiple literacies have been developed within these groups (Rogers, 2002).

In an attempt to capture the notion of literacies, literacy practices, and group membership, Gee (1996) has distinguished between discourse and Discourse. Discourse, with a lower case *d*, is defined as a connected stretch of language that is unified (coherent) and meaningful to some social group. This view of discourse is similar to the way "text" was defined in chapter 2 when we explored the linguistic dimension of literacy. Discourse, with an upper case *D*, signifies the appropriate way to use discourse within a particular social setting and as part of a particular social group. It represents not only what is said, but also how it is expressed. As a form of behavior or action in the world, the Discourse of the individual always displays affiliation with, and characteristics of, a particular group. Discourse is always associated with "ways of thinking, believing, and valuing" (Rogers, 2002, p. 252) that are connected with group membership.

Literacy as a social practice has received increased attention during the last decade. This attention has focused on both the functions (purposes) and forms (linguistic characteristics) of group literacy activity. A. Anderson and Stokes (1984), for instance, studied the literacy events or practices displayed by three cultural groups (African American, Mexican American, and European American) in homes with preschool children. The focus in this research was on the various literacy functions, types, and uses, such as those depicted in Table 9.1. The examination of your own literacy practices, as well as the practices of the professor and the artist, highlighted such patterns. The actual linguistic form of the texts produced by particular groups and the relation of these forms to the cognitive and interactional demands made on the individuals involved in the literacy event have also received attention. Moss (1994), for example, examined the linguistic features of dialogic sermons within certain Evangelical African American churches.

Although the literacy practices of a number of different social configurations have been investigated, cultural groups have received special attention. Culture is a particularly powerful social framework that can significantly impact the nature of other social groups, such as gender and religious. Educational groups or institutions (e.g., schools) have received attention as well. Schools are a primary sponsor of literacy development and use within society and have developed their "own particular brand of learning" (Hull & Schultz, 2001, p. 577). The relationship between the function, form, and performance of school literacy events to the function, form, and performance of nonschool literacy events, especially those in the home or other institutions, has been of particular interest. It is an understanding of this intersection between home and school that holds the most promise for those of us interested in promoting literacy development among all students.

As we examine the literacy of various groups in this chapter, it is important to avoid stereotyping group characteristics, literacy practices, and literacy forms. The practices and forms displayed by any group should not be generalized to such an extent that within-group variations are obliterated. Variation is part of the human experience, and individual behavior is influenced by identities, contexts, and circumstances.

LITERACY IN SCHOOL AND OUT

Schools are a principal site for literacy sponsorship in U.S. society. Both adults and children expect that literacy will be formally taught, learned, and sustained throughout students' academic careers. As cultural sites of literacy activity, the

TABLE 9.7

Characteristics of School-Based Essay Texts

Explicitness:	Meanings are stated in a direct, overt, and unambiguous manner.
	Emphasis on truth value.
	Assume no shared knowledge between the reader and the writer; state information that may already be known.
	Important relationships to be signaled are those among sentences, not those among speakers or sentences and speakers.
Boundaries:	There are fixed distinctions between the reader and the writer; writer is expected to construct a coherent text that exists as an entity that is independent from the reader.
	Texts are read individually and independently; the reader is expected to process the text by him/herself.
Context:	Meanings are expected to stand on their own, without support from the immediate environment.
	Audience and author are fictionalized.
	Text transcends social and cultural differences; communicates logically, rationally, and dispassionately.
Ownership:	The text and its meanings are owned by the writer.
Cognition:	Promotes and requires abstract, logical, and decontextualized thinking; the ability to view text as an object of study.

schools have specific rules or norms for how language is to be used and how texts are to be formed. These rules and forms may affirm, build on, and extend the way in which language is used in the child's home; may require adaptation in language rules and forms; or may directly contradict home language patterns (Heath, 1983; Scollon & Scollon, 1981).

A common and privileged school literacy form or genre is that of the essay. Like all texts, there are specific characteristics that this type of discourse must fulfill and display. As indicated in Table 9.7, in school-based essays, meanings are stated in a direct, overt, and unambiguous manner. Typically, these texts are constructed as if there is no shared knowledge between reader and writer. This is the case even when the writer is fully aware that the reader is knowledgeable. In other contexts, such explicitness would, at best, be considered insensitive and rude and, at worst, condescending and arrogant (Gee, 1990).

The explicitness of meanings within essays reflects the fixed boundary between the reader and the writer often found in school-based literacy events. The writer is expected to construct a coherent text that exists as an entity independent from the reader. In the monologic structure of such essays, meanings are decontextualized in that they are to stand on their own without support from the immediate environment. In what Moss (1994) termed radical individualism, essay texts are to be processed

TABLE 9.8

Initiation–Reply–Evaluation Structure

Initiation:	Teacher initiates the IRE sequence by asking a question. In contrast to authentic questions, it is clear to all involved that the teacher knows the answers to the questions being asked.
Reply:	A student is then identified to respond or reply to the question.
Evaluation:	The teacher explicitly evaluates the adequacy of the response. Again, in contexts other than the classroom, it would be considered inappropriate for a questioner to openly evaluate the acceptability of a provided answer.

individually and independently; that is, the reader is expected to construct text meanings without assistance.

Finally, there is often the belief that essays by their very nature transcend social and cultural differences. Essays are to present their claims in a logical, rational, and dispassionate manner. This separation of text from culture is thought to require as well as promote abstract, logical, and decontextualized thinking. As is more fully developed shortly, those cultures without literacy or those communities that value other discourse forms may be perceived as having less civilized thinking. Once again, the form and function of literacy of dominant groups becomes linked with superior forms of thinking.

Not only does school-based discourse have a particular structure and content, but there are also rules for how students are to interact with such discourse. That is, there are regulations for school-based literacy performance. This is especially true in the early grades, when the classroom is highly focused on initial literacy teaching and learning. A central feature in classroom lessons is the initiation–reply–evaluation (IRE) sequence. Table 9.8 sets forth the essential characteristics of this mode of classroom interaction and performance. As documented by Cazden (1988, 2001) and Heath (1983), the teacher initiates the IRE sequence by asking a question. In contrast to authentic questions, it is clear to all involved that the teacher knows the answers to the questions being asked. A student is then identified to respond or reply to the question, and the teacher explicitly evaluates the adequacy of the response. Again, in contexts other than the classroom, it would be considered inappropriate for a questioner to openly evaluate the acceptability of a provided answer.

As with norms for school texts and lessons, there are also rules for what text meanings are to be the focus of attention within the IRE lesson sequence. In the early grades, much attention is given to the asking and answering of "what" questions (e.g., What did the boy do after he planted the seed?). Selective attention is given to the segmentation of items and meanings in the text as they are discussed and analyzed. Students are expected to listen as an audience to the questions and answers and then to respond and display what they know when called on. This display of knowledge, however, may be limited to the factual meanings in the text that the teacher has solicited; the incorporation of nonschool experiences into the answers is often discouraged.

Of course, all texts, whether located in or out of school, have their own codes and conventions for how they are to be constructed, interacted with, and understood (Smagorinsky, 2001). Texts are products of group activities and as such reflect the social and literacy practices of the groups that created them. However, as we shall see, because of the power and dominance of the schools in regard to literacy learning, the discourse practices of the classroom often come to be viewed as the norm. Alternate practices are conceived as deviant as well as deficient in nature.

Regardless of their cultural identity or socioeconomic status, most children in the United States enter school having encountered numerous literacy events within the home. Few children are initiated into the schooling experience without some knowledge of literacy. The nature of these events and the degree to which the children have directly participated in them, however, may vary. That is, there may not be a one-to-one correspondence between the form and function of literacy performed in the home and that found in the classroom setting. Heath (1982a, 1982b, 1983) examined language use in three different settings in the southeastern United States: Maintown, Roadville, and Trackton. Maintown was a mainstream, middle-class, school-oriented community. Both African Americans and European Americans resided in Maintown. Roadville was a European American, working-class mill community, and Trackton was an African American, working-class mill community.

In terms of school literacy development and school success, there were distinct differences among these three groups. The Maintown children were the most successful, whereas the Roadville children performed well in the primary grades and then began to fall behind during the intermediate years. The Trackton children experienced failure almost from the very beginning.

The reason for the differential impact of school instruction on literacy growth can be found, according to Heath (1983), in the "ways with words" in the home settings. To a large extent, the manner in which literacy was used in Maintown homes paralleled that found in the school. In this case, school literacy lessons built directly on the home literacy events experienced by the child. For example, in Maintown homes, the mother and child book-reading episodes displayed the IRE sequence found in school lessons. The adult typically asked "what" questions, focused on and labeled individual items in the illustrations with attention to particular features, and insisted that the child display the facts known about the text. Throughout the reading, the adult engaged in a running commentary on past and current meanings. Given these experiences, the children from Maintown came to school already knowing how to interact with print in a way that the school would value. In effect, the children had been socialized at home to interact with language in a manner that paralleled that of formal school instruction. Doing or performing literacy in the home was replicated in the school context.

Many of the home literacy events encountered by the Roadville children were similar to those of the Maintown children. This was particularly the case with the frequent use of "what" questions. Parents in this community saw their role as teaching their children to talk, and during initial book-reading experiences they focused on such conventions as letters, numbers, and the names of items pictured in books. Children were encouraged to engage with the books through questions that focused on these conventions and items and to display their knowledge by "doing it right." The adults did not, however, as was done in Maintown, provide a running commentary of responses as they read to the children. At around 3.5 years of age, the orientation changed. At this point, the children were restrained from responding. Instead, adults insisted that the children sit and listen quietly as the adults read stories to them. It was not expected that the children were able to contribute knowledge to the literacy event or to link the event to other aspects of the environment.

During the early school years, when school literacy practices and those of the home were in parallel, the Roadville children made progress in their literacy development. They did, however, encounter difficulties responding to affective questions (e.g., What did you like?) or alternative responses (e.g., What would you have done?). This difficulty appears to be directly related to the fact that in home literacy events, such interactions were not present—and in some cases, they were actually discouraged. After third grade, as the focus of the school literacy curriculum shifted to linking book knowledge to other experiences and to more active participation by the students in general, the Roadville children began to fall behind. In this setting, school literacy instruction and successful literacy learning required adaptation in language rules and forms that the children had encountered and developed in the home.

For the Trackton children, home literacy events were the most distant from literacy events within the school. In general, there was a lack of books or book-based items or games within the home. The adults tended not to read to or with their children. When adults did read, they typically did so as a group; reading was a social event. The children in these homes learned to tell stories by creating a context and inviting the audience to participate. The structure of these stories was vastly different from that found in schools. There was an absence of formulaic beginnings—for example, "Once upon a time"—and endings were open-ended. Stories did not conclude until the audience shifted its attention to something or someone else. Consequently, the teller of the story was required to be assertive in gaining the floor and then, to maintain attention and involvement, was required to invite the audience to respond to and evaluate the unfolding story.

As Trackton adults interacted with their children, they also tended not to segment or highlight aspects of the environment through such behaviors as pointing, labeling, or asking "what" questions. Adults did not request or demonstrate the features that were used or shared when comparing one item or event to another. Rather than having the child decontextualize meanings, the adults heavily contextualized the meanings. Adults did, however, ask their children analogical questions that called for nonspecific comparisons of one thing with another. This resulted in children who were able to make comparisons but who were not capable of specifying the features on which such comparisons were grounded.

Upon entering school, the Trackton children immediately encountered unfamiliar types of questions and behavioral demands. They were asked to respond to "what" questions, to isolate and identify items, to label features, and in general to respond to an array of questions about what has been read. Without explicit instruction for how these new linguistic and content demands were to be met, the children failed to learn the social interactional rules and the content under consideration. It was not uncommon for the Trackton students to link book events with their personal experiences and to provide affective responses. However, these links and responses were not always requested or valued during early literacy instruction. Such responses were viewed as being "off track." In contrast to the Maintown students, who found school literacy events to be familiar, and the Roadville students, who initially were able to connect to school instruction, the Trackton students were out of sync from the first day, because school language use directly contradicted that of their homes.

In their work with Athabaskan Native Americans living in Northern Canada and Alaska, Scollon and Scollon (1981) found similar conflicts between home and school discourse patterns. Athabaskans tend not to express their views on a topic unless they first are aware of the views of their audience. Children are not to display knowledge to adults but rather to observe and learn from their superiors. In typical school literacy lessons, however, children are frequently requested and expected to display their knowledge and views. This expectation runs counter to cultural and discourse rules of Athabaskan children. Their response in such situations often is to remain silent. In a sense, these children cannot successfully participate in such lessons unless they take on norms and values that are in direct conflict with their own, their families,' and their culture's. Learning school literacy becomes possible only by unlearning the home culture.

The inability or unwillingness to display knowledge that is shared among students and teachers is not just related to early literacy learning contexts or to nonmainstream students. Such situations can emerge whenever learners find themselves within new environments. In a graduate class that I teach, students are engaged in a research study in which they examine their own miscues made when reading an unfamiliar short story. As the instructor, I take them through a series of steps on how to engage in the reading and how to identify and mark their various miscues, such as substitutions, insertions, and deletions. Students are then asked to explore a particular pattern of miscues, such as when they do and do not correct miscues. I also provide them with a number of such patterns that they may find interesting to examine. Finally, when students present their findings in a research paper, the issues that need to be addressed, such as describing the reader, the conditions under which the reading took place, and how the data were analyzed and interpreted, are identified. Much of this process reflects my understanding of what it means to "do research" as well as the guidelines set forth in the *Publication Manual of the American Psychological Association* (APA, 2001).

Interestingly, when writing the paper, many students fail to elaborate on or even address certain issues. This is particularly the case when students discuss how miscues were collected, marked, and coded. Even though they have been explicitly asked to do so, because the students are fully aware that I know how they collected, marked, and coded their miscues—I taught them how to do it—they fail to display this information. They either ignore these issues altogether or provide only the sketchiest of descriptions. When I ask them why this information was not provided, given my explicit instructions to do so, they readily tell me that I already knew what they did. Why should they discuss information that was already shared? Like the Trackton students, my students entered into a new discourse community—that of researchers—and struggled with both the functions and forms of this new community.

Heath (1983) suggested that in meeting the needs of both the Roadville and Trackton students, the schools need to build on and extend the abilities that the children of both communities bring to the classroom. For the Roadville children, this might mean teaching them how to apply their labeling abilities to other domains besides books and how to assume both exhibitor and questioner roles. Additionally, Roadville students need to reexperience what it means to be interactive with book meanings. For the Trackton students, who face difficulty from the first day of school, Heath suggested that students be taught the specific basis for making links among items or events. They must also learn to recount factual events in a straightforward, time-sequenced manner.

In a related study, A. Anderson and Stokes (1984) examined literacy use within the homes of three working-class ethnic communities in San Diego: European Americans, African Americans, and Mexican Americans. All homes had at least one preschooler. The focus of the research was to document the types, frequency, and duration of literacy activities that the children encountered within the home environment. The types of literacy events were classified by domain, which are largely reflected in the categories found in Table 9.1. One additional category, however, was included: literacy techniques and skills. This category represented those times when the focus of the literacy activity was explicitly on the teaching and learning of particular literacy skills.

Although A. Anderson and Stokes (1984) found different patterns of literacy across the domains, only four were statistically significant: daily living, entertainment, religion, and literacy techniques. African American families tended to use literacy more frequently for daily living and religious purposes than did European Americans and Mexican Americans. European Americans were most likely to use print to investigate what entertainment was available (e.g., using a television guide) and most likely to initiate literacy instruction with their preschoolers.

In contrast, the African American and Mexican American families usually waited for the preschool child to initiate literacy instruction. Interestingly, however, when children in the African American and Mexican American homes did initiate literacy interactions, they tended to last longer than in the European American homes. In general, and perhaps surprisingly, book reading represented a minor activity across all ethnic groups and the IRE sequence within this domain represented only a portion of the parent–child interaction. Finally, although European Americans were more likely to engage in activities that involved print than the other two groups, they did not actually spend more time involved with print. Children in these families may see a greater frequency of reading and writing, but the duration of these activities is not as long as those in the African American and Mexican American families.

Homes are not the only environment in which literacy may be used in a manner that differs from that found in the schools. In a study of literacy events within African American churches, Moss (1994, 2001) examined the form and function of sermons. For the most part, these sermons were based on written discourse. In contrast to school-based essays, the discourses of the sermons did not represent or function as independent entities. Rather, sermons had a dialogic quality and were created and sustained through a collaboration between the minister and the congregation. Therefore, there was not a fixed boundary between the minister and the congregants. In fact, the active participation and contributions of the congregants were needed to complete the text.

Similar to what was found in the homes of the Trackton families, the sermons were also heavily contextualized. The pastor sought to build community through the involvement of the believers. References were made to both current and historical events of relevance to the African American fellowship. According to Moss (1994, 2001), these references served to lessen the distance between the pastor and the worshipers. It was through the sermon itself that the pastor attempted to demonstrate that he was not above or beyond the worshipers, but rather one with them.

Within an Israeli Orthodox Jewish context, Elster (2003) has documented similarly different understandings of, and interactions with, sacred texts from those commonly found in secular schools. For the most part, the texts under study are restricted to the *Torah* and *Talmud*, are continually and orally reread and studied, and are regulatory in their function. That is, the texts seek to impact moral behavior and spiritual aspirations. The ritual oral reading of the *Torah* scroll is to be accomplished without "deviation from the words of the written text" (p. 674). Secular schools, in contrast, involve the reading of a continually evolving variety of texts reflecting a variety of functions. Oral reading, although a strategy used in early reading instruction, seldom continues into the upper grades. And, miscues—that is, deviations—at least as understood in the previous chapter, are a natural part of the reading process.

Such an emphasis on exact or accurate readings occur within the context of U.S. religious communities as well. I recently taught a graduate psycholinguistics course for classroom teachers, of whom several were Orthodox Jews. We had been examining the miscues of adult proficient readers and the tendency for all readers to make miscues and for these miscues to maintain the author's meaning. Almost as an aside, one Orthodox teacher commented that such miscues were fine when reading secular texts, but would be considered "sacrilegious" if they occurred during the reading of the *Torah*. Similarly, I have been at religious services conducted by Catholic Benedictine monks when miscues occur in the individual oral reading of particular sacred passages. In such circumstances, the Benedictine doing the reading asked the religious community's forgiveness for his error. Regardless of what the community of psycholinguists might believe about the "naturalness" of miscues, many religious communities have a much different understanding of this phenomenon.

It is important to note that the forms and functions of the written discourse in these various communities are not deficient in nature. The forms and functions simply reflect different rules and norms for the use of particular written texts in particular contexts by particular discourse communities. It is critical that teachers are sensitive to the ways of literacy knowing that children bring with them into the classroom. Ultimately, it is on these ways that teachers will build new literacy learnings and understandings. Rather than valuing middle-class literacy norms as cultural capital and all other norms as insufficient or even as barriers to literacy development, teachers must value and extend literacy forms and functions in all of their children. I have more to say about the teaching and learning implications in chapter 12.

Care should also be taken, however, not to automatically assume that children of color or from low-income communities will automatically reflect nonschool literacy norms. This may or may not be the case. In an interesting examination of literacy use among twenty poor, inner-city families, Purcell-Gates (1996; Purcell-Gates, L'Allier, & Smith, 1995) found great variation. The families represented a range of ethnicities—European American, African American, Latino/a American, Asian American—as well as a range of literacy use and frequency. In the homes that Purcell-Gates labeled high-literacy families, literacy use permeated the lives of the participants. Print material, such as storybooks, religious materials, and newspapers, abounded. Literacy was used not only for entertainment but also involved storybook reading between parent and child and the direct teaching of literacy conventions.

In contrast, there was a tendency among low-literacy families to use literacy for entertainment—usually related to television viewing—and daily living, such as reading ingredients for a recipe. When storybooks and writing materials were available, they were seldom utilized. On average, the low-literacy families engaged in literacy once every 3 hours. This is in contrast to 2.5 literacy events per hour for the high-literacy families. In total, the high-literacy families engaged in literacy eight times more often than the low-literacy families. Purcell-Gates concludes by arguing that socioeconomics is not a very reliable variable on which to predict home literacy use or preschooler literacy preparation.

Farr (1994) made similar observations in her work with Mexican American immigrant families living in Chicago. For the most part, the adults had limited formal education and encountered English as a second language. Although few of the immigrants in this particular community brought Spanish literacy abilities with them when they came to the United States, they soon developed the motivation to learn and use literacy, especially writing. For the most part, these literacy abilities were developed outside of formal schooling. The knowledge of the writing system was passed on from trusted friends. Men in particular learned to write in this informal way—called Lirico—so that they could communicate with their families in Mexico. In fact, the men usually learned to write first and often did not see their decoding abilities as reading. For them, in contrast to writing, reading was something that was learned formally in school. When the need to read arose on the job, the men relied heavily on the use of their background knowledge. They would identify words known and then supplement any gaps with their on-the-job experiences.

Within this Mexican American community, literacy was viewed as a community rather than as an individual resource, and it was shared among those who were and were not literate. This sociocultural understanding is in contrast to school notions of literacy that emphasize individual and independent acquisition and the display of cognitive abilities and formal teaching and learning. In fact, Farr (1994) noted that adults did not respond positively to educational programs that emphasized individual accomplishments over family relationships or other community networks. In such contexts, there frequently was a reluctance to exhibit literacy knowledge because of a concern for others. This reluctance to demonstrate individual abilities is reminiscent of the Athabaskan Native Americans previously discussed (Scollon & Scollon, 1981). Therefore, although the Mexican American community clearly valued written discourse and demonstrated literacy use to their children on a regular basis, the norms were not always aligned with those of the schools.

All of this, however, is not to say that economics and social class are unrelated to literacy use and its development. Neuman and Celano (2001) explored the availability of, or access to, print in two low-income and two middle-income urban communities. Their focus was not so much on how people in these communities used print, but rather on what print was actually on hand in the social and physical environment beyond the home. Perhaps not surprisingly, the disparities in both the amount and quality of print available between the low-income and middle-income communities were profound.

In the lower-income neighborhoods, there were relatively few children's books, magazines, comics, etc., available in such local businesses as drug stores, grocery stores, and bodegas. Coloring books tended to predominate. Although environmental print—that is, street signs, product labels, store signs—was far more plentiful than in the middle-class communities, much of it was frequently difficult to read. Many signs lacked the use of color, shapes, and pictures that children might use to "decode" the print and oftentimes the print was covered with graffiti. Neuman and Celano (2001) also documented the public places, such as restaurants, coffee shops, public and school libraries, where reading might take place. Many of the eating establishments in the lower-income neighborhoods were not conducive to reading. Take-out orders were common, seating was uncomfortable and used primarily for waiting, and employees encouraged a quick turnover of customers. Libraries, both public and school, were limited in the quantity and quality of reading materials. Materials were frequently in poor condition and library hours were limited. Trained and experienced librarians typically did not staff the libraries.

The amount and quality of print available to individuals living in the middle-class communities were radically different. Local businesses contained a great variety of print resources, both in terms of the kinds of reading materials sold and the number of titles available. Environmental print, although less plentiful, was easier to read due to the use of pictures, shapes, and color. In the middle-income communities, there were also numerous sites that encouraged reading. Restaurants and coffee shops afforded customers comfortable, well-lit, and welcoming environments in which to read. Newsstands were usually located directly outside of the eating establishments and customers frequently purchased newspapers and magazines before entering. Reading for long periods of time was commonplace and waitresses intruded only when requested by the diner. School and public libraries contained far more reading materials in terms of kind—books, magazines, newspapers—choice, and quality. Staffing was usually by certified and experienced librarians. Unfortunately, such disparities in the quality of print experiences and environments based on socioeconomics too often continue within the schools (Duke, 2000).

As these various studies clearly document, literacy is intimately woven into the very fabric of daily life in most communities within the United States. The relationship between home and community literacy use, and that of the school, may not always be an easy one. Researchers such as Heath (1982a, 1982b, 1983), Henson and Gilles (2003), and Comber (2000) have suggested a number of ways in which teachers can help children enter the discourse community of the schools. A mismatch between home and school, however, need not necessarily lead to difficulties in literacy development. Other avenues exist. Schieffelin and Cochran-Smith (1984) investigated home literacy use in three very different contexts: a Philadelphia multiethnic, middle-class, school-oriented community; a nonliterate community in Papua New Guinea; and working-class Sino-Vietnamese families in Philadelphia. The forms and functions of literacy use, regardless of ethnicity, of the middle-class community were largely similar to the Maintown families studied by Heath. What is of interest here is the literacy development of the two communities in which literacy use did not reflect that of the schools and the factors that contributed or distracted from this development.

In Papua New Guinea, literacy was introduced to a largely nonliterate society by Christian missionaries. The focus of literacy instruction was on learning to read religious texts, including the *Bible*. Writing was not emphasized; nor was literacy connected to other aspects of daily life within the community. Additionally, a government boarding school for older children existed. After 5 years of literacy classes, there was little literacy use within the villages. Except for those with strong missionary interests, most villagers did not perceive literacy as relevant to their lives.

Even more interesting was the impact of literacy on the configuration of village life. For those adults who had learned literacy for religious purposes, literacy tended to separate them from traditional Papua New Guinea ways. Because the mission was located at some distance from the village, a great deal of time was spent traveling to and from the site, as well as engaging in the activities at the mission. This resulted in greater gardening and other food-collecting activity responsibilities for those adults who stayed behind. Given that literacy was viewed as an adult activity, parents tended not to engage or encourage literacy interests on the part of the children. Literacy engagements were typically initiated by the children, as parents did not want their children handling literacy materials because they were in short supply, highly valued, and viewed as being for adults.

There was also a discontinuity between parent–child oral and written language interactions. Parental requests for the naming and labeling of objects in the environment were not part of this community's oral language development pattern. However, during the few times when adults and children did interact with print, there was a tendency for both the child and adult to name objects in the illustrations. Consequently, there did not exist oral discourse patterns in parent–child interactions that were built on and extended during joint book-related activities. The interactions in the two settings were significantly different.

The lack of home literacy use as a part of daily living need not necessarily serve as a barrier to child literacy learning. In a community of Chinese Americans from Vietnam living in west Philadelphia, some literacy artifacts, such as books, magazines, and newspapers—written in Chinese but not in English—were present in the homes. For the most part, however, these homes were not literate environments. There was no evidence of joint book-related activities between parent and child, nor was there significant home instruction in written Chinese. Additionally, because many of the adults were not proficient in spoken English, parent–child interaction in the language of the school was absent. The children of these families did, however, successfully learn both spoken and written English.

The literacy success among the children in this community was, in part, due to the ability of the children to develop a range of social relationships outside of the family network to support their literacy needs. Because the children in these families were the only proficient users of spoken English, they frequently were relied on to translate, negotiate, and mediate their parents' interactions with various institutions. As noted by Schieffelin and Cochran-Smith (1984), this responsibility resulted in a literacy role reversal. It was the young children who facilitated their parents' entrance into a new society, "a role usually restricted to parents in English-speaking families" (p. 15). The child's development of English literacy, therefore, became critical to the survival of the family.

These literacy-learning examples serve as a much needed reminder that there are many paths to becoming literate in our society. Middle-class norms for reading and writing may, in fact, reflect the literacy norms found in many schools. They are not, however, the only route to becoming a reader and writer. Teachers must be cognizant of this fact when they are tempted to lament the "poor preparation" for school that they perceive in some of their students. Just as there are many types of literacies—multiple literacies—there are many avenues to these literacies. Most parents and children, regardless of their backgrounds, expect that schools will build on and extend student abilities. Teachers must be willing to seek out and affirm the aptitudes of their children if such continuity is to occur.

LITERACY AND ITS RELATIONSHIP TO COGNITIVE
AND SOCIOECONOMIC DEVELOPMENT

Historically, a variety of claims have been made about the positive impact of literacy on cognitive, social, and economic development. Scribner and Cole (1978, 1981) termed this perspective "literacy as development" and contrasted it with the sociocultural view they labeled "literacy as practice." A summary of these two views is represented in Table 9.9. For the most part, the claims of each perspective are directly linked to the previous discussion on the nature of essay texts and the manner in which readers and writers are expected (i.e., taught) to interact with them.

From a developmental perspective, literacy is believed to create a "great divide" between those who are and are not print oriented (Goody, 1977; Goody & Watt, 1963). Literacy, it is argued, produces a unique form of logical and rational thinking—that is, the ability to conceptualize in an abstract, decontextualized manner. This impact is thought to affect general mental functioning, promoting higher order abilities and advancing cognitive development. Because of the very nature of essay texts (e.g., explicitness, fixed boundaries, decontextualization), literates come to regard meaning as residing in the written discourse itself. They are able to draw conclusions based solely on the evidence provided in the text, without reference to outside sources of information. Of course, it might be asked both why we would want readers to ignore their backgrounds when interacting with texts and whose agenda is being served when such an ability is promoted.

As well as making cognitive and linguistic claims, developmentalists assert that literacy promotes social, moral, and economic development and responsibility (Gee, 1996; Hull, 1993; F. Smith, 1989; Willis & Harris, 2000). This view was recently expressed by a student in a university class that I was teaching. Historically, this claim was made—at least implicitly—by many religious leaders in the United States. Learning to read was promoted so that the "Word of God" via the *Bible* would be available to all. Similarly, in today's workplace, it is not uncommon to hear that the supposed inability of the United States to compete with other industrialized countries is due to workers who are deficient in basic literacy skills. Poor literacy abilities are linked to poor job performance, which in turn is

TABLE 9.9

mpact of Literacy: Two Views

Impact On	Literacy as Development	Literacy as Practice
Cognition	Written language produces a unique form of logical competencies: abstract, decontextualized thinking.	Literates are not significantly different from nonliterates on any measures of general cognitive ability.
	Literacy effects general mental capacities—abstract thinking or logical operations—rather than specific skills.	Effects of literacy are restricted to the practice actually engaged in or generalized only to closely related practices; particular skills are promoted by particular kinds of literacy practices in particular contexts.
	Literacy promotes higher-order capacities which contribute to more advanced stages of development; mental growth is arrested in cultures without literacy; lack of literacy leads to primitive thinking.	Written language and literacy abilities are context-dependent; a tendency to confound literacy with schooling, that teaches students to treat individual learning problems as instances of general classes of problems.
Language	Literate individuals regard meaning as residing in the text, e.g., can draw conclusions solely from the linguistic evidence without regard to truth or fact.	Literate individuals regard text meaning and its truth or fact in light of their purpose and the function of the text within the particular context.
	Literate individuals develop a metalinguistic awareness; are able to analyze and understand language as an "object."	Literacy has not been found to promote general metalinguistic or metacognitive skills.
Social, Moral, and Economic Development	A nation's social and economic health is based on the literacy rates of the citizens; literacy promotes individual social, economic, and moral development.	Myriad complex forces impact a nation's social and economic health; individual social, economic, and moral development is a consequence of numerous interrelated factors.

linked to national economic problems. The current national campaign to promote literacy development in our children frequently asserts similar links among illiteracy, poverty, crime, and unproductive lives. These links are often portrayed not as simply correlational but causative as well.

Given such a view, it is not much of a leap to begin to associate the lack of literacy with a negative view of those individuals who are less than proficient in reading and writing (Gee, 1996; Hull, 1993). Deficiencies in literacy become associated with deficiencies in human character, and this association is implicitly connected to people of color. Interestingly, those citizens who are the most vulnerable and least powerful come to be blamed for national economic and social woes simply because they are perceived as lacking particular literacy skills. As noted by F. Smith (1989), "when literacy is promoted as the solution to all economic, social, and educational problems, it is easy to assume that inability to read and write creates those same economic, social, and educational problems" (p. 355). Therefore, whereas literates are viewed as being rational, logical, and abstract in their thinking, nonliterates are perceived as concrete and context-dependent. The great divide essentially is between the civilized thinking and being of literates and the primitive thinking and being of nonliterates.

Gee (1996) argued that this view of literacy as development reflects a "master myth." Master myths represent a culture's or social group's favored views of reality. Entering a particular culture or group means becoming acculturated in these views of thinking and knowing. In some cases, master myths of the dominant group within a society may reflect and enforce values that are complicit with the oppression of nonmainstream groups. Because schools reflect the values of dominant groups, literacy instruction reflects these values. Becoming literate, therefore, often requires taking on the master myths of those in control. For children from nondominant groups, this may actually require the acceptance of beliefs and practices that are, in fact, used to subjugate them.

Literacy as practice directly challenges the master myths of our society. As reflected in Table 9.9, understanding literacy as practice means understanding literacy as embedded and operating within the social practices (e.g., economic, religious, occupational, schooling) of various groups. Literacy cannot be understood as an entity isolated from the world but rather as being part of human activities and endeavors. As part of social activities, literacy is rarely the only or determinant factor in the outcome of such activities.

Scribner and Cole (1978, 1981), through their study of the Vai, were among the first researchers to challenge the assumptions of literacy as development. The Vai, a traditional African people living in Liberia, invented an indigenous script for their spoken language approximately 150 years ago. The Vai script is used in most daily living activities, such as writing to friends and relatives, recording business transactions, and documenting the activities of various social organizations. In contrast to the way literacy is learned in much of the world, the Vai script is acquired in nonschool settings. This learning of literacy in nonschool settings allowed Scribner and Cole to investigate the impact of literacy on the individual separate from the impact of schooling. At least in the early grades, literacy learning and use are often the primary focus of classroom activities.

In contrast to the claims of developmentalists, Scribner and Cole (1978, 1981) found that Vai literates were not significantly different from nonliterates on various cognitive tasks. Any difference was associated with the number of years of schooling, not with literacy per se. For example, there was no across-the-board evidence that the literates were more linguistically or cognitively aware than nonliterates. Literates were not, in general, more abstract, advanced, or civilized in their reasoning. This is not to say that literacy had no psychological consequences; however, these consequences were related to specific and similar tasks rather than to general effects across a wide range of dissimilar literacy events.

Vai literates, for example, were far better at explaining the rules of a game than were nonliterates. This ability was not due to a generalized consequence of literacy, but rather to specific experiences the Vai had with written language. It was a common practice for Vai to write letters to relatives who lived at some distance. An important element in these letters was beginning with a general introduction that contextualized the ideas to be discussed. This specific use of literacy allowed Vai literates to contextualize their explanations of game rules such that the other individual could successfully play the game. Specific use, therefore, promoted specific abilities that were effective in specific situations.

Hull (1993), Smith (1989), and Gee (1996) made similar claims in regard to the workplace and the economy. Just as literacy does not have a generalizable impact on all types and uses of literacy, literacy itself does not have a generalizable impact on economic development: "There are myriad complex forces—political economic, social, personal—that can either foster or hinder literacy's potential to bring about change, as can the variety of literacy that is practiced" (Hull, 1993, p. 30). Although literacy has been touted as a curative for economic woes, Graff (1979, 1987) clearly documented its limited impact on such development. He noted that during the Middle Ages and the 18th century, Europeans made significant economic advances without high rates of literacy. Conversely, at the end of the 1700s, Sweden had obtained near universal literacy for both men and women. Literacy development and use was sponsored by the church in response to the Reformation and Lutheran Protestantism. At the time, there was little formal schooling in the country. Despite the high rates of literacy, Sweden was a country of widespread poverty, and the achievement of literacy had little impact on the economy. Again, specific literacy practices promoted specific abilities in specific contexts.

Although the extent to which literacy impacts cognitive, social, and economic development has been challenged, the master myths of a society exert powerful influences on the individual. Mahiri and Godley (1998) investigated a university student, Viviana, who was highly literate but had lost her ability to write due to carpal tunnel syndrome (CTS). With the onset of CTS, Viviana began to revise her sense of self in terms of being a good student, a good daughter, and a good mediator.

A woman of Mexican descent, Viviana had come to accept the dominant culture's values for education and literacy. As she lost her ability to write, Viviana came to assume that other people saw her as less intelligent, as less educated. She, too, believed that the loss of writing caused her to become less connected to her courses. Viviana asserted that she could not understand, connect, or retain as much information in class and that she was also unable to read as well as she once had. This view contrasted with the fact that her course examination grades as well as her Graduate Record Examination scores were high.

The onset of CTS also impacted Viviana's view of herself as a good daughter. She frequently assisted her father with his paperwork and in the translation of Spanish documents into English. This "helper" role also extended to her boyfriend and to her involvement in a variety of Latino/a organizations. As she lost her ability to write, Viviana could not fulfill this helper role in ways that she once had. In fact, Viviana was now in the position of needing to ask others for assistance, a role she had great difficulty accepting. Related to her role as a good daughter was her sense of being a good cultural mediator. Because she was bilingual as well as bicultural, she was able to move back and forth between two worlds and two languages with some ease. However, she believed this movement was challenged by her inability to write. Viviana experienced difficulty, for example, in taking notes for her parents when talking over the telephone with an insurance agent. She had to request that the agent talk slower so that she was able to write down what he said. The agent responded as if, according to Viviana, "I was mentally retarded" (Mahiri & Godley, 1998, p. 428).

It is clear that the consequences of literacy—or lack thereof—impacted the social meanings to which literacy had become connected for Viviana. Because literacy was viewed as providing capital that could be used to advance one's place in the world, she felt disempowered intellectually and socially. The link among literacy and achievement, intelligence, and success was so strong that when her literacy was challenged, so too were social meanings and her self-identity.

CONCLUSIONS

Literacy involves more than a text and a mind. Additionally, various groups are always represented—looking over the shoulder—when an individual literacy user transacts with written discourse. These groups significantly impact the experiences of the individual and consequently the acts of reading and writing. Group norms and values exist for literacy events, governing how texts are to be constructed and used as the individual makes his or her way in the world. Although literacy is a currency that impacts cognitive, social, and economic development, it is not determinant in nature. A host of factors influence the degree to which the individual is successful in any endeavor. Equal if not more significant than literacy are the various groups in which the individual finds membership.

10

The Authority of Written Discourse

In the previous chapter, we examined how various social groups made use of literacy, the patterns of their interactions with written texts, and the characteristics of the texts themselves. The individual as text user was understood as a reflection of membership within these various groups. In this chapter, the focus shifts to an analysis of the nature of knowledge itself—epistemology—and text interpretation—hermeneutics. Here, we are interested in the individual as text critic. Although knowledge can be realized through a variety of sign systems (e.g., art, music, dance), written language continues to be a primary avenue through which ideas are expressed and promoted in Western cultures. Therefore, the written texts that are actually produced and consumed within a society and the knowledge reflected in these texts are critical parts of the sociocultural dimension of literacy.

At this point, you may be wondering what such an exploration of knowledge has to do with literacy instruction. Literacy curricula, it might be argued, are focused on helping students learn to generate meanings from written discourse. This involves the development of various linguistic understandings and cognitive strategies for successfully transacting with text. In this view, educational methods or techniques become the key to helping students unlock the meanings underlying the printed page. However, the very nature of the texts encountered—and the understandings that children construct through transacting with the texts made available—significantly impact both literacy and concept development. As will be discovered, the texts used in classrooms are the product of power relationships within the society. Texts are sponsored by particular groups representing particular ideologies.

Additionally, the background knowledge applied to the text by the reader does not only represent idiosyncratic, particularistic experiences. Rather, background knowledge also reflects the beliefs, ideologies, and experiences of the groups of which the individual is a member. Gender, ethnicity, and socioeconomic status, for example, all influence the reader's interpretation of any piece of written discourse. Finally, the interpretation of the text is directly and explicitly taught by the sponsors—other groups—of literacy learning. In the classroom, significant literacy sponsors are teachers, publishers, evaluative instruments such as standardized tests, and administrators who hire and fire teachers. More recently, with the passage of the No Child Left Behind legislation (United States Department of Education, 2001), the federal government has become a significant sponsor as well.

From this perspective, it is not so much the individual, using his or her implicit knowledge of the systems of language and cognitive processes, that links the surface structure to deep structure. Rather, it is the groups in which the individual is a member that constructs the links. This is why the variability in comprehension illustrated in Fig. 7.3, in the discussion on understanding written discourse, so frequently is not evident. The groups to which we belong often inform us in very direct as well as indirect ways what a text is to mean or how it is to be interpreted.

This is not to say that the participants in literacy teaching and learning are always or even usually aware of the ways in which knowledge is conceived and texts interpreted. Rarely, in fact, is the positioning of reader, text, and writer made explicit in the classroom setting. This, of course, makes the entire enterprise all the more problematic because participants are largely not cognizant of their contributions to the construction of stance, interpretation, and knowledge. The purpose of this chapter, therefore, is to uncover the ideologies that undergird texts and literacy sponsorship and the knowledge that results from such sponsorship.

THE NATURE OF KNOWLEDGE

Recently, much media attention has been given to the so-called culture wars that are emerging around particular issues. These wars are centered on sites where there is a struggle for dominance among conflicting ideologies. Participants, as members of specific groups, vie over whose views and meanings are to find representation and therefore validation in the marketplace of ideas. On a national level, the skirmish over whose voices are to be heard within the setting of the classroom was recently played out with the development of standards for United States history. Commissioned by Congress, the history standards guide was to set parameters for both what was to be taught and how in Grades 5 through 12. The initial guide was especially sensitive to the role of women and people of color in the development of the United States. Additionally, rather than focusing on facts and figures, the standards attempted to help students develop historical knowledge of larger themes, generalizations, and concepts. The development of this knowledge was to move beyond teacher and text "telling" to the use of original sources and inquiry techniques. Students were not only to encounter a wider range of historical content but also to learn how to think and behave like historians. The history standards guide, therefore, proposed a shift in both the texts to be experienced as well as the very nature of the experience.

The response to the initial guide was immediate and divided. Many educators, politicians, and social critics praised the document as a much needed attempt to include seldom heard voices in the history of the nation. Others, such as Lynne Cheney, former head of the National Endowment for the Humanities, were quick to assert that the guide represented "just the sad and the bad" and painted a "gloomy" picture of the nation (Hancock, 1994, p. 54). Cheney noted that national heroes of distinction were not mentioned or were given slight attention. Christopher Columbus became the poster boy for all that was shameful about the nation's historical roots. Identity politics were relentlessly emphasized and the very origins of United States history challenged (Ravitch, 2003a,b). In response to the critics and the forces they represented, the standards were revisited and revised.

Similarly, various ideologies have come into conflict over the most appropriate ways to teach young children how to read. University researchers, teachers, parents, and school boards have struggled over this issue. These struggles, however, are not just disagreements over methods. They also represent very different worldviews. The response of Evangelical Christians to whole language curricula perhaps best demonstrates this phenomenon. Putting aside for the moment the overtly political agenda of such groups as the Christian Coalition, Evangelical Christians came into conflict with whole language curricula because of their basic beliefs concerning texts and how they are to be interpreted—hermeneutics. In this case, the text in question is the *Bible*, and the conflict concerns what the *Bible* represents and how it is to be read.

For Evangelical Christians, the *Bible* contains the revealed truth of God. Epistemologically speaking, it is the authoritative and controlling text in the life of the believing community. Becoming literate, therefore, is crucial because it allows the individual direct access to God's Word. Given the nature of the text, becoming literate necessarily involves learning to read closely and carefully the written discourse. Each word must be correctly understood, for not to do so results in a misunderstanding of God's plans and intentions for humankind. Predicting, guessing, or skipping words simply will not do. The very idea of encouraging various responses or interpretations is anathema because it may lead to the spiritual downfall of the individual (Brinkley, 1998; K. Goodman, 1998; Weaver & Brinkley, 1998). Evangelical Christians, therefore, are sympathetic and predisposed to the use of phonics and literal comprehension questions as primary tools for literacy learning. They see such instruction as supporting the kind of reading the *Bible* requires.

These textual understandings of Evangelical Christians are reminiscent of our discussion of literacy as social practices in the previous chapter. Just as parents in Maintown, Roadville, and Trackton (Heath, 1982a, 1982b, 1983), and schools (Cazden, 1988, 2001; Gee, 1990) have norms for interacting with texts, so too do Evangelical Christians. Elster (2003) and Sarroub (2002) have documented similar conflicts between secular and sacred readings in other religious groups, such as Orthodox Jews and Muslims.

Given such beliefs, and a concern for the spiritual growth of their children, it was perhaps inevitable that Evangelical Christians would become increasingly vocal about curricula they perceived as threatening their worldview. In California, for example, they were a potent force in the ultimate rejection of the state's *English-Language Arts Framework* (California State Department of Education, 1981) and corresponding assessment procedures. Today, children in California are experiencing very different kinds of literacy instruction and encountering very different kinds of texts because of the power of such groups.

Debates of this kind, although not always played out in such a public way, are of no small consequence to what knowledge children ultimately encounter and develop in the classroom. There are various sponsors of literacy learning (Brandt, 1998, 2001; Willis & Harris, 2000) who play significant roles in knowledge construction. Literacy is a primary avenue through which this knowledge is developed and conveyed. Sponsorship, therefore, ultimately serves as a gatekeeper for the generation, promotion, and maintenance of knowledge in our society. It impacts what knowledge is to be privileged or deemed "official" and what is to be disparaged or ignored. As demonstrated with the history standards and whole language debates, patronage is not limited to the classroom teachers. Publishers, test developers, and teacher educators all play a role. Political leaders and activists, researchers, and the media are involved as well.

Because meanings are seldom if ever neutral—they always assert a particular perspective related to a particular individual as a member of a particular group— meanings reflect the particular worldviews of particular groups (Fairclough, 2001; Meacham & Buendia, 1999; Pennycook, 2001; Smagorinsky, 2001; Willis & Harris, 2000). However, the impact of group meanings on knowledge (i.e., "truth") is only a potential one. Not all meanings or truths are created equal. Some meanings or versions of the truth and reality—and the language used for their expression— are dominant over others and may be deemed "official."

Just as importantly, meanings also have the ability to cover up other meanings, to suppress other stories and other voices. Meanings conceal as well as illuminate. The Eurocentric knowledge that many Americans have about colonial explorations of the Western Hemisphere, for example, covers, hides, or dominates meanings that represent an indigenous perspective (Bigelow, 1989; Bigelow, Miner, & Peterson, 1991; Bigelow & Peterson, 1998). Use of the words *discover*, *New World*, *savage Indians*, and *America* position both Europeans and native peoples. Alternative positions and perspectives are reflected in such words as *steal*, *homeland*, *one with nature*, and *civilized*. These words and the views and voices they represent, however, are often not encountered in school and other institutional discourses.

When the origin and nature of knowledge is considered from this perspective, the "socialness" of knowing is made visible. Knowledge is understood to be communally constructed and promoted by like-minded individuals. The general characteristics of this view—social constructionism—are represented in the right-hand column of Table 10.1. Many readers may be unaware of social constructionism

TABLE 10.1

Two Views Concerning the Nature of Knowledge

Characteristics	Foundationism	Social Constructionism
	(e.g., Structuralism, Modernism, New Criticism)	(e.g., Poststructuralism, Postmodernism, Critical Theory)
Nature	Knowledge as truth; objective, universal, and stable; exists across space and time; exists independent of human beings; transcends human differences and experiences	Knowledge as perspective; subjective, particular, and changeable; reflects how a particular group intertextually explains and interprets reality at a particular point in time
Change	Knowledge changes when it is found to be invalid (untrue)	Knowledge changes when it is no longer useful to the community that generated it, when the community disbands, or when its members die
Types	True; singular	Multiple truths or realities; various types of knowledge: personal/cultural, popular, mainstream academic, transformative academic, and school
Origin	Knowledge as a given; exists in and of itself regardless of whether it is known to humankind; knowledge is discovered (uncovered)	Knowledge as a social construct; a product of group activity; groups are knowledge producing social systems
	Author as the creator of the text	Author, colleagues, editor, publisher, other texts as the creators of the text
Criteria/Standard	Justification based on objective, reliable evidence	Socially justified; serves the rhetorical, historical, and ideological needs of the group; historical circumstances of ethnicity, gender, socioeconomics, culture, nationality, etc., determine whose truth is accepted
Language	Language as neutral	Language as subjective, reflecting perspective, ideology, and positions of power
Canonical Texts	Particular texts are universally supreme across space and time; the supremacy of such texts is self-evident; the texts speak to all of us; texts represent singular meanings	Particular texts are revered by the community that generated and maintains them; texts speak to particular community needs; texts represent multiple meanings across various interpretative communities

229

because it represents a view that contradicts much of what we have been taught and may believe about reality. In general, advocates of critical theory, such as critical pedagogy, feminist theory, critical race theory, critical theology, queer theory, and postmodernism, take a social constructivist view toward knowledge (e.g., Belenky, Clinchy, Goldberger, & Tarule, 1986; Bizzell, 1991; Bruffee, 1986; Fairclough, 2001; Giroux, 1983; Haight, 1999; Honeychurch, 1996; Kuhn, 1970; Meacham & Buendia, 1999; Pennycook, 2001; Rand, 2001; Taylor, 1999; West, 1993).

Constructionists conceive of knowledge as a product of human activity. As such, knowledge, and the language used for its expression, reflects a particular view, a particular position of writer and reader, at a particular point in time, and operates within a particular context. There is no neutral position from which truth claims can be made. Knowledge exists because it is needed by a community; it tells a story that needs to be told. Evidence for justifying the truth of assertions rests not only on the evidence provided. In fact, even what counts as evidence, facts, or data will vary from group to group. Also involved in truth justification is the status of the advocate(s) within the community and the impact of the truth on the community itself.

Whether the knowledge of a particular community receives a hearing by the broader society and ultimately finds acceptance is influenced by those in a position of power. According to social constructionists, dominant groups have significantly less difficulty finding forums for their ideas and language because they have ready access to and control over these forums. Also, the ideas and language of dominant groups frequently serve to maintain their positions of power or authority. There is a vested interest in providing a hearing for their ideas. Less dominant or disenfranchised groups, on the other hand, may find it difficult to create public forums for themselves. Their views may challenge positions of privilege and entitlement and therefore may come under attack by mainstream groups.

Social constructionists also believe that knowledge changes not so much because it is found to be untrue but because it no longer fulfills the needs of the community or the group that generated it. A group may have its knowledge suppressed because, as already mentioned, it threatens the status quo. Additionally, rather than there being only a single kind of knowledge (i.e., truth) various forms of knowledge exist. According to Banks (1993), there is knowledge that is personal and cultural, popular, mainstream academic, transformative academic, and school-based. Table 10.2 elaborates on these various types of knowledge. Because these "knowledges" are social constructs, more than an author is involved, regardless of whose name is on the text. Colleagues, editors, publishers, and advocacy groups all contribute to (i.e., sponsor) the production of text.

Although constructionists acknowledge that all communities have their revered texts, these texts are just that—the valued discourses of a particular group. Canonical texts do not represent universal qualities, meanings, or forms of knowledge that are supreme across space and time. Texts that appear to be universally supreme, such as those by Shakespeare for example, are texts that have been privileged or given status by those groups in power. This is not to say that the works of

TABLE 10.2

Types of Socially Constructed Knowledge

Type	Definition
Personal and Cultural	Knowledge that individuals construct from personal experiences in their homes, families, and community cultures, e.g., doing well in school means violating kinship norms and "acting White."
Popular	Knowledge that is institutionalized within the mass media and other institutions that are part of the popular culture, e.g., you can realize your dreams in the United States if you are willing to work hard and pull yourself up by the bootstraps.
Mainstream Academic	Traditional Westerncentric knowledge in history and the behavioral and social sciences. Based on a foundationist view of knowledge, e.g., Europeans discovered America.
Transformative Academic	Knowledge that challenges mainstream academic knowledge and expands and substantially revises established canons, paradigms, theories, explanations, and research methods. Based on a social constructionist view of knowledge, e.g., the history of the United States has not been one of continuous progress toward democratic ideas.
School	Knowledge presented in textbooks, teacher guides, other media forms, and lectures by teachers.

Shakespeare lack valuable linguistic and conceptual qualities. Rather, it is to note that texts from other, non-Western cultures have similar qualities. However, because non-Western societies frequently lack the status and power of Western cultures, their texts similarly lack status and power.

Recently, a social constructionist view of reality has received increased attention within academic circles. However, a number of critics have found this view of knowledge to be problematic (e.g., Hirsch, 1987; Rauch, 1993; Ravitch, 2003a, 2003b; Sokal & Bricmont, 1998). To a large extent, these critics represent a perspective that has been termed foundationism. (See the left-hand column of Table 10.1.) In general, a foundationist stance toward knowledge represents the norm within our society. Schools, governments, religious institutions, media, and the like all tend to promote a foundational view of knowledge.

Foundationism is known as such because of the belief that knowledge or truth exists in and of itself. Truth is present whether known or not; its existence is independent of human activity. Because of its very nature, knowledge is conceived as objective, universal, and stable across space and time. Given its a priori existence, rather than being constructed, truth is dis[un]covered. Rather than creating knowledge, it is found or located. When change in knowledge occurs, it is because what was thought to be true is found to be invalid and false. New truths come to replace the invalid or false truths. Foundationism, therefore, sees truth as the primary focus and ultimate goal in the seeking of knowledge.

Information is judged to represent truth when it can be justified with objective, reliable evidence. Although different disciplines may utilize varying methodologies, researchers frequently attempt to model their endeavors on the scientific paradigm. Hypotheses may be generated and then data collected, analyzed, and interpreted in light of the hypotheses. Analyses and interpretations are to be reliable in the sense that other researchers would come to the same conclusions if they were to examine the data. "Credit" for the knowledge generated through such methodologies is assigned to the individual(s) doing the research. The existence of copyrights and patents, or the fray between U.S. and French scientists over who first discovered the AIDS virus, reflects the notion that ideas can be discovered and owned by an individual.

Finally, just as some knowledge is viewed as truth, it is common for foundationists to conceive of particular texts—especially those found in literature—as universally supreme. Discourse is identified as canonical when its qualities are so superior that they are preeminent across space, time, and cultures (Ravitch, 2003a, 2003b). The texts of Shakespeare, for example, are regarded by some individuals as canonical because they contain internal qualities and themes that are thought to speak to all cultures. These self-evident qualities are why Shakespeare is valued throughout the world, not because his texts have been imposed on others by Western cultures or because non-Western cultures have the desire or need to emulate dominant cultures.

THE NATURE OF TEXTS AND TEXT INTERPRETATION

In general, most classrooms assume a foundationist perspective toward knowledge and texts. This stance is reflected in and reinforced by the way in which students are taught to interpret the texts that they read. We have already seen in the previous chapter how children are "normed" to interact with texts in particular ways in elementary school settings. It is important to note, however, that the word interpret is used here rather than the word comprehend. As discussed in chapter 7, readers construct meanings from their transactions with written discourse. This transaction is conceived as being among reader, text, and author. As part of this transaction, the reader's own particular background knowledge impacts in a very direct way how any text is understood.

However, as we also saw in the previous chapter, readers and writers have multiple social identities. These identities reflect and are formed by the particular experiences that members of the group have had with one another and with other groups in the wider society. The background that a reader brings to the page is a reflection not simply of his or her own unique experiences, but also of the experiences of the various groups in which the individual holds membership.

These group identities impact how the individual interprets and writes any piece of written discourse. In general, shared experiences lead to shared understandings. The transaction, therefore, is widened beyond the individual and conceives of reader, writer, and text as reflections and products of relevant interpretive communities.

As demonstrated in chapter 2 in the *Alice in Wonderland* example and the burglar–homebuyer story in chapter 7, texts can be understood in a multitude of ways. Just as individuals have a number of identities, texts have many layers of meaning as well. Texts display a multitude of ideas both directly and indirectly. In the remainder of this chapter, I examine the relation between these identities and layers.

Pigs and Wolves

We begin with a look at two stories that, as a text set, explicitly and consciously highlight the notion of identities and layers of meaning in written discourse. The first, "The Three Little Pigs," is a well-known British folktale. In the story, three pigs leave home and each builds a house for himself. One builds a house of straw, one a house of sticks, and one a house of bricks. As you probably recall, a big, bad wolf blows in the house of the first and second little pigs. They run off to the home of the third little pig. Although he huffs and he puffs, the wolf is unable to blow in the house of the third little pig. He slides down the chimney but the pigs have a boiling pot of water waiting for him.

The second story in the text set is "The True Story of the Three Little Pigs" (Scieszka, 1989). This story may not be as familiar to some readers as "The Three Little Pigs." "The True Story" is told by the wolf, and he offers another perspective on his encounters with the pigs. He explains that the entire incident was a simple misunderstanding. The wolf was only trying to borrow a cup of sugar to bake a birthday cake for his dear old granny. However, because he had a terrible sneezing cold, he ended up huffing and puffing and blowing in the two houses. The police were called and the reporters jazzed up the story to make it more interesting to their readers.

The difference between the two stories that readers typically find to be the most obvious and significant is that of the facts and intentions. In the "Three Little Pigs" (3LP), the intention of the wolf is to eat the pigs, and all of his behaviors are attempts to reach this goal. In "The True Story of the Three Little Pigs" (TS), the intention of the wolf is to borrow a cup of sugar. However, a cold and a sneeze interfere with his goal. These differences are fairly obvious, and young children love pointing them out when discussing the stories.

What is more interesting—and significant—are the other, more hidden differences between the stories. As indicated in Table 10.3, the storyteller in 3LP assumes the stance that truth will emerge from the facts. Although not identified, the teller is positioned as one who is all-knowing. This omniscient presentation and the use

TABLE 10.3
An Analysis of Pigs and Wolves

	The Three Little Pigs	*The True Story*
Story Teller	Unidentified and uninvolved, but one that is all knowing	Wolf who was a participant in the story and has a point of view
Story Teller's Agenda	To retell the "facts" of an event	To persuade an audience to accept a different set of "facts"
Discourse Strategies	"Facts" are presented in an "objective" manner; use of "distant" and uninvolved language	"Facts" are presented in a persuasive manner; use of involved language inviting understanding and sympathy
Intended Audience	An audience that is fearful of wolves but not of pigs	An audience that has heard the pig's but not the wolf's perspective
	An audience that can be easily persuaded by the "facts" told in an objective manner	An audience sympathetic with the pig's perspective. An audience skeptical or hostile to the wolf's perspective. An audience that is more fearful of wolves than pigs
Historical Context	An audience that historically is fearful of wolves	An audience that historically is fearful of wolves

of unbiased, distant, and uninvolved language implies a sense of objectivity on the part of the narrator. Just the facts are being presented and the reader can determine for himself or herself who is in the right. Of course, for all we know, one of the pigs might be retelling the story. Reporters for newspapers, magazines, and television and radio news programs typically position themselves in such a way and take on the language that accompanies this position.

Additionally, the storyteller in 3LP takes for granted the sympathy of the reader. The original audience—most probably peasants living in a rural environment—had a historical fear of wolves—both for themselves and their livestock—before the story was even encountered. They are ready to believe the worst about this animal, and the wolf is guilty until proven innocent. The pigs, on the other hand, are viewed as harmless creatures that provide food and on which a family's survival might depend. The author is aware of the fears of this group and uses it to his or her advantage when presenting the story. Not until the very end, when the wolf is described as <bad>, is there an explicit attempt to analyze or interpret the events for the reader. The author knows that the reader is already on the narrator's side. If we were to find this account in a newspaper, we might describe it as an unbiased report of a particular event.

All of this is in marked contrast to the task faced by the storyteller in TS. First, we know that a participant—the wolf—is the narrator. Just this fact is likely to make the reader somewhat wary. Given the position of the wolf, the reader wonders if the presentation is going to be objective. This skepticism is only reinforced by the historical fear of wolves that is brought to the printed page. Even the summary provided on the copyright page of the book reflects this bias: "The wolf gives his own outlandish version of what really happened when he tangled with the three little pigs."

Given such skepticism and fear, the wolf feels compelled to explicitly mark his perspective. His task is not simply to tell a story, but to counteract the events in the existing text, to persuade the reader of an alternative truth. Therefore, the language used is overtly partisan in nature as the author attempts to develop a sympathetic reader who will accept or at least consider a different set of truths. In fact, the wolf frames the story as a simple attempt to obtain sugar to bake a cake for his <dear old granny>. Of course, it is the very use of such rhetorical devices that may convince many readers that they are being had by the wolf. Such a suspicion fits the reader's already strongly held view that wolves are wily and not to be trusted.

I have intentionally selected these two texts to contrast because of the very different views of reality that are made explicit in both content and form. Recently, a number of educators (e.g., Leland, Harste, Ociepka, Lewison, & Vasquez, 1999) have proposed that text sets of this type be used to help younger children understand different group perspectives. Schools, they argue, should support students in developing critical literacy abilities. Texts are not so much to be comprehended in the traditional sense but rather interpreted and critiqued for the perspectives and positions they represent. Haight (1999) has even gone so far as to assert that "all understanding is at the same time interpretation" (p. 120). Although the use of such text sets as "The Three Little Pigs" and "The True Story of the Three Little Pigs" might be a good place to begin, I think that the power dynamics reflected in most texts are usually far more subtle, far less visible to readers and writers. With this in mind, we briefly take a look at another text set and consider the position of readers and writers.

Turnips, Carrots, and Other Texts

The texts considered here are "The Great Big Enormous Turnip" (Tolstoy, 1976) and "The Carrot Seed" (Kraus, 1945). We have already examined "The Great Big Enormous Turnip" (GBET) from a linguistic perspective in chapter 2. (See Table 2.16.) "The Carrot Seed" (CS) is shown in Table 10.4. Once again, read through the two stories and consider what "lessons" are being taught—both explicitly and implicitly—and how.

In GBET, it might be argued, the reader is taught that the power of the individual exists as part of a collaborative, cooperative relationship with others. (See Table 10.5.) Working together to accomplish tasks that could otherwise not be

TABLE 10.4

"The Carrot Seed"

A little boy planted a carrot seed. His mother said, "I'm afraid it won't come up."
His father said, "I'm afraid it won't come up." And his big brother said, "It won't
come up." Every day the little boy pulled up the weeds around the seed and
sprinkled the ground with water. But nothing came up. And nothing came up.
Everyone kept saying it wouldn't come up. But he still pulled up the weeds around
it every day and sprinkled the ground with water. And then, one day, a carrot came
up just as the little boy had known it would.

TABLE 10.5

A Sociocultural Analysis of Two Texts

	Turnip	*Carrot Seed*
Power	Individual efforts may not lead to success; power is realized through collaboration	Individual persistence and hard work leads to success; power is realized through individual initiative
Interpersonal relationships	Individuals are part of a community; all members of a community have a valuable role to play; the community can accomplish tasks that an individual cannot; individuals of diverse backgrounds can collaborate in order to accomplish a goal; community involves helping an individual accomplish his/her goal	The community attempts to thwart individual efforts; do not expect support from community members
Initiative	Initiative is demonstrated by seeking assistance and support when necessary; lack of success calls for seeking additional support and trying again	Initiative is demonstrated by the individual persevering in the face of opposition; success takes time
Discourse strategies	The repetition of episodes with a new character being added each time reflects the collaborative nature of the community	The repetition of episodes with a new family member voicing discouragement
Intended audience	A community whose existence depends on collaboration among its members	A community whose existence depends on each member seeking his/her own success

accomplished is presented as a valued norm. The community is there to support the initiative of the individual. Although persistence may often be necessary—even the repetition of the language demonstrates this belief—it is the perseverance of the group rather than the isolated individual that is critical. When failure is encountered, not only does the group try again, but its members also seek to expand the individuals involved in the effort. At no point in the story does a character indicate that he or she is too busy, too tired, or too disinterested to lend a hand. These underlying messages may not be highlighted during instruction if the focus is solely on surface-level meanings. However, with repeated encounters with such texts, children may nonetheless come to take on the values accompanying discourse of this type. Texts reflect as well as create cultural norms.

A very different view of the relationship between the individual and group is presented in CS. In marked contrast to GBET, the reader is "taught" that the group—in this case the family—is there to obstruct or at least discourage individual initiative. Success, therefore, is not so much overcoming a difficult task, but rather overcoming the attempts of the group to thwart the individual. With persistence and hard work, the individual can triumph. Once again, repeated encounters with these types of texts have the potential to impact the values and perspectives of those doing the reading.

In developing literacy in young children, it is important that students be helped to understand not only explicit meanings but also the more subtle and nuanced messages, positions, and stances that the discourse presents or assumes. Teachers also need to be cognizant of the values and norms that children bring to the learning experience. This recognition moves beyond a simple affirmation of the diversity of experiences children have had. Too often, these experiences reflect dominant norms of our society, which continues to struggle with such "isms" as racism, sexism, classism, and homophobia. Simply to affirm childhood learning risks missing the opportunity to take a more critical look at societal values in terms of justice and equity.

That children themselves bring ideologies and positional frameworks to the classroom that are reflected in what they read and write has been demonstrated by a number of researchers. Kamler (1993) analyzed the self-selected writing of two young children—a girl and a boy—just learning how to write. Almost from the first text written, gendered patterns emerged. Examples of these patterns are presented in Table 10.6. Although both children tended to write about personal experiences, their positions in these experiences varied. The stories authored by the boy tended to focus on behaviors within events that positioned him as an actor and doer. He depicted himself as an agent acting in and on his world. Use of description was uncommon in the boy's texts, as was the use of commentary. In contrast, the girl situated herself as a describer and commentator. Her role was more passive and reflective in nature, and she frequently expressed her personal feelings and emotions about an event. As noted by Kamler, these positions are not idiosyncratic or by happenstance. Rather, they are aligned with gender stereotypes: males as active and females as passive.

TABLE 10.6
Gendered Story Writing Samples

Girls	Boys
• A description of the event; a focus on details: *Christa got a bluebird bracelet in a velvet bag with a yellow ribbon.*	• Action-oriented events dominate; a focus on acting and doing: *My dad and me are going on a boat ride with lots of water animals.*
• Descriptions dominate; observing the event: *The string was tied in a knot. It had silver writing on it. It was brown.*	• Descriptions were rare: *There was a real bike and a toy bike.*
• Many comments reflecting attitudes; discussion of feelings and emotions were common: *I like ballet. I love my baby.*	• Few comments reflecting attitudes; discussion of feelings and emotions were infrequent: *It was a great day yesterday.*
• Comments were based on events that impacted her: *My presents had pretty paper.*	• Comments were based on his actions and behaviors: *When I fell off my bike I got hurt on the knee and back and arm.*
• Frequent involvement in quiet activities: *I am going to brush my teeth. I am going to sleep in Kate Roger's bedroom. I am going to bed.*	• Frequent involvement in active activities: *We are going to destroy ant houses. I am going to take my superman suit. We are going to play superfriends.*
• A focus on the giver: *Grandma gave me some pretty ribbons. Santa gave me the game Connect Four.*	• A focus on the receiver: *I got a football from mum and dad. I got a dot-to-dot book.*

Positioning also was reflected in the very language the children used to convey their experiences. The boy tended to <take, put, play, destroy, get>, whereas the girl <slept, gave, left, finished, and came>. When both children described receiving a gift, the boy positioned himself as the focus of the event. His <getting> is emphasized. In contrast, the girl focused on the giver of the gift rather than on herself as the recipient. Thus, the very language used by the boy places the focus on himself, whereas the language employed by the girl places the focus on others. Other researchers have found similar gendered patterns in student writing (e.g., Dyson, 1997, 1998; Gilbert, 1989; Orellana, 1995; Poynton, 1985; Solsken, 1992). Still other researchers have noted the existence of similar gendered patterns in children's books and in the types of stories boy and girls select to read (e.g., Adler, 1993; Barrs & Pidgeon, 1994; Bender-Peterson & Lach, 1990).

Although many progressive educators have advocated the use of student-selected writing topics as a mainstay of literacy instruction, studies such as

Kamler's (1993) should give us pause. The work of Henkin (1995) and Dyson (1997, 1998) only highlights this concern. Henkin investigated the organizational practices of writing workshops within a first-grade classroom. In particular, she focused on issues of participation and equity. Because writing conferences are intended to impart knowledge about the composing process and because knowledge can be viewed as a form of currency, it is critical that all children have opportunities to encounter such knowledge.

Henkin (1995) found that access to writing conferences was skewed along ethnic and gender lines. There were, in effect, two literacy clubs in the classroom—girls and boys—and the boys' club dominated. The boys refused to conference with the girls, explaining that their interests were too different. Even when the girls wrote about such topics as sports, the boys continued to insist that they were not adequate conference partners. Additionally, boys who did not fit the norm—European American, cooperative—were also excluded from the boys' conferences. The club was hierarchical in nature, and a single child—Bart—dominated, conferring membership and status on those boys who cooperated with him. Bart invented many of the literacy club rules and resisted participating in conferences in ways the teacher had demonstrated.

Similarly, resistance to critiques of gender stereotypes, as well as to the nature of power, was found by Dyson (1997, 1998) in her study of the impact of superheroes on student writing in the primary grades. For many students, shared knowledge of superheroes served as a bonding experience and contributed to a sense of collective identity in the classroom. Children used this shared knowledge "to bond with each other and to learn about and play with powerful societal images (e.g., the warrior, the lover, the rescuer, the victim in distress)" (Dyson, 1998, p. 395). Because superheroes characteristically reflect society's biases and stereotypes, superheroes that found their way into student writing tended to reflect these same biases and stereotypes. Characters were oftentimes active males who exhibited their power through the use of physical force. Student authored texts reflected as well as responded to these shared cultural experiences of the classroom community.

In appropriating their out of school experiences with superheroes, however, students also demonstrated authorial agency. Students actively as well as selectively drew upon other sources of knowledge, such as classroom activities and classroom texts, as they made textual choices. For example, several students objected to the positioning of females within many superhero stories. One student, Tina, was bothered by the fact that most of the student-authored superhero texts were male oriented. Female roles, when presented, were relatively short and storylines always concluded with the boys winning. When Tina noted that these textual choices were not fair to girls, a classmate, Victor, argued that it was not fair to the boys (presumably because the boys were feeling pressure to expand their text world possibilities). Another student, Holly, authored a story in which most of the superhero characters were female who had become tired of "fighting bad guys" (Dyson, 1998, p. 398). When her story was performed by the students in an

Author's Theater production, however, many boys refused to follow the "script." They immediately began to demonstrate their powers through the use of physical force. Tina and Holly had challenged and even violated the dominant and normative classroom community stories and their stories were resisted by some members of their community. It was only through active intervention by the teacher that the class came to fully appreciate the various linguistic and textual options and choices that were available to them.

Societal norms that have been constructed by dominant groups also find their way into reader response conferences. Like self-selected writing topics and conferences, the use of reader response groups has been advocated by progressive educators as a way in which to affirm the multitude of experiences that children bring to the classroom. Most educators would agree that this is a worthy instructional goal. However, as documented by Enciso (1994), interwoven with many of these experiences are dominant views on such issues as race and culture. That is, the experiences that children bring to the classroom are not solely individualistic or particularistic; they are also grounded in the various social groups of which the students are members.

Enciso (1994) investigated the responses of an ethnically diverse group of intermediate elementary students to the book *Maniac Magee* (Spinelli, 1990). The book's main character, Jeffrey Lionel Magee, is a 12-year-old boy who is involved with two racially divided communities—African American and European American. The plot focuses on the boy's attempts to negotiate his way through these two groups. As expected, students responded to the text and interpreted the characters and events based on their personal experiences. However, as Enciso quickly discovered, these responses and experiences also reflected numerous cultural references related to race and ethnicity. Such references framed both the identity of the children and the identity of the characters within the story.

Initially, the use of racial and ethnic ideologies in student responses was implicit. Their ideologies were not openly acknowledged or critiqued. However, when Enciso (1994) highlighted race and ethnicity within the story, the children began to make explicit their underlying beliefs. In one response session, for example, students were discussing the physical divide between the African American and European American communities. Based on Enciso's explicit marking of this divide, students began to discuss the concept of segregation. One European American boy, Mark, presented what he knew about the civil rights era in a standup comic-like routine. In his presentation, he made reference to a song from the musical *West Side Story*. Although popular, this play depicts the Puerto Rican community in stereotyped ways. Additionally, Mark appeared to believe that African Americans were unaware that certain kinds of exclusions were occurring within society. Although Mark's responses were certainly based on his background, his background represented the dominant groups to which he belonged. According to Enciso, to allow such views to go unchallenged is to implicitly affirm a distorted view of history and reality.

TABLE 10.7

Reader and Critical Response

Reader Response	Critical Response
A focus on the uniqueness of the individual	A focus on the social identities of the individual; the individual as part of various social groups
A privileging of the particular experiences that the individual brings to the text	A privileging of the socially based experiences that the individual brings to the text
Responses reflect the personal experiences of the reader	Responses reflect the social experiences of the reader
Reading and comprehension represent an interaction between an individual reader and an individual author	Reading and interpretation represent a transaction between the social identities of the reader and the social identities of the author
An implicit affirmation of the individual's personal knowledge	A critique of the reader's personal, popular, and cultural knowledge
	An interrogation of writer and text in terms of stance and power
	Transforms mainstream knowledge so as to create a more equitable and just society

We should not be surprised by the fact that our children read, write, and think in ways that reflect their social identities. Gender, ethnicity, and class support as well as constrain student work. Because engagement with print requires the use of background knowledge, teachers will want to encourage their students to draw on their experiential resources. Active teacher intervention, however, is also required when such experiences run counter to the promotion of a more equitable and just society. Not to do so runs the risk that process classrooms, which are intended to affirm diversity, will in the end legitimize existing cultural norms and power relationships (Dyson, 1997, 1998; Orellana, 1995; Spears-Bunton, 1990, 1992; Willis, 2001).

The work of these and other critical theorists calls for an instructional shift from reader response to critical response. As indicated in Table 10.7, traditionally, classroom reader response activities focus on helping students connect their personal experiences with the text being read (e.g., Rosenblatt, 1978, 1991a, 1991b). We know from our examination of the cognitive dimension of literacy that comprehension involves the active use and linking of the individual's background knowledge with what is being read. In an attempt to encourage the use of this background knowledge, as well as to validate multiple understandings of a text, teachers typically affirm student reactions and the experiences that undergird them. In many respects, during response activities the individual reader comes to dominate both text and author.

Critical response acknowledges the experiences that students bring to the text. However, these responses are understood to reflect not just personal knowledge, but also popular and cultural knowledge (Banks, 1993). The responses may mirror as well as reproduce the values and norms of dominants groups within society. Rather than simply comprehending the text, students are conceived as actually interpreting it based on their own sociocultural identities and histories. Critical response activities, therefore, seek to analyze and critique issues of power and perspective that weave their way through any text and any response. Hidden or taken for granted ideologies are exposed, interrogated, and challenged so as to transform student understandings of their world. The focus extends beyond simply affirming student meanings, with the goal of creating a more just and equitable society.

Bigelow (1989), a public school teacher, documented such attempts to help students critique a dominant view of society. In this case, the goal was to help his students understand the "discovery" of the "New World" from a Native American perspective. As previously noted, the very use of such language places both the terms "discoverers" and "discovered" in particular positions. This placement represents the views of the most dominant group. That is, the history—or his story—told represents the victor's understanding. Bigelow quickly discovered that students frequently resisted his attempts to "deconstruct" the Eurocentric view represented in their history books. The alternative view presented by Bigelow ran counter to not only the books the students had read, but also the representations found in such popular cultural texts as movies, television programs, songs, and holidays. In many respects, Bigelow was the big, bad wolf trying to tell the "true story," and some students viewed his attempts at presenting alternative perspectives with skepticism.

In an interesting article that serves as a companion piece to Bigelow's (1989), J. Hoffman (1992) related the story of his young daughter returning home from school distraught. She had been studying Christopher Columbus and encountered ideas that challenged her established beliefs. According to what she had learned, Columbus was not so much a hero and a great man as he was cruel and selfish. The existing textbooks on Columbus were "full of lies . . . because they don't think that children should know the truth" (p. 121). She was unable to distance herself emotionally from what she had learned.

J. Hoffman (1992) suggested that one way to avoid such student reactions, as well as to highlight the notion that much knowledge represents perspective, is through the use of inquiry charts. In inquiry, or I-charts, the issue under study is considered through the use of multiple questions and multiple resources (e.g., books, magazines, movies). One goal of the I-charts is not so much to locate the "right" answer as it is to represent various voices, perspectives, and positions, depending on the resources utilized. With mediation from the teacher, students identify questions of interest related to a particular topic. These guiding questions are listed across the top of a grid. A sample of what these questions might be is shown in Table 10.8.

To support students in their explorations of these questions and to provide them with alternative viewpoints, the teacher gathers a wealth of material on the topic. This material reflects different perspectives or "answers" to the questions and might come from a variety of resources—books, magazines, newspapers, movies, songs, television, and radio programs, for example. The materials utilized are listed in the far left-hand column of the chart. Students are then given the opportunity either individually or in groups to research the questions and to list the "answers" provided by various resources. As indicated in Table 10.8, "answers" vary depending on the source. Through the use of this chart, students quickly come to see that knowledge frequently is dependent on perspective. The same event may represent very different meanings to different groups. As noted by Ravitch (2003a), "...there is seldom, if ever, a single interpretation of events on which all reputable historians agree. The soul of historical research is debate..." (p. 134).

CONCLUSIONS

In this chapter, the power of written discourse has been explored. Of course, it is not so much the discourse itself that is powerful, but rather the groups behind the discourse. Nonetheless, it is not uncommon to hear individuals assert the truth of their statements with "I read it." As has been demonstrated, the truths encountered in print are directly related to who controls the printing presses, so to speak. Additionally, what truths in print are accepted as such are impacted by the social identities of the reader. The authority of written discourse, therefore, varies as the groups involved with the discourse vary.

THE SOCIOCULTURAL DIMENSION OF THE LITERACY STORY

The previous analyses of the language story first introduced in chapter 1 focused on the linguistic and cognitive dimensions of literacy. I now turn attention to the sociocultural. Here, the focus is on how the various groups in which I hold membership impact my use and critique of literacy within the workplace.

The fact that I had the need to write academic papers and the desire to use a computer software program to do so was directly related to my social identity. I was an assistant professor who worked at a university that required publication for tenure and promotion. Therefore, if I wanted to keep my job, I knew that writing was required. Besides the threat of dismissal if I did not publish, the university sponsored my literacy endeavors through the purchase of a computer and printer for my use. All of my colleagues were similarly sponsored and engaged in comparable academic writing pursuits. Most faculty in my department were aware of who was writing what and, although not explicitly acknowledged, to a certain extent

TABLE 10.8

Inquiry Chart on Christopher Columbus

GUIDING QUESTIONS

SOURCES		1. Why did Columbus sail?	2. What did he find?	3. What important things did he do while he got there?	4. How was Columbus regarded by others?	Other Interesting Facts & Figures	New Questions
	WHAT WE KNOW	to prove the world was round	America	...not sure	He was a hero	He sailed in 1492. He was Spanish	Did he have a family?
1. Meet Christopher Columbus, de Kay, New York: Random House, 1989		He was trying to find a new route to the Indies.	He found friendly Indians... some pieces of gold... different islands. He found America	He named the islands. He claimed the land for Queen Isabella and King Ferdinand. He brought back gold for Isabella.	At the beginning people regarded him as a normal person. Later, when he got back, they thought he was a great man.	C.C. had asked the King of Portugal for ships. He was turned down. When he came back he landed in Portugal and was taken to the King. The King was mad that he didn't help him.	Whatever happened to his son?
2. The World Book Encyclopedia, World Book Childcraft Inc. 1979		to find riches... and a shorter route to the Indies. He wanted to be famous... to be known as a great sailor and explorer.	He found America... Indians... new islands.	He named the islands. He captured some Indians as slaves. He became the governor.	He was an "understanding..." dreamy person. It sounds like he had a lot of friends	In other books I've read he wasn't very popular. He had 2 sons, not 1. Six brothers and a sister. He was born in Italy.	Whatever happened to his sons?
3. Where do you Think You're Going Christopher Columbus? Jean Fritz, New York: G.P.Putnam's Sons, 1980		Because he liked to travel and explore. they said they would give a big reward for finding a new route to the Indies	He found Indians... Some small hunks of gold	He talked to the Indians. He asked for directions to the Palace of the Khan. He named the islands	Before he went he was wealthy because he had married a rich woman. He was famous after. He sailed, but a couple of years later, everyone forgot about him.	Columbus sounded greedy in this book. He said he saw land first and claimed the prize money. He claimed that all of this was God's work.	Was he really cruel to the Indians? whatever happened to the slaves he brought back to Spain?
SUMMARY		To find a new route to the Indies... He hoped to find riches and become famous as an explorer. He already knew the world was round.	He found America with Indians living there. He found a little gold.	He claimed the land for Spain. He named the islands. He met with the Indians. He took some back to Spain as slaves. He became Governor.	Before he sailed he was normal. a dreamer. After he came back he was famous and a hero. He seemed greedy. Everyone forgot about him after a while.	He claimed he was doing God's work. His family supposedly helped him. He tried to get money for his voyage from lots of people. Everyone forgot about him. Born an Italian.	Find out more about his family and what happened to them. Was he cruel to the Indians? What happened to the slaves?

244

evaluated their own writing accomplishments in the light of what others were doing.

The fact that I was even attempting to learn WordPerfect was also socially based. I had been using an older software program that I found quite satisfactory when new software was purchased for my department—another form of sponsorship. The staff, graduate assistants, and other faculty immediately began to learn the program, and I felt pressure to do so as well. The norms had shifted in the workplace, and I knew that staying with the older program would limit my interaction with those around me. People would wonder why I alone had not made the switch. As a voluntary club member, I wanted to remain in good standing with my tenured colleagues. Additionally, the new software actually allowed me to do things that the older program had not, such as constructing columns and tables.

Finally, I also engaged in critique of the computer guide and the group that had generated it. At times, I felt the text was not very user friendly—inconsiderate, to use Tierney and LaZansky's (1980) term. I remarked to colleagues that such guides should not be written by "techies" but rather by people who knew something about the writing process and audience. However, if I wanted to learn the program, I needed to submit to the dominance, both conceptually and linguistically, of the author. Other guides and authors were no more user friendly. Of course, my own dislike of reading and following directions was certainly part of the difficulty that I was experiencing. Interestingly, once I learned the software program, the guide became easy to understand.

V

The Developmental
Dimension of Literacy

11

Constructing the Written Language System

At this point in your reading, you have developed a fairly extensive knowledge of three of the dimensions of literacy first encountered in Fig. 1.1. Linguistically, you understand that written language consists of rule-governed systems that build on and extend oral language. The particular operating rules of these systems vary across individuals and groups. There are many norms for what constitutes "correct" usage, and these norms vary as groups and situations vary. Additionally, the building of meaning, the ultimate goal of literacy events, is a selective and constructive process that involves the use of numerous mental strategies and processes. This cognitive dimension conceives of meaning as the outcome of a generative, symbiotic transaction among reader, writer, text, and context. Finally, from a sociocultural perspective, we know that literacy represents social practices. These practices, which include both language forms and language content, reflect the actions of various groups as they interact with their world. Literacy practices vary from group to group and always involve issues of authority, power, and control.

As we shift our attention to how literacy is developed, it is important to keep these three dimensions in mind. Contrary to popular beliefs, literacy learning involves far more than the mere acquisition of graphophonemic relations and orthographic knowledge. More significantly, development reflects growth in the individual's ability to effectively and efficiently engage the linguistic, cognitive, and sociocultural dimensions of literacy in an ever widening range of contexts. As Dyson (2003) notes, growth in written language involves the learner's ability to maneuver and orchestrate the various levels (dimensions) of language "with more control, more flexibility, on expanding landscapes" (p. 174). These dimensions are negotiated and grappled with all at once, not within neat and tidy, linear, and step-by-step stages.

As shown in Fig. 11.1, the learner initially has limited knowledge of these dimensions and is able to effectively and efficiently apply this knowledge in only a relatively narrow range of contexts. For example, a young child may be able to

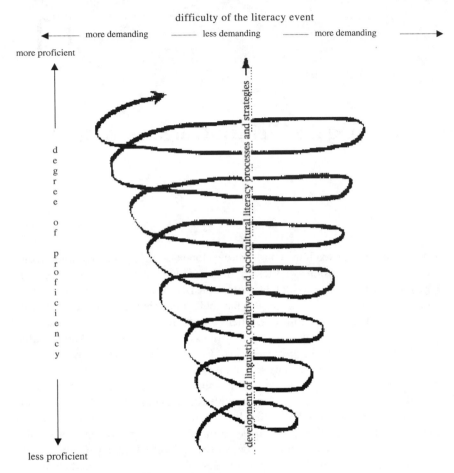

FIG. 11.1.   Profile of literacy development.

proficiently read a number of predictable books, such as "The Great Big Enormous Turnip" (Tolstoy, 1976), yet may appear to know little about literacy when given less supportive texts to read. This disparity in the child's interaction with various types of texts is not necessarily an indication that the child is unable to "really read," as is frequently asserted. Rather, it may simply demonstrate the child's narrow range of developed linguistic, cognitive, and sociocultural strategies and the limited settings in which he or she can proficiently apply these strategies. Of course, this can be said about most of us reading this book. Development typically continues throughout the course of one's life as long as literacy is encountered and used in new or novel ways. In fact, as previously noted, *becoming literate* rather than *being literate* more accurately describes our relationship with written language (Leu, 2000).

Additionally, there always exist literacy contexts in which we are less than proficient, if only because we lack experience in these situations. At times, we may even seek to avoid such contexts. I, for example, eschew reading the tax codes and forms sent to me from the Internal Revenue Service. Rather, I employ an accountant to read them for me. Before the invention of the printing press and the wider distribution of literacy, it was common for scribes to be employed to read and write for those who were unable to do so. Today, this tradition continues in a somewhat modified form.

As yet, there is no fully articulated theory of literacy learning that can account for how all three dimensions of literacy are developed. There are, however, a number of principles that we know guide the development of language, both spoken and written. General patterns exist, with individual as well as group variations due to such circumstances as culture, class, and family. Despite different experiences, children learn language in surprisingly similar ways. In this chapter, I examine the patterns and principles of language learning, the interrelationships between reading and writing development, and cultural variations. Although the focus is on written language, throughout the discussion, concepts are also taken from oral language to demonstrate the many similarities that exist between the development of the two modes. First, however, it is important that we consider what might motivate a child to begin, and sustain an adult to continue, the long and demanding process of learning language. The "answer" to this "why" holds significant implications for classroom literacy instruction.

WHY LEARN LANGUAGE?

No young child awakens one morning and suddenly says to himself or herself, "I think I'll learn some language today!" For the most part, learning language is not a conscious decision on the part of the young learner; nor does the child learn language for its own sake. Rather, children are born into a world in which the use of oral language is everywhere. In literate cultures such as our own, print is plentiful as well. Language is immediately used with the child by those in the discourse community in which the child is immersed. People talk to and with the child as if he or she were fully capable of understanding what is being said. Language is used as a communicative tool and serves as a functional system. As such, language creates and expresses meanings and is used to act on the world. The child is not oblivious to the role of language in the environment and quickly develops a desire to enter into this world.

Linked to the desire to communicate is the need to be social, to interact and emotionally bond with others. This need represents a second motivating force for language learning. Human beings are social beings, and language facilitates the interactive process among individuals. Once again, the child experiences the socializing effects of language not only personally, but also vicariously as language as a social vehicle is used among others in the immediate, observable environment.

Both the communicative and social nature of language are represented in Halliday's (1973) functions of language, which were presented in Table 2.2 when the pragmatic system of language was examined. Children come to understand the various dimensions of literacy only if they have a sense of these functional and social purposes of literacy (Dyson, 2003).

It is important for those of us who are engaged in the teaching of literacy to consider the links between need, motivation, and learning. Too often, literacy is taught to young children in a manner that appears to be literacy learning for its own sake. Of course, if teachers were asked the purpose for teaching reading and writing, most would give functional, real-world reasons. However, the way in which reading and writing are taught often fails to reflect the purpose for which literacy is learned and used. As noted by Dewey (1938), this disconnect between purpose and instruction can be problematic. The manner in which learning occurs frequently influences the manner in which what has been learned can be used in other spaces and times. Learning and the learned are fused in that the learning lives on in the use of the learned. The instructional implication is that literacy teaching and learning are best promoted when written language is engaged for communicative and social purposes.

Keeping in mind the motivating forces behind language learning, we shift our attention to the patterns and principles of literacy development.

DEVELOPMENTAL PATTERNS AND PRINCIPLES

Four language learning patterns and principles are explored in this section. The first concerns the actions of the child and the second the recursive nature of development. We then shift our attention to the mediations provided by more proficient language users and conclude with a look at how children negotiate their meanings. It is important to note at this time that although most of the literacy examples to follow come from English monolingual children, the same basic developmental processes apply to bilingual children as well (Hudelson & Poynor, 2003). Bilingual children are active agents and negotiators in their language learning and adult mediators, especially teachers, need to respond accordingly.

The Learner as Scientist and Construction Worker

The child goes about learning language knowledge much as a scientist goes about developing scientific knowledge: through data collection, rule generation, rule testing, and rule modification. The dimensions of language—linguistic, cognitive, sociocultural—are actually constructed or built by the child through a process of induction. The child discovers the abstract regularities of the language based on past communicative experiences, the language data available, and the mediation provided. Actively involved in the developmental process, the learner is anything but a passive recipient of the language. Rather, the child experiences or encounters

TABLE 11.1

Types of Constructionism

Type of Constructionism	Characteristics
Linguistic	The individual as actively constructing the systems of language from and into the surface structure of the text based on language knowledge.
Cognitive	The individual as actively constructing meaning from and into the surface structure of the text based on prior conceptual experiences.
Sociocultural	The individual as actively constructing an understanding of the text as a member of various social groups.
Developmental	The individual as actively constructing linguistic, cognitive, and sociocultural competence through demonstrations, mediations, and data collection → data analysis → hypothesis generating → hypothesis testing → and hypothesis revision.

language data expressed by others within a communicative context. In an attempt to make sense of these data, the learner generates or constructs hypotheses, rules for how a particular aspect of the language might operate. Using these hypotheses as a guide, the child engages in language use and receives feedback from others. Based on the feedback provided, the hypotheses are modified as warranted.

"Constructivism" or the "constructivist classroom" has received increased attention by the educational community. The concept, however, has oftentimes been used in a variety of ways to characterize a variety of behaviors. In Table 11.1, these various characterizations are delineated. Common to all these types of constructivism, however, is the active engagement of an involved individual. As we saw in the chapter on the nature of language, as well as in the chapters on the reading, comprehending, and writing processes, the individual actively assembles the text. The individual makes use of linguistic and cognitive resources to build a linguistic and conceptual understanding of the language encountered. We also saw that this building of meaning and knowledge are impacted or sponsored by the various groups or "clubs" to which the individual is a member. Personal meanings reflect social meanings. In this sense, various types of constructivism are involved in every act of literacy.

Developmentally, which is our focus in this chapter, constructivism refers to the individual's active building of an understanding for how written language operates linguistically, cognitively, and socioculturally. Therefore, when interacting with a text, the individual is simultaneously involved in two acts. The individual is constructing meaning using available linguistic, cognitive, and sociocultural resources.

At the same time, the individual is also constructing a fuller understanding for how the linguistic, cognitive, and sociocultural dimensions of the language operate.

In the past, it was thought that proficient language users (i.e., parents, caregivers, teachers) were largely responsible for or determined language learning. The child was conceived to be a passive and empty recipient, filled with language by those who already knew it. However, as illustrated here, research conducted during the last three decades has clearly demonstrated that language development involves a transaction between the child and the environment (e.g., Bruner, 1974; Clay, 1975; DeFord, 1981; Dyson, 1997, 1998, 2003; Harste et al., 1984; Teale, 1984; Wells, 1986). Both the learner and environment act and are acted on.

Not only is language development an inductive process, but the rules governing the various dimensions of language (e.g., systems of language, cognitive processes, cultural norms) are learned tacitly. Initially, the child's focus is on trying to understand the intentions and meanings that undergird the language being used. The rules governing the language are constructed during the process of attempting to understand. Because of this indirect learning, the child's knowledge is largely implicit; that is, the child is capable of employing the rules, processes, and norms to generate and use language, but is unable to verbalize them. For many children,

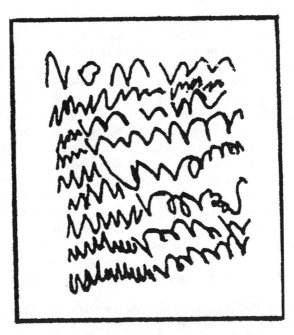

FIG. 11.2.   Dawn's initial writing sample. From Harste, J., Woodward, V., and Burke, C. (1984). *Language stories and literacy lessons* (p. 82). Portsmouth, NH: Heinemann.

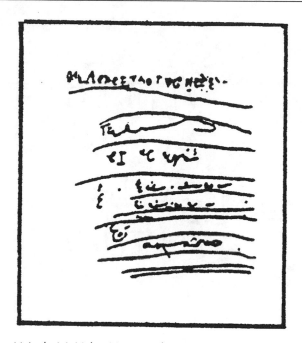

FIG. 11.3.   Najeeba's initial writing sample. From Harste, J., Woodward, V.,
and Burke, C. (1984). *Language stories and literacy lessons* (p. 82). Portsmouth,
NH: Heinemann.

schools are the first context in which what is known implicitly must be made
explicit to be counted as knowledge.

Just as we discovered that miscues reveal the underlying rules and processes
used by proficient readers, so too the "errors" in language use reveal the rules and
processes used by developing readers and writers. Unconventional writings, for
instance, display the thought processes and regulatory systems of the young child.
To demonstrate the rule-revealing nature of errors, we examine a number of initial
writing samples from preschool children. Many of these samples come from the
seminal early literacy research of Harste et al. (1984).

In the first set of examples (Figs. 11.2, 11.3, and 11.4), three 4-year-olds (Dawn,
Najeeba, and Ofer, respectively) were asked to write anything they knew on a piece
of unlined paper. At this point in their lives, the three children had not yet received
any form of direct explicit literacy instruction. In fact, their parents were surprised
and delighted at what their children actually knew about print. Look closely at these
three samples and jot down what each child appears to understand about the writing
process. Keep in mind that this "knowing" may be different from the "knowing"
of more proficient language users. Nevertheless, consider what hypotheses each
child has generated about how the written language system operates.

FIG. 11.4.   Ofer's initial writing sample. From Harste, J., Woodward, V., and Burke, C. (1984). *Language stories and literacy lessons* (p. 82). Portsmouth, NH: Heinemann.

Although not formally introduced to the written language system, all three children had clearly encountered written language in their environments. Dawn, an American child, did her "writing" from top to bottom and from left to right. Najeeba, a child from Saudi Arabia, first drew lines across the blank paper and then produced a script that contained curlicue formations and numerous dots. His understanding of written language differed from Dawn's because the language data to which he was exposed differed. Although difficult to see in Najeeba's sample, the top line contains letters of the English alphabet. Najeeba had recently come to the United States with his parents, who were attending a local university. Finally, Fig. 11.4 was produced by Ofer, an Israeli preschooler. His parents were also in the United States attending college. As is the convention in Hebrew, he wrote from right to left and then, as is the convention in English, from left to right.

These samples clearly demonstrate that the three children were all actively engaged in generating hypotheses from the written language data that they had encountered in their environments. Najeeba, in fact, demonstrated developing knowledge of two written systems—Arabic and English. Although not conventional, the children's very different representations of their languages reflect very active attempts to understand how their respective language systems operate.

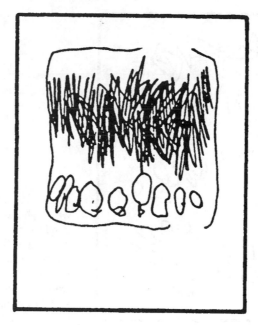

FIG. 11.5.   Shannon's writing and illustration sample. From Harste, J., Woodward, V., and Burke, C. (1984). *Language stories and literacy lessons* (p. 82). Portsmouth, NH: Heinemann.

Beginning around the age of three years old, young children also begin to understand the difference between the symbolic system of writing and the iconic system of drawing. Shannon, a 3-year-old in the Harste et al. (1984) study, was asked to draw a picture of his family and then to write his name underneath the picture. Figure 11.5 represents his response. Never explicitly taught to write and draw, Shannon nonetheless had already begun to tease out the differences between the two communication systems. It should be noted at this point in our discussion that young children use various forms to represent both their knowledge of written language and of drawing. As Shannon's writing sample demonstrates, scribbling is not the only way to represent writing; the use of circles will work just as well.

In the second pair of writing examples (Figs. 11.6 and 11.7), a preschool child named Megan was asked to write a story and a letter. If you are unable to read her attempts, her oral readings of the texts accompany each sample. Once again, examine the two samples and consider what rules Megan generated about written language.

As illustrated by these writings, Megan had already begun to formulate understandings of the differences in both the structure and content of stories and letters. She began her story with the typical <Once upon a time> and finished with

Once upon a time there
was a ghost. Three ghost
family. One day they went
out for a walk. They honked
the horn cause they saw Mrs.
Wood and said "Hi." They
went back to Mrs. Corners
and they honked the
horn and said "Hi." The end.

FIG. 11.6.   Megan's story sample. From Harste, J., Woodward, V., and Burke, C. (1984). *Language stories and literacy lessons* (p. 109). Portsmouth, NH: Heinemann.

<The end>, a marking of the conclusion frequently used by young children. Although hers is not a fully formed story as defined in chapter 2, Megan is well on her way to developing such a form. Her letter is even more revealing. Initially, she forgot the greeting of a letter and reverted to the more familiar <Once upon a time> introduction found in some stories, especially fairy tales. Suddenly, she remembered that she was writing a letter and switched to the use of a greeting— in this case, <Dear Mary>. In concluding, Megan used both a storylike marking (<The end>) and a letterlike marking (<Megan>).

Finally, we take a look at a piece of writing by Susan (source unknown), a 3-year-old preschooler. She was asked to write a shopping list for the grocery store. As clearly shown in Fig. 11.8, Susan's writing visually resembles what might be a list. When asked to read her list and point to each item, Susan read one item per line.

Until recently, the notion of the learner generating rules for understanding written language was largely ignored. Written language development was thought to come about through direct, skill-by-skill instruction. However, we now know that children also attempt to make sense of the print that surrounds them. Children appropriate, negotiate, and orchestrate the data encountered. In the next series of

Once upon a time
there was—wait, uh,
uh. Dear Mary, I would
like you to bring me
here every day.
The end. Megan.

FIG. 11.7.   Megan's letter sample. From Harste, J., Woodward, V., and Burke,
C. (1984). *Language stories and literacy lessons* (p. 109). Portsmouth, NH:
Heinemann.

examples, we look more closely at the various hypotheses the young child has
generated about particular writing conventions.

In the first example shown in Fig. 11.9, a preschool child wrote the following
sentence: <Hi, I like to eat because I am hungry> (source unknown). The child
clearly understands that word boundaries are marked in English but uses lines rather
than spaces. Similarly, Matt (Harste et al., 1984), nine years of age, understands
word boundaries as well (Fig. 11.10). He simply used another convention—dots—
to mark such boundaries. Although both children encountered word boundaries in
print, their hypotheses are not mere imitations or copies of what they have observed.
Clearly, the preschool child had not seen word boundaries marked by lines. Matt
had certainly encountered the use of dots to mark sentences—periods—but not
words. However, the stance of these two children is to understand the rule system
through the generation and testing of hypotheses, not to simply reproduce what is
seen.

Hypothesis generating and testing do not necessarily end in the early grades. I
asked a child entering the fifth grade to write a story to accompany the pictures in
the wordless picture book *Ah-choo*, by Mayer (1976). When he read his writing
(as shown in Fig. 11.11), the child read <hiccup> for each pair of quotation marks.

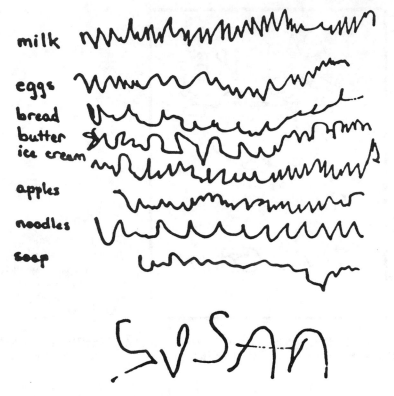

milk

eggs
bread
butter
ice cream

apples

noodles

soap

FIG. 11.8.   Susan's grocery list sample. Source unknown.

FIG. 11.9.   Using lines to demarcate word boundaries.

The child had essentially combined the use of quotation marks with ditto marks and created a new convention for the use of repeated words. This remixing and recontextualizing—or transporting and transforming—of material encountered in previous settings to new situations is typical of the active child at work (Dyson, 2003). We fail to appreciate such active behavior, however, if the efforts of the child are judged only in terms of conventionality.

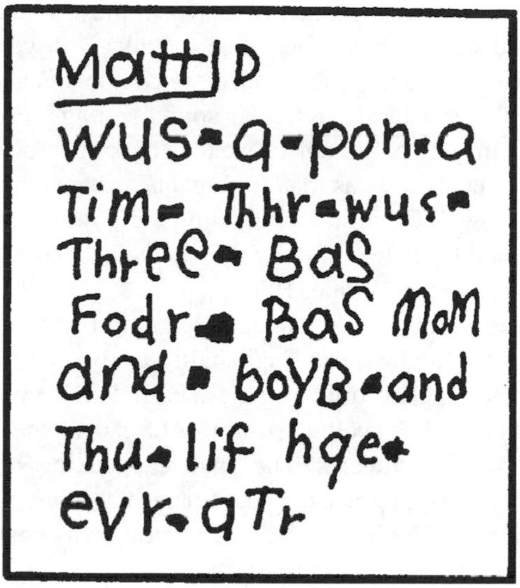

FIG. 11.10.   Using dots to demarcate word boundaries. From Harste, J., Woodward, V., and Burke, C. (1984). *Language stories and literacy lessons* (p. 87). Portsmouth, NH: Heinemann.

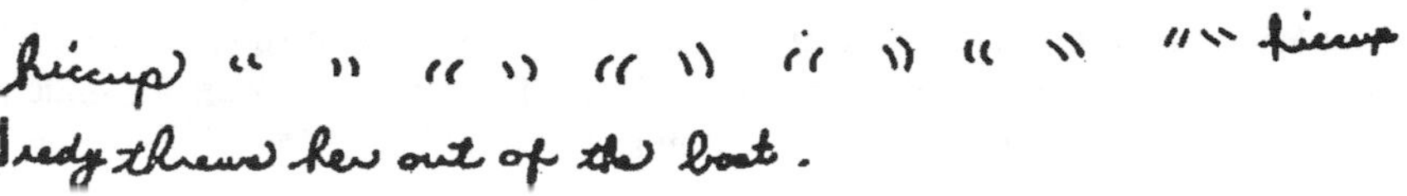

FIG. 11.11.   Using quotation marks to repeat sounds.

Even learning to spell, which was largely thought to be a process of memorization and application of phonic rules, reflects the activity of a constructive mind. Through his investigation of the spelling of young children, Read (1971, 1975) discovered rule-governed, systematic, orthographic patterns that were not necessarily based on adult logic. In their spelling attempts, children tended to use the sounds contained in the letter names—both vowels and consonants—as opposed to letter sounds. For example, <cherry> was represented as <hare>, <museum> as <muzm>, and <day> as <da>. To represent short vowels, the children used the position of the mouth and tongue. The vowel's name and the sound to be represented in print were matched when the position of the mouth and tongue were similar. <Bed> was spelled as <bad>, <fish> as <fes>, and <fell> as <fall>.

Children also apply their understanding of the language's phonological system in determining how a word is to be represented in print. For example, the sounds of affricatives (e.g., /tr/ and /dr/) are more often the property of /ch/ and /g/ than

/t/ and /d/. Therefore, children frequently represent these sounds in print through the use of <ch> and <g>. <Truck> becomes <chruk>, <drive> becomes <griv>, and <dragon> becomes <jragin>. There also are circumstances in which children are unaware as to which letter a particular sound belongs. Preconsonant nasals, such as /n/ and /m/, may be omitted because they are not perceptually salient. The difference between such words as /pat/ and /pant/, for example, is understood as a difference in the vowel. Or children may omit the vowel before /l/, /m/, and /n/ because the consonant tends to "swallow up" the vowel: <from> becomes <frm> and <open> becomes <opn> (Wilde, 1992).

This constructive stance toward language learning is also evident in bilingual children learning to read and write in English. In a study examining the interaction between Spanish and English orthographies, Fashola, Drum, Mayer, and Kang (1996) compared the English spelling patterns of Spanish-speaking children with those of English-speaking students. The Spanish-speaking students were in the second, third, fifth, and sixth grades; spoke Spanish at home; and were classified by the schools as limited English proficient. The English-speaking students were native speakers and nonproficient in Spanish.

All students were given a list of forty common English words to spell. In an examination of the spelling errors of Spanish-speaking students, two patterns were discovered. First, students produced misspellings by actively adjusting their perceptions of English phonology to fit within the Spanish phonological system. Sounds that exist in English but not in Spanish, such as the sound of /oo/ in /look/ and the /b/ in /cable/, were mapped onto the closest Spanish sounds, such as /o/ and /v/. Second, with sounds that exist in both English and Spanish, students frequently applied Spanish phonological and orthographic rules rather than English rules. For example, the English word /hero/ was spelled <jero>, because the sound represented by /h/ in English corresponds to the sound that is marked by <j> in Spanish. In both cases, the children were not slavishly attempting to memorize the English orthographic system. Rather, they were drawing on their Spanish linguistic resources to make sense of a new English written language system.

As you may have guessed by now, there is little evidence to suggest that language is learned through imitation to any great extent. The child's stance is not to replicate or copy the language that is encountered. Rather, the child attempts to understand the meanings being expressed and the systems of language that serve as the avenue for their expression. Through such attempts at understanding, the language is constructed. As the previous examples indicate, we know that imitations play a minor role in language learning because children generate language forms and conventions that they have never before encountered. Most children have not seen their parents use lines or dots to demarcate word boundaries. Such behaviors are the reflection of an active, constructing mind, the mind of a learner who is generating and testing hypotheses for the data encountered.

Second, even if the child wanted to imitate the language, most rules for the linguistic, cognitive, and sociocultural dimensions of language are not directly displayed. For example, the rules of the syntax that underlie every sentence are not explicitly evident. Nor, given the great variability of letter–sound relationships, are the rules for graphophonemics readily apparent. They are not directly articulated in the surface structure. In fact, if most adult language users were asked to make explicit their knowledge of the various dimensions of literacy, they would be unable to do so. Such knowledge is implicit and has been learned tacitly.

Finally, as documented by Keenan-Ochs (1977), in oral language, much of what appears to be imitation in fact is repetition. The repeating of what has been heard is used by both parents and children as a strategy for communication. For example, the parents or children may repeat what they heard as a communicative check, to verify that he or she has heard and understood correctly. Repetition may also serve as a vehicle for topic extension. Even among adults, there is a concept known as the given–new contract. The responder repeats part of what has been said (given) and then builds on additional information (new). Children engage in the same kind of behavior. Finally, information may be repeated to signal agreement or to make counterclaims.

In the process of language learning, it has been suggested by Bruner (1990) that the child comes "prewired" with structures or tools that support development. This prewiring is not the language itself or even so much linguistic in nature. Rather, the tools support the learner in understanding the events that are unfolding in the immediate environment. This understanding or meaning is then mapped onto the language itself. According to Bruner, the child is born with an interest in human action, interaction, and the resulting outcomes. The child also attempts to establish order in the environment through a sensitivity to temporal sequence, causation, or correlation. In addition, the child seeks to understand perspective or voice. Finally, special attention is given to the marking of unusual events and actions to distinguish them from the usual.

Development as a Recursive Process

A second principle of language learning highlights the recursive, interactive nature of development. It is commonly thought that learning is a process that involves improvement over time; that is, the child's attempts at using language become more and more conventional as time passes. However, at least on the surface, this may not always be the case. The ongoing development and refinement of hypotheses may cause the child to appear to have taken a step backward. Therefore, a distinction must be made between surface-level behaviors and deeper level hypotheses.

In spoken language, the development and testing of hypotheses have been found to follow a fairly typical pattern. Initially, the learner may use a particular word or structure correctly. This occurs because the child has not yet encountered enough data to begin the formulation of rules for the language. Much of the child's vocabulary is initially learned in this fashion. The child may conventionally use, for example, such words as /sheep/, /fish/, /go/, and /daddy/.

With additional language encounters, the child begins to formulate hypotheses for how the linguistic system operates. The child learns the /s/ rule for plurality, the /ed/ rule for past tense, and additional semantic features that define a word (for example, /daddy/ is a man with glasses). At this point, /sheep/ becomes /sheeps/, /fish/ becomes /fishes/, /go/ becomes /goed/, and any man wearing glasses becomes /daddy/. Many parents view such behavior as a step backward in the language development of their child. These surface-level behaviors look like regressions rather than advancements. However, just the opposite has occurred. The child has been actively attempting to understand how the language operates and has generated a number of viable and valid rules. The rules have simply been overgeneralized or overextended. The child simply needs to learn the exceptions. Over time and with linguistic feedback, the child modifies the rules as the exceptions are learned.

Overgeneralizations occur in writing as well. A primary school teacher was concerned that her students suddenly started to spell unconventionally words that they had previously spelled correctly. The word <blow> became <blowe>, <corn> became <corne>, and <toy> became <toye>. In talking with the teacher, the researcher discovered that she had recently introduced her students to the "silent e" found in such consonant–vowel–consonant–e words as <bake> and <lake>. The children, thinking that many of the words they were writing might contain a silent <e>, began adding <e>'s to the endings of their words.

The evolving signature of a young child named Alison (Fig. 11.12), documented by Harste et al. (1984), also illustrates this recursive phenomenon. At 3.0, Alison demonstrates control of the manuscript <n> in her name. However, at 3.7, the letter appears to have been written in cursive, although all other letters are represented in manuscript. It is not until 4.8 that the formation of the letter becomes stabilized. Similarly, although initially problematic for her, Alison comes to produce a well-formed <s> at 4.1. At 4.8, the <s> becomes reversed; it is not until 5 years of age that the <s> is conventionally formed. Most interesting is Alison's sudden use of a <u> in her name at age 5.0, a letter that had not previously been used. Rather than taking a step backward, Alison is actually demonstrating some newfound knowledge. She is becoming increasingly aware that the sounds in her spoken language are represented in the letters of written language. Rather than simply writing her name "from memory," Alison attempts to use her evolving understanding of sound–letter relations in her spelling.

There is a second and related reason that advances in the surface structure may suddenly appear to be abandoned and old forms returned to. As we found in our analysis of the cognitive nature of language, there are always limits to the cognitive resources available to any language user. When new learnings are developing, energy and attention must be allocated to these learnings. This results in fewer resources being available for other aspects of language and thought. When such situations occur, it is not uncommon for the more recent learnings to become unstable because energy is not available to control them. In the case of Alison, the positioning of the <s> continued to be a challenge for her throughout first grade.

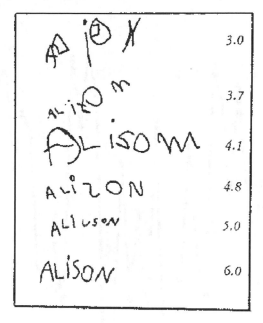

FIG. 11.12.   Spelling over time. From Harste, J., Woodward, V., and Burke, C. (1984). *Language stories and literacy lessons* (p. 12). Portsmouth, NH: Heinemann.

Whenever she was engaged in a demanding writing task, such as composing a make believe story, Alison would experience difficulty controlling the *s* because her focus was on other aspects of the written discourse.

Graves (1983) proposed that the last aspect of writing learned is the first aspect to be lost when the demands of the writing task overload the writer. Over a two-year period, Graves documented the writing development of six- to ten-year-old elementary students. Each piece of writing produced by the students was holistically evaluated in terms of the use of information, organization, and language. Although the general quality of the writing improved over the two years, not every piece was better than the one before. As illustrated by the writing of Andrea, shown in Fig. 11.13, such factors as the topic, text structure, and audience impacted the quality of the piece and which aspects of the writing process the writer was able to control. Writing ability was not monolithic, a process that the child was able to uniformly control across texts, contexts, and contents.

Not limited to young children, the to-and-fro nature of development is found in more proficient language users as well. For example, the ability of a group of university students to control coherence, or the overall organization of a text, during the course of a semester-long composition course was examined (Kucer, 1983a, 1983b). Regardless of any student's overall writing ability in general, and command

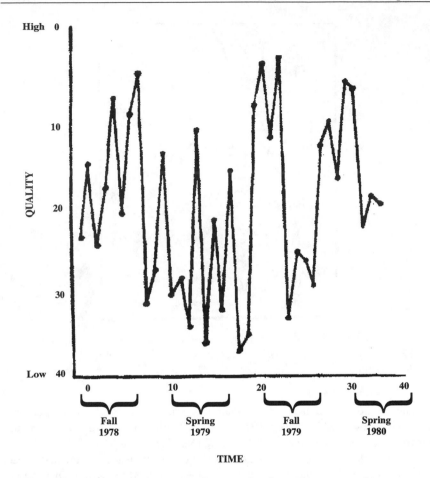

FIG. 11.13.   The recursive nature of writing development. Reprinted by
permission from *Writing: Teachers and children at work* by Donald H. Graves.
Copyright © 2003 by Donald H. Graves. First published © 1983 by Donald H.
Graves. Published by Heinemann, a division of Reed Elsevier, Inc., Portsmouth,
NH. All rights reserved.

of coherence in particular, control of coherence within one writing activity was not
predictive of control within another. Even the most proficient writers in the class
did not demonstrate consistent proficiency on all writing assignments; nor did those
writers having the least control over coherence always produce highly incoherent
texts. There existed conditions under which both groups of writers displayed a
high degree and a low degree of control over the process. Furthermore, different
writers were impacted differently by different tasks. Throughout the course of the
semester, it was not uncommon for a writer to produce one of the most coherent

texts in the class under one writing condition and then produce one of the most incoherent texts under another condition.

The Adult as Demonstrator, Mediator, and Guide

Although the child is intimately involved in the process of language learning, adults or more capable "others" are not passive viewers. Just as we found that various cultural groups, institutions, or worksites sponsor various kinds of literacy development in adults (see chapter 9), parents also sponsor language learning in their young children. Adults—usually the parents and primary caregivers at first—are actively involved, demonstrating the dimensions of language to and for the child as well as mediating and supporting the child's attempts to use language. Together, the parent and child participate in a communicative event and negotiate and create shared meanings. Therefore, the adult and child socially and collaboratively construct the dimensions of literacy. This focus on meaning allows the child to take risks without fear of rejection.

Brown (1973) was one of the first researchers to document the behavior of parents as they verbally interacted with their young children. The following example (Table 11.2) involves a conversation between a mother and her preschool

TABLE 11.2
Typical Parent–Child Language Interaction

EVE:	Have that?
MOTHER:	No, you may not have it.
EVE:	Mom, where my tapioca?
MOTHER:	It's getting cool. You'll have it in just a minute.
EVE:	Let me have it.
MOTHER:	Would you like to have your lunch right now?
EVE:	Yeah. My tapioca cool?
MOTHER:	Yes, it's cool.
EVE:	You gonna watch me eat my lunch?
MOTHER:	Yeah, I'm gonna watch you eat your lunch.
EVE:	I eating it.
MOTHER:	I know you are.
EVE:	It time Sarah take a nap.
MOTHER:	It's time for Sarah to have some milk, yeah. And then she's gonna take a nap and you're going to take a nap.
EVE:	And you?
MOTHER:	And me too, yeah.

child (Eve). As you read through the transcript, consider the intentions of each, the language of the child, and the language used in response by the mother.

As the transcript makes clear, the mother's focus was on getting Eve to eat her lunch—before eating the dessert—and then to take a nap. Eve also had her own intentions and wanted to eat the tapioca first. As the event unfolds, the mother could either focus on the conflicting intentions or on taking the opportunity to teach Eve some language. Most of Eve's sentences were not fully formed syntactic structures, and the mother might want to teach grammar to her child. However, as anyone who has had a young child knows, little would get accomplished if the parent responded to every "mistake" the child made when talking. Additionally, we can easily understand what Eve is saying even though her language was not fully formed.

The mother, as do most adults, elected to focus on the meanings and intentions behind Eve's utterances. Her responses, however, also provided important linguistic feedback for Eve. For example, in reply to Eve's /Have that?/, which lacks a subject, the mother provided the subject with /No, you may not have it/. Or, when Eve omitted the verb in /Mom, where my tapioca?/, her mother did not admonish her to include verbs in her sentences. However, she did demonstrate the use of verbs in her response, /It's getting cool/.

There is little evidence of deliberate and extensive direct instruction on the part of most parents. Many parents may explicitly teach polite expressions such as /thank you/ or /please/. Even there, however, the focus is more on helping the child to remember to use the expression in the appropriate contexts than to teach the child new words. Vocabulary "instruction" may occur at the end of two years when the child suddenly realizes that objects have names. The child, however, is usually the initiator, asking the /What is this?/ question.

Although a focus on meaning is typical of most parents, on occasion parents may attempt to "help" the child use the language correctly. In most cases, however, the instruction may not have the intended effects. Table 11.3 contains two samples (Braine, 1971; Cazden, 1972) in which a parent is attempting to help the child "say it right."

In both of these examples, it is clear that the parent understands what the child is saying. The first parent responds with a typical teaching strategy—simplify and reduce the language to smaller and smaller pieces—to help the child speak conventionally. In the first case, the child is able to say /spoon/ in isolation but quickly reverts back to the rule-governed structure when asking for the /other one spoon/. The second parent is a bit more sophisticated and provides the word /held/ for the child to imitate. However, the second child has overgeneralized the past tense marker /ed/ to words that are the exception: /hold, held/. Once again, because the child's language is based on a rule rather than on imitation, the child continues with the overgeneralization. In oral language, Nelson (1973) found the children whose parents responded to form rather than to meaning developed language more slowly. Direct instruction failed.

TABLE 11.3

Attempts at Correcting

• *Sample 1*	
CHILD:	Want other one spoon, Daddy.
FATHER:	You mean, you want the other spoon?
CHILD:	Yes, I want other one spoon, please daddy.
FATHER:	Can you say, "The other spoon?"
CHILD:	Other . . . one . . . spoon.
FATHER:	Say "other."
CHILD:	Other
FATHER:	"Spoon."
CHILD:	Spoon
FATHER:	"Other spoon."
CHILD:	Other . . . spoon. Now, give me other one spoon?
• *Sample 2*	
CHILD	My teacher holder the baby rabbits and we patted them.
ADULT:	Did you say your teacher held the baby rabbits?
CHILD:	Yes.
ADULT:	What did you say?
CHILD:	She holded the baby rabbits and we patted them.
ADULT:	Did you say she held them tightly?
CHILD:	No, she holded them loosely

Children do not, however, learn language all on their own, independent from those more capable language users with whom they engage. Children are not simply immersed in a garden of oral or written discourse and then left to independently construct the language (K. Goodman & Y. Goodman, 1979). Adults or more capable others play a critical role in the construction through their demonstrations and their mediations. F. Smith (1981) suggested that observing language being used in the environment is the start of language development. Initially observed are demonstrations, displays of how something operates or is accomplished, in this case language use. Displays occur in meaningful, functional contexts and provide the observer with a variety of linguistic, cognitive, and sociocultural information.

Repeated encounters with a particular demonstration, such as parent–child book reading, afford the learner the opportunity to attend to new aspects within the demonstration. The child develops an evolving sensitivity or awareness to particular aspects of the demonstration that influences the kind of engagement that occurs. The engagement represents the child's involvement with the demonstration. It is a coming together of learner and event. Such engagements with various discourse communities—for example, home, school, church—inform the child about the nature of the dimensions of literacy. Therefore, "what counts as valid knowledge, as valid ways of coming to know, and as valid ways of being in the world" (Novinger, 2003, p. 427) is shaped by the discourse communities in which the child is engaged.

In addition to demonstrating language use, the adult is also directly involved in mediating or guiding language development. Building on the learning and developmental concepts first set forth by Vygotsky (1962, 1978), a number of researchers have examined how adults interact with and promote their children's language growth (e.g., Teale, 1984; Wells, 1986; Wertsch, 1985). As illustrated in Fig. 11.14, language learning begins on a social, collaborative plane, termed *interpsychological* by Vygotsky. Interpsychological or potential abilities are processes and strategies that the child can successfully accomplish only with the help and support of more capable others. The darker portions in the upper left-hand corner of the figure indicate significant degrees of support. These abilities are potential in that they will, with time, with experience, and with continued support, eventually become independent or internal abilities (intrapsychological). Vygotsky described potential abilities as similar to buds on a tree that with time and nourishment will bloom into flowers and ultimately bear fruit.

The distance between what the child can accomplish with the support of others and can accomplish independently is what Vygotsky termed the *zone of proximal development* (ZPD). Movement through the ZPD—depicted by the developmental arrow in Fig. 11.14—is movement from collaborative to independent abilities. This movement is both sponsored and facilitated by the supportive, interactive environment that adults provide for the child. Often called scaffolding (Bruner, 1974), the adult structures the language or literacy event such that the child is able to participate in a meaningful way.

As the child begins to learn and internalize particular aspects of the dimensions of language, the adult modifies or begins to deconstruct the support structure. This modification requires that the child take on those aspects of language that have been developed, that is, are independent. The adult continues to provide support for other language features that are in the state of development. This pattern of interaction ensures that the child can participate in the communicative event as fully as possible. In Fig. 11.4, as the developmental arrows move towards the lower right-hand corner—towards independence—the background becomes lighter. The support provided by the adult progressively decreases and the child assumes more responsibility. Independent abilities, the ultimate goal of development, are those language behaviors that the child is able to employ without the support or assistance of others. Language strategies or processes, once social and external in nature, are now internal, autonomous, and self-governing.

Various types of support for language and literacy development have been identified. Table 11.4 contains some of those support structures found to be the most common within the home environment (Cazden, 1988, 2001; Wells, 1986).

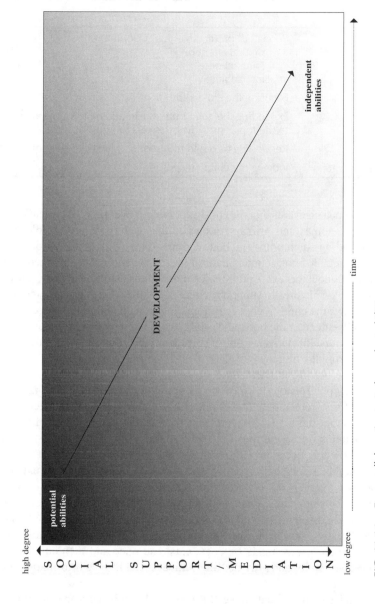

FIG. 11.14.   From collaborative to independent abilities.

TABLE 11.4

Adult–Child Interactional Patterns

Pattern	Characteristics
Routines	Repeated, predictable interactional events: mutual attention joint action intersubjectivity
Attentional	Focusing the child's attention
Expansions	Expanding the child's utterance; adding new information to the topic; providing answers to questions, etc.
Questioning	Requesting the child to respond; asking clarifying questions
Feedback/Evaluation	Judging the child's response

Routines are repeated events that the child experiences over time. A typical routine found in many homes and primary grades is the reading of predictable books to—shared reading—and with—guided reading—the young child. As defined in chapter 5, predictable books contain natural language patterns that are recurrent or built upon throughout the text. Additionally, the pictures parallel the story, allowing the child to use the pictures to support the reading of the print. The repeated use of such texts allows the child to engage in joint action with the adult. The child and parent mutually attend to the book and establish a shared focus and understanding of the event (intersubjectivity). Both the child and the adult are aware of what is to transpire during the literacy event.

For example, during the rereading of the predictable book "The Great Big Enormous Turnip" (Tolstoy, 1976) with my young niece, I focused her attention. I asked her if she remembered what the story was about and engaged her in a discussion about the book. As we began the reading, she was asked to point to particular items in the pictures (e.g., old woman, old man, turnip) and their corresponding words in the text. Such attentional focusing assured that both she and I were on the "same page," so to speak. Throughout the reading, I expanded her responses to the story, adding new information as necessary. When the dog was introduced in the story, she commented that dogs do not like cats. Based on this comment, we discussed the neighbor's dog and the relationship between their dog and her cat. Finally, I questioned her about the story and evaluated her responses. I asked what sounds were made by dogs, cats, and mice and then confirmed or disconfirmed her replies and provided alternative and additional information when necessary.

Mediational structures that move the learner through the zone of proximal development have been proposed for school-based literacy instruction as well (e.g., Carrasquillo, Kucer, & Abrams, 2004; Fountas & Pinnell, 1996; Kucer & Silva, in progress). Table 11.5 presents a series of instructional literacy strategies

TABLE 11.5
Strategy Lessons and Mediation

Most Support

Reading and Writing To

Teacher Reading: The teacher reads aloud a text to the children, responding at various places and encouraging the children to respond as well.	*Teacher Writing:* The teacher demonstrates the writing of a text, discussing his/her thinking as s/he writes.
Shared Reading: The teacher reads aloud a text to the children, asking them to predict upcoming meanings when appropriate or to chorally read with her/him particular parts.	*Shared Writing:* The teacher records a text that the children dictate; the teacher supports student generation of ideas by asking questions and reflecting on text content, development, organization, conventions, etc.

Reading and Writing With

Choral Reading: The teacher and the children orally read a text together.	*Choral Writing:* The teacher and the children write a text together; the teacher and individual students take turns generating and recording new ideas.
Guided Reading: Individual children read a text aloud with support provided by the teacher as necessary.	*Guided Writing:* Individual children write a text with support provided by the teacher as necessary.

Reading and Writing By

Paired Reading. Two children orally read a text aloud together.	*Paired Writing.* Two children write a text together.
Independent Reading: Each child silently reads a text independently.	*Independent Writing:* Each child silently writes a text independently.

Least Support

that correspond to varying degrees of support. As with the previous table, the darker portions of the table indicate more support and the lighter portions less support. Teacher reading and writing, for example, are the most supportive in nature with the teacher assuming most of the processing responsibility. As instruction moves to shared, choral, guided, and paired reading and writing, the child is held more accountable for the processing. Finally, in independent reading and writing, the child is largely processing the text on his or her own. Stated somewhat differently, in Teacher and Shared strategy lessons, the teacher is reading and writing *to* the students. In Choral and Guided lessons, the teacher is reading and writing *with* the students. And, in Paired and Independent strategy lessons, the reading and writing is *by* the students.

Once again, we should remember that the forms of mediation provided may vary by culture. Ethnographers such as Heath (1982a, 1982b, 1983), Wells (1986), A. Anderson and Stokes (1984), and Schieffelin and Cochran-Smith (1984) have all demonstrated that there are no universal types of mediation. Different groups sponsor literacy learning in different ways. Adults do, however, expect that children will enter their oral and written language communities. Their interactions and mediations with children reflect this assumption. Therefore, regardless of culture, children are immersed in a world that is organized, supportive, and steeped in symbols (Nelson, 1996).

Finally, it is also important to keep in mind the active participation of the learner in this entire enterprise. Children do not simply and passively fit into the scaffolds constructed for them. Rather, they bring their own experiences and interpretations to each communicative event and these may not always match those of the mediator. In her seminal book, *Children's Minds*, Donaldson (1978) describes a young child's confusion during her first day at school. In an attempt to learn the students' names, as well as to take attendance, the teacher asks the child, "Is your name Laurie Lee?" The child replies, "Yes," and the teacher responds, "Fine, now just sit there for the present time." From an adult perspective, it is clear that the directive to the child is intended to help the teacher take attendance in an orderly fashion. However, the child interprets "present" as a gift, misses the teacher's intention entirely, and returns home in the afternoon fuming about being lied to. Intersubjectivity clearly had not been established between teacher and learner.

A number of researchers have investigated both the process of establishing intersubjectivity (e.g., Barnes & Todd, 1995; Dyson, 2003; Kucer, 1992; McCarthey, 1998; Searle, 1984) as well as learner resistance to scaffolds that have been developed without their participation (e.g., Abowitz, 2000; Ashley, 2001; Delpit, 1995; Finders, 1996; Kohl, 1994; Kucer, 1998, 1999; Labbo, et al., 1995; McDermott, 1987, 1995). This body of research suggests that creating shared understanding and meaningful involvement always involves a give and take between the learner and the adult. Intersubjectivity, scaffolds, and engagement are mutually constructed, negotiated, and sustained among the participants.

Negotiating Meaning

Both in oral and written language development, children use a variety of cues to generate meaning from and through language. In the following language story, consider how both the young boy and his sister are able to understand what is being said.

> An English woman is in the company of an Arab woman and her two children, a boy of seven and a little girl of thirteen months who is just beginning to walk but is afraid to take more than a few steps without help. The English woman speaks no Arabic, the Arab woman and her son speak no English. The little girl walks to the English woman and back to her mother. Then, she turns as if to start off in the direction of

the English woman once again. But, the latter now smiles, points to the boy and says, "Walk to your brother this time." At once the boy, though he understands not a word of the language, holds out his arms. The baby smiles, changes direction, and walks to her brother (Donaldson, 1978, p. 37).

Although the boy was not a speaker of English and the little girl was just beginning her learning of language, both were able to "understand" what was said. Contributing to their understanding was the pointing of the English woman to the brother. The brother holding out his arms provided additional cues to the girl. Also, a routine of walking from one adult to another had been established. Finally, although we are unable to hear how the sentence—/Walk to your brother this time/— was spoken, we can imagine that the intonation of a command might have been used. These various oral language cues, categorized in Table 11.6, allow the language learner to build an understanding of the meaning behind the utterances. As previously discussed, this understanding supports the child in mapping meaning onto the language.

Because young children are actively engaged with their environment, they also use various cues to help them understand the print that is encountered. Environmental print, the written language found on signs, food products, games, and so on, is typically located in situations that provide a wealth of cues for reading. Children see the print on milk cartons, fast-food soda cups, and stop signs. They also observe the relation between the print and what the object contains or what

TABLE 11.6

Oral and Written Language Cues

Oral Language Cues	Written Language Cues
Linguistic Anything that is part of the language itself, e.g. systems of language	*Linguistic* Anything that is part of the language itself, e.g. systems of language
Paralinguistic Cues that are part of language but are not linguistic in nature, e.g. pitch, intonation, stress, rhythm	*Paralinguistic* Cues that are part of the language but are not linguistic in nature, e.g. exclamation points, questions marks, bold face, italics, print/font size, print display
Intent Underlying purpose/function of the language, e.g. command, request, question	*Intent* Underlying purpose/function of the language, e.g. command, request, question
Extralinguistic Cues that accompany the use of the language, e.g. facial expressions, gestures, physical movements, setting, objects in the environment	*Extralinguistic* Cues that accompany the use of the language, e.g. pictures, illustrations, charts, use of color
Background Knowledge What is known in terms of past interactions with the person, language, setting, event	*Background Knowledge* What is known in terms of past interactions with the person, language, setting, event

people do in response to the print. As indicated in Table 11.6, these written language cues parallel those found in oral language and provide a base for early reading experiences for the young child. Harste et al. (1984) found that preschool children from a variety of socioeconomic and cultural backgrounds were able to read much of the environmental print on such objects. Even when they could not, they frequently provided functional responses. When asked to read the environmental print <Kroger> on a milk carton, for example, some children responded with /something that holds milk in it/. K. Goodman, Y. Goodman, and Flores (1979) found that bilingual children are also sensitive to environmental print and respond in similar ways.

The use of various cues or communication systems to negotiate meaning occurs in the child's writing as well. I recently worked with a primary child who was writing a story to accompany a wordless picture book (title unknown). After writing <She sees a>, the boy wanted to write <crazy> but was unsure how the word was spelled. In place of the word, he drew a picture of a face with a bubble full of stars, circles, and spirals (see Fig. 11.15). When asked to explain the illustration, he said that it was similar to cartoons he had seen that used bubbles to indicate a character's anger.

FIG. 11.15.   Using art to support the writing process.

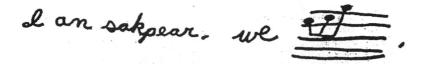

FIG. 11.16.   Using music to support the writing process.

FIG. 11.17.   Using mathematics to support the writing process.

Even older children negotiate their meanings with alternative communication systems. Writing a story to accompany a Mercer Mayer (1974) wordless picture book, one child drew a musical scale for the word <music> (see Fig. 11.16). Finally, a kindergartner was asked to write down what kind of book she wanted from the school library. As shown in Fig. 11.17 (source unknown), she wanted a book on numbers, was unsure how the word was spelled, and substituted real numbers for the word.

INTERRELATIONSHIPS BETWEEN READING AND WRITING DEVELOPMENT

In chapter 8, we found that there were a number of cognitive similarities between reading and writing, set forth in Fig. 8.3. Not only are there cognitive parallels between reading and writing, but there are developmental links as well (Kucer, 1987; Langer & Flihan, 2000; Tierney & Shanahan, 1996). As illustrated in Fig. 11.18, encounters with and learnings from reading are used to advance the writing process, and encounters with and learnings from writing are used to advance the reading process (Kucer & Harste, 1991). Potentially, each process impacts and

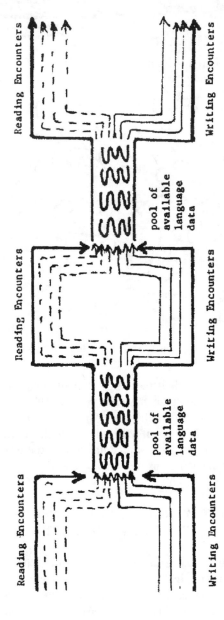

FIG. 11.18.　Common literacy data pool. From Kucer, S. B., and Harste, J. (1991). The reading and writing connection: Counter-part strategy instruction (p. 127). In B. Hayes (Ed.), *Effective strategies for teaching reading.* Boston, MA: Allyn & Bacon.

spurs growth in the other. For example, the discovery that writing involves the integration of meaning into an organized whole sets up expectations by the child that meanings generated through reading should similarly form an organized whole.

In attempting to understand the development of the written language system, a number of researchers have focused on the particular contributions of each process to the other (Kucer, 1987). Interestingly, if the researcher's primary interest was in reading, he or she tended to see reading contributing to writing. If the interest was in writing, then reading development was spurred by developments in writing. It is most likely the case that the type of mediations provided by the teacher significantly influences the degree to which one process impacts the other as well as the direction(s) of the contributions.

DeFord (1981) and Eckhoff (1983) examined the influence that instructional reading material had on the writing development of primary schoolchildren. Both found that the children's writing reflected features of the materials read in the classroom. As DeFord's examples in Fig. 11.19 clearly illustrate, reading instruction does make a difference. Reed, whose writing is at the top of the figure, was in a classroom in which phonics as an instructional strategy was emphasized. This emphasis was found both in the decoding lessons presented by the teacher and in the reading materials that were constrained by letter–sound patterns, such as that found in the decodable text, "A Pin for Dan" (Fries et al., 1966), discussed in chapter 5. The production of such texts by the children was a common occurrence in this classroom.

Similarly, the students in the classroom using a basal reader in which particular words were introduced and used repeatedly in the stories tended to produce stories such as Jeffrey's. It is interesting to note Jeffrey's sensitivity to sentence placement. As found in many beginning readers, each line of the text was limited to one sentence. Finally, Jason came from a classroom in which literature was the primary material used for reading instruction. Children in this classroom tended to produce a wider variety of literary forms, such as stories, songs, and poetry, because these forms were encountered throughout the day. Eckhoff (1983) found similar relations between what children read and what they wrote. Children who encountered reading materials with constrained graphophonemic, morphemic, and syntactic patterns produced writing displaying similar patterns. Children exposed to materials containing more elaborate and varied linguistic patterns tended to include these patterns in their own writing.

Reading has also been shown to contribute to children's use of text structures when writing. Children have been found to spontaneously incorporate certain textual patterns into their writing after they have encountered the patterns in their reading (Blackburn, 1982; Geva & Tierney, 1984; Tierney & Leys, 1986). This is especially the case if the stories contain predictable organizational sequences. According to Blackburn (1982), the use of such sequences is initiated only after the child's conception of "storiness" has begun to develop. That is, the beginnings of story structure in reading precede the use of the structures in writing. The

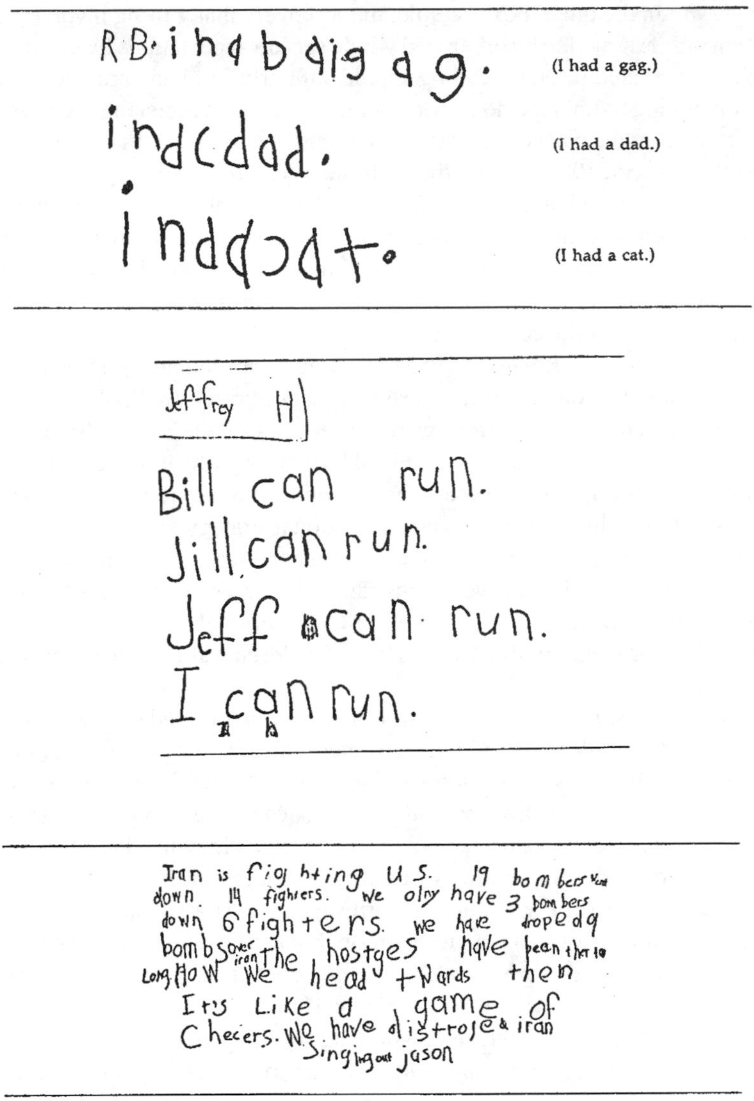

RB· i hd b djg d g.   (I had a gag.)

i ndcdad.   (I had a dad.)

i ndd⊃d+.   (I had a cat.)

Jffroy H)

Bill can run.
Jill can run.
Jeff can run.
I can run.

Iran is fighting U.S.   19 bombers
down.   14 fighters.   we olny have 3 bombers
down 6 fighters.   we have droped a
bombs over the hostges have bean thr to
Long How we head twards then
Its Like a game of
Checers. We have distrojea iran
singing out jason

FIG. 11.19.   The impact of reading materials on writing. From Deford, D.
(1981). Literacy: Reading, writing, and other essentials (pp. 356–357).
Language Arts, 58, 652–658. Copyright © 1981 by the National Council of
Teachers of English. Reprinted with permissions.

280

subsequent use of these structures in writing allows the child to "move forward without a lot of organizational decision-making" (p. 3). Finally, Blackburn noted that when children first use a particular story pattern in their writing, they frequently include meanings from the story to help them control the pattern.

F. Smith (1983a,b) investigated the role that reading plays in the child's understanding of written language conventions. He asserted that writing requires specialized knowledge of spelling, punctuation, capitalization, and syntax that cannot be learned through writing alone. Hypothesis generating and testing require enormous amounts of information and feedback, and the schools simply do not provide enough writing experiences to support such a process. Instead, children must learn the conventions of written language through the texts they read. Because all existing texts display the relevant conventions, it is by reading these texts with the eye of a writer that children come to control the conventions.

A second line of research has examined the contribution of writing to the child's strategy use in reading. In a number of school-based studies with young children (Graves & Hansen, 1983; Hansen, 1983a, 1983b), it has been found that a developing sense of authorship influenced the stances that children took toward published texts. As the children grew in their ability to reflect on what they had written, they began to reflect on what they read. As they learned to generate options in their production of written language and to make revisions, the children also began to read and reread with a sense of options. According to Graves and Hansen (1983), the children initially approached the reading of text with a sense of distance and accepted the author's message as stated. However, as the children learned to question the meanings in their own texts, they also began to question the meanings in those texts they read. Through first engaging in the activity during writing, the children learned to read for layered meanings and to look for part–whole relations in text content.

Finally, Newkirk (1982) and Boutwell (1983) examined how young children learn to distance themselves from their writing and the effect of this distancing on children's ability to distance themselves from what they read. Paralleling the findings of Graves and Hansen (1983), the children in these studies usually had difficulty disembedding the text they wrote from their experiences. Experience and text were fused, and evaluations of the text became evaluations of the experience. Through writing conferences, however, the children developed the ability to distance themselves from what they wrote, and the bonds between experience and text loosened. They became strategic readers of their own texts, reading to evaluate the sense of what they had written, and rewording, deleting, and adding new information to clarify their meanings. This same sense of strategic reading also became apparent in the children's reading of published texts. They became critical readers and used the same strategies to generate meanings from what they were reading.

To a certain extent, the interactive and supportive relationship of reading and writing development is made possible and supported by the intertextual nature of written language. As addressed in chapter 6, intertextuality reflects the linguistic

TABLE 11.7

Intertextual Contributions of Reading to Writing and Writing to Reading

Knowledge of the various systems of language: pragmatic, text type, genre, text structure, semantic, syntactic, morphemic, orthographic, graphophonemic, graphemic
Knowledge of written language conventions: punctuation, capitalization, directionality
Use of background knowledge to support the generation and organization of meaning
Monitoring and evaluation of continuity: informativity, logic, coherence, intentionality, situationality, intertextuality
Revision of meaning as a natural part of language use

and conceptual links among various texts. Texts share particular features based on type (narration, exposition, poetry, drama), genre (novels, folktales, letters, directions), and structure (temporal order, attribution, adversative, covariance, response), as well as the meanings that they include. No text stands alone; rather, it contains linguistic characteristics and meanings found in other texts serving similar purposes in similar contexts. Because of these links, the child comes to learn that the textual patterns encountered when reading narratives, for example, are expected to be employed when writing narratives. Similarly, as the child learns about writing directions, he or she expects to encounter similar features when directions are read. This symbiotic relationship among texts allows the child to use reading to fine-tune his or her writing and to use writing to fine-tune his or her reading. Table 11.7 summarizes the intertextual contributions of each process to the development of the other.

VARIATIONS ON A THEME: CULTURE
AND LITERACY DEVELOPMENT

The previous developmental patterns and principles were presented and discussed in a fairly general manner so as to capture the common themes represented across a variety of literacy learning settings. However, as we found in our examination of dialects, comprehension, and sociocultural characteristics of literacy use, difference is a natural part of the dimensions of written discourse. We should not be surprised, therefore, that variation exists in literacy learning as well. In fact, according to Dyson (2003), variation in development is the norm. In particular, variation is evident when we look at the kinds of literacy activities young children encounter and experience in their homes. In an examination of these home experiences, our focus is on parent–child storybook reading because of the claims that have been made concerning the relationship between this cultural practice and school literacy development.

An assumption held by many Americans, including elementary school teachers, is that difficulty in learning to read is frequently due to a lack of reading in the homes of children. Most commonly, these particular children are of color and come from impoverished environments. This assumption represents what Gee (1990, 1996) termed a master myth, a cultural belief held by many or most individuals within a society that serves as an orienting framework. One American master myth is that reading to young children provides a foundation and entree into school literacy learning. Related to this belief is the assumption that parent–child book reading occurs more frequently in middle-class than in lower-class homes. This difference is thought to exist due to a lack of literacy use in the homes of those living in poverty. Parents in these homes, it is thought, are less engaged in literacy activities, especially when it comes to reading books to their children.

This literacy master myth must be analyzed in a number of ways. The first concerns the amount and kinds of literacy activities occurring in middle-class and lower-class homes. The second analysis is the impact of home literacy activities on the written discourse knowledge of preschool children. The final issue is the relationship between the preschool children's knowledge of literacy and the learning of school-based literacy.

A great deal of research has investigated the use of literacy in a wide variety of homes. As we discovered in chapter 9, these studies leave little doubt that in most U.S. homes, literacy activities permeate the lives of family members (e.g., Leseman & de Jong, 1998; Purcell-Gates, 1996; Purcell-Gates, L'Allier et al., 1995; Taylor, 1983; Taylor & Dorsey-Gaines, 1988; Teale, 1986). Even non-English-speaking children living in isolated areas, such as Native Americans in the desert Southwest, experience literacy use in their homes (K. Goodman et al., 1979). Additionally, as a much needed reminder that variation exists as much within groups as between them, Taylor (1983) and Taylor and Dorsey-Gaines (1988) found a range in the amount of literacy use within both suburban, middle-class European-American and inner city, working-class African American families. Purcell-Gates (1996; Purcell-Gates, L'Allier et al., 1995) reported similar findings. Therefore, regardless of class, ethnicity, and language background, it is the exception rather than the rule when children enter school having encountered little if any literacy in their homes.

Because schools, even in the early grades, emphasize and value book literacy, it is important to consider the kinds of literacy activities preschoolers actually experience. Although most children encounter various forms of literacy in the home, there does appear to be a discrepancy in the degree to which children encounter book reading. As discussed in chapter 9, many children enter school having few experiences with being read to. The lack of such experience can have a direct impact on the kinds of literacy knowledge preschoolers develop before the onset of formal literacy instruction. Wells (1986) found that when preschool children were engaged in shared book reading, they had opportunities to experience the sustained building and organization of meaning and developed a familiarity with book language. Stories also provided children with vicarious experiences and served as a starting point for collaborative talk between parent and child. In most conversational language, the words fit the world or the context in which the language is evolving. In contrast, written language uses words to create the world, in this case a world of book meaning.

The knowledge gained from shared book reading at home directly impacts the ease with which children are able to learn school-based (i.e., book-based) literacy practices (Purcell-Gates, 1996; Wells, 1986). Although children may experience a variety of home literacy activities, it is book reading that appears to be the significant activity that results in the successful development of school literacy. As noted by Scarborough and Dobrich (1994), success in early school literacy development tends to have positive long-term effects on continued literacy growth and subsequent academic achievement.

This is not to say that all forms of book reading necessarily have the same impact on the child's emerging knowledge of literacy. Reese and Cox (1999), for example, found three styles of adult book reading with preschoolers. A describer style focused on discussing the pictures accompanying the print during reading. A style they labeled comprehender was concerned with the meaning of the text. Performance-oriented style involved an introduction of the text followed by a discussion of its meaning after it was read. The describer style most significantly impacted the child's learning of vocabulary and developing knowledge of print. However, when the children being read to had a more developed vocabulary, they benefited more from the performance-oriented style.

In summary, it would appear that the "truth" of the master literacy myth is a complex one. First, in general, most students, regardless of ethnicity or socioeconomic background, have experiences with various forms of literacy in the home. However, there are a significant number of preschool children who do not experience shared book reading. In turn, home literacy activities do positively impact the literacy knowledge that young children bring to their early school experiences. However, it is experience with shared book reading and the literacy knowledge it engenders that most readily affords children access to school literacy.

This having been said, we need to be cognizant of the significant exceptions to these truths. Researchers such Heath (1982a, 1982b, 1983), Moss (1994), and Farr (1994)—discussed in chapter 9—have argued that difficulty in literacy development occurs because schools fail to acknowledge, value, and build on the literacy experiences and knowledge that some children bring to the school setting. The problem, they argued, is not with the homes, but rather with the instruction. A. Anderson and Stokes (1984) went a step further and noted that in their research, there was no statistical difference in the amount of book reading across various ethnic groups.

We must also be mindful of the research of Schieffelin and Cochran-Smith (1984). They examined the literacy learning of children of Sino-Vietnamese immigrants. In general, there was little literacy activity in the homes, there was no evidence of shared book reading, and the children came to school knowing little spoken English. However, these children became successful literacy learners and speakers of English in the schools. Additionally, in her work with bilingual Mexican American children, Hudelson (1994) found that home literacy was not the only factor that impacted school literacy learning. Children who came from homes in which storytelling was a valued and frequent event were more likely to create written texts that moved beyond personal narratives. These children were the first to create fiction and fantasy tales in their writings. Lest we give too much credit to shared book reading, other factors such as the socioeconomic status of the home and the child's attitude toward literacy have been found to significantly contribute to literacy development as well (Scarborough & Dobrich, 1994; Wells, 1986).

Finally, we must remember that the current cultural norm of reading with young children is of some recency. When I was growing up in the 1950s, shared book reading was not a common occurrence in my neighborhood. I came from a middle-class Eastern European-American home and my father was a high school economics teacher. Although my parents frequently read books, magazines, and newspapers, and even though there were Golden Books around the house, I never remember any adult sitting down and reading to me; nor did I have friends whose parents read to them. At least in my neighborhood, learning to read was viewed as something that would take place in first grade.

Given the benefits that shared book reading may have for school literacy learning, what is a teacher to do with children who lack these experiences? Interestingly, the response often seems to be to provide such children with myriad phonics and skill worksheets. Unfortunately, this response is becoming all the more common with the use of high stakes testing and performance standards, driven in part by No Child Left Behind legislation (U.S. Department of Education, 2001) and *The Report of the National Reading Panel* (NICHD, 2000). I suppose the thinking behind such a response is that the children need to "catch up" with the children who bring book knowledge to the classroom. However, as noted by Wells (1986), only rarely did book-reading parents directly instruct their children on such things as the alphabet or letter sounds. I believe that a more appropriate response to these children is to provide them with what they missed at home—shared book reading—through the use of such materials as predictable big books. This is not to say that more focused instruction, such as guided reading, should not also occur. However, it only seems sensible to also provide that which we lament the children lack—experiences with being read to.

THE PHONICS QUESTION

The previous discussion brings us to the constantly debated issue concerning the role of phonics in learning to read and write. As illustrated in Table 11.8, there are actually a variety of issues that must be taken into account when the "phonics question" is considered. First is the linguistic dimension of phonics. As we saw in earlier chapters on the nature of language, in the relationship between oral and

TABLE 11.8

The Phonics Question

Dimension	Question
Linguistic	What is the relationship between letters and sounds in written language?
Cognitive	What is the role of letters and sounds in the reading and writing processes?
Sociocultural	What value do various social groups and sponsors of literacy use place on letter–sound knowledge?
Developmental	What knowledge of letter–sound relationships is necessary to learn in order to become a proficient reader and writer?
	How are letter–sound relationships learned in beginning reading and writing development?

written language, as well as language variation, there is only a loose relationship between letters and sounds in English. Written language is not speech written down and there are numerous rules that link graphemes to phonemes. The degree to which any letter–sound rule is effective is dependent on the letter and sound being considered. Letter–sound relationships vary as the morphemic context in which particular graphemes are located vary. Additionally, meaning as well as the alphabetic principle impact how words are ultimately spelled.

Cognitively, we found that proficient readers only selectively sample the print on the page. Readers are especially sensitive to the beginnings and endings of words and find consonants particularly useful in word identification. The identification of words, however, is not just a matter of sampling the print. Readers also use previous linguistic and conceptual context as well as their background knowledge to construct an interpretation for the text being processed. Of course, for writers, the task is far different. Writers must fully display all letters in a word, regardless of whether they are beginnings, middles, or endings, and must supply the reader with both consonants and vowels.

Socioculturally, various communities or social groups emphasize the use of letter–sound relationships and "close" readings to varying degrees. Certain religious communities, for example, see the use of phonics and the exact rendering of particular texts to be vitally linked to their salvation. Similarly, home literacy practices tell the child in very direct ways the degree to which letters and sounds are of import.

Finally, as demonstrated throughout the present chapter, knowledge of letter and sound relationships is developed through the child acting as a scientist. Through demonstrations and mediations by more capable adults, the learner actively builds an understanding of the graphophonemic system within meaningful, communicative-based contexts. Acting as a scientist, the child constructs hypotheses for how letters and sounds relate, tests these hypotheses when reading and writing, and receives feedback. Based on this feedback, the hypotheses are revised as necessary. Of course, the child is able to begin learning to read and write before a full grasp of letters and sounds has been acquired. Shared book reading activities, predictable books, environmental print, and the use of invented spellings, for example, allow the child to be engaged as a "reader" or "writer" from the very beginning. And, as we have seen, the degree to which the learner must develop and employ letter–sound knowledge varies between reading and writing.

CONCLUSIONS

In contrast to what is commonly thought, the development of literacy involves a number of very active participants. Children are less interested in imitating the language around them and more concerned with attempting to understand how the language system itself operates. Adults support these efforts by providing the child with language data, feedback, and structured, predictable environments. The driving force behind the efforts of both children and adults is the desire to make meaning, to interact, and to communicate with their discourse community. Educators would be wise to be cognizant of these forces as they develop literacy curricula for young children.

THE DEVELOPMENTAL DIMENSION OF THE LITERACY STORY

As we have seen, literacy development does not necessarily have an endpoint, a time when we have learned all there is to know about the reading and writing processes. The literacy story first introduced in chapter 1 clearly demonstrates that I continued to expand my control over the reading process long after I left grade school. In my interactions with the *Microref Quick Reference Guide* (Microref Systems, Inc., 1988), I quickly discovered that I was unable to use (i.e., read) the program independently. At work, I had observed my colleagues' demonstrations as they went about using the guide. Based on these observations and demonstrations, I wanted to become a member of this club. I was motivated to learn and employ the guide for authentic purposes—to write an article—and engaged various strategies to make sense of the print. Despite all of this, I was largely unsuccessful.

Like the experiences of a young child first learning literacy, I sought the support or sponsorship of a more knowledgeable colleague who I knew would be sensitive to my needs as a learner. My colleague was proficient in the use of the program and her sensitivity allowed me to take risks without fear of making "public" mistakes. As I interacted with the program, she provided various mediational structures to assist me in learning the program. Her support—scaffolds—was based not only on what she knew about the program but also on my needs as a learner. I was not a passive recipient in this process: I explained my areas of confusion, asked questions, and sought clarification when necessary. As the colleague provided me with information and feedback, I would immediately try out her suggestions on the computer and inform her of my success or failure. Once I fulfilled my immediate needs, we would end the call and I would return to writing on the computer. When I encountered a new block, I would first attempt to solve the problem based on my new knowledge of the program. If my attempts were unsuccessful, I would return to my colleague once more for assistance. I also found that as I became more knowledgeable of the program, new questions arose and new answers were provided.

VI

The Educational Dimension
of Literacy

The Dimensions of Literacy: Implications
for Reading and Writing Instruction

In this concluding chapter, the issue of school-based literacy teaching and learning is addressed. I focus on schools because they continue to serve as the initial site for and primary sponsor of formal reading and writing instruction for most children. I begin with a brief review concerning what literacy entails, a review grounded on our previous analysis of the dimensions of literacy. You are then asked to revisit the Literacy Beliefs Profile first introduced in chapter 1. Following this reexamination, we turn our attention to an analysis of both the old and new literacy debates and consider what a dimensional view of literacy might contribute to this dispute. Finally, the political challenges to an expanded view of literacy teaching conclude the chapter and the book.

SUMMARIZING THE DIMENSIONS OF LITERACY

Throughout the previous 11 chapters of this book, literacy was examined through a number of different lenses. The linguistic (text focus), cognitive (mind focus), sociocultural (group focus) and developmental (growth focus) dimensions of literacy and their interrelationships were addressed. Proficient users of literacy employ these dimensions in a simultaneous, transactive, symbiotic manner. In particular contexts, their employment is accomplished in an effective and efficient manner.

An understanding of these dimensions is important not just for academic or intellectual reasons. Such an understanding can also serve as a guide for literacy instruction. Children must come to command these various aspects of reading and writing if they are to be successful literacy users in their worlds. Similarly, schools must introduce and teach many of these various aspects if they are to be learned. It is certainly the case that some children may come to learn some aspects of the dimensions of literacy without direct instructional support. This is especially true of middle-class students whose home literacy practices and sponsorships typically reflect the practices and sponsorships of the school. Many other children, however, will need the schools to provide demonstrations, mediations, and guidance if such learning is to be developed. Based on this need, Table 12.1 summarizes the knowledge involved in each dimension that has been discussed throughout the book.

REEXAMINING OUR BELIEFS ABOUT LITERACY

In chapter 1, you were asked to reflect on your beliefs about the reading and writing processes. Guiding your reflection was a Literacy Beliefs Profile (Table 1.1) that you completed. Take a moment to return to this profile and once again answer the questions based on what you currently know about reading and writing. Compare and contrast your literacy beliefs—then and now.

If you are similar to most students in my classes, you have greatly expanded your understanding of reading and writing. Some of your past beliefs may have been rejected and replaced by others, some may have been modified, and others may have been solidified. More importantly, you most likely have a fuller, more layered view of what it means to be a reader and writer. Therefore, even if you believed and continue to believe, for example, that knowledge of graphophonemics is necessary to be a proficient reader and writer, you now realize that there exists a wealth of additional knowledge that must accompany graphophonemics.

Such an expanded view of literacy is critical because our society tends to conceive of reading and writing in rather reductionistic ways. All too frequently, newspaper articles, radio talk shows, and politicians discuss literacy in terms of whether words are best learned through the use of phonics or through a sight approach. Not surprisingly, this narrow focus on graphophonemics and morphemics frames the kinds of instructional materials, mediational strategies, and assessment instruments that are considered appropriate for solving the so-called literacy crisis. When entering these discussions, teachers must have the knowledge necessary to expand what is conceived as being involved in literacy teaching and learning.

Although Americans continue to focus on the "best" methods for teaching literacy—the old debate—there is a second debate brewing on the horizon that incorporates much of what was addressed in our analysis of the sociocultural dimension of literacy (chapters 9 and 10). We now turn our attention to these debates, old and new.

THE LITERACY DEBATES: OLD AND NEW

Most readers are well aware of the "great debate" concerning which instructional model best promotes literacy learning among young children. In many respects, this debate has intensified during the last decade (e.g., Adams, 1990; Cazden, 1992; K. Dahl, Scharer, & Lawson, 1999; K. Goodman, 1993, 1996; McIntyre & Freppon, 1994; Pearson, 1989; Purcell-Gates, McIntyre, & Freppon, 1995; F. Smith, 1994a, 2003; Stahl & Miller, 1989). Not limited to the teaching of literacy to English-speaking European American students, the debate has occurred within

TABLE 12.1

Becoming Literate: What Needs to Be Learned

Linguistic Knowledge (text focus)	Cognitive Knowledge (mind focus)	Sociocultural Knowledge (group focus)	Developmental Knowledge (growth focus)
The various systems of language that are used to make meaning: pragmatic, text type, genre, text structure, semantics, syntax, morphology, orthography, graphophonemics, graphemes	The active, selective, and constructive nature of reading and writing	How the purposes and patterns of literacy practices vary within and across social groups, sponsors, and institutions, e.g., ethnic, cultural, class (SES), religious, family, recreational, occupational, schools, governmental, etc.	The active and constructive role of the learner in literacy development
How written language is similar and different from oral language	The use of relevant background knowledge to build meaning		The use of various strategies and processes to construct the dimensions of literacy, e.g., data gathering, hypothesis generating, hypothesis testing, hypothesis modification
How the systems of language vary (dialects) across social groups, sponsors, and institutions, e.g., ethnic, cultural, class (SES), religious, family, recreational, occupational, schools, governmental, etc.	The use of various mental processes and strategies to generate meaning, e.g., predicting, monitoring, evaluating, revising, responding, inferencing, building coherence, using various systems of language, etc.	An understanding of the rules and norms for transacting with written language within and across social groups, sponsors, and institutions, e.g., ethnic, cultural, class (SES), religious, family, recreational, occupational, schools, governmental, etc.	Observations of, and transactions with, literacy demonstrations of more proficient literacy users within and across social groups, sponsors, and institutions, e.g., ethnic, cultural, class (SES), religious, family, recreational, occupational, schools, governmental, etc.
	The use of various mental processes and strategies to overcome "blocks" during reading and writing, e.g., stop and rethink, reread/rewrite previous portions of the text, skip it and read/write on and return when necessary, put something in that makes sense, seek assistance from an outside source, etc.	Knowledge of the linguistic features of various texts used for various purposes within and across social groups, sponsors, and institutions e.g., ethnic, cultural, class (SES), religious, family, recreational, occupational, schools, governmental, etc.	

(continued on next page)

TABLE 12.1 (continued)

Linguistic Knowledge (text focus)	Cognitive Knowledge (mind focus)	Sociocultural Knowledge (group focus)	Developmental Knowledge (growth focus)
	Varying the use of the mental processes and strategies based on the text, purpose, and audience	How to use literacy to produce, consume, maintain, and control knowledge within and across various social groups, sponsors, and institutions, e.g., ethnic, cultural, class (SES), religious, family, recreational, occupational, schools, governmental, etc. Knowledge of the particular literacy forms and functions that are valued and supported by various social groups, sponsors, and institutions, e.g., ethnic, cultural, class (SES), religious, family, recreational, occupational, schools, governmental, etc. Ability to critique texts of various social groups, sponsors, and institutions—e.g., ethnic, cultural, class (SES), religious, family, recreational, occupational, schools, governmental, etc.—for the values and agendas embedded within them	How to use the support and mediation provided by more proficient literacy users within and across social groups, sponsors, and institutions, e.g., ethnic, cultural, class (SES), religious, family, recreational, occupational, schools, governmental, etc. The use of knowledge gained through reading to support the development of writing; the use of knowledge gained through writing to support the development of reading How to negotiate textual meanings through the use and support of alternate communication systems, e.g., art music, mathematics, etc.

TABLE 12.2

The Great (Old) Debate: Decoding, Skills, and Whole Language Paradigms

<————————————— Continuum —————————————>		
Decoding	*Skills*	*Whole Language*
An initial focus on graphophonemics as the base for literacy development	An initial focus on morphemes as the base for literacy development	An initial focus on meaning as the base for literacy development
Literacy development = graphophonemics → morphemes → meaning	Literacy development = morphemes + graphophonemics + meaning	Literacy development = meaning → syntax → graphophonemics
Literacy development as part-to-whole process	Literacy development as a part-to-whole process	Literacy development as a whole-to-part process
Literacy teaching and learning as a deductive process	Literacy teaching and learning as a deductive process	Literacy teaching and learning as an inductive process
Literacy development = learning about literacy → learning literacy → learning through literacy	Literacy development = learning about literacy → learning literacy → learning through literacy	Literacy development = learning through literacy + learning literacy + learning about literacy
Literacy learning as an individual process	Literacy learning as an individual process	Literacy learning as a collaborative process

the multicultural and bilingual communities as well (e.g., Delpit, 1990, 1995; Edelsky, 1986; Y. Freeman & D. Freeman, 1992; Perez, 1994; Reyes, 1991; Teale, 1991).

It is beyond the scope of this chapter to delineate in a detailed manner the differences among the three instructional paradigms—decoding, skills, and whole language—that have dominated the national discussion over literacy. Ample literature exists that has already done so (e.g., Adams & Bruck, 1995; Edelsky, Altwerger, & Flores, 1991; K. Goodman, 1986; Mayher, 1990; Pressley, 1998; F. Smith, 2003). Rather, at the risk of oversimplifying a complex issue, a brief overview of the three paradigms is provided for the purpose of contrasting their common concerns with what some see as an emerging fourth paradigm—critical literacy. Table 12.2 presents some of the key beliefs involved in the old debate.

On a general level, the decoding and skills paradigms have a good deal in common. Both conceive of literacy learning as a part-to-whole process, although the system(s) of language emphasized varies. Decoding proponents believe that graphophonemes serve as the entree into literacy. It is by first learning about letter–sound relationships that children are able to form words. As the reader learns to say and blend the sounds of the letters and hears the words that the sounds form, he or she is able to connect the print to meaning. For skill advocates, vocabulary—morphemes—is the base for learning to read. Much of the early instruction emphasizes the mastering of sight words and connecting the child's spoken vocabulary to a print vocabulary. At the same time, the child is also introduced to graphophonemes and comprehension skills. Comprehension skills give particular attention to new vocabulary development—words not in the child's oral language repertoire. Therefore, although various linguistic aspects of literacy are addressed, it is the morphemic system of language that receives primary attention during initial instruction within the skills instructional model.

In contrast, the whole language model rejects the isolated and systematic instruction of particular systems of language and instead places primary emphasis on the process of meaning construction. As its name indicates, whole language advocates believe that children should encounter whole, authentic texts. These texts are primarily read for understanding and for the learning of new ideas. The various systems of language—including graphophonemic and morphemic—and the various cognitive processes—such as sampling, predicting, and integrating—are believed to be best developed as the child focuses attention on text meanings.

Both the decoding and skills paradigms conceive of literacy learning as largely a deductive process. Typically, the learner is formally introduced to particular linguistic or cognitive rules (e.g., i before e except after c; when you encounter an unknown word, sound it out) and then is expected to apply the rules in all relevant contexts. For both paradigms, to learn literacy, the child must first learn about literacy—its systems of language and strategies for cracking the code. Once these learnings have occurred, the child is then able to use literacy to learn. Throughout this entire process, the focus is on the literacy knowledge that the individual is able to acquire and display independently.

Whole language advocates believe that, like learning oral language, written language learning involves a process of induction. The child, by experiencing a wealth of written language data within meaningful, purposeful, and mediated contexts, actively constructs an understanding of the regularities of the systems of language. This construction involves data collection, hypothesis generation and testing, feedback, and hypothesis modification. Whole language rejects the developmental sequence of learning about literacy → learning literacy → and then learning through literacy. Instead, it is thought that every literacy event offers the child the opportunity to learn about any of the three aspects of literacy, depending on what is foregrounded and what is backgrounded. The child, the text, the purpose, and the mediator all influence what is learned. This process involves the collaborative construction and display of literacy knowledge among and between the learners and the mediators.

Although the great debate continues to capture much of the attention of the academic community as well as the public, critical literacy theorists offer an alternate analysis and solution (e.g., Bartolome, 1994; Comber & Simpson, 2001;

Creighton, 1997; Fehring & Green, 2001; Ladson-Billings, 1994, 1995; Lewison, Flint, & Sluys, 2002; Luke, 1995, 1998; Willis, 2001). As represented in the left-hand column of Table 12.3, critical theorists argue that the great debaters, regardless of theoretical orientation, tend to limit their concerns to the linguistic and cognitive dimensions of literacy development. Methods and materials for the promotion of these dimensions are the sites of contention among the adversaries.

The new debaters maintain that the discussion of literacy and its development within school contexts must be expanded to incorporate the sociocultural dimension. Although methods and materials are to be considered, they alone are not sufficient conditions for literacy learning. Literacy instruction must also include, in fact must emphasize, the critique of texts as they relate to issues of power, dominance, and intergroup relationships. Instruction must examine how texts, readers, and writers operate within various sociocultural contexts. As we discovered in chapter 10 with our analysis of "The Great Big Enormous Turnip" (Tolstoy, 1976) and "The Carrot Seed" (Kraus, 1945), texts are positioned socioculturally in terms of the ideologies, discursive forms, and the values they reflect. Frequently, these ideologies, forms, and values are "hidden" in that they are not the primary focus that the author foregrounds. In many respects, this "hiddenness" is all the more insidious because beliefs that are in the background tend not to be critiqued. Furthermore, as we have already seen, such ideologies may have to be implicitly accepted by students for them to successfully participate in the school-based activities that surround the discourse.

Although not highlighted or critiqued, hidden ideologies are not without their impact. According to critical literacy theorists, these ideologies, especially when repeatedly encountered, often come to be accepted as reflections of reality. They are reflections of the way things are supposed to be. This is especially the case if the text reflects or is aligned with, as is frequently the case, broader cultural norms and values. The discussion on gender and race in chapter 10 provides two such examples. The writing of young children tended to position males in active and doer roles and females in commentator, reflective roles (Kamler, 1993). Similarly, Enciso (1994) found that students typically drew on stereotypic popular cultural knowledge as well as their own cultural identities to interpret characters within the stories read in class. From a critical perspective, there are no innocent children, no innocent teachers, and no innocent texts.

An uncritical acceptance of dominant norms can lead to a reproduction of existing sociocultural dimensions within the classroom. School texts and activities often reflect the values, beliefs, and knowledge of those groups that are dominant. Additionally, a privileging of the personal through such instructional activities as reader response and student-selected writing topics may only reinforce existing dominant norms. Some students bring experiences and narratives to school that reflect dominant cultural and linguistic norms. When they do not, instruction may attempt to normalize them. That is, literacy learning and success becomes a domesticating literacy. Therefore, texts—both student and published—must be evaluated

TABLE 12.3

The Literacy Debates

←———————— Continuum ————————→

Methods as Solution (The Great [Old] Debate) *<—Decoding—Skills—Whole Language—>*	*Critical Literacy as Solution* *(The New Debate)*
A focus on the linguistic and cognitive dimensions of literacy teaching and development	A focus on the sociocultural dimension of literacy teaching and development
Teaching and learning through the use of various methodologies, technologies, and materials	Teaching and learning through high academic achievement expectations, acknowledging and valuing the cultural competence of students, and the development of sociopolitical consciousness of teachers and students
Values the individual experiences of the student	Values the experiences of the various groups in which the student is a member
A focus on the personal; expression of self through individual narratives	A focus on the socialized; expression of self through group–group relationship narratives and critique
Critique of text as it relates to personal experiences	Critique of text as it relates to issues of power, dominance, and group–group relationships
A tendency to see students as "individuals" and classrooms as unrelated to the realities of the society	A tendency to see students as part of various sociocultural groups and classrooms as reflecting the realities of the society

A reproduction of sociocultural aspects of society	A conscious attempt not to reproduce in the classroom the stratified realities of the society, e.g., the rich get rich and the poor get poorer, dominance of males over females; a critique and challenge of sociocultural aspects of society based on principles of justice, equity, and access
One size fits all approach to teaching; methods are implemented in a vacuum	Many sizes for many types of students; methods are embedded within particular sociocultural contexts and histories
Evaluates the impact of various methodologies on students' literacy learning	Evaluates the impact of the curriculum on students' ability to critique texts and contexts
Student failure is due to not finding the "right" teaching methods or to disengaged students and the groups to which they hold membership	Student failure is due to the failure of the dominant culture to support nondominant groups; need a critical sociohistorical view of educational institutions, teachers, and learners
A reductionistic view of education	An expansive view of education
Methods as the necessary and sufficient condition for learning	Methods as a necessary but insufficient condition for learning
Literacy teaching and learning as individual linguistic and cognitive actions	Literacy teaching and learning as social practices and group actions
Literacy learning as an avenue through which to compensate for societal inequities	Literacy learning as part of a complex social, cultural, political, and economic puzzle by and through which groups are constructed and positioned

based on the principles of justice, equity, and access. Rather than domesticating literacy, we have critical literacy (Finn, 1999).

Finally, critical theorists hope that the critique of text and context as an integral part of schooling can begin to address the notion that school success equals "acting White." Ogbu (1992, 1999; Ogbu & Matute-Bianchi, 1986) documented how some cultural groups within our society, fully aware of the discrepancies between their own ways of knowing and being and those of the school, have developed what he termed oppositional identities. To maintain a sense of self, students resist attempts of the schools to form them in ways that run counter to their own identities. Rather than perceiving school knowledge as an "adding on" process, students view schooling as a "subtracting" process. Of course, this frequently is the case. Critical literacy, it is hoped, will help students accommodate themselves to the norms of the schools without having to assimilate.

A critical stance, however, will not by itself produce a just society; nor will literacy learning itself stop people from committing crimes or being unfairly imprisoned. Literacy is only one factor that contributes to the complexities of a postindustrial society. As a single factor, literacy instruction and learning cannot by itself compensate for societal inequities; nor will critical literacy necessarily produce competent readers and writers. What is also required is economic, political, and social support by dominant groups and institutions for a more just society.

TEACHING THE DIMENSIONS OF LITERACY

Although critical literacy theorists insist that there is no single pathway to literacy, it is likely that some pathways are more profitable and enjoyable than others. Additionally, as has been made clear throughout this book, there are various dimensions of literacy, of which the sociocultural is just one. Therefore, we want to avoid any reduction of literacy to the teaching and learning of a single dimension. We have been down that path far too many times.

Fortunately, there appears to be a growing body of evidence from a variety of sources concerning the types of literacy experiences that are believed to be beneficial for students in elementary school settings. Table 12.4 summarizes these literacy experiences in a general curricular framework. In this framework, the goal is to promote both literacy and critical concept development—learning about literacy, learning literacy, and learning through literacy. The degree to which such learnings must be made explicit for students will vary, depending on the students, what is to be learned, and the context in which teaching and learning are operating. Similarly, the exact nature of literacy activities and the degree of explicit instruction will also vary based on student need. We want to avoid the standardization of the curriculum because as Ohanian (1999) reminds us, "one size fits few" (p. 5) and development is facilitated "when we allow many starting points for learning and many paths to progress" (Hull & Schultz, 2001, p. 595).

TABLE 12.4

Literacy Curricular Components

Component	Characteristics	Time
Thematic or Inquiry Units	Students explore and critique topics and issues of interest using various disciplines (literature, social science, science) and multiple communication systems (language, art, music, mathematics, movement). Materials include diverse types of texts (narratives, expositions, dramas, poems) and various resources (magazines, newspapers, records, audiotapes, songs, computer programs, books, filmstrips, videotapes, movies, simulation games). The focus is on literacy development (learning about literacy, learning literacy, and learning through literacy) and critical content development (generalizations, concepts, and facts).	1 to $2\frac{1}{2}$ hours
Teacher Reading and Student Response	Teacher oral reading of theme-related books, stories, articles, etc. Students are given opportunities to respond and to critique the reading.	15 to 45 minutes
Independent Reading and Student Response	Student silent reading of self-selected books, stories, magazines, student published texts, etc. Students are given opportunities to share and to critique what is read with the class.	15 minutes to 1 hour
Independent Writing, Conferencing, and Publishing	Student writing, conferencing, revision and editing, and publishing on self-selected topics.	30 minutes to $1\frac{1}{2}$ hours

Regardless of the nature of the activities and degree of explicitness, however, it is also important to keep in mind that authentic, real-world literacy events always involve the four dimensions of literacy, as first illustrated in Fig. 1.1. One goal of teaching and learning should be to keep these dimensions operating in a transactive, symbiotic fashion, lest both teachers and students lose sight of the very nature of literacy itself.

It is most likely that various students will need various types of demonstrations and mediations based on the content or strategies under consideration. This is particularly the case as teachers attempt to develop a critical stance in their students (Bigelow, 1989; Creighton, 1997). As we have already seen, unmediated student responses typically reflect the ideologies of the home community and the dominant culture. These ideologies oftentimes will need to be directly and explicitly addressed and even challenged if students are to encounter and consider alternative ways of viewing reality.

The mixed results of the research that has examined the impact of different types of curricula on student literacy development highlight the complex nature of literacy learning and instruction (e.g., K. Dahl et al., 1999; Edelsky, 1986; Kucer & Silva, 1999; McIntyre & Freppon, 1994; Perez, 1994; Purcell-Gates, McIntyre, et al., 1995; Stahl & Miller, 1989). Clearly, it is overly simplistic to assert that significant growth in certain dimensions of literacy will not occur without direct instruction. Similarly, it is overly simplistic to assert that students will improve their literacy abilities by being immersed in a garden of print; that is, students will improve in their reading and writing due to the maturation and experiential process, regardless of the mediation provided.

The uneven student literacy development across various kinds of curricula has been termed differentiated mediation (Kucer & Silva, 1999, in progress), instructional detours (Cazden, 1992), or overt instruction (New London Group, 1996; Pappas & Pettegrew, 1998). In instruction of this type, students continue to be engaged in ongoing authentic and meaningful literacy activities. However, when it is determined that a child is encountering difficulty with a particular dimension of written language, focused instructional events would be developed that explicitly teach over time the matter with which the child is experiencing difficulty. In these lessons, not only is the child shown what to do but also how and when it is to be accomplished. Such mediation is differentiated because not all children receive the instruction, only those in need. Additionally, the degree of explicitness varies depending on the child. Such instruction is a detour in that it does not represent the majority of literacy activities experienced by the student. Finally, the instruction is overt in that an explicit and conscious attempt is made to highlight particular dimensions of literacy for examination and reflection on the part of the student. Two examples of such instruction are retrospective miscue analysis (Y. Goodman & Marek, 1996; Moore & Aspegren, 2001) and language studies (Y. Goodman, 2003). Retrospective miscue analysis, for example, engages students in examining their miscues—types, locations, causes, impact on meaning—and considering alternative strategies for transacting with text.

In addition to taking into account what instructional strategies might best help students to develop school literacy—that is, the literacy of dominant societal groups—we must also consider what curricular modifications might support more varied forms of literacy. As demonstrated in our examination of the cultural dimension of literacy, there are often significant discrepancies between home and school literacy practices. Too often, the child is expected to take on the functions and forms of school literacy with little regard for what literacy knowledge the learner brings to the classroom. The common use by teachers of the IRE pattern is one such example. Rather than simply acculturating the child into such norms, the teacher will also want to utilize other types of interactional patterns that both build on the child's home experiences and expand the various stances that all students learn to take toward written discourse (Dyson, 2003; Moje, 2000).

On a curricular level, many educators have advocated that students encounter four types of literacy experiences on a regular basis: thematic or inquiry units; teacher reading and student response; independent reading and student response; and independent writing, conferencing, and publishing (see Table 12.4). A range of instructional time that has been found to be appropriate is specified for each curricular component. What follows is a general discussion of each curricular component and corresponding strategies. Easily accessible references are provided to assist those readers who are interested in developing more in-depth knowledge of the components and strategies.

Thematic or Inquiry Units

In many respects and in contrast to other disciplines, reading and writing have no inherent content in and of themselves. A wide range of materials and experiences can be used for the teaching and learning of literacy. Going back to at least the time of Dewey (1938), many educators have proposed the use of themes as the basis for instruction. Given a variety of names (e.g., integrated units, project approach, inquiry studies) and theoretical orientations, the general focus being advocated here is on the exploration of topics or issues to promote the development of both literacy and conceptual knowledge (Banks, 1991; Kucer & Silva, in progress; Kucer et al., 1995; Manning, Manning, & Long, 1994; Short, Harste, & Burke, 1996). When selecting topics of study, it is important to consider the quality of experiences that the topic can provide. Dewey (1938) suggested that quality experiences are those that take up something from those experiences that have gone before and modify in some way the quality of those experiences that come after. Quality experiences promote desirable future experiences in the students.

Recently, critical theorists have pushed this approach from simply a "study of" to a "critique of" (e.g., Buckingham & Sefton-Green, 1994; Comber & Simpson, 2001). In their review of critical literacy research and professional literature, Lewison, Flint, and Sluys (2002) propose that inquiry units reflect four overlapping and interrelated qualities. First, the units help students to understand "the everyday through new lenses" (pp. 382–383). Current knowledge and beliefs are examined and even challenged. Second, the units also help students to understand the topic from multiple viewpoints or through various lenses. Perspectives not commonly considered or heard are given consideration. Thirdly, inquiry units help students to move beyond their own personal experiences to those that are more group or

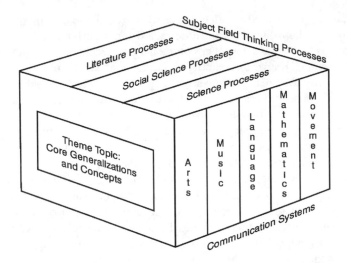

FIG. 12.1. An integrated view of the curriculum. From Kucer, S. B., Silva, C., and Delgado-Larocco, E. (1995). *Curricular conversations: Themes in multilingual and monolingual classrooms* (p. 8). York, ME: Stenhouse.

socially based. Topics are examined in terms of power, dominance, and privilege. Finally, inquiry units involve "taking a stand and promoting social justice" (p. 387). Students are engaged in activities that have an impact on their worlds (Edelsky, 1999).

A limitation of many themes has been their focus on facts and figures rather than more global forms of knowledge. As we saw in the discussion on the nature of knowledge in chapter 7 (see Fig. 7.2), although facts and figures can begin to form the basis for understanding, they fall short in offering the depth of knowledge necessary for a fuller and more textured knowing to occur. Themes must also support students in the development of higher types of knowledge in the form of concepts and generalizations. As illustrated in Fig. 12.1 (Kucer et al., 1995), the development of a critical understanding of higher forms of knowledge is at the center of the thematic curriculum. The communication systems—art, music, language, mathematics, and movement—as well as the thinking processes commonly used in the disciplines— literature, social sciences, and sciences—are the vehicles through which such critical understandings are developed. The content or "stuff" of the curriculum is drawn from those disciplines that are relevant to the topic.

Conceptual and generalizable knowledge is developed and refined throughout the theme as students recycle and revisit key ideas and meanings in different contexts using different lenses and materials in different activities. No one experience, no one text can result in a well-formed concept or generalization; the experiences and texts interacted with must be numerous and ongoing. Additionally, concepts and generalizations are dynamic, not static in nature. For all of us, children as

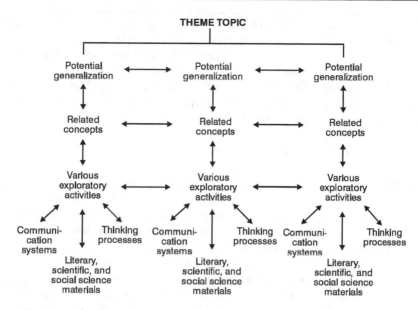

FIG. 12.2. The interrelationship among theme topic, generalizations, concepts, activities, materials, thinking processes, and communication systems. From Kucer, S. B., Silva, C., and Delgado-Larocco, E. (1995). *Curricular conversations: Themes in multilingual and monolingual classrooms* (p. 59). York, ME: Stenhouse.

well as adults, knowledge evolves over time; the notion of mastering a concept or generalization makes little sense. Rather, knowledge continues to grow and change as students experience various exploratory activities using various communication systems and thinking processes. Figure 12.2 (Kucer et al., 1995) illustrates this transactive process.

In one third-grade bilingual and bicultural class in Southern California, for example, the students explored the topic of immigration (Kucer et al., 1995; Silva & Kucer, 1997). Given the controversial nature of the issue in California and the wealth of material available, it would have been relatively easy for the teacher to focus on individual instances in which immigration was an issue. However, the teacher built on and extended these firsthand experiences of the students and helped them to develop broader forms of knowledge. In addition to learning facts and figures about immigration, students also developed knowledge about a number of generalizations (e.g., immigrants have made significant contributions to society; immigration can lead to conflict and change among various groups within a society; there are many reasons why people immigrate to one country from another).

A final characteristic of thematic teaching as it is proposed here is that the activities be functional, authentic, or "real to life" in nature. As we discovered when the nature of language was examined, a driving force behind language learning is the child's desire to make meaning so as to interact with the world around him or her. We also found that the pragmatic system of language was the most powerful language system, influencing the operation of all other systems, such as text type, genre, semantics, and syntax. If themes are to connect to the world as experienced by the child, the activities need to be more than traditional skill and drill lessons covered up by a topic. Table 12.5 sets forth various literacy activities as they relate to various functions of language. These activities are fairly general in nature so that they can be easily adapted to the content of the theme under study.

Teacher Reading and Student Response

Teachers, regardless of the age of their students, should read to them. Students need to hear the sounds of language and the expression of ideas in forms they may not yet be able to read on their own. This oral reading may be related to the theme under study or something the students have requested; it may be chapter books, short stories, magazines, newspaper articles, or poems.

Teacher reading allows for the demonstration of various strategies, processes, and stances involved in reading and comprehending. If the teacher reads a sentence that does not make sense, the sentence can be reread and followed by a discussion of the strategy employed. If a word is changed without altering the author's meaning, the behavior can be highlighted and evaluated by the teacher. If a particular idea evoked an internal response, it can be shared. As well as reading and demonstrating, teachers should provide time for students to critically respond to what they have heard. Like the stance of critique taken in the thematic units, teachers should help students critically analyze what is being read, regardless of who is doing the reading.

Independent Reading and Student Response

On a regular basis, students need occasion to explore their own interests and read for the pure pleasure of reading. The block of time devoted to independent reading and the chance to share their critical responses to what they have read demonstrates the value placed on self-selected reading. In our society, we often hear various groups—teachers, parents, politicians—decry the lack of reading abilities of the population in general. Certainly, it is the case that many individuals continue to find reading to be problematic in their lives. Just as important and problematic is the desire to read or the lack thereof. It probably would not be an overstatement to say that there exist just as many individuals who can read but do not—reluctant readers—as there are individuals who cannot read but want to—struggling readers. Providing students with regular and ongoing opportunities to read for pleasure and to share this pleasure with others is one avenue to address motivational issues (Gambrell, 1996). Interest can motivate even struggling or reluctant readers to pursue texts that may be beyond their reading abilities (Allen, 2000). Finally, because we tend to become good at what we enjoy doing, research has consistently

TABLE 12.5

Functions of Literacy Activities

Language Function	Classroom Literacy Activities
Instrumental: "I want" Literacy used as a means of getting things; satisfying material needs	Sign-up charts for activities or interest centers; picture collages with captions: things I want for my birthday, Christmas, etc.; play stores, gas stations, etc.; posters and advertisements; use of paper money; ordering supplies; things I want lists; listing of things needed for a project; shopping lists; birthday and holiday lists; library book lists; want ads; yellow pages; recipe ingredient lists
Regulatory: "Do as I tell you/How it must be" Literacy used to control the behaviors, feelings, or attitudes of others	Directional and traffic signs; rules for care of pets, plants, etc.; written directions; schedules, notes to and from others; laws and rules; letter writing to governmental officials; newspaper editorials and letters to the editor; suggestion box; instructions and recipes; arts and crafts "how to" books; road maps
Interactional: "Me and you/Me against you" Literacy used to interact with others; forming and maintaining personal relationships; establishing separateness	Letters, e-mails, and faxes to and from friends and relatives; friendship books; message boards; notes between and among teachers and students; class post office; pen pals; shared reading experiences; notes on home bulletin board or refrigerator; Dear Abby column
Personal: "Here I come" Literacy used to express individuality and uniqueness; awareness of self; pride and shame	Books about self and family; pictures of self and family with captions; personal experience stories; family or class albums with captions; writing and illustrating "about me" books; what I want to be when I grow up stories; journals and diaries; student of the week bulletin board; autobiographies; family histories; Dear Abby column
Heuristic: "Tell me why" Literacy used to explore the environment; to ask questions, to seek and test knowledge	Question box; concept books; science experiments; research/inquiry projects; surveys and interviews; predicting the weather; model building; question and answer books
Imaginative: "Let's pretend" Literacy used to create new worlds; to leave the here and now	Creative dramatics; Readers Theatre; story telling and writing; puppetry; science fiction books; jokes, riddles, and puns; comic books; word games; crossword puzzles
Informative: "I've got something to tell you" Literacy used as a means of communicating information to someone who does not possess the information	Bulletin boards; notes to others; reference materials; encyclopedias and dictionaries; newspapers and magazines, expert groups; book, record, movie reviews, television and movie guides; concept books; web sites

demonstrated that increased amounts of reading are related to increased student reading achievement (Allington, 2001).

For self-selected reading to be successful, there needs to be a wide range of reading materials on various topics, in different text types and genres, and from various resources (e.g., books, magazines, newspapers). If students are developing biliteracy, written materials in various languages should also be available. It is important to keep in mind that the purpose of this reading experience is to help students to discover and explore their interests. Therefore, care should be taken not to require students to demonstrate and display their knowledge of what has been read. Book reports, written summaries, and the like are best avoided. Teacher time is better spent helping students locate materials that are appropriate to their abilities and interests (Fielding & Roller, 1992).

Independent Writing, Conferencing, and Publishing

Blocks of time when students can engage in self-selected writing topics, conferencing, and publishing must also be part of the daily classroom routine. If our goal is to develop independent writers, students must be provided multiple writing experiences on topics about which they care deeply. Additionally, children, as we have learned from writing teachers such as Atwell (1990, 1998), Calkins (1994), and Graves (1983), need regular and frequent time in which to engage in the process. Students need to know that they will have both opportunities and periods of time to compose and to reflect on their writing. Although independent writing and much of the writing that occurs as part of a thematic unit differ as to topic, they do not differ in terms of process. Self-selected writing and thematic writing both involve a cycle in which students compose, share their work through conferencing with others, revise, edit, publish, and celebrate (Short et al., 1996).

For students who lack the experience in writing about topics they choose, the teacher may need to provide additional support to make this curricular component effective. Developing a list of possible writing topics with students can be a helpful first step. Even more important, the teacher should help students discover where writers locate or discover their topics. Almost any experience, topic, and interest holds the possibility for writing, if students develop and live a "writerly life" (Calkins, 1994). Dyson (2003) has argued that such open-ended writing and reading activities are critical in that they serve as points in the school day where "unofficial" literacy topics can enter the classroom. However, as Moje (2000) notes, students often will not automatically bring into the classroom setting such unsanctioned forms of literacy. Teachers may need to explicitly encourage their use.

CHALLENGES TO TEACHING THE DIMENSIONS OF LITERACY: THE POLITICS OF INSTRUCTION

Instruction in general, literacy pedagogy in particular, and reading instruction specifically, are impacted by various forces operating within our society. These forces mediate and sponsor what occurs in the classroom. How children are taught to read and write, therefore, may not be directly related to what we know about the dimensions of literacy. As we saw in previous chapters, for example, deep divisions exist over the very nature of the reading process and how knowledge is most appropriately characterized. Accordingly, there are also deep divisions over how reading and knowledge can best be facilitated within classroom settings (Routman, 1996). As noted by Willis and Harris (2000), "politics and literacy... remain inseparable" (p. 72) in the United States and these divisions are long standing. In fact, literacy, literacy teaching, and literacy learning can never be "ideologically neutral or culturally unbiased" (p. 78).

As well as "in-house" academic literacy debates, there are other stakeholders or gatekeepers involved. Because most Americans are the product of public education, where much of their initial literacy learning occurred, there is a tradition and culture of schooling that permeates our society (Eisner, 1994). "This is how I was taught to read and it worked!" is a common response when more progressive or alternative instructional paradigms are put forth. Suggestions for change are perceived as violating cultural norms and as being deviant in nature. Even students have been found to resist attempts to realign the curriculum and their interactions with written discourse (Fawcett, 1998; Henson & Gilles, 2003; Kucer, 1998, 1999). Of course, as F. Smith (1975) pointed out, there may be a difference or gap between how something was taught and how it was actually learned. There may not be a one-to-one correspondence between teaching and learning within the classroom setting.

The federal government has also become a significant gatekeeper in determining the nature of reading, reading curricula, and reading materials especially in the early grades. Through its funding of the National Reading Panel and support of the Panel's findings (NICHD, 2000), as well as the No Child Left Behind legislation (United States Department of Education, 2001), the instructional options available to the schools are increasingly limited. In practice, "scientifically based reading research" has come to be defined as that which focuses on phonemic awareness and decoding processes (Coles, 1998, 2000; McQuillan, 1998; Taylor, 1999). Similarly, "scientifically based reading instruction" is associated with the use of such programs and materials as Success for All, Direct Instruction, Saxon Phonics, and Open Court. Unfortunately, the impact of such reductionistic instruction has especially affected those in need of the richest instruction—children living in poverty (Kohn, 2000, 2002), and "serves to revictimize the most needy children ... " (Willis & Harris, 2000, p. 80). Access to the dimensions of literacy as defined here is much more likely to be available to and experienced by middle- and upper-class children.

Somewhat paradoxically, a second response to curricular change has been that "We already tried that and it didn't work. We need to go back to the basics." This reflects the belief that schools are always engaging in the latest fad rather than focusing on what really counts and works. According to Cuban (1990), however, for much of 20th century, instruction has looked pretty much the same. In fact, given the advent of technology, the ability to segment, sequence, and drill-and-skill students has become far easier than it was in the early 1900s. This stability of instruction at first may appear puzzling given the press that many advocated innovations receive, but this is just the point. Although much is made in public and academic circles about better ways to educate our children, in general, very little trickles down to the students.

In contrast to these more traditional concerns, there is a new agenda behind many of today's most persistent critics of U.S. education and their constituents— teachers, students, curricula, unions, teacher education programs, and schools of education (Allington, 2001; Berliner & Biddle, 1995; Y. Freeman, D. Freeman, & Fennacy, 1997; K. Goodman, 1998; Shannon, 1990; Taylor, 1999). The agenda, largely political, religious, or both in nature, appears to be the very weakening of public schools so as to promote a particular ideology for educational reform. Reform would consist of public support (monies) for private education through such programs as vouchers. Proponents of this reform perceive today's public education as largely a failure and argue that only competition (i.e., capitalism) or religion will produce more effective teaching and learning.

In response to these critics, researchers, Berliner and Biddle (1995) in particular, have argued that for most students, schools for the most part are as effective as they have ever been. Allington (2001) and McQuillan (1998) have made the same argument concerning reading in particular. Most Americans are supportive of their children's schools, even though they may be critical of schools in general (Routman, 1996). This is not to ignore the real challenges and failures that teachers and students face within impoverished school contexts. Schools that face society's most formidable social and economic problems are often the very schools that lack the necessary resources. Rather, it is to acknowledge that school performance has not significantly declined during the last several decades, regardless of the types of assessments employed to measure student growth, and that socioeconomics is a primary factor in school success—as well as in school failure.

CONCLUSIONS

As demonstrated in this concluding chapter, an understanding of the dimensions of literacy has direct implications for classroom reading and writing instruction. Rather than simply focusing on one dimension of literacy, students must encounter a variety of experiences that will support their development of a literacy that is rich and multilayered in nature. The teaching of literacy in all of its complexity, however, faces challenges on a number fronts—from teachers, parents, politicians, religious leaders, and the like. These challenges are not likely to disappear in the near future. The task to which literacy educators are called is to help others understand the multidimensional nature of reading and writing without reducing complex processes to simple slogans and sound bites.

References

Abowitz, K. (2000). A pragmatist revisioning of resistance theory. *American Educational Research Journal, 37*, 877–907.

Adams, M. (1990). *Beginning to read: Thinking and learning about print.* Cambridge, MA: MIT Press.

Adams, M., & Bruck, M. (1995, Summer). Resolving the "great debate." *American Educator, 7*, 7–20.

Adler, S. (1993). Aprons and attitudes: A consideration of feminism in children's books. In H. Claire, J. Maybin, & J. Swann (Eds.), *Equality matters* (pp. 111–123). Bristol, England: Multilingual Matters.

Alexander, P., & Jetton, T. (2000). Learning from text: A multidimensional and developmental perspective. In M. Kamil, P. Mosenthal, P. D. Pearson, & R. Barr (Eds.), *Handbook of reading research* (Vol. 3, pp. 285–310). Mahwah, NJ: Lawrence Erlbaum Associates.

Allen, J. (2000). *Yellow brick roads: Shared and guided paths to independent reading 4–12.* Portland, ME: Stenhouse.

Allen, P. D., & Watson, D. (Eds.). (1976). *Findings of research in miscue analysis: Classroom implications.* Urbana, IL: National Council of Teachers of English.

Allen, V. (1991). Teaching bilingual and ESL children. In J. Flood, J. Jensen, D. Lapp, & J. Squire (Eds.), *Handbook of research on teaching the English language arts* (pp. 356–364). New York: Macmillan.

Allington, R. (1983). The reading instruction provided readers of differing reading ability. *Elementary School Journal, 83*, 548–559.

Allington, R. (2001). *What really matters for struggling readers: Designing research-based programs.* New York: Longman.

Allington, R., & Woodside-Jiron, H. (1998). Decodable text in beginning reading: Are mandates and policy based on research? *ERS Spectrum, 16*, 3–11.

Alvermann, D. (2002). Effective literacy instruction for adolescents. *Journal of Literacy Research, 34*, 189–208.

Alvermann, D., & Phelps, S. (1998). *Content reading and literacy: Succeeding in today's diverse classrooms.* Boston: Allyn & Bacon.

Anderson, A., & Stokes, S. (1984). Social and institutional influences on the development and practice of literacy. In H. Goelman, A. Oberg, & F. Smith (Eds.), *Awakening to literacy* (pp. 24–37). London: Heinemann.

Anderson, R., & Nagy, W. (1996). Word meanings. In R. Barr, M. Kamil, P. Mosenthal, & P. D. Pearson (Eds.), *Handbook of reading research* (Vol. 2, pp. 690–724). Mahwah, NJ: Lawrence Erlbaum Associates.

Anderson, R., Reynolds, R., Schallert, D., & Goetz, E. (1977). Frameworks for comprehending discourse. *American Educational Research Journal, 14*, 367–382.

Anderson, R., & Shifrin, Z. (1980). The meaning of words in context. In R. Spiro, B. Bruce, & W. Brewer (Eds.), *Theoretical issues in reading comprehension* (pp. 331–348). Hillsdale, NJ: Lawrence Erlbaum Associates.

Anderson, R., Spiro, R., & Anderson, M. (1978). Schemata as scaffolding for the representation of information in connected discourse. *American Educational Research Journal, 14*, 367–382.

American Psychological Association (APA). (2001). *Publication manual of the American Psychological Association* (5th ed.). Washington, DC: Author.

Ashley, H. (2001). Playing the game: Proficient working-class student writers' second voices. *Research in the Teaching of English, 35*, 493–524.

Atwell, M. (1980). *The evolution of text: The interrelationship of reading and writing in the composing process.* Unpublished doctoral dissertation, Indiana University, Bloomington.

Atwell, N. (1990). *Coming to know.* Portsmouth, NH: Heinemann.

Atwell, N. (1998). *In the middle: New understandings about writing, reading, and learning.* Portsmouth, NH: Heinemann.

Au, K. (1993). *Literacy instruction in multicultural settings.* Orlando, FL: Holt, Rinehart, & Winston.

Bailey, M. H. (1967). The utility of phonic generalizations in grades one through six. *The Reading Teacher, 20*, 413–418.

Banks, J. (1991). *Teaching strategies for ethnic studies.* Boston: Allyn & Bacon.

Banks, J. (1993, June–July). The canon debate, knowledge construction, and multicultural education. *Educational Researcher, 22*, 4–14.

Bank Street College of Education (Ed.). (1965). Bills Evers and the Tigers. In *My city* (pp. 237–243). New York: Macmillan.

Barnes, D., & Todd (1995). *Communication and learning revisited.* Portsmouth, NH: Heinemann.

Baron, D. (1992, July 1). Why do academics continue to insist on "proper English?" *Chronicle of Higher Education*, pp. B2–B3.

Baron, D. (1997, January 24). Ebonics is not a panacea for students at risk. *Chronicle of Higher Education*, pp. B4–B6.

Barrs, M., & Pidgeon, S. (Eds.). (1994). *Reading the difference: Gender and reading in elementary classrooms.* York, ME: Stenhouse.

Bartolome, L. (1994). Beyond the methods fetish: Toward a humanizing pedagogy. *Harvard Educational Review, 64*, 173–194.

Baumann, J., Kame'enui, E., & Ash, G. (2003). Research on vocabulary instruction: Voltaire redux. In J. Flood, D. Lapp, J. Squire, & J. Jensen (Eds.), *Handbook of research on teaching the English language arts* (2nd ed., pp. 752–785). Mahwah, NJ: Lawrence Erlbaum Associates.

Bazerman, C. (2004). Intertextuality: How texts rely on other texts. In C. Bazerman & P. Prior (Eds.), *What writing does and how it does it* (pp. 83–96). Mahwah, NJ: Lawrence Erlbaum Associates.

Beach, R., Appleman, D., & Dorsey, S. (1994). Adolescents' uses of intertextual links to understand literature. In R. Ruddell, M. Ruddell, & H. Singer (Eds.), *Theoretical models and processes of reading* (4th ed., pp. 695–714). Newark, DE: International Reading Association (IRA).

Belenky, M. F., Clinchy, B. M., Goldberger, N. R., & Tarule, J. M. (1986). *Women's ways of knowing: The development of self, voice, and mind.* New York: Basic Books.

Bender-Peterson, S., & Lach, M. (1990). Gender stereotypes in children's books: Their prevalence and influence on cognitive and affective development. *Gender and Education, 2,* 111–123.

Berdiansky, B., Cronnel, B., & Koehler, J. (1969). *Spelling–sound relations and primary form–class descriptions for speech-comprehension vocabularies of 6–9 year-olds* (Tech. Rep. No. 15). Inglewood, CA: Southwest Regional Laboratory for Educational Research and Development.

Bereiter, C., & Engelman, S. (1966). *Teaching disadvantaged children in the preschool.* New York: Prentice Hall.

Berliner, D., & Biddle, B. (1995). *The manufactured crisis: Myths, fraud, and the attack on America's public schools.* New York: Addison-Wesley.

Bernhardt, E. (2000). Second-language reading as a case study of reading scholarship in the 20th century. In M. Kamil, P. Mosenthal, P. D. Pearson, & R. Barr (Eds.), *Handbook of reading research* (Vol. 3, pp. 791–811). Mahwah, NJ: Lawrence Erlbaum Associates.

Bigelow, W. (1989). Discovering Columbus: Rereading the past. *Language Arts, 66,* 635–643.

Bigelow, W., Miner, B., & Peterson, R. (Eds.). (1991). *Rethinking schools.* Milwaukee, WI: Rethinking Schools.

Bigelow, W., & Peterson, B. (Eds.). (1998). *Rethinking Columbus: The next 500 years.* Milwaukee, WI: Rethinking Schools.

Bizzell, P. (1991). Beyond anti-foundationalism to rhetorical authority: Problems defining cultural literacy. *College English, 52,* 661–675.

Blackburn, E. (1982). *Borrowing words: Children use literature to improve writing.* Unpublished manuscript, Great Falls School, Somersworth, NH.

Blackburn, M. (2003). Exploring literacy performances and power dynamics at The Loft: Queer youth reading the world and the word. *Research in the Teaching of English, 37,* 467–490.

Boutwell, M. (1983). Reading and writing processes: A reciprocal agreement. *Language Arts, 60,* 723–730.

Bovair, S., & Kieras, D. (1996). Toward a model of acquiring procedures from text. In R. Barr, M. Kamil, P. Mosenthal, & P. D. Pearson (Eds.), *Handbook of reading research* (Vol. 3, pp. 206–229). Mahwah, NJ: Lawrence Erlbaum Associates.

Braine, M. (1971). The acquisition of language in infant and child. In C. Reed (Ed.), *The learning of language* (pp. 7–95). New York: Appleton-Century-Crofts.

Brandt, D. (1990). *Literacy as involvement: The acts of writers, readers, and text.* Carbondale: Southern Illinois University Press.

Brandt, D. (1998). Sponsors of literacy. *College Composition and Communication, 49,* 165–185.

Brandt, D. (2001). Literacy learning and economic change. In S. Beck & L. Olah (Eds.), *Perspectives on language and literacy: Beyond the here and now* (pp. 201–220). Cambridge, MA: Harvard Educational Review.

Bransford, J., & Johnson, M. (1973). Considerations of some problems of comprehension. In W. Chase (Ed.), *Visual information processing* (pp. 383–438). New York: Academic.

Brinkley, E. (1998). What's religion got to do with attacks on whole language? In K. Goodman (Ed.), *In defense of good teaching* (pp. 57–71). York, ME: Stenhouse.

Britton, J., Burgess, T., Martin, N., McLeod, A., & Rosen, H. (1975). *The development of writing abilities*. London: Macmillan.

Brown, R. (1973). *A first language: The early stages*. Cambridge, MA: Harvard University Press.

Bruce, B. (1980). Plans and social action. In R. Spiro, B. Bruce, & W. Brewer (Eds.), *Theoretical issues in reading comprehension* (pp. 367–384). Hillsdale, NJ: Lawrence Erlbaum Associates.

Bruffee, K. (1986). Social construction, language, and the authority of knowledge: A bibliographical essay. *College English, 48*, 773–790.

Bruner, J. (1974). The ontogenesis of speech acts. *Journal of Child Language, 2*, 1–19.

Bruner, J. (1990). *Acts of meaning*. Cambridge, MA: Harvard University Press.

Buck, C. (1977). Miscues of non-native speakers of English. In K. Goodman (Ed.), *Miscue analysis: Applications to reading instruction* (pp. 91–96). Urbana, IL: National Council of Teachers of English.

Buckingham, D., & Sefton-Green, J. (1994). *Cultural studies goes to school: Reading and teaching popular media*. Bristol, PA: Taylor & Francis.

Burke, C. (1973). Dialect and the reading process. In J. Laffey & R. Shuy (Eds.), *Language differences: Do they interfere?* (pp. 91–100). Newark, DE: International Reading Association.

Burke, C. (1976). *Reading: What it is and what it isn't* [videotape]. Bloomington: Indiana University, Language Education Department.

California State Department of Education. (1981). *English-language arts framework*. Sacramento, CA: Author.

Calkins, L. (1994). *The art of teaching writing* (2nd ed.). Portsmouth, NH: Heinemann.

Cambourne, B., & Rousch, P. (1979). *A psycholinguistic model of reading proficiency as it relates to proficient, average, and low-ability readers* (Tech. Rep.). Wagga Wagga, NSW, Australia: Sturt University, Riverina College of Advanced English.

Carey, R., Harste, J., & Smith, S. (1981). Contextual constraints and discourse processes: A replication study. *Reading Research Quarterly, 6*, 382–410.

Carrasquillo, A., Kucer, S. B., & Abrams, R. (2004). *Beyond the beginnings: Literacy interventions for upper elementary English language learners*. Clevedon, England: Multilingual Matters LTD.

Carroll, L. (1988). *Alice in wonderland*. New York: Scholastic.

Carroll, J. B., Davies, P., & Richman, B. (1971). *The American Heritage word frequency book*. New York: Houghton Mifflin.

Cattell, J. M. (1885). The inertia of the eye and brain. *Brain, 8*, 295–312.

Cazden, C. (1972). *Child language and education*. New York: Holt, Rinehart, & Winston.

Cazden, C. (1988). *Classroom discourse: The language of teaching and learning*. Portsmouth, NH: Heinemann.

Cazden, C. (2001). *Classroom discourse: The language of teaching and learning* (2nd ed.). Portsmouth, NH: Heinemann.

Cazden, C. (1992). *Whole language plus*. New York: Teachers College Press.

Chafe, W., & Danielewicz, J. (1987). Properties of spoken and written language. In R. Horowitz & S. J. Samuels (Eds.), *Comprehending oral and written language* (pp. 83–113). New York: Academic.

Chall, J. (1983). *Stages of reading development*. New York: McGraw-Hill.

Chomsky, C. (1970). Reading, writing, and phonology. *Harvard Educational Review, 40*, 287–309.

Chomsky, N. (1957). *Syntactic structures*. Hague, The Netherlands: Mouton.

Clay, M. (1975). *What did I write?* London: Heinemann.

Clymer, T. (1996). The utility of phonic generalizations in the primary grades. *The Reading Teacher, 50*, 182–187.

Coles, G. (1998). *Reading lessons: The debate over literacy*. New York: Hill & Wang.

Coles, G. (2000). *Misreading reading*. Portsmouth, NH: Heinemann.

Comber, B. (2000). What *really* counts in early literacy lessons. *Language Arts, 78*, 39–49.

Comber, B., & Simpson, A. (Eds.). (2001). *Negotiating critical literacies in classrooms*. Mahwah, NJ: Lawrence Erlbaum Associates.

Creighton, D. (1997). Critical literacy in the elementary classroom. *Language Arts, 74*, 438–445.

Cuban, L. (1990). Reforming again, again, and again. *Educational Researcher, 19*, 3–13.

Cummins, J. (1988). Language proficiency, bilingualism and academic achievement. In P. Richard-Amato (Ed.), *Making it happen: Interaction in the second language classroom* (pp. 382–395). New York: Longman.

Cummins, J. (1991). Interdependence of first- and second-language proficiency in bilingual children. In E. Bialystok (Ed.), *Language processing in bilingual children* (pp. 70–89). Cambridge, England: Cambridge University Press.

Cummins, J. (1994). Knowledge, power, and identity in teaching English as a second language. In F. Genesee (Ed.), *Educating second language children* (pp. 33–58). Cambridge, England: Cambridge University Press.

Cunningham, P. (2000). *Phonics they use: Words for reading and writing* (3rd ed.). New York: HarperCollins.

Dahl, K., Scharer, P., & Lawson, L. (1999). Phonics instruction and student achievement in whole language first-grade classrooms. *Reading Research Quarterly, 34*, 312–341.

Dahl, R. (1974). Poison. In R. Dahl, *The Roald Dahl omnibus* (pp. 128–144). New York: Barnes & Noble.

Daiute, C. (2000). Writing and communication technologies. In R. Indrisano & J. Squire (Eds.), *Perspectives on writing: Research, theory, and practice* (pp. 251–276). Newark, DE: International Reading Association.

D'Angelo, F. (1975). *A conceptual theory of rhetoric*. Cambridge, MA: Winthrop.

Danielewicz, J. (1984). The interaction between text and context: A study of how adults and children use spoken and written language in four contexts. In A. Pellegrini & T. Yawkey (Eds.), *The development of oral and written language in social contexts* (pp. 243–260). Norwood, NJ: Ablex.

de Beaugrande, R. (1980). *Text, discourse, and process*. Norwood, NJ: Ablex.

de Beaugrande, R. (1984). *Text production*. Norwood, NJ: Ablex.

DeFord, D. (1981). Literacy: Reading, writing, and other essentials. *Language Arts, 58*, 652–658.

DeFord, D. (1985). Validating the construct of theoretical orientation in reading. *Reading Research Quarterly, 20*, 351–367.

Delpit, L. (1990). Language diversity and learning. In S. Hynds & D. Rubin (Eds.), *Perspectives on talk and learning* (pp. 247–266). Urbana, IL: National Council of Teachers of English.

Delpit, L. (1995). *Other people's children: Cultural conflict in the classroom*. New York: New Press.

Delpit, L., & Dowdy, J. K. (Eds.). (2002). *The skin that we speak: Thoughts on language and culture in the classroom*. New York: The Free Press.

Devine, J. (1994). Literacy and social power. In B. Ferdman, R. M. Weber, & A. Ramirez (Eds.), *Literacy across languages and cultures* (pp. 221–237). Albany: State University of New York Press.

Dewey, J. (1938). *Experience and education*. New York: Collier.

Donahue, P., Voelkl, K., Campbell, J., & Mazzeo, J. (1999). *The NAEP 1998 reading report card for the nation and the states*. Washington, DC: National Center for Education Statistics.

Donaldson, M. (1978). *Children's minds*. Glasgow, Scotland: William Collins.

Duke, N. (2000). For the rich it's richer: Print experiences and environments offered to children in very low- and very high-socioeconomic status first-grade classrooms. *American Educational Research Journal, 37*, 441–478.

Dyson, A. H. (1997). *Writing superheroes: Contemporary childhood, popular culture, and classroom literacy*. New York: Teachers College Press.

Dyson, A. H. (1998). Folk processes and media creatures: Reflections on popular culture for literacy educators. *The Reading Teacher, 51*, 392–402.

Dyson, A. H. (2003). *The brothers and sisters learn to write: Popular literacies in childhood and school cultures*. New York: Teachers College Press.

Eckhoff, B. (1983). How reading affects children's writing. *Language Arts, 60*, 607–616.

Edelsky, C. (1986). *Writing in a bilingual program: Habia una vez*. Norwood, NJ: Ablex.

Edelsky, C. (Ed.) (1999). *Making justice our project*. Urbana, IL: National Council of Teachers of English (NCTE).

Edelsky, C., Altwerger, B., & Flores, B. (1991). *Whole language: What's the difference?* Portsmouth, NH: Heinemann.

Ehrlich, S., & Rayner, K. (1981). Contextual effects on word perception and eye movements during reading. *Journal of Verbal Learning and Verbal Behavior, 20*, 641–655.

Eisner, E. (1994). *Cognition and curriculum reconsidered*. New York: Teachers College Press.

Elster, C. (2003). Authority, performance, and interpretation in religious reading: Critical issues of intercultural communication and multiple literacies. *Journal of Literacy Research, 35*, 663–692.

Emans, R. (1967). The usefulness of phonic generalizations above the primary grades. *The Reading Teacher, 20*, 419–425.

Enciso, P. (1994). Cultural identity and response to literature: Running lessons from Maniac Magee. *Language Arts, 71*, 524–533.

Engelman, S., & Carnine, D. (1982). *Theory of instruction: Principles and applications*. New York: Irvington.

Erickson, F. D. (1987). Transformation and school success: The politics and culture of educational achievement. *Anthropology and Education Quarterly, 18*, 335–356.

Faigley, L., & Witte, S. (1981). Analyzing revision. *College Composition and Communication, 32*, 400–414.

Fairclough, N. (2001). *Language and power* (2nd ed.). Harlow, England: Pearson.

Farnan, N., & Dahl, K. (2003). Children's writing: Research and practice. In J. Flood, D. Lapp, J. Squire, & J. Jensen (Eds.), *Handbook on research on teaching the English language arts* (2nd ed., pp. 993–1076). Mahwah, NJ: Lawrence Erlbaum Associates.

Farr, M. (1991). Dialects, culture, and the teaching of the English language arts. In J. Flood, J. Jensen, D. Lapp, & J. Squire (Eds.), *Handbook of research on teaching the English language arts* (pp. 365–371). New York: Macmillan.

Farr, M. (1994). En los dos idiomas: Literacy practices among Chicago Mexicanos. In B. Moss (Ed.), *Literacy across communities* (pp. 9–47). Cresskill, NJ: Hampton.

Farr, M., & Daniels, H. (1986). *Language diversity and writing instruction*. Urbana, IL: National Council of Teachers of English.

Fashola, O., Drum, P., Mayer, R., & Kang, S. (1996). A cognitive theory of orthographic transitioning: Predictable errors in how Spanish-speaking children spell English words. *American Educational Research Journal, 33*, 825–843.

Fawcett, G. (1998). Curricular innovations in literacy instruction: How students respond to change. *Journal of Literacy Research, 30*, 489–514.

Fehring, H., & Green, P. (Eds.). (2001). *Critical literacy: A collection of articles from the Australian Literacy Educators Association*. Newark, DE: IRA.

Ferdman, B. (1990). Literacy and cultural identity. *Harvard Educational Review, 60*, 181–204.

Fielding, A., Schoenbach, R., & Jordan, M. (2003). *Lessons from reading apprenticeship classrooms, Grade 6–12: Building academic literacy*. San Francisco, CA: Wiley.

Fielding, L., & Roller, C. (1992). Making difficult books accessible and easy books acceptable. *The Reading Teacher, 45*, 678–685.

Fillmore, C. J. (1968). The case for case. In E. Bach & R. T. Harms (Eds.), *Universals in linguistic theory* (pp. 1–88). New York: Holt, Rinehart, & Winston.

Finders, M. (1996). "Just girls." Literacy and allegiance in junior high school. *Written Communication, 13*, 93–129.

Finn, P. (1999). *Literacy with an attitude: Educating working-class children in their own self-interest*. Albany: State University of New York Press.

Fitzgerald, J. (1995). English-as-a-second-language learners' cognitive reading processes: A review of research in the United States. *Review of Educational Research, 65*, 145–190.

Flores, B., Cousin, P., & Diaz, E. (1991). Transforming deficit myths about learning, language, and culture. *Language Arts, 68*, 369–379.

Flower, L. (1979). Writer-based prose: A cognitive basis for problems in writing. *College English, 41*, 19–37.

Flower, L., & Hayes, J. (1981). A cognitive process theory of writing. *College Composition and Communication, 32*, 365–387.

Fountas, I., & Pinnell, G. S. (1996). *Guiding reading: Good first teaching for all children*. Portsmouth, NH: Heinemann.

Freeman, D., & Freeman, Y. (1994). *Between worlds: Access to second language acquisition*. Portsmouth, NH: Heinemann.

Freeman, Y., & Freeman, D. (1992). *Whole language for second language learners.* Portsmouth, NH: Heinemann.

Freeman, Y., Freeman, D., & Fennacy, J. (1997). California's reading revolution: What happened? *The New Advocate, 10*, 31–47.

Fries, C., Fries, A., Wilson, R., & Rudolph, M. (1966). A pin for Dan. In *Merrill linguistic readers* (Reader 2). Columbus, OH: Merrill.

Gambrell, L. (1996). Creating classroom cultures that foster reading motivation. *The Reading Teacher, 50*, 14–25.

Gee, J. (1990). *Social linguistics and literacies: Ideology in discourses.* New York: Falmer.

Gee, J. (1996). *Social linguistics and literacies: Ideology in discourses* (2nd ed.). New York: Falmer.

Gee, J. (1999). *An introduction to discourse analysis: Theory and method.* New York: Routledge.

Geva, E., & Tierney, R. (1984, April). *Text engineering: The influence of manipulated compare-contrast selections.* Paper presented at the annual meeting of the American Educational Research Association, New Orleans, LA.

Gilbert, P. (1989). *Writing, schooling, and deconstruction: From voice to text in the classroom.* London: Routledge.

Giroux, H. (1983). *Theory and resistance in education: A pedagogy for the opposition.* London: Heinemann.

Glass, G., & Stanley, J. (1970). *Statistical methods in education and psychology.* Englewood Cliffs, NJ: Prentice Hall.

Glasswell, K., Parr, J., & McNaughton, S. (2003). Four ways to work against yourself when conferencing with struggling writers. *Language Arts, 80*, 291–298.

Goodman, K. (1967). Reading: A psycholinguistic guessing game. *Journal of the Reading Specialist, 6*, 126–135.

Goodman, K. (Ed.). (1977). *Miscue analysis: Applications to reading instruction.* Urbana, IL: National Council of Teachers of English.

Goodman, K. (1986). *What's whole in whole language?* Portsmouth, NH: Heinemann.

Goodman, K. (1993). *Phonics phacts.* Portsmouth, NH: Heinemann.

Goodman, K. (1996). *On reading.* Portsmouth, NH: Heinemann.

Goodman, K. (Ed.). (1998). *In defense of good teaching.* York, ME: Stenhouse.

Goodman, K., & Buck, C. (1997). Dialect barriers to reading comprehension revisited. *The Reading Teacher, 50*, 454–459.

Goodman, K., & Goodman, Y. (1978). *Reading of American children whose language is a stable rural dialect of English or a language other than English* (NIE-C-00-3-0087). Washington, DC: U.S. Department of Health, Education and Welfare.

Goodman, K., & Goodman, Y. (1979). Learning to read is natural. In L. Resnick & P. Weaver (Eds.), *Theory and practice of early reading* (pp. 137–154). Hillsdale, NJ: Lawrence Erlbaum Associates.

Goodman, K., Goodman, Y., & Flores, B. (1979). *Reading in the bilingual classroom: Literacy & biliteracy.* Rosslyn, UA: National Clearinghouse for Bilingual Education.

Goodman, Y. (2003). *Valuing language study: Inquiry into language for elementary and middle schools.* Urbana, IL: National Council of Teachers of English.

Goodman, Y., & Burke, C. (1980). *Reading strategies: Focus on comprehension.* New York: Holt.

Goodman, Y., & Marek, A. (1996). *Retrospective miscue analysis: Revaluing readers and reading.* New York: Owens.

Goodman, Y., Watson, D., & Burke, C. (1987). *Reading miscue inventory: Alternative procedures.* New York: Owens.

Goody, J. (1977). *The domestication of the savage mind.* Cambridge, England: Cambridge University Press.

Goody, J., & Watt, I. P. (1963). The consequences of literacy. *Comparative Studies in History and Society, 5,* 304–345.

Gough, P. (1972). One second of reading. In J. F. Kavanagh & I. G. Mattingly (Eds.), *Language by ear and by eye* (pp. 331–358). Cambridge, MA: MIT Press.

Graessner, A., Golding, J., & Long, D. (1996). Narrative representation and comprehension. In R. Barr, M. Kamil, P. Mosenthal, & P. D. Pearson (Eds.), *Handbook of reading research* (Vol. 3, pp. 171–205). Mahwah, NJ: Lawrence Erlbaum Associates.

Graff, H. J. (1979). *The literacy myth: Literacy and social structure in the nineteenth-century city.* New York: Academic.

Graff, H. J. (1987). *The legacies of literacy: Continuities and contradictions in western culture and society.* Bloomington: Indiana University Press.

Graves, D. (1983). *Writing: Teachers and children at work.* Portsmouth, NH: Heinemann.

Graves, D. (1994). *A fresh look at writing.* Portsmouth, NH: Heinemann.

Graves, D., & Hansen, J. (1983). The author's chair. *Language Arts, 60,* 176–183.

Greenleaf, C., Jimenez, R., & Roller, C. (2002). Conversations: Reclaiming secondary reading interventions: From limited to rich conceptions, from narrow to broad conversations. *Reading Research Quarterly, 37,* 484–496.

Greenleaf, C., Schoenbach, R., Cziko, C., & Mueller, F. (2001). Apprenticing adolescent readers to academic literacy. *Harvard Educational Review, 71,* 79–125.

Groff, P. (1978). Children's spelling of features of Black English. *Research in the Teaching of English, 12,* 21–28.

Haas, C. (1991). Composing in technological contexts: A study of notemaking. *Written Communication, 7,* 512–547.

Haight, R. (1999). *Jesus, symbol of God.* Maryknoll, NY: Orbis.

Hall, W., & Guthrie, L. (1980). On the dialect question and reading. In R. Spiro, B. Bruce, & W. Brewer (Eds.), *Theoretical issues in reading comprehension* (pp. 439–450). Hillsdale, NJ: Lawrence Erlbaum Associates.

Halliday, M. A. K. (1973). *Explorations in the functions of language.* London: Arnold.

Halliday, M. A. K. (1974). *Language and social man.* London: Longman.

Halliday, M. A. K. (1987). Spoken and written modes of meaning. In R. Horowitz & S. J. Samuels (Eds.), *Comprehending oral and written language* (pp. 55–82). New York: Academic.

Halliday, M. A. K., & Hasan, R. (1976). *Cohesion in English.* London: Longman.

Halliday, M. A. K., & Hasan, R. (1980). *Text and context.* Tokyo: Sophia University.

Hancock, L., with Biddle, N. (1994, November). Red, white—and blue. *Newsweek, 130,* p. 54.

Hansen, J. (1983a). Authors respond to authors. *Language Arts, 60,* 970–976.

Hansen, J. (1983b). First grade writers who pursue reading. In P. Stock (Ed.), *Forum: Essays on theory and practice in the teaching of writing* (pp. 155–162). Upper Montclair, NJ: Boynton/Cook.

Harste, J., & Burke, C. (1978). Toward a socio-psycholinguistic model of reading comprehension. *Viewpoints in Teaching and Learning, 45*, 9–34.

Harste, J., Woodward, V., & Burke, C. (1984). *Language stories and literacy lessons.* Portsmouth, NH: Heinemann.

Hartman, D. (1992). Intertextuality and reading: The text, the reader, the author, and the context. *Linguistics and Education, 4*, 295–311.

Hartman, D. (1994). The intertextual links of readers using multiple passages: A postmodern/semiotic/cognitive view of meaning making. In R. Ruddell, M. Ruddell, & H. Singer (Eds.). *Theoretical models and processes of reading* (4th ed., pp. 616–663). Newark, DE: IRA.

Hartman, D., & Hartman, J. (1993). Reading across texts: Expanding the role of the reader. *The Reading Teacher, 47*, 202–211.

Hayes, J. (2000). A new framework for understanding cognition and affect in writing. In R. Indrisano & J. Squire (Eds.), *Perspectives on writing: Research, theory, and practice* (pp. 6–44). Newark, DE: IRA.

Heath, S. (1982a). Protean shapes in literacy events: Evershifting oral and literate traditions. In D. Tannen (Ed.), *Spoken and written language: Exploring orality and literacy* (pp. 91–117). Norwood, NJ: Ablex.

Heath, S. (1982b). What no bedtime story means: Narrative skills at home and school. *Language in Society, 11*, 49–76.

Heath, S. (1983). *Ways with words: Language, life, and work in communities and classrooms.* Cambridge, England: Cambridge University Press.

Henkin, R. (1995). Insiders and outsiders in first-grade writing workshops: Gender and equity issues. *Language Arts, 72*, 429–434.

Henson, J., & Gilles, C. (2003). Ali's story: Overcoming beliefs that inhibit learning. *Language Arts, 80*, 259–267.

Hillocks, G. (1986). *Research on written composition: New directions for teaching.* Urbana, IL: ERIC/National Conference on Research in English.

Hillocks, G., & Smith, M. (2003). Grammars and literacy learning. In J. Flood, D. Lapp, J. Squire, & J. Jensen (Eds.), *Handbook of research on teaching the English language arts* (2nd ed., pp. 721–737). Mahwah, NJ: Lawrence Erlbaum Associates.

Hirsch, E. (1987). *Cultural literacy.* Boston: Houghton Mifflin.

Ho, C. S., & Bryant, P. (1997). Learning to read Chinese beyond the logographic phase. *Reading Research Quarterly, 32*, 276–289.

Hodges, R. (2000). Mental processes and the conventions of writing: Spelling, punctuation, handwriting. In R. Indrisano & J. Squire, (Eds.), *Perspectives on writing: Research, theory, and practice* (pp. 187–211). Newark, DE: International Reading Association.

Hoffman, D. (1996). Culture and self in multicultural education: Reflections on discourse, text, and practice. *American Educational Research Journal, 33*, 545–569.

Hoffman, J. (1992). Critical reading/thinking across the curriculum: Using I-charts to support learning. *Language Arts, 69*, 121–127.

Honeychurch, K. (1996). Researching dissident subjectivities: Queering the grounds of theory and practice. *Harvard Educational Review, 66*, 339–355.

Hudelson, S. (1994). Literacy development of second language children. In F. Genesee (Ed.), *Educating second language children* (pp. 129–158). Cambridge, England: Cambridge University Press.

Hudelson, S., & Poynor, L. (2003). Teaching bilingual and ESL children and adolescents. In J. Flood, D. Lapp, J. Squire, & J. Jensen (Eds.), *Handbook of research on teaching the English language arts* (2nd ed., pp. 421–434). Mahwah, NJ: Lawrence Erlbaum Associates.

Huey, E. (1968). *The psychology and pedagogy of reading*. Cambridge, MA: MIT Press. (Originally published by Macmillan in 1908.)

Hughes, L. (1995). Subway rush hour. In A. Rampersad & D. Roessel (Eds.), *The collected poems of Langston Hughes* (p. 423). New York: Knopf.

Hull, G. (1993). Hearing other voices: A critical assessment of popular views on literacy and work. *Harvard Educational Review, 63*, 20–49.

Hull, G., & Schultz, K. (2001). Literacy and learning out of school: A review of theory and research. *Review of Educational Research, 71*, 575–611.

Irwin, P., & Mitchell, J. (1983). A procedure for assessing the richness of retellings. *Journal of Reading, 26*, 391–396.

Jacobs, A. (1997, June 16). Novice newscasters get voice therapy. *New York Times*, p. D11.

Jenkins, J., Pany, D., & Schreck, J. (1978). *Vocabulary and reading comprehension: Instructional effects* (Tech. Rep. No. 100). Urbana-Champaign, IL: Center for the Study of Reading.

Jimenez, R., Garcia, G., & Pearson, P. D. (1995). Three children, two languages, and strategic reading: Case studies in bilingual/monolingual reading. *American Educational Research Journal, 32*, 31–61.

Jimenez, R., Garcia, G., & Pearson, P. D. (1996). The reading strategies of bilingual Latino/a students who are successful English readers: Opportunities and obstacles. *Reading Research Quarterly, 31*, 90–112.

Jimenez, R., & Gersten, R. (1999). Lessons and dilemmas derived from the literacy instruction of two Latina/o teachers. *American Educational Research Journal, 36*, 265–301.

Johnson, C. (1998). Holding on to a language of our own: An interview with linguist John Rickford. In T. Perry & L. Delpit (Eds.), *The real Ebonics debate: Power, language, and the education of African-American children* (pp. 59–65). Boston: Beacon.

Johnston, F. (2001). The utility of phonic generalizations: Let's take another look at Clymer's conclusions. *The Reading Teacher, 44*, 132–143.

Just, M. A., & Carpenter, P. (1987). *The psychology of reading and language comprehension*. Newton, MA: Allyn & Bacon.

Kamil, M., Intrator, S., & Kim, H. (2000). The effects of other technologies on literacy and literacy learning. In M. Kamil, P. Mosenthal, D. Pearson, & R. Barr (Eds.), *Reading research* (Vol. 3, pp. 771–788). Mahwah, NY: Lawrence Erlbaum Associates.

Kamler, B. (1993). Constructing gender in the process writing classroom. *Language Arts, 70*, 95–103.

Keenan-Ochs, E. (1977). Making it last: Repetition in children's discourse. In S. Ervin-Tripp & C. Mitchell-Kernan (Eds.), *Child discourse* (pp. 125–138). New York: Academic.

Keene, E., & Zimmermann, S. (1997). *Mosaic of thought: Teaching comprehension in a reader's workshop*. Portsmouth, NH: Heinemann.

Kinzer, C., & Leander, K. (2003). Technology and the language arts: Implications of an expanded definition of literacy. In J. Flood, D. Lapp, J. Squire, & J. Jensen (Eds.), *Handbook on research on teaching the English language arts* (2nd ed., pp. 546–565). Mahwah, NJ: Lawrence Erlbaum Associates.

Kintsch, W. (1998). *Comprehension: A paradigm for cognition.* Cambridge, England: Cambridge.

Kligman, D., Cronnel, B., & Verna, G. (1972). Black English pronunciation and spelling performance. *Elementary English, 49,* 1247–1253.

Kohl, H. (1994). I won't learn from you! Confronting student resistance. In B. Bigelow, L. Christensen, S. Karp, B. Miner, & B. Peterson (Eds.), *Rethinking our classrooms: Teaching for equity and justice* (pp. 134–135). Milwaukee, WI: Rethinking Schools.

Kohn, A. (2000). *The case against standardized testing.* Portsmouth, NH: Heinemann.

Kohn, A. (2002). Poor teaching for poor kids. *Language Arts, 79,* 251–255.

Kolers, P. (1969). Reading is only incidentally visual. In K. Goodman & J. Fleming (Eds.), *Psycholinguistics and the teaching of reading* (pp. 8–16). Newark, DE: International Reading Association.

Kolers, P. (1973). Three stages of reading. In F. Smith (Ed.), *Psycholinguistics and reading.* (pp. 28–49). New York: Holt.

Krashen, S. (1999). *Three arguments against whole language and why they are wrong.* Portsmouth, NH: Heinemann.

Kraus, R. (1945). *The carrot seed.* New York: Scholastic.

Kucer, S. B. (1983a). Text coherence from a transactional perspective. In J. Niles & L. A. Harris (Eds.), *Searchers for meaning in reading/language processing and instruction* (pp. 104–110). Rochester, NY: National Reading Conference.

Kucer, S. B. (1983b). *Using text comprehension as a metaphor for understanding text production: Building bridges between reading and writing.* Unpublished doctoral dissertation, Indiana University, Bloomington.

Kucer, S. B. (1985a). The making of meaning: Reading and writing as parallel processes. *Written Communication, 2,* 317–336.

Kucer, S. B. (1985b). Predictability and readability: The same rose with different names? In M. P. Douglas (Ed.), *Claremont reading conference yearbook* (pp. 229–246). Claremont, CA: Claremont Graduate School.

Kucer, S. B. (1986). Helping writers get the "big picture." *Journal of Reading, 30,* 18–32.

Kucer, S. B. (1987). The cognitive base of reading and writing. In J. Squire (Ed.), *The dynamics of language learning: Research in the language arts* (pp. 27–51). Urbana, IL: National Conference on Research in English and ERIC Clearinghouse on Reading and Communication Skills.

Kucer, S. B. (1989a). Evaluating literacy processes: On listening to children thinking. In M. P. Douglas (Ed.), *Claremont reading conference yearbook* (pp. 170–190). Claremont, CA: Claremont Graduate School.

Kucer, S. B. (1989b). Reading a text: Does the author make a difference? In B. Lawson, S. Sterr Ryan, & W. R. Winterowd (Eds.), *Encountering student texts: Interpretive issues in reading student writing* (pp. 159–168). Urbana, IL: National Council of Teachers of English.

Kucer, S. B. (1991). Authenticity as the basis for instruction. *Language Arts, 68,* 532–540.

Kucer, S. B. (1992). Six bilingual Mexican-American students' and their teachers' interpretations of close literacy lessons. *Elementary School Journal, 92,* 555–570.

Kucer, S. B. (1994). Real world literacy activities for real world kids. *The California Reader, 27,* 3–10.

Kucer, S. B. (1995). Guiding bilingual students "through" the literacy processes. *Language Arts, 72,* 20–29.

Kucer, S. B. (1998). Engagement, conflict, and avoidance in a whole language classroom. *Language Arts, 75*, 90–96.

Kucer, S. B. (1999). Two students' responses to, and literacy growth in, a whole language curriculum. *Reading Research and Instruction, 38*, 233–253.

Kucer, S. B., Brobst, K., & Bolgatz, J. (2002). *Literacy Evaluation Report.* CSD 10–Fordham University Partnership, School Improvement and Literacy in the Middle Schools, New York City Schools.

Kucer, S. B., & Harste, J. (1991). The reading and writing connection: Counterpart strategy instruction. In B. Hayes (Ed.), *Effective strategies for teaching reading* (pp. 123–152). Boston: Allyn & Bacon.

Kucer, S. B., & Silva, C. (in progress). *Teaching the dimensions of literacy.* Mahwah, NJ: Lawrence Erlbaum Associates.

Kucer, S. B., & Silva, C. (1996, November). *Reader response strategies in a whole language bilingual classroom and their effects on student comprehension.* Paper presented at the meeting of the National Council of Teachers of English, Chicago.

Kucer, S. B., & Silva, C. (1999a, April). *The English literacy development of bilingual students within a transition whole language curriculum.* Paper presented at the meeting of the American Educational Research Association, Montreal, Canada.

Kucer, S. B., & Silva, C. (1999b). The English literacy development of bilingual students within a transition whole language curriculum. *Bilingual Research Journal, 23*, 339–364.

Kucer, S. B., Silva, C., & Delgado-Larocco, E. (1995). *Curricular conversations: Themes in multilingual and monolingual classrooms.* York, ME: Stenhouse.

Kucer, S. B., & Tuten, J. (2003). Revisiting and rethinking the reading process. *Language Arts, 80*, 38–44

Kuhn, T. S. (1970). *The structure of scientific revolutions* (2nd ed.). Chicago: University of Chicago Press.

Kutz, E. (1997). *Language and literacy: Studying discourse in communities and classrooms.* Portsmouth, NH: Boynton/Cook-Heinemann.

Labbo, L., Hoffman, J., & Roser, N. (1995). Ways to unintentionally make writing difficult. *Language Arts, 72*, 164–170.

Labov, W. (1970). The logic of nonstandard English. *Georgetown Monographs of Language and Linguistics, 22*, 1–22.

Labov, W. (1972). *Language in the inner city: Studies in Black English vernacular.* Philadelphia: University of Pennsylvania.

Labov, W. (1973). The boundaries of words and their meanings. In C. J. Bailey & R. Shuy (Eds.), *New ways of analyzing variation in English* (pp. 340–373). Washington, DC: Georgetown University Press.

Labov, W., & Harris, W. (1983). *De facto segregation of Black and White vernaculars.* Paper presented at the Annual Conference on New Ways of Analyzing Variation in English, Montreal, Canada.

Ladson-Billings, G. (1994). *The dreamkeepers: Successful teaching for African American students.* San Francisco: Jossey-Bass.

Ladson-Billings, G. (1995). Toward a theory of culturally relevant pedagogy. *American Educational Research Journal, 32*, 465–491.

Ladson-Billings, G. (2002). I ain't writin' nuttin': Permissions to fail and demands to succeed in urban classrooms. In L. Delpit & J. K. Dowdy. (Eds.), *The skin that we speak: Thoughts on language and culture in the classroom* (pp. 107–120). New York: The Free Press.

Langer, J. (1984). The effects of available information on responses to school writing tasks. *Research in the Teaching of English, 18,* 27–44.

Langer, J., & Flihan, S. (2000). Writing and reading relationships: Constructive tasks. In R. Indrisano & J. Squire (Eds.), *Perspectives on writing: Research, Theory, and Practice* (pp. 112–139). Newark, DE: International Reading Association.

Lankshear, C., & Knobel, M. (2002). Do we have your attention? New literacies, digital technologies, and the education of adolescents. In D. Alvermann (Ed.), *Adolescents and literacies in a digital world* (pp. 19–39). New York: Peter Lang.

Lawless, K., Brown, S., Mills, R., & Mayall, H. (2003). Knowledge, interest, recall, and navigation: A look at hypertext processing. *Journal of Literacy Research, 35,* 911–934.

Lee, C., & Jackson, R. (1992). *Faking it: A look into the mind of a creative learner.* Portsmouth, NH: Boynton/Cook-Heinemann.

Leland, C., Harste, J., Ociepka, A., Lewison, M., & Vasquez, V. (1999). Exploring critical literacy: You can hear a pin drop. *Language Arts, 77,* 70–77.

LeMoine, N. (2001). Language variation and literacy acquisition in African American Students. In J. Harris, A. Kamhi, & K. Pollock (Eds.), *Literacy in African American communities* (pp. 169–194), Mahwah, NJ: Lawrence Erlbaum Associates.

Leseman, P., & de Jong, P. (1998). Home literacy: Opportunity, instruction, cooperation and social-emotional quality predicting early reading achievement. *Reading Research Quarterly, 33,* 294–318.

Leu, D. (2000). Literacy and technology: Deictic consequences for literacy education in an information age. In M. Kamil, P. Mosenthal, D. Pearson, & R. Barr (Eds.), *Reading research* (Vol. 3, pp. 743–770). Mahwah, NY: Lawrence Erlbaum Associates.

Lewison, M., Flint, A., & Sluys, K. (2002). Taking on critical literacy: The journey of newcomers and novices. *Language Arts, 79,* 382–392.

Luke, A. (1995). When basic skills and information processing just aren't enough: Rethinking reading in new times. *Teachers College Record, 97,* 95–115.

Luke, A. (1998). Getting over method: Literacy teaching as work in "new times." *Language Arts, 75,* 305–313.

Mahiri, J., & Godley, A. (1998). Rewriting identity: Social meanings of literacy and "revisions" of self. *Reading Research Quarterly, 33,* 416–433.

Mandler, J., & Johnson, N. (1977). Remembrance of things parsed: Story structure and recall. *Cognitive Psychology, 9,* 111–151.

Manning, M., Manning, G., & Long, R. (1994). *Theme immersion: Inquiry-based curriculum in elementary and middle schools.* Portsmouth, NH: Heinemann.

Mayer, M. (1974). *Frog goes to dinner.* New York: Dial.

Mayer, M. (1976). *Ah-choo.* New York: Dial.

Mayher, J. (1990). *Uncommon sense: Theoretical practice in language education.* Portsmouth, NH: Heinemann.

McCarthey, S. (1988). Constructing multiple subjectivities in classroom literacy contexts. *Research in the Teaching of English, 32,* 126–160.

McDermott, R. (1987). The explanation of minority school failure, again. *Anthropology and Education Quarterly, 18,* 361–364.

McDermott, R. (1995). Culture as disability. *Anthropology and Education Quarterly, 26,* 324–348.

McIntyre, E., & Freppon, P. (1994). A comparison of children's development of alphabetic knowledge in a skills-based and a whole language classroom. *Research in the Teaching of English, 28*, 391–417.

McNeal, K. (2003). *Comprehensive examination.* Unpublished manuscript, Fordham University-Lincoln Center, New York.

McQuillan, J (1998). *The literacy crisis: False claims, real solutions.* Portsmouth, NH: Heinemann.

Meacham, S., & Buendia, E. (1999). Modernism, postmodernism, and post-structuralism and their impact on literacy. *Language Arts, 76*, 510–516.

Merriam, E. (1984). One, two, three—gough! In J. Cole (Ed.), *A new treasury of children's poetry: Old favorites and new discoveries* (p. 120). New York: Doubleday.

Meyer, B. (1982). Reading research and the composition teacher: The importance of plans. *College Composition and Communication, 33*, 37–49.

Michaels, S. (1981). Sharing time: Children's narrative styles and differential access to literacy. *Language and Society, 10*, 423–442.

Michaels, S., & Cazden, C. (1986). Teacher–child collaboration as oral preparation for literacy. In B. Schieffer (Ed.), *Acquisition of literacy: Ethnographic perspectives* (pp. 132–154). Norwood, NJ: Ablex.

Microref Systems, Inc. (1988). *Microref quick reference guide.* Chicago: Author.

Moje, E. (2000). "To be part of the story": The literacy practices of gangsta adolescents. *Teachers College Record, 102*, 651–690.

Moje, E., Young, J., Readence, J., & Moore, D. (2000). Reinventing adolescent literacy for new times: Perennial and millennial issues. *Journal of Adolescent and Adult Literacy, 43*, 400–410.

Moore, D., Bean, T., Birdyshaw, D., & Rycik, J. (1999). *Adolescent literacy: A position statement for the Commission on Adolescent Literacy of the International Reading Association.* Newark, DE: IRA.

Moore, R., & Aspegren, C. (2001). Reflective conversations between two learners. Retrospective miscue analysis. *Journal of Adolescent and Adult Literacy, 44*, 492–503.

Morgan, A. (1983). Context: The web of meaning. *Language Arts, 60*, 305–314.

Moss, B. (1994). Creating a community: Literacy events in African-American churches. In B. Moss (Ed.), *Literacy across communities* (pp. 147–178). Cresskill, NJ: Hampton.

Moss, B. (2001). From the pews to the classrooms: Influences of the African American church on academic literacy. In J. Harris, A. Kamhi, & K. Pollock (Eds.), *Literacy in African American communities* (pp. 195–211). Mahwah, NJ: Lawrence Erlbaum Associates.

Murray, D. (1978). Internal revision: A process of discovery. In C. Cooper & L. Odell (Eds.), *Research on composing* (pp. 85–103). Urbana, IL: National Council of Teachers of English.

Nagy, W., & Scott, J. (2000). Vocabulary processes. In M. Kamil, P. Mosenthal, P. D. Pearson, & R. Barr (Eds.). *Handbook of reading research* (Vol. 3, pp. 269–284). Mahwah, NJ: Lawrence Erlbaum Associates.

Nejad, A. I. (1980). *The schema: A structural or functional pattern* (Tech. Rep. No. 159). Urbana: University of Illinois, Center for the Study of Reading.

Nelson, K. (1973). Structure and strategy in learning to talk. *Monographs of the Society for Research in Child Development, 38* (pp. 1–2, Serial No. 149).

Nelson, K. (1996). *Language in cognitive development: Emergence of the mediated mind.* Cambridge, England: Cambridge University Press.

Neuman, S., & Celano, D. (2001). Access to print in low-income and middle-income communities: An ecological study of four neighborhoods. *Reading Research Quarterly, 36,* 8–26.

Newkirk, T. (1982). Young writers as critical readers. *Language Arts, 59,* 451–457.

New London Group. (1996). A pedagogy of multiliteracies: Designing social futures. *Harvard Educational Review, 66,* 60–92.

NICHD (2000). *The report of the National Reading Panel: Teaching children to read.* Washington, DC: National Institute of Health.

Novinger, S. (2003). "I want her to know me": The ways adults position young children. *Language Arts, 80,* 425–434.

Ogbu, J. (1992). Understanding cultural diversity and learning. *Educational Researcher, 21,* 5–14.

Ogbu, J. (1999). Beyond language: Ebonics, proper English, and identity in a Black-American speech community. *American Educational Research Journal, 36,* 147–184.

Ogbu, J., & Matute-Bianchi, M. (1986). Understanding sociocultural factors: Knowledge, identity, and school adjustment. In Bilingual Education Office (Ed.), *Beyond language: Social and cultural factors in schooling language minority students* (pp. 73–142). Los Angeles: California State University Evaluation, Dissemination, and Assessment Center.

Ohanian, S. (1999). One size fits few. *Rethinking Schools, 13,* p. 5.

O'Neal, V., & Trabasso, T. (1976). Is there a correspondence between sound and spelling? In D. Harrison & T. Trabasso (Eds.), *Black English: A seminar* (pp. 171–190). Hillsdale, NJ: Lawrence Erlbaum Associates.

Orellana, M. F. (1995). Literacy as a gendered social practice: Tasks, text, talk, and take-up. *Reading Research Quarterly, 30,* 674–708.

Ortony, A. (1980). Metaphor. In R. Spiro, B. Bruce, & W. Brewer (Eds.), *Theoretical issues in reading comprehension* (pp. 349–384). Hillsdale, NJ: Lawrence Erlbaum Associates.

Pappas, C., & Pettegrew, B. (1998). The role of genre in the psycholinguistic guessing game of reading. *Language Arts, 75,* 36–44.

Paris, S., Wasik, B., & Turner, J. (1996). The development of strategic readers. In R. Barr, M. Kamil, P. Mosenthal, & P. D. Pearson (Eds.), *Handbook of reading research* (Vol. 2, pp. 609–640). Mahwah, NJ: Lawrence Erlbaum Associates.

Pearson, P. D. (1989). Reading the whole-language movement. *The Elementary School Journal, 90,* 231–241.

Pease-Alvarez, C., & Vasquez, O. (1994). Language socialization in ethnic minority communities. In F. Genesee (Ed.), *Educating second language children* (pp. 82–102). Cambridge, England: Cambridge University Press.

Pennycook, A. (2001). *Critical applied linguistics: A critical introduction.* Mahwah, NJ: Lawrence Erlbaum Associates.

Perez, B. (1994). Spanish literacy development: A descriptive study of four bilingual whole-language classrooms. *Journal of Reading Behavior, 26,* 75–94.

Perl, S. (1979). The composing process of unskilled college writers. *Research in the Teaching of English, 13,* 313–336.

Perry, T., & Delpit, L. (Eds.). (1998). *The real Ebonics debate: Power, language, and the education of African-American children.* Boston: Beacon.

Pianko, S. (1979). A description of the composition processes of college freshman writers. *Research in the Teaching of English, 13,* 5–22.

Pichert, J. W., & Anderson, R. C. (1977). Taking different perspectives on a story. *Journal of Educational Psychology, 63,* 309–315.

Piestrup, A. (1973). *Black dialect interference and accommodation of reading instruction in first grade* (Monograph No. 4). Berkeley, CA: Language-Behavior Research Laboratory.

Poynton, C. (1985). *Language and gender: Making the difference.* Geelong, Australia: Deakin University.

Pratt, M. (1977). *Toward a speech act theory of literary discourse.* Bloomington: Indiana University Press.

Pressley, M. (1998). *Reading instruction that works: The case for balanced teaching.* New York: Guilford.

Purcell-Gates, V. (1989). What oral/written language differences can tell us about beginning instruction. *The Reading Teacher, 42,* 290–294.

Purcell-Gates, V. (1996). Stories, coupons, and the TV Guide: Relationships between home literacy experiences and emergent literacy knowledge. *Reading Research Quarterly, 31,* 406–428.

Purcell-Gates, V. (2002). "... As soon as she opened her mouth!" Issues of language, literacy, and power. In L. Delpit & J. K. Dowdy (Eds.), *The skin that we speak: Thoughts on language and culture in the classroom* (pp. 121–141). New York: The Free Press.

Purcell-Gates, V., L'Allier, S., & Smith, D. (1995). Literacy at the Harts' and the Larsons': Diversity among poor, inner city families. *The Reading Teacher, 48,* 572–578.

Purcell-Gates, V., McIntyre, E., & Freppon, P. (1995). Learning written storybook language in school: A comparison of low-SES children in skills-based and whole language classrooms. *American Educational Research Journal, 32,* 659–685.

Rand, L. (2001). Enacting faith: Evangelical discourse and the discipline of composition studies. *College Composition and Communication, 52,* 349–367.

Rand Reading Study Group. (2002). *Reading for understanding.* Santa Monica, CA: Rand.

Rauch, J. (1993). *Kindly inquisitors: The new attacks on free thought.* Chicago: University of Chicago.

Ravitch, D. (2003a). *The language police: How pressure groups restrict what students learn.* New York: Knopf.

Ravitch, D. (2003b, summer). Thin gruel: How the language police drain the life and content from our texts. *American Educator,* 6–19.

Rayner, K. (1997). Understanding eye movements in reading. *Scientific Studies in Reading, 1,* 317–339.

Rayner, K., & Pollatsek, A. (1989). *The psychology of reading.* Hillsdale, NJ: Lawrence Erlbaum Associates.

Read, C. (1971). Pre-school children's knowledge of English phonology. *Harvard Educational Review, 41,* 1–34.

Read, C. (1975). *Children's categorization of speech sounds in English.* Urbana, IL: National Council of Teachers of English.

Reder, S. (1994). Practice-engagement theory: A sociocultural approach to literacy across languages and cultures. In B. Ferdman, R. M. Weber, & A. Ramirez (Eds.), *Literacy across languages and cultures* (pp. 33–74). Albany: State University of New York Press.

Reese, E., & Cox, A. (1999). Quality of adult book reading affects children's emergent literacy. *Developmental Psychology, 35,* 20–28.

Reinking, D., & Bridwell-Bowles, L. (1996). Computers in reading and writing. In R. Barr, M. Kamil, P. Mosenthal, & P. D. Pearson (Eds.), *Handbook of reading research* (Vol. 11, pp. 310–340). Mahwah, NJ: Lawrence Erlbaum Associates.

Resnick, L. (1987). Learning in school and out. *Educational Researcher, 16*, 13–20.

Reyes, M. de la Luz. (1991). A process approach to literacy using dialogue journals and literature logs with second language learners. *Research in the Teaching of English, 25*, 219–313.

Rhodes, L. (1979a). Comprehension and predictability: An analysis of beginning reading materials. In J. Harste & R. Carey (Eds.), *New perspectives on comprehension* (pp. 100–131). Bloomington: Indiana University, School of Education.

Rhodes, L. (1979b). *The interaction of beginning reader's strategies and texts reflecting alternate models of predictability*. Unpublished doctoral dissertation, Indiana University, Bloomington.

Rhodes, L. (1981). I can read! Predictable books as resources for reading and writing. *Reading Teacher, 34*, 511–519.

Richards, J., & McKenna, M. (2003). *Integrating multiple literacies in K-8 classrooms*. Mahwah, NJ: Lawrence Erlbaum Associates.

Rogers, R. (2002). Between contexts: A critical discourse analysis of family literacy, discursive practices, and literate subjectivities. *Reading Research Quarterly, 37*, 248–277.

Rose, M. (1994). Rigid rules, inflexible plans, and the stifling of language: A cognitivist analysis of writer's block. In S. Perl (Ed.), *Landmark essays on writing process* (pp. 65–97). Davis, CA: Hermagoras.

Rosenblatt, L. (1978). *The reader, the text, the poem*. Carbondale: Southern Illinois University Press.

Rosenblatt, L. (1991a). Literary theory. In J. Flood, J. Jensen, D. Lapp, & J. Squire (Eds.), *Handbook of research on teaching the English language arts* (pp. 57–62). New York: Macmillan.

Rosenblatt, L. (1991b). Literature—S.O.S.! *Language Arts, 68*, 444–448.

Rousch, P. (1976). Testing. In P. D. Allen & D. Watson (Eds.), *Findings of research in miscue analysis: Classroom implications* (pp. 132–136). Urbana, IL: National Council of Teachers of English.

Routman, R. (1996). *Literacy at the crossroads*. Portsmouth, NH: Heinemann.

Ruddell, M. R. (1994). Vocabulary knowledge and comprehension: A comprehension-process view of complex literacy relationships. In R. Ruddell, M. R. Ruddell, & H. Singer (Eds.), *Theoretical models and processes of reading* (4th ed., pp. 414–468). Newark, DE: International Reading Association.

Rumelhart, D. (1975). Notes on a schema for stories. In D. Bobrow & A. Collins (Eds.), *Representation and understanding: Studies in cognitive science* (pp. 211–236). New York: Academic.

Rumelhart, D. (1980). Schemata: The building blocks of cognition. In R. Spiro, B. Bruce, & W. Brewer (Eds.), *Theoretical issues in reading comprehension* (pp. 33–58). Hillsdale, NJ: Lawrence Erlbaum Associates.

Rumelhart, D. (1984). Understanding understanding. In J. Flood (Ed.), *Understanding reading comprehension* (pp. 1–20). Newark, DE: International Reading Association.

Rumelhart, D. (1994). Toward an interactive model of reading. In R. Ruddell, M. R. Ruddell, & H. Singer (Eds.), *Theoretical models and processes of reading* (4th ed., pp. 864–894). Newark, DE: International Reading Association.

Sankoff, G. (1980). *The social life of language*. Philadelphia: University of Pennsylvania Press.

Santman, D. (2002). Teaching to the test?: Test preparation in the reading workshop. *Language Arts, 79*, 203–211.

Sarroub, L. (2002). In-betweenness: Religion and conflicting visions of literacy. *Reading Research Quarterly, 37*, 130–148.

Sawkins, M. (1970). *The oral responses of selected fifth grade children to questions concerning their written expression*. Unpublished doctoral dissertation, State University of New York, Buffalo.

Scarborough, H., & Dobrich, W. (1994). On the efficacy of reading to preschoolers. *Developmental Review, 14*, 245–302.

Schieffelin, B., & Cochran-Smith, M. (1984). Learning to read culturally: Literacy before schooling. In H. Goelman, A. Oberg, & F. Smith (Eds.), *Awakening to literacy* (pp. 3–23). London: Heinemann.

Schoenbach, R., Greenleaf, C., Cziko, C., & Hurwitz, L. (1999). *Reading for understanding: A guide to improving reading in middle and high school classroom*. San Francisco: Jossey-Bass.

Scieszka, J. (1989). *The true story of the three little pigs*. New York: Penguin.

Scollon, R., & Scollon, S. W. (1981). *Narrative, literacy, and face in interethnic communication*. Norwood, NJ: Ablex.

Scribner, S., & Cole, M. (1978). Literacy without schooling: Testing for intellectual effects. *Harvard Educational Review, 48*, 448–461.

Scribner, S., & Cole, M. (1981). Unpackaging literacy. In M. Whiteman (Ed.), *Variation in writing: Functional and linguistic-cultural differences* (pp. 71–87). Hillsdale, NJ: Lawrence Erlbaum Associates.

Searle, D. (1984). Scaffolding: Who's building whose building? *Language Arts, 61*, 480–483.

Shannon, P. (1990). *The struggle to continue: Progressive reading instruction in the United States*. Portsmouth, NH: Heinemann.

Shaughnessy, M. (1977). *Errors and expectations: A guide for the teacher of basic writing*. New York: Oxford University Press.

Short, K., Harste, J., & Burke, C. (1996). *Creating classrooms for authors and inquirers* (2nd ed.). Portsmouth, NH: Heinemann.

Siegel, M. (1995). More than words: The generative power of transmediation for learning. *Canadian Journal of Education, 20*, 455–475.

Silva, C., & Delgado-Larocco, E. (1993). Facilitating learning through interconnections: A conceptual approach to core literature units. *Language Arts, 70*, 469–474.

Silva, C., & Kucer, S. B. (1997). Expanding curricular conversations through unification, diversity, and access. *Language Arts, 74*, 26–32.

Simons, H., & Ammon, P. (1989). Child knowledge and primerese text: Mismatches and miscues. *Research in the Teaching of English, 23*, 380–398.

Sims, R. (1976). What we know about dialects and reading. In P. D. Allen & D. Watson (Eds.), *Findings of research in miscue analysis: Classroom implications* (pp. 128–131). Urbana, IL: National Council of Teachers of English.

Sims, R. (1982). Dialect and reading: Toward refining the issues. In J. Langer & R. Burke-Smith (Eds.), *Reader meets author/Bridging the gap* (pp. 222–236). Newark, DE: International Reading Association.

Smagorinsky, P. (2001). If meaning is constructed, what is it made from? Toward a cultural theory of reading. *Review of Educational Research, 71*, 133–169.

Smith, E. (2002). Ebonics: A case history. In L. Delpit & J. K. Dowdy (Eds.), *The skin that we speak: Thoughts on language and culture in the classroom* (pp. 15–27). New York: The Free Press.

Smith, F. (1975). *Comprehension and learning*. Katonah, NY: Owen.

Smith, F. (1977). The uses of language. *Language Arts, 54*, 638–644.

Smith, F. (1981). Demonstrations, engagement, and sensitivity: A revised approach to language learning. *Language Arts, 52*, 103–112.

Smith, F. (1983a). *Essays into literacy*. Portsmouth, NH: Heinemann.

Smith, F. (1983b). Reading like a writer. *Language Arts, 60*, 558–567.

Smith, F. (1988). *Joining the literacy club*. Portsmouth, NH: Heinemann.

Smith, F. (1989, January). Overselling literacy. *Phi Delta Kappan*, 353–359.

Smith, F. (1994a). *Understanding reading* (5th ed.). Hillsdale, NJ: Lawrence Erlbaum Associates.

Smith, F. (1994b). *Writing and the writer* (2nd ed.). Hillsdale, NJ: Lawrence Erlbaum Associates.

Smith, F. (2003). *Unspeakable acts, unnatural practices: Flaws and fallacies in "scientific" reading instruction*. Portsmouth, NH: Heinemann.

Smith, F. (2004). Understanding reading (6th ed.). Mahwah, NJ: Lawrence Erlbaum Associates.

Snow, C., Barnes, W., Chandler, J., Goodman, I., & Hemphill, L. (1991). *Unfulfilled expectations: Home and school influences on literacy*. Cambridge, MA: Harvard University Press.

Sokal, A., & Bricmont, J. (1998). *Fashionable nonsense: Postmodern intellectuals' abuse of science*. New York: Picador.

Solsken, J. (1992). *Literacy, gender, and work: In families and school*. Norwood, NJ: Ablex.

Sommers, N. (1994). Revision strategies of student writers and experienced adult writers. In S. Perl (Ed.), *Landmark essays on writing process* (pp. 75–84). Davis, CA: Hermagoras.

Sowers, S. (1979). *A six-year-old's writing process: The first half of first grade*. Unpublished doctoral dissertation, Boston University, Boston.

Spache, G. (1978). *Good reading for poor readers* (10th ed.). Champaign, IL: Garrard.

Spears-Bunton, L. (1990). Welcome to my house: African American and European American students' responses to Virginia Hamilton's *House of Dies Drear*. *Journal of Negro Education, 59*, 566–576.

Spears-Bunton, L. (1992). Literature, literacy, and resistance to cultural domination. In C. Kinzer & D. Leu (Eds.), *Literacy research, theory and practice: Views from many perspectives*. 41st yearbook of the National Reading Conference (pp. 393–401). Chicago: National Reading Conference.

Spencer, M. M. (1988). *How texts teach what readers learn*. Victoria, Canada: Abel.

Spinelli, J. (1990). *Maniac Magee*. Boston: Little, Brown.

Spiro, R. (1977). Remembering information from text: Theoretical and empirical issues concerning the "State of Schema" reconstruction hypothesis. In R. Anderson, R. Spiro, & W. Montague (Eds.), *Schooling and the acquisition of knowledge* (pp. 137–165). Hillsdale, NJ: Lawrence Erlbaum Associates.

Stahl, S., & Miller, P. (1989). Whole language and language experience approaches for beginning reading: A quantitative research synthesis. *Review of Educational Research, 59,* 87–116.

Stanovich, K. (2000). *Progress in understanding reading: Scientific foundations and new frontiers.* NY: Guildford.

Stanovich, K. (1998). Twenty-five years of research on the reading process: The grand synthesis and what it means for our field. In T. Shanahan & F. Rodriquez-Brown (Eds.), *Forty-seventh yearbook of the National Reading Conference* (pp. 44–58). Chicago: National Reading Conference.

Stanovich, K. (1996). Word recognition: Changing perspectives. In R. Barr, M. Kamil, P. Mosenthal, & P. D. Pearson (Eds.), *Handbook of reading research* (Vol. 2, pp. 418–452). Mahwah, NJ: Lawrence Erlbaum Associates.

Steffensen, M., Joag-Dev, C., & Anderson, R. (1979). A cross-cultural perspective on reading comprehension. *Reading Research Quarterly, 15,* 10–29.

Stein, N., & Glenn, C. (1979). An analysis of story comprehension in elementary school children. In R. O. Freedle (Ed.), *Advances in discourse processes: Vol. 2. New directions in discourse processing* (pp. 53–120). Norwood, NJ: Ablex.

Stein, N., & Trabasso, T. (1982). What's in a story: An approach to comprehension and instruction. In R. Glaser (Ed.), *Advances in instructional psychology* (Vol. 2, pp. 213–267). Hillsdale, NJ: Lawrence Erlbaum Associates.

Steiner, E. (1978). *Logical and conceptual analytic techniques for educational researchers.* Washington, DC: University Press of America.

Strauss, S. (2001). An open letter to Reid Lyon. *Educational Researcher, 30,* 26–32.

Strauss, S. (2003). Writing and reading: A reply to Wolf and Kennedy. *Educational Researcher, 32,* 31–32.

Street, B. (1984). *Literacy in theory and practice.* New York: Cambridge University Press.

Stubbs, M. (2002). Some basic sociolinguistic concepts. In L. Delpit & J. K. Dowdy (Eds.), *The skin that we speak: Thoughts on language and culture in the classroom* (pp. 63–85). New York: The Free Press.

Taylor, D. (1983). *Family literacy: Young children learn to read and write.* Portsmouth, NH: Heinemann.

Taylor, D. (1999). Beginning to read and the spin doctors of science: An excerpt. *Language Arts, 76,* 217–231.

Taylor, D., & Dorsey-Gaines, C. (1988). *Growing up literate: Learning from inner-city families.* Portsmouth, NH: Heinemann.

Teale, W. (1984). Toward a theory of how children learn to read and write naturally. In J. Jensen (Ed.), *Composing and comprehending* (pp. 127–142). Urbana, IL: National Council of Teachers of English.

Teale, W. (1986). Home background and young children's literacy development. In W. H. Teale & E. Sulzby (Eds.), *Emergent literacy: Writing and reading* (pp. 173–206). Norwood, NJ: Ablex.

Teale, W. (1991). A conversation with Lisa Delpit. *Language Arts, 68,* 541–547.

Templeton, S. (1992). New trends in an historical perspective: Old story, new resolution—Sound and meaning in spelling. *Language Arts, 69,* 43–52.

Templeton, S., & Morris, D. (2000). Spelling. In M. Kamil, P. Mosenthal, D. Pearson, & R. Barr (Eds.), *Reading research* (Vol. 3, pp. 525–543). Mahwah, NY: Lawrence Erlbaum Associates.

Thorndyke, P. (1977). Cognitive structures in comprehension and memory of narrative discourse. *Cognitive Psychology, 9*, 77–110.

Tierney, R., & LaZansky, J. (1980). *The rights and responsibilities of readers and writers: A contractual agreement* (Reading Education Rep. No. 15). Urbana: University of Illinois, Center for the Study of Reading.

Tierney, R., & Leys, M. (1986). What is the value of connecting reading and writing? In B. Petersen (Ed.), *Convergences: Transactions in reading and writing* (pp. 15–29). Urbana, IL: National Council of Teachers of English.

Tierney, R., & Pearson, P. D. (1994). Learning from text: A framework for improving classroom practice. In R. Ruddell, M. Ruddell, & H. Singer (Eds.), *Theoretical models and processes of reading* (4th ed., pp. 496–513). Newark, DE: International Reading Association.

Tierney, R., & Shanahan, T. (1996). Research on the reading–writing relationship: Interactions, transactions, and outcomes. In R. Barr, M. Kamil, P. Mosenthal, & P. D. Pearson (Eds.), *Handbook of reading research* (Vol. 2, pp. 246–280). Mahwah, NJ: Lawrence Erlbaum Associates.

Tolstoy, A. (1976). *The great big enormous turnip*. Glenview, IL: Scott Foresman.

Tovani, C. (2000). *I read it, but I don't get it: Comprehension strategies for adolescent readers*. York, ME: Stenhouse.

United States Department of Education. (2001). *No child left behind* (PL107-110). Washington, DC: Government Printing Office.

van den Broek, P., & Kremer, K. (2000). The mind in action: What it means to comprehend during reading. In B. Taylor, M. Graves, and P. van den Broek (Eds.), *Reading for meaning: Fostering comprehension in the middle grades* (pp. 1–31). New York: Teachers College Press.

van Dijk, T. A. (1980). *Macrostructures*. Hillsdale, NJ: Lawrence Erlbaum Associates.

van Dijk, T. A., & Kintsch, W. (1983). *Strategies of discourse comprehension*. New York: Academic.

Venesky, R. (1980). From Webster to Rice to Roosevelt. In U. Frith (Ed.), *Cognitive processes in spelling* (pp. 9–30). London: Academic.

Vygotsky, L. S. (1962). *Thought and language*. Cambridge, MA: MIT Press.

Vygotsky, L. S. (l978). *Mind in society*. Cambridge, MA: Harvard University Press.

Walczyk, J. (2000). The interplay between automatic and control processes in reading. *Reading Research Quarterly, 35*, 554–566,

Waller, R. (1996). Typography and discourse. In R. Barr, M. Kamil, P. Mosenthal, & P. D. Pearson (Eds.), *Handbook of reading research* (Vol. 2, pp. 341–380). Mahwah, NJ: Lawrence Erlbaum Associates.

Weaver, C. (Ed.). (1998). *Lessons to share on teaching grammar in context*. Portsmouth, NH: Heinemann

Weaver, C. (2002). *Reading process and practice* (3rd ed.). Portsmouth, NH: Heinemann.

Weaver, C., & Kintsch, W. (1996). Expository text. In R. Barr, M. Kamil, P. Mosenthal, & P. D. Pearson (Eds.), *Handbook of reading research* (Vol.2, pp. 230–245). Mahwah, NJ: Lawrence Erlbaum Associates.

Weaver, C., & Brinkley, E. (1998). Phonics, whole language, and the religious and political right. In K. Goodman (Ed.), *In defense of good teaching* (pp. 127–141). York, ME: Stenhouse.

Weber, R. (1996). Linguistic diversity and reading in American society. In R. Barr, M. Kamil, P. Mosenthal, & P. D. Pearson (Eds.), *Handbook of reading research* (Vol. 2, pp. 97–119). Mahwah, NJ: Lawrence Erlbaum Associates.

Wells, G. (1986). *The meaning makers*. Portsmouth, NH: Heinemann.

Wells, M.C. (1995). *Literacies lost: When students move from a progressive middle school to a traditional high school*. New York: Teachers College Press.

Wertsch, J. (Ed.). (1985). *Culture, communication, and cognition*. London: Cambridge University Press.

West, C. (1993). *Race matters*. Boston: Beacon.

West, R. F., Stanovich, K., & Cunningham, A. (1995). Compensatory processes in reading. In R. Dixon & L. Backman (Eds.), *Compensating for psychological deficits and declines: Managing losses and promoting gain* (pp. 275–296). Hillsdale, NJ: Lawrence Erlbaum Associates.

Whiteman, M. F. (1981). Dialect influence in writing. In M. F. Whiteman (Ed.), *Variation in writing: Functional and linguistic-cultural differences* (pp. 153–166). Hillsdale, NJ: Lawrence Erlbaum Associates.

Wilde, S. (1992). *You ken red this! Spelling and punctuation for whole language classrooms, K–6*. Portsmouth, NH: Heinemann.

Wilhelm, J. D. (1996). *"You gotta be the book"; Teaching engaged and reflective reading with adolescents*. New York: Teachers College Press.

Willis, A. I. (2001). Reading the world of school literacy: Contextualizing the experience of a young African American male. In S. Beck & L. N. Olah (Eds.), *Perspectives on language and literacy: Beyond the here and now* (pp. 399–417). Cambridge, MA: Harvard Educational Review.

Willis, A., & Harris, V. (2000). Political acts: Literacy learning and teaching. *Reading Research Quarterly, 35*, 72–88.

Wolf, M., & Kennedy, R. (2003). How the origins of written language instruct us to teach: A response to Steven Strauss. *Educational Researcher, 32*, 26–30.

Wolf, S., & Wolf, K. (2002). Teaching *true* and *to* the test in writing. *Language Arts, 79*, 229–240.

Wolfram, W., Adger, C., & Christian, D. (1999). *Dialects in schools and communities*. Mahwah, NJ: Lawrence Erlbaum Associates.

Wysocki, F. (2004). The multiple media of texts: How onscreen and paper texts incorporate words, images, and other media. In C. Bazerman & P. Prior (Eds.), *What writing does and how it does it: An introduction to analyzing texts and textual practices* (pp. 123–163). Mahwah, NJ: Lawrence Erlbaum Associates.

Young, E. (1992). *Seven blind mice*. New York: Philomel.

Zola, D. (1984). Redundacy and word perception during reading. *Perception and psychophysics, 36*, 277–284.

Author Index

Subject Index